Meister Eckhart

Meister Eckhart

Philosopher of Christianity

Kurt Flasch

Translated by Anne Schindel
and Aaron Vanides

Yale

UNIVERSITY PRESS

NEW HAVEN AND LONDON

The translation of this work was funded by Geisteswissenschaften International—Translation Funding for Humanities and Social Sciences from Germany, a joint initiative of the Fritz Thyssen Foundation, the German Federal Foreign Office, the collecting society VG WORT, and the Börsenverein des Deutschen Buchhandels (German Publishers & Booksellers Association).

Published with assistance from the Ronald and Betty Miller Turner Publication Fund.

Published with assistance from the Mary Cady Tew Memorial Fund.

Originally published as *Meister Eckhart: Philosoph des Christentums*, 3rd ed. Copyright © Verlag C.H. Beck oHG, München 2011.

Yale University Press books may be purchased in quantity for educational, business, or promotional use. For information, please e-mail sales.press@yale.edu (U.S. office) or sales@yaleup.co.uk (U.K. office).

Set in Fournier type by IDS Infotech, Ltd.
Printed in the United States of America.

ISBN: 978-0-300-20486-5 (cloth; alk. paper)

Library of Congress Control Number: 2015943082

A catalogue record for this book is available from the British Library.

This paper meets the requirements of ANSI/NISO Z39.48–1992 (Permanence of Paper).

10 9 8 7 6 5 4 3 2 1

For
Maria Antonietta Terzoli
November 27, 2009

One must speak wholly differently of the grounds of being of things and the knowledge of them, differently also of the things outside in nature. Likewise, it is to be spoken differently of substance and differently of accident. Those who fail to consider this will often fall into error.
—Meister Eckhart, *In Ioh.*, LW 3, n. 514, 445

All things, or almost all, that we ask about God are easily solved. And what is written about God—often also the obscure and difficult things—is explained clearly through natural reason.
—Meister Eckhart, *Prologus generalis*, LW 1, n. 2, 39.3–4

Everything that is written or taught about the blessed Trinity is not necessarily so or true.
—Meister Eckhart, Latin sermon 4, LW 4, n. 1, 31

It is a kinship of the divine kind. It is one within itself. It does not have anything in common with anything. In this matter, many a great scholar stumbles.
—Meister Eckhart, German sermon 28, DW 2, n. 66, 4–5

If only they understood what mind is.
—Meister Eckhart, DW 4, n. 1, 652.211, stating his reason for rejecting all the theologians of his time

We are concerned here with a thinker who presents—granted, at times more casually than we are accustomed to demand—thoughts, not impressions, and strives to prove them by a strict method. He would believe that he was merely treading water if he were to keep his sentences unexplained and unproven.
—Adolf Lasson, *Meister Eckhart: Der Mystiker* (Berlin, 1868), 3

Contents

Translators' Preface

Every act of translation requires negotiation and compromise, especially with two translators collaborating on the same text. We agreed from the outset that we wanted to re-create as closely as possible the experience of reading the German original. Both of us are fluent in English and German, but both of us are also native speakers of just one language. We naturally disagreed about nuances of tone and style in the original and the translation, though we were in agreement about the content and the direction of the argument. Kurt Flasch's style is unique, subtle, and careful: how he says something is nearly as important as what he says. It is in terms of the "how" that we had to make compromises. A subtlety in the German that one of us found important could not always be re-created without introducing alienating diction into the English version, and we therefore decided to retain Flasch's idiosyncrasies only where the German is equally peculiar.

A few of these idiosyncrasies merit special mention. Flasch's style oscillates between the formal and the conversational and is aimed at a learned and curious general audience, not just specialists. At times his tone may border on the irreverent, and Flasch delights in wordplay and vivid images, some of them taken from German daily life. In our translation we have attempted to keep the text equally whimsical.

Flasch's style also relies on a flexible terminology: the same philosophical concepts are often presented with German synonyms. We have collapsed some of these synonyms to make the text more readable in English, but without sacrificing variation completely. In this context our use term "being" deserves a special note. It represents the German terms *Wesen*, *Sein*, and *Seiendes* to avoid unnecessary complications. We have followed Flasch more closely in his use of compounds by breaking them apart and translating each part literally wherever possible. Flasch often eschews Latinisms in favor of words with Germanic roots to avoid the impression of loftiness and mysticism attached to many modern interpretations of Eckhart. Latinate words have a more elevated sense in German than they do in English, but we have also tended to avoid Latinisms where possible—with the caveat that they were sometimes inevitable. Readers familiar with Eckhart scholarship will therefore encounter certain terms that seem new or different from those to which they are accustomed.

Finally, two typographical decisions deserve mention. First, Kurt Flasch repeatedly uses colons to connect main clauses. We have kept this important facet of his style to preserve the author's unique voice. Second, we have chosen to capitalize certain nouns, such as Oneness, Wisdom, and Justice, when they refer to the primary determinations. The precise relationship between these primary determinations and their existence in specific entities is developed throughout Flasch's reading of Eckhart, but those who wish to acquaint themselves with the distinction between "Wisdom" and "wisdom," for example, can refer to Flasch's discussion of the prologues to the *Opus Tripartitum* on pages 77 to 82 for a preliminary explanation.

We are indebted to our copyeditor Kip Keller and the anonymous reader for their attentive reading of the manuscript. They offered many suggestions for improvement, prevented us from introducing inconsistencies, and caught various typos. Their invaluable comments helped us wade through and rethink many thorny issues, and both their eye for detail and their deep understanding of the content helped us improve the text at several stages.

Preface

Meister Eckhart attracts. His radical thinking and the force of his words still fascinate us. We are moved by his tragic fate: his death in Avignon, his trial, his condemnation by the church. And then there is his immense impact: from Henry Suso to Nicholas of Cusa, from Hegel to Heidegger, from Robert Musil to Paul Celan. And beyond.

His image has fluctuated throughout history. Studies from the past few decades have changed it. This book attempts to take stock.

It is an introduction to his thinking. It is an invitation to read Eckhart and to think along with his propositions without divorcing him from the historical world from which he came and against which he positioned himself. I have tried to do this as transparently, as verifiably, and as succinctly as possible. A more comprehensive account would have gone beyond the intended scope of this work.

Like all arguments and texts, Eckhart's are grounded in his life and times. Yet we possess too few securely datable sources to reconstruct the progression of Eckhart's thinking. Surely there were shifts in both Eckhart's ideas and his literary output. He spoke differently in different types of texts (tractates, commentaries, sermons), in front of different audiences (learned readers of Latin writings, the laity as readers of German works), and in different environments (Paris, Erfurt, Strasbourg, Cologne) as a professor or as a preacher. Every detail is precious, but we cannot write an intellectual biography of Eckhart in the same way that we can of Goethe. I peruse Eckhart's works in their currently accepted chronological order, but the chapters are laid out in a way that will make it possible to rearrange them should the need arise in the future because of additional research on the chronology of Eckhart's writings.

Despite the excellent works that already exist on the subject, a new and complete exposition of Eckhart seems necessary. Apart from the fact that philosophical topics can never be exhausted, recent scholarship has allowed for greater precision than before. Since 2006, we have had access to Eckhart's trial records, thanks to the critical edition by Loris Sturlese (*Die lateinischen Werke* 5); in 2007, Sturlese's *Homo divinus* was published in Stuttgart, including many new details. Georg Steer reedited and explained Eckhart's German sermons (*Die deutschen Werke* 4 [Stuttgart, 2003]). Reliable commentaries on Eckhart's German sermons have been published continually in the series *Lectura Eckhardi* since 1998, under the direction of Georg Steer and Loris Sturlese.

Our understanding of the Middle Ages has become increasingly multifaceted, variegated, and regional. Past centuries and regions were more diverse than formerly assumed. Today, Eckhart's intellectual environment is better known than ever before, especially his involvement with Albertus Magnus and Dietrich of Freiberg, who occupied key roles in Eckhart's thinking. Both the condemnation in 1277 and the intellectual milieu of the 1280s and 1290s in Paris have been studied more carefully, with a focus, for example, on Giles of Rome, Henry of Ghent, and Godfrey of Fontaines. In addition, the development of medieval German philosophical thought has been documented in detail since Loris Sturlese and I founded the Corpus Philosophorum Teutonicorum Medii Aevi (Hamburg, 1985–).

To add a short personal note: I gave my first academic talk on Meister Eckhart exactly sixty years ago. I am lucky to have benefited from conversations with friends who are the most eminent Eckhart scholars. I will name only a few: Raymond Klibanski, Josef Koch, and Kurt Ruh, and, among the younger generation, Ruedi Imbach, Alain de Libera, Burkhard Mojsisch, and Loris Sturlese. And yet in writing this book I did not look backward, not even to my own previous work on Eckhart. Instead, I reread all of Eckhart's texts, and I am presenting a new approach—not a specialized study of a particular topic, but an attempt at an overall picture. I am subsuming it under the (nowadays uncommon) title "philosopher of Christianity." Chapter 2 explains what this means. There I define this title as a hypothesis that is tested in subsequent chapters through a reading of Eckhart's texts.

My publisher and I agreed on a book of modest proportions. I have cut some notes, some sources, and some engagement with previous interpretations of Eckhart for the sake of brevity. My focus is on presenting new and original material and limiting historical retrospectives to the bare necessities. One of these is Eckhart's connection with Dietrich of Freiberg. I presented his engagement with Aristotle, Avicenna, Averroës, Moses Maimonides, Albertus Magnus, and Thomas Aquinas in my previous study *Meister Eckhart: Die Geburt der "Deutschen Mystik" aus dem Geist der arabischen Philosophie* (Munich, 2006). A continuation of my study can be found in Loris Sturlese, ed., *Studi sulle fonti di Meister Eckhart* (Fribourg, 2008).

I refer only occasionally to the general state of philosophy, theology, and the natural sciences around 1300 and the educational training of Dominicans; they are described in my work *Dietrich von Freiberg: Philosophie, Theologie, Naturforschung um 1300* (Frankfurt am Main, 2007).

Finally, I would like to thank my friends and colleagues Ruedi Imbach (Paris) and Loris Sturlese (Lecce). Both have been of great help to me: Ruedi Imbach prompted me to write this book and carefully read and corrected its penultimate version; Loris Sturlese and I spent three days discussing the question of how his discoveries about Eckhart's life and works have influenced and changed our current image of Meister Eckhart. I must also thank my sister Monika and her husband, Walter Schäfer, both of whom meticulously edited my manuscript.

It is likely that Eckhart would have called the epigraphs to this book his spicy nutmegs. Anyone who bites into them will need a drink.

Kurt Flasch
Mainz, December 2009

PART ONE

1. Life and Works around 1300

Eckhart's Life—"Hidden in God"?

No one spoke ill of the Danish bishop Hans Lassen Martensen (1808–1884)—except Søren Kierkegaard. Martensen, a famous Lutheran theologian, had been professor of theology since 1840. In 1845, he was made court chaplain and, finally, bishop. He never grew tired of arguing for the peaceful relationship between Christianity and reason, between church and state. He proclaimed to have left Hegel behind, but whenever he wrote or spoke, he praised, in diluted Hegelian terms, the harmony of the New Testament, "reason," and public offices. In 1854, during the official eulogy for Bishop Jacob Peter Mynster, he pronounced the deceased a "witness to the Truth"—and Kierkegaard was seized with rage. He was disgusted by Martensen's form of Christianity, which he considered conformist, "affirmative," and riddled with reason. Kierkegaard's entire life was bound up with Martensen's, as Joakim Garff's biography of Kierkegaard (Munich, 2005) shows, and now he attacked Martensen in a series of articles entitled *The Moment*. For Kierkegaard, only a "martyr" could be a "witness to the Truth," and there were no martyrs in the state-supported Christianity of Denmark. Kierkegaard wrote: "Truly, there is something more adverse to Christianity and its very nature than any heresy, any schism, more adverse than all heresies and schisms taken together, and that is: to play at Christianity."[1] For Kierkegaard, to play at Christianity meant robbing it of its opposition to the "world," attributing a false harmony to it, taking away its asceticism, its poverty, its eschewal of power and riches. Bishop Martensen played at Christianity and mistook the miter for the martyr.

A radical, authentic Christianity, renunciation of the world, and poverty have a great deal to do with Meister Eckhart. He belonged to a mendicant order whose ideal church was a poor one. By 1310, it had admittedly lost its radically reformist zeal, as Dante confirms when he has Thomas Aquinas say in *Paradiso* 11, "Little cloth is needed for the frocks of poor friars" (l. 132). We are again approaching Eckhart, but I have to return once more to Bishop Martensen. Martensen, who, incidentally, was from Flensburg, published a German monograph on Eckhart in 1842 called *Meister Eckhart: Eine theologische Studie* (Hamburg, 1842). From the very beginning, Martensen had a preconceived notion of who Eckhart was—a mystic. He begins his work by lamenting the divergent assessments of "mysticism." He demonstrates right away how damaging the concept of mysticism had been, and perhaps still is, in scholarly debates. He remarks, "We know hardly anything about the external history of these mystics. Their lives were hidden in God."[2]

But seen from the outside, did Eckhart not also live a little? Did he not, as a historical figure, exist in the world? And not just anywhere, but in the most populous European cities, such as Paris and Cologne; even Erfurt was not all that small. Martensen gets caught up in playing with the opposition of external history and internalized mysticism; he sets out to write about Eckhart and immediately conflates him with other "mystics"; instead of increasing the knowledge of Eckhart's life, still sparse among his contemporaries, Martensen hides his complacency behind a veil of solemn awe: "Their lives were hidden in God." But Eckhart is a subject of history. Martensen is unctuous, not scholarly: he only plays at scholarship.

Traces of an Earthly Life

Eckhart had an earthly life, and we know much about it thanks to the studies by Josef Koch and Loris Sturlese.[3] A brief outline of their results will suffice here; the reader can also refer to the time line in the back of the book.

Life lurks behind historical dates. I try to make it visible here in broad strokes. But first, a methodological remark: when we state what we know, we also reveal the gaps in our knowledge. Some of Eckhart's works are lost; others he talked about but likely never wrote; some he labored over for a long time, making it difficult to fit them into a chronology of his works. This is especially true of his German sermons, and probably also for his *Opus tripartitum*. Eckhart's date of birth is not attested, but is inferred from the regulations stipulating that a Parisian *magister* had to be at least thirty-five years old. But there were exceptions. Hence, there are some weak spots in the chronology.

Eckhart was from Tambach, near Gotha. Dietrich of Freiberg, an important influence on Eckhart's life and thought, was born twelve years earlier in Freiberg, a silver-mining town in Saxony. Before 1250, the central German states did not produce any notable scholars: Albertus Magnus was from Lauingen, by the Danube; Bonaventure from Bagnoregio; Thomas Aquinas from Aquino, near Frosinone.[4] After about 1230, the Dominican order altered the cultural landscape of Europe by reorganizing its educational structure—putting a lector in every convent and providing the laity with access to their teachings. Afterward, central Germany produced scholars who achieved the highest rank attainable for any academic: the position of *magister* at Paris. After all, *Meister* Eckhart means that he was a master, a *magister* at Paris—just like the Germans Albertus Magnus and Dietrich of Freiberg.

Eckhart, like Albertus Magnus, was a Dominican. The Dominican and Franciscan orders had been founded in response to the ever-growing prosperity of the cities in central and northern Italy, Provence, the Île-de-France, southern England, and the Rhine Valley; even thirteenth-century Erfurt was on the rise. The poverty of the new orders served as a reminder that Jesus had had no place to rest his head and that the expression "apostolic life" still essentially meant "life without possessions." Several Christian protest movements rebelled against the wealth of the church. Poverty was an ideal in ancient philosophy, too. At his trial, Socrates defended himself by saying that he had but one witness—his poverty. At the beginning of the twelfth century, Abelard reclaimed the philosophical ideal of poverty for Christianity—long before Il Poverello, St. Francis.

The twelfth and thirteenth centuries brought about an extraordinary economic and social boom that ended only around the middle of the fourteenth century. Rich overseas merchants competed with the feudal and ecclesiastical rulers of cities on the one hand and with the emergent class of craftsmen on the other. Bloody struggles followed, especially in large cities such as Cologne. The Rhenish League, founded originally by Mainz and Worms, stretched as far as Bremen and Aachen and eventually comprised all the German lands; from 1256 onward, it proved that there was a fourth major power in addition to the king, the territorial princes, and the lesser lords. Its goals were peace and secure trade routes; supraregional commerce was expanding. The new wealth increasingly made poverty appear scandalous; it was to remain a hotly debated issue until the end of the Middle Ages. A proper friar like Albertus Magnus traveled on foot, even from Cologne to Paris; in Dante's *Divine Comedy*, St. Peter scoffs from heaven that he had always walked everywhere and been satisfied with the simplest of food, but that now the highest clerics were always seen well nourished and grand, riding high on their horses and accompanied by a large entourage. The so-called mendicant orders were looking for a new form of Christian life, but soon turned rich and plump; they competed with other orders and the secular clergy for money, power, and chairs at the University of Paris. Dominicans and Franciscans developed opposing philosophical and theological doctrines in order to distinguish themselves from each other: Franciscans considered themselves the heirs of St. Francis in their praise of compassion; as early as 1286, Dominicans explicitly aligned themselves with Thomas Aquinas and taught the superiority of the intellect over the will. Eckhart could not ignore the rivalries and debates around him. He speaks of them even in his German sermons.

An Empire in Disarray

Eckhart was born during the time of the Interregnum (1254–73).[5] There was no longer a centralized force in the aged empire, and the princes, especially the increasingly influential prince-electors of the thirteenth century, consolidated their power. From 1273 onward, a king ruled again: Rudolf of Habsburg. He was greatly occupied, however, with securing and expanding his power base, which was becoming an indispensable measure for exercising kingship. The princes, themselves in the process of expanding their territorial sovereignty, resisted. After Rudolf's death, they elected Count Adolf of Nassau, whose minor house did not have the resources to assert itself. A mere six years after his election, Adolf was deposed and died at the Battle of Göllheim, defeated by his successor, Albert of Habsburg, who in 1308 was himself murdered by his nephew. It was once assumed that Eckhart had sent his *Book of Divine Consolation* to Albert's daughter Agnes on the occasion of her father's death in 1308, but this is impossible to prove. At the very least, we know that Eckhart did indeed send Agnes the book. He was familiar with the bloody history of the German kings: 1298, 1308, 1313. These were turbulent times: Albert was succeeded in 1308 by Henry VII of Luxembourg, whom Dante praised as the liberator of Italy. After five years of ruling the empire, Henry died on his way to Rome in 1313. His son John laid claim to

Bohemia, marking the beginning of Luxembourg's reign in Bohemia and Brandenburg. After 1347, Emperor Charles IV successfully built upon this influence, but he could not prevent the dissolution of order within the empire. The time had come for the powerful prince-electors and competing royal families that were to determine Germany's future: the Habsburg, Luxembourg, and Wittelsbach dynasties. Their splintered territorial bases lay far apart. New administrative measures and economic and military needs called for a realignment of their borders, leading to continual battles throughout the German lands in the fourteenth century. In 1317, the great famine, which had not struck for decades, returned. By 1348, Christians in the West were praying for deliverance from hunger, war, and the plague.

Corruption in the Church

In 1294, Eckhart preached his Easter sermon in Paris, and on Christmas Eve, Boniface VIII came to power in Rome. He had pressured his predecessor, Celestine V, the "angelic" pope, to abdicate. Boniface's portrait sculpture in Florence, by Arnolfo da Cambio, is a sight to behold. A powerful personality, he thought of himself as God's representative on earth, Europe's sovereign, and feudal lord of the emperors. He carried the idea devised by Gregory VII and Innocent III of the pope's absolute supremacy over all earthly power to an extreme: the bull *Unam sanctam* represents its most explicit formulation. But France resisted and humiliated the pope at Anagni with a slap in the face. Boniface was a broken man; he died shortly thereafter, in October 1303.

Philip the Fair's conflict with Boniface showed that papal ambitions for worldly dominion were increasingly futile. While the empire grew weaker, new powers were on the rise in the form of nation-states, first France, then Spain and England. One hundred years later, Nicholas of Cusa could still remark that the Curia was financially exploiting the empire, which lacked both fiscal autonomy and military power; the Western monarchies, on the other hand, knew how to shield themselves better. Dante placed all the popes who had reigned during his lifetime in hell—primarily because they ruined Italy's peace, but also because of their financial policies and their imperiousness, self-indulgence, and hunger for power. Since 1309, the popes had resided at Avignon, in Petrarch's "Babylon." They were subject to the French secular powers, a common practice after the fated massacre of the Knights Templar by Philip IV, who had been heavily indebted to the rich order. Pope John XXII, a financial genius, heaped strict monetary demands on Western Christendom, denounced the unwavering Franciscans, spoke about Jesus and his poverty as if he had owned real estate, and condemned Meister Eckhart in 1329.

John XXII was elected in 1316 after a two-year *sede vacante*. He was about seventy-two, and his enemies were hopeful about the future. But they were wrong: he lived and ruled until 1334. And he ruled with an iron fist. One of the great church historians, Albert Hauck, characterizes him thus: "An unimpressive little man; short, skinny, pale, bald, with unattractive features and a thin voice. Constantly busy, the weariness of old age seemed to elude him. He was interested in everything: politics and dogmatics, arts and sciences, the quarrels of monks and the dealings of intellectuals, the Crusades, and especially everything to do with money."[6]

John XXII was the cause of civil unrest in the final decades of Eckhart's life: two German kings were simultaneously elected in 1314; the pope supported Frederick the Fair of Austria against Louis IV of Bavaria. Count Heinrich II of Virneburg, archbishop of Cologne, had crowned Frederick, and he continued to support him even after Frederick was defeated by Louis at the Battle of Mühldorf in 1322. Concerning the relations of power, the Avignonese pope was allied with Paris and the Habsburgs; the alliances of the German bishops fluctuated, but Cologne stood behind Avignon and against Emperor Louis, who in turn was supported by the more affluent towns. The Dominicans were split: their leaders stood by the pope, but some German preachers were reprimanded in 1325 and 1327 in the *capitulum generale* for preaching against the pope. The final years of Eckhart's life saw a dramatic escalation of political activity: at the end of 1323, Louis IV of Bavaria began to attack the pope publicly, filed a lawsuit against him, and appealed to the Holy See against the pope. In 1324, the pope excommunicated him. Yet in the same year, Louis got married in Cologne with the citizens' approval; the archbishop did not attend. In May 1324, the king contested his excommunication with the so-called Appeal of Sachsenhausen; soon thereafter, the pope excommunicated both Louis and his followers. In 1327, Louis left for Rome. He arrived there in January 1328, declared the pope a heretic based on his stance on poverty, and deposed him, which had no real consequences in the ecclesiastical realm. We may wonder where Eckhart stood among these struggles. Did the archbishop intend to attack the Dominicans for their relationship with the citizens? Did Eckhart choose a side? Occasionally, he calls for people to honor their father and mother as well as those who possess

spiritual power (German sermon 51, DW 2:468.1–3), but he does not explicitly name the pope, the archbishop, or Louis. In the few instances in which he
does mention the pope, he speaks of him as a distant, powerful, and rich man,
as in his *Book of Divine Consolation* (DW 5:58.18–23); in Sermon 25 (DW
2:18.1–2), he describes the importance of intent by using a papal example:
"If I accidentally killed the pope, I could still approach the altar without any
repercussions." Another time he preaches that one need not envy the pope;
everyone can have the same virtue as the pope, and without the turmoil that
surrounds him (Sermon 27, DW 2:46.2–6).

The pope does not feature as a religious figure in Eckhart's works.
Dante was more political in his thinking: he raged against the politics of the
papacy, but recognized its spiritual function. Eckhart ignored the pope completely, as both spiritual sovereign and politician.

Intellectual Developments

Eckhart's lifetime was marked by bloody incidents and military and intellectual conflicts within the church and the empire. We turn our focus now to the
scholarly world. Eckhart profited from the substantial intellectual developments of thirteenth-century Europe. Despite warnings and prohibitions,
Christian academics studied the vast knowledge transmitted by the Greco-
Arabic world and, after some controversy, largely absorbed it. A new rationality had developed through centuries of training in Aristotelian logic. That
reason could successfully create order could be seen in the administration of
the church across regional borders, in the restructuring of public finance, in
the organization of trade networks, and in innovations in the military and in
city planning. Aristocrats and artisans alike developed a new trust in reason,
bolstered by the Greco-Arabic arts and sciences, which opened up new
branches of knowledge: metaphysics, ethics, chemistry and optics, econom-
ics and politics. As professor of theology, Albertus Magnus interpreted
Aristotle for two decades, beginning in 1248. The curriculum adopted by the
Dominicans in 1259, developed in part by Albertus Magnus and Thomas
Aquinas, emphasized philosophy as an important part of their training, including even the previously prohibited natural philosophy.

We can assume that Eckhart's educational career must have resembled
the following: reading and writing were prerequisites for anyone entering
the novitiate, as were understanding and speaking Latin, so Eckhart must

have finished his training in grammar before he started his year as a novice, which was supposed to instill in him a monastic mindset and familiarize him with the rules of his order. Two to three years of studying logic, followed by two to three years of training in natural philosophy, must have been next; and then, finally, theology. Just like philosophy, theology had seen rapid and vibrant changes and new developments since the discovery of the Greco-Arabic texts. Albertus Magnus had harshly criticized the failings of Latin scholars: he did not merely want to incorporate Aristotle, Avicenna, and Averroës into the seemingly harmonious collective wisdom of Christianity, but instead strove to rebuild all the sciences, including theology, from the ground up. He emphasized the autonomous method of philosophy. He complained about obscurantism, something especially prevalent among the Dominicans; he showed that miracles had no place in matters of physics. His autonomous philosophical research became a model for Siger of Brabant and Boetius of Dacia. Thomas Aquinas instead opted for a middle course. His approach was criticized for its inconsistency, especially after his death in 1274. His handling of Augustine and Aristotle was too imprecise, according to Henry of Ghent, Dietrich of Freiberg, and John Duns Scotus. The church, however, increasingly made Aquinas a prominent figure of authority: it sanctioned his understanding of the soul as the form of the body, and of the blessed soul's endowment with a special kind of enlightenment in the afterlife, the *lumen gloriae*. Efforts to turn Aquinas into a figurehead of the church through his canonization in 1323 were never completely successful, despite the church's repeated threat of severe penalties. Critiques of Aquinas by Dietrich of Freiberg and Durandus of Saint-Pourçain were discussed but soon suppressed. The new political philosophy of Dante's *Monarchia* and Marsilius of Padua's *Defensor Pacis* of 1324 was banned. It never reached Eckhart.

There is one more intellectual shift worth mentioning. Since the twelfth century, Western Europe had been developing a new sense of the human individual and his rational and organizational abilities. It was no longer taken for granted that people were subjects to be ruled. Lords had to justify themselves. Authority could be challenged. Several classical authors (Aristotle in his *Logic*, Cicero, Seneca, the early Augustine, and especially Boethius) all contributed to a heightened trust in reason within the more progressive regions of Europe. The experience of urban life, the organization of corporations, legislation not based on customary law or decisions by episcopal lords, supraregional trade and monetary transactions, encounters with foreign cultures, religions, and values—all these created the need for a new way of explaining the world that took in everything, including secular rulers and religious topics. The still-flexible authority of the church participated in this change, but tried to control it to its own advantage: the second half of the twelfth century saw the formation of a new and organized dogmatic framework (Peter Lombard) as well as the comprehensive gathering and structuring of canon law (Gratian). Rules were developed for electing the pope and for the presence of papal delegations throughout the Christian world. Popes and bishops strove to support and control the universities. New ideas and developments were no longer automatically stigmatized. Authors composed their works fully conscious that innovation was legitimate. Public opinion became more diverse, and people across regional borders were constantly discussing and evaluating it: in short, a new literary public, engaged in critical dialogue, had come into existence. People paid more attention to themselves than ever before and attributed value to their own being, even in written form for others to read. Man was not just the paragon of wretchedness, the individual not just another link in a long chain of sinners. There was something divine about him. The Bible states that God created man in his own image, and this sentiment now sanctified all forms of social, urban, intellectual, and religious productivity, the pace of which was rapidly accelerating. Twenty years—that meant something rather different around 1300 from what it had around 900. In science, philosophy, and organization, Christian self-awareness was constantly re-creating itself in different and often opposing directions through continual debate. Without these historical and cultural multiplications and disturbances, Meister Eckhart would not have been possible. Far too often he has been viewed in isolation, as though— to recall Bishop Martensen's phrase—his life had been hidden in God.

A Look Ahead at Reception

An evaluation of historical events must include a consideration of their reception. How was Eckhart perceived by his contemporaries? How was he received? By paying attention to reception history, we can lessen the chance of getting stuck in the seemingly unavoidable anachronism of our modern patterns of thought. By now, we know quite a bit about the influence that Eckhart exerted.[7] He was immensely important for Henry Suso and Johannes

Tauler. Because of their proximity to Eckhart, they were denied academic careers, but they continued some of Eckhart's themes in their vernacular writings as well as in the practice of pastoral care. Nicholas of Cusa studied Eckhart's works early in his career and expanded on them with diplomatic deftness.

Later, an edition of Tauler's works, printed in Basel in 1522 and reprinted by me in 1966, became one of the most significant attestations of Eckhart's works: it contained several of his sermons, albeit under Tauler's name. In the nineteenth century, Franz von Baader rediscovered it and pointed Hegel in Eckhart's direction. Hegel is said to have exclaimed enthusiastically, "Now here is the thing we have been looking for."

The beginning of the twentieth century saw an Eckhart renaissance. Robert Musil and Karl Mannheim, Martin Buber and Martin Heidegger, Gustav Landauer and György Lukács, even Alfred Rosenberg: they all read Eckhart's German works. Roughly a third of Rosenberg's *Der Mythus des 20. Jahrhunderts* (*The Myth of the Twentieth Century*) is essentially a book about Eckhart. This renewed interest in Eckhart within German literature, philosophy, and sociology occurred outside the Catholic Church. Within it, Pope John XXII's condemnation of Eckhart still held, and it was unambiguous and harsh: the pope had called Eckhart's teachings "devil's seed." We will examine Eckhart's trial at length in later chapters; here I am concerned with the overall picture. Between the initial accusations in Cologne in 1325/6 and the end of the trial in 1329 lay three years of close scrutiny and examination. The pope stressed that he had had "many" learned theologians investigate Eckhart's teachings, and that he and his cardinals had reexamined them once more. Eckhart was a respected theologian and had occupied several high-level positions within a powerful order; the situation demanded thoroughness. The pope was careful to highlight that the investigation had not only focused on individual sentences, but also taken into account their context, the *connexio sententiarum* (LW 5:599.99). The pope did not accept all the articles that had come under suspicion in Cologne; he singled out certain ones and distinguished them according to their degree of reprehensibility. He identified three groups of sentences: fifteen were wholly heretical, eleven were suspected of being so, and two Eckhart denied ever having taught. During his interrogation in Avignon, Eckhart admitted that he had taught the twenty-six sentences listed in the first two groups, of which at least seventeen were clearly heretical. Eckhart's trial was conducted professionally and with proper care; other heretics were not so lucky.[8] The extent to which Eckhart was personally affected by the trial is discussed in the final chapter.

Only his death protected Eckhart from a worse fate. My study shows that Eckhart's teaching of the deified man, the *homo divinus*, was incompatible with the official theology of the time and the beliefs of the Curia in Avignon. The great Eckhart scholars writing before 1950 confirmed this view: Heinrich Denifle, Martin Grabmann, and Gabriel Théry. Nicholas of Cusa defended Eckhart, saying that he never taught that Creator and creature were the same. Nonetheless, Nicholas wanted Eckhart's writings removed from public libraries.

After 1980, there were attempts to reopen the trial. They led nowhere. Eckhart's case was different from Galileo's: the church brusquely rejected his teachings. And there are good reasons to believe that it will not—that it cannot—overturn the condemnation of Eckhart as devil's seed. Those reasons will reveal themselves in the process of our textual analysis.

2. A Forgotten Concept: Philosophy of Christianity

A Conciliatory Proposal, an Initial Hypothesis

The works and ideas of influential thinkers, because of their rich complexity, seem different to every historical age; they oscillate, unconcerned with how we categorize them. But anyone who starts to work historically looks for order; he needs labels, and so he clings to disciplinary affiliations, intellectual currents, titles. Historical thinking thrives on rebelling against this initial manner of categorizing, classifying, and designating, especially in philosophy, where certain labels—like idealism, realism, and so forth—are almost never used without doing injustice. They drown the individual thinker in "currents."

Our task here is to try to grasp Eckhart's intellectual world, the private world of a misfit, through his writings; other labels we may bring to the text are dismissible and of no real value, except perhaps for their preparatory and didactic nature as aids to a first approach. Nothing can be inferred from them about Eckhart. At best, they are heuristic tools.

The utility of any such label must be proved through a close and thorough reading of Eckhart's texts, and I propose—only hypothetically for now—to try out the phrase "Eckhart as philosopher of Christianity" instead of the label "mystic." Perhaps this phrase may lead us closer to Eckhart's way of thinking than does "mystic," a term that has no grand origin and cannot, after all, invoke Dionysius the Areopagite as its source. I am asking the reader to forget about Eckhart the "mystic" for now and to attempt instead to read Eckhart as a "philosopher of Christianity." Let me provide a preliminary explanation of the phrase here; whether this designation indeed fits his writings better, only a close reading of Eckhart's works can show. The following facts may provide cause for revision: the label "mystical theology" existed long before Eckhart, and yet, as the next chapter will show, he never said in any of his self-portrayals or defenses: you will only understand me once you recognize that I am engaging in a "mystical theology." There is nothing authentic about the label "mystic" in Eckhart's case. It began to circulate before anyone could have been familiar with Eckhart's Latin writings and when scholars were under the impression that they had detected a second school of thought, a medieval corollary to "scholasticism," namely, "mysticism."

The phrase "philosophy of Christianity" sounds strange today, or is associated with Hegel. It reeks of philosophical idealism and of anachronism. It sounds as if ideas from the early nineteenth century are being applied to an earlier period.

In a philosophy of Christianity, Christian beliefs would be explained via a strict methodology, through pure reason. A philosophy of Christianity would mean an attempt to prove Christian ideas rationally in such a way that believers and unbelievers alike would come to recognize them as true, and not merely as culturally contingent constructs of Christian communities of faith. Someone developing such proofs could be a believer, but need not be; either way, he would be creating a new methodological realm in which certain universal premises of humanity would replace the creed as the basis of proof. Let us assume that such a philosopher of Christianity was praying for enlightenment while he was constructing and putting forth such proofs. No matter how fierce his prayers, or how seriously he took them, he would evaluate them like a mathematician praying to the Holy Spirit for inspiration in attempting to solve a complex mathematical problem. The prayer in this scenario would not enter into the argument, an argument that would have to be entirely mathematical, or the prayer would have been in vain.

A philosopher of Christianity would subscribe to a similarly strict method of proving his arguments. The article of Christian faith to be proved would vary according to place and time. It has a history, and we must not imagine it as a stable given existing outside time. Even an author saying that he is proving the main tenets of the Bible may mean different things, and we must ask ourselves which ones they are. *Sacra Scriptura*, Holy Scripture, was simply another word for theology in the Middle Ages, and hence meant not just the Bible. The creeds of Christianity developed late and only after immense struggles. They lack some of the most important tenets, such as the justification. They were interpreted in various ways. They were the cause of much strife. Do purgatory and confirmation, for example, belong to the doctrinal teachings of Christianity?

So, too, "purely rational proofs" were not always the same everywhere. Reason itself was not always the same. Even the strictest standards of proof could not always prevent contingency, which was due to group affiliations and contemporary trends, the books one had read, what else one knew about science or the world, and the mission that one subscribed to.

Therefore, to practice a philosophy of Christianity can mean only this: a thinker attempts to prove those theses generally considered essential tenets of Christian thought with what he considers to be a purely rational method. And yet he could not do so unless he started from the philosophical status quo, even if he wanted to improve it. He developed a method that he was able to plausibly defend against authorities of the time as a purely rational procedure; he made use of the concepts of reason and the rules of knowledge creation that were relatively uncontested in his intellectual milieu and that were known for their methodological separability from mere beliefs.

As is immediately recognizable, such a procedure was threatened by objections from two sides: Christians protested that what was squeezed into a rational mold was not the real and true Christianity, and philosophers objected that what was claimed to be purely rational was in reality highly illogical and philosophically untenable.

Philosophers of Christianity were constantly faced with this war on two fronts. But they could console themselves; their opponents did not possess the definite and successful form of philosophy either.

I take the label "philosophy of Christianity" to be programmatic. It does not have to carry this designation. There were authors who understood theology in emphatically scientific or philosophical terms. They claimed that they were practicing the true, the speculative theology; others may have called it "philosophical dogmatics." The terms we use and our departmental affiliations do not matter; what matters is the strict adherence to a specific methodology.

What Is Philosophy?

What does philosophy mean in the context of a philosophy of Christianity? The term "philosophy," in my opinion, should not be used too vaguely here, in the everyday sense that it carries in expressions like "the philosophy of the Pentagon." At the same time, it would be too limiting to insert a term denoting a specific school of thought, as though we recognized only Kantian epistemology, neoscholastic ontology, or Anglo-American analysis of language as philosophy. These special forms may have their own value, but anyone who recognizes only one of them as philosophy will consider the phrase "philosophy of Christianity" a paradox.

We are concerned here with the universal concept of philosophy. It is a love for *sophia* and is recognizable as the habit to justify one's statements, to argue most precisely according to a set of common rules. We can approach philosophy as a universal concept via the following deliberation:

Insofar as we know historical life, humans have always placed their daily needs, wants, and experiences into a complex conceptual framework. They developed a unified worldview. They told each other stories about their origins; they explained their hierarchies through images, buildings, or poems. They created models for what one must and must not do. They found ways to explain their experiences of natural phenomena like day and night, summer and winter.

To establish some connection with Eckhart, I illuminate my point about the production of universal conceptual frameworks through the example of religion. There are several ways of generalizing one's religion beyond a single proscription or statement, and it happens even in everyday life, not just as an academic exercise. Some people, for example, think of everything religious as a form of venerating their ancestors. Or as adhering to the church calendar. A third model portrays the kingdom of God as a royal court and subsumes individual rituals and statements under this image. God, in this scenario, is called the Lord. He is conceptualized in the same terms as those used to describe a pharaoh or the Persian Great King. He is surrounded by heavenly hosts who execute his will in quasi-military ways. He demands obedience; questioning his commands is taboo. Part of the royal-court model of religion is: the ruling Lord is seen, admired, and applauded by his servants. He wants to be praised. His staff function as messengers, they intervene when necessary, they acclaim him constantly. There is a clear hierarchy, even among the servants. Such a unified picture shapes a person's interpretation and conduct of life. Gaining and retaining the Lord's favor is important; his wrath is terrible. A victory in war is a sign of God's favor. If one asks what is right, the answer is: whatever the Lord wants is right. If one asks what thunder is: a sign of God's anger; a rainbow signals his reconciliation.

Other cultures gave other answers: "right," people determined, was what arose from reason or from what the people wanted. In historical time (I mean: for as long as we have had written sources), there have always been competing views of society and concepts of religion. Some of these could be combined, for example, the royal-court image with a religious calendar and a commitment to sing praise. But when adherents of these competing views started to quarrel with one another, philosophy was born: it is to be distinguished from the production of myths, epic stories, and general rules as a later phenomenon. It is a Greek invention, arising between the time of Homer and that of Parmenides as a self-commitment to justify one's assertions. When someone asks for the justification for these rules, new debates arise; their other preconditions, and they do have them, appear difficult to pin down; they trail off into indefiniteness; nobody can survey them all. And thus the discussion continues. These controversies form the history of philosophy.

Philosophy interfered with Greek religion. It told the Homeric gods that a new time had come, one in which they were no longer able to do whatever they pleased. It stipulated fixed criteria for them. If they wanted to continue to be seen as gods, they had to be considerate, just, and good. Otherwise they would not be true gods, but popular fantasies or inventions of the poets. And as Aristotle—and Heraclitus and Plato before him—had said: poets often lie. The one God worthy of adoration was the one that adhered to the criteria of Truth, Goodness, and Justice. A purifying storm had come to cleanse both popular religion and Homer. Homer should have been whipped, counseled Heraclitus; and while Plato was more polite, he still had him moved to the fringes of the state and honorably deposed. In his book *Die Theologie der frühen griechischen Denker* (Stuttgart, 1953; translated into English as *The Theology of the Early Greek Philosophers* [1947]), Werner Jaeger described the beginnings of philosophy up to Plato as this type of work: correcting the royal-court model of religion; replacing the feuding heavenly clans with a single God; stressing wisdom over capriciousness, and ungrudging goodness and justice over incontestable power; the world as *kosmos* and *physis*, not a mere footstool for God.

Truly, a new time had begun. Now philosophers determined, though at first only for an intellectual elite, what a real and true God could be. Their actions were at once pious and rebellious. God, Plato says, has to be good. He does not observe human skills with envy; he is not angry with us for wanting to know. The philosophers' God once was a god of purification, of ethical sublimation of the popular and Homeric gods. His arrival marked the end of courtly religion, and the Stoics and Neoplatonists pushed this agenda consistently, albeit in different ways; the Skeptics criticized and laughed.

Everything looked different after this philosophical revolution, nature and polis. It changed the way people thought about themselves. They now knew: they were both reason and soul; and they demanded of a God that he be reason and be related to them as soul. The meaning of "soul" changed: soul was no longer a vapor of the blood, a breath of life, or the presence of one's ancestors. Soul became the essence of the criteria. It was subjected to the rule that it had to become as similar to God as possible, a God conceptualized as mind and as wholly good. Greek philosophy dematerialized and ethically ennobled both God and the human soul. God and soul became "mind," *nous*. Now it was a matter of explaining what "mind" meant. As elsewhere, there were variations. Plato's *Republic* developed the idea of the Good: it was not an individual good, but the indeterminate Good that humans could and should employ to judge everything, even the gods. For the conduct of life, that is, for ethics and politics, that meant man was supposed to live in a way that would make him as similar to the Godhead as possible. Plato's *Timaeus*, especially at 29b, concluded regarding the creation of the world that its creator shaped it, without jealousy, as beauty, order, and accordance with reason. Plato's differentiation between perception and knowledge was momentous for the period that followed: in the *Theaetetus*, it led him to the discovery that the soul was the ground of unity for the sense perceptions: the eye cannot hear, the ear cannot see, and yet we often assign what we have seen and heard to the same being. Therefore, there had to exist a faculty of differentiation and consolidation above sense perceptions. The soul is active, harmonizing and evaluating what has been perceived, especially whether it is good or bad. It is indispensable for finding commonalities among wholly different perceptions. Whether these perceptions are similar or dissimilar, one or many, good or bad, is decided not by individual perceptions themselves, but only by the thinking soul itself. It engages in dialogue with itself; which means: it thinks. The soul is the reason that sense perceptions do not just bump about within us like the Greek heroes in the Trojan horse. It relates the multitude of its impressions to one coherent point of reference (*Theaetetus* 184d). And to do that, it needs concepts that apply evenly to different sense modalities. These concepts are primary determinations that are not derived from sensory perception, but that are necessary for our thinking about what we have perceived when we consult ourselves about whether our impressions are similar or dissimilar. Plato calls these concepts *koina*, common things. But they could also be called primary determinations. Plato lists several different ones: Being or Nonbeing, One-Many and Number, Similar-Dissimilar. "Soul," then, means two things: that which consolidates the many sense perceptions coherently, and that which consults with itself about which of the common determinations are true (*Theaetetus* 184d–185e).

This Platonic deliberation is important for two reasons. First, it refutes the false impression we have of certain epochs, that is, the legend of antiquity—and even more so of the Middle Ages—as "objective ages" that had no knowledge of the productive nature of the mind-soul, of "consciousness" or the "subjectivity" of knowledge.[1] And second, because Plato's analysis of knowledge, among many other Platonic legacies, was channeled through Aristotle, Plotinus, Proclus, Augustine, Avicenna, Averroës, Albertus Magnus, and Dietrich of Freiberg, and influenced Eckhart's concepts of the soul and, especially, of the intellect.[2]

Within this family of ideas, man embodied mind. Mind, *nous*, *intellectus*, was seen as essential and as the true human. We can read it thus in Aristotle; Albertus Magnus and Thomas Aquinas adopted his position. Living according to the mind is the right kind of living; it is the life that pleases God. Mind is the possession of those criteria that determine what a true God must be and how a rational human has to conceptualize himself. Mind is an active ground of unity; it is synthesis. And it means having primary determinations such as One-Many, Being or Nonbeing, Good or Evil.

Greek "Mind" and Judeo-Christian Revelation

Aristotle, who wanted to know more about what mind was, defined it more precisely in the third book of *De anima*. The text is a complicated one; apart from Plato's *Theaetetus* 184d–186 and *Timaeus* 29b, it is the best remote preparation for a study of Eckhart; I provide a necessarily simplified summary:

Mind has nothing in common with anything else. It is not a natural thing; none of the determinations with which we define the world apply to it. It is essentially energy and activity. It is the active nothingness of the world; it is the energy not to be like the world, to have it as its counterpart and to rule over it intelligently.

Mind is the possession of the universal. Everything is its object. Because it is not part of anything, it posits reality as a unified whole in opposition to itself, and can turn anything into an object.

It is the possession of its contents. It is its contents. It becomes what it thinks.

It is divine; it is the divine. Since Plato and Aristotle, European philosophy has based its general view of humanity, of nature, of politics, and of religion on *nous* as its model. Instead of being represented as a royal court, religion became the relationship between God and the mind-soul. God is good to the mind-soul; he granted it its privileges, that is, its capacity and license to evaluate the world and its religions. It cannot be bothered with things contrary to it; it is justified in applying its criteria—regarding nature, politics, and religions. If revelatory texts contain something that does not fit its criteria, for example, when they command a father to kill his own son, then the text is interpreted figuratively and in the end becomes evidence for schizophrenia. The multiple senses of scripture and allegorical exegesis developed this way. It made the passion-driven, chaotic nature of Homer's gods more rational; it defended the Hebrew Bible against objections based on its barbarity—as evidenced in Philo of Alexandria, Origen, Ambrose, and the younger Augustine.

Augustine increasingly moved away from an allegorical interpretation of the Bible, but he could never quite rid himself of it completely. Inspired by Plotinus and Porphyry, he sanctioned for Christians the Aristotelian metaphysics of the mind and the ideas, which Plotinus had developed further. He taught that we are God's image, *imago*, through the mind, *mens*. Since nobody has seen God, we rely on this image to conceptualize God and divine truth. Augustine established this God-Soul type as the universal concept of religion, but the model never existed in isolation. The models of the royal court, of the cult of one's ancestors, and of the ferial calendar continued to exist, but the concept of true religion was now inextricably linked with the mind-soul's self-awareness; its task was to judge false elements, even within religion. Augustine saw in Christianity a kind of Platonism for the people;

everyone heard preachers explain what the true God was—in distinction to the false gods. For Augustine, the rational soul represented the essence of all criteria. He expressly taught: when we talk about God, we can say that he has always done that which, after careful deliberation, we must consider the better option. God is the true God only if he adheres to the rules of reason. It was Augustine who created this standard, and it was he who later destroyed it. Eventually, he had to recognize that God said of himself that he hated Esau and loved Jacob before they ever could have done anything good or evil. It created a rift in his thinking. Augustine passed on a conflicting view of religion and man, of nature and politics. Greek philosophy had put the gods under certain criteria. In part, Augustine broke with them when he praised God's actions as free from criteria. And while he initially adopted and furthered a philosophy of religion, his doctrine of original sin limited and partly negated such a way of thinking, though he never abandoned it completely.

"Intellect" in the Middle Ages:
A Note on Albertus Magnus of Cologne

Late antique philosophy and Islamic interpreters of Aristotle streamlined the Aristotelian theory of the mind: they developed it further into a cosmology. In the second half of the thirteenth century, they presented the Christian academics in the West with the question whether to adopt or reject this tradition, which had survived via Augustine in only a fragmentary state, as a normative religious concept. Individual parts of the tradition were challenged. Christians rejected the idea of the intellect's unicity for all people, but overall assimilation was the norm. Albertus Magnus declared that he agreed with Averroës in "almost everything"; Thomas Aquinas, Henry of Ghent, and Dietrich of Freiberg attempted different combinations of Aristotle with Avicenna, Augustine with Averroës.

Eckhart was aware of this intellectual milieu. He knew how effective a philosophy of the mind could be in unlocking the interpretive secrets of Christianity: he had read Albertus Magnus of Cologne, with whom he was acquainted.

Albertus Magnus explains what the intellect is in a supplement to his commentary on the third book of Aristotle's *De anima.*

For Albertus Magnus, the object of the intellect is the universal, a universal that exists in reality, which is the foundation of the individual things, *cum universale sit intellectus proprium obiectum*, an object that precedes the things, that is *ante rem* (Lib. I tr. 2 c. 3 IX 494b). This universal informs the particular things; it makes them into what they are. The mind already holds all content within itself beforehand, *praehabet in seipso omnia intellecta* (Lib. II tr. unic. 508a). It is the possession of the principles from which all knowledge develops. That is why the intellect finds itself in all objects. It is the reason why Plato's definition of philosophy is quintessentially true: philosophy is the knowledge of one's self, *verissima philosophiae diffinitio est suiipsius cognitio* (ibid., 515a). The intellect finds the absolute Good and absolute Truth within itself as its immanent principles. The human mind is image, equivalence, and likeness of the first Truth. Its greatest joy, and one most in accordance with its nature, is the contemplation of the contents that it has perceived through the senses. This contemplation becomes the mind's very reason for its existence. Man's entire nature flourishes in it, *in ea tota refloret natura hominis* (515b). Within this context, man is pure intellect, *inquantum homo solus est intellectus*. Like the first Truth, the highest Good is present within the intellect. It is its nature to rejoice in it. It is why it should shun the particular, transient good, *a bono ut nunc* (515b). At times the intellect melds with the first Truth and the highest Good; it receives prophetic insight and to a certain extent can be called "God," *et quasi Deus quidem esse perhibetur* (417a). It brings along its own rules, and everything that happens in relation to it has to adhere to its power of perception. If, through understanding, the intellect is linked to the first Truth and Good, then it is itself divine, *divinus*, and as Homer says, it no longer seems like the son of a man, but the son of God. That is why Hermes Trismegistus says of the intellect that it is the link between God and the world, *homo nexus est Dei et mundi* (5174b).

Albertus Magnus wrote a hymn on the human intellect made divine. This hymn, an exercise in philosophy of mind, alludes to Homer in calling the deified intellect the "son of God." Philosophy of mind qua relationship with God is simultaneously recognition of nature and ethics. The deified human is distinguished through knowledge and virtue: he is *optimus in scientiis et virtutibus*. The intellect is man, and it connects God and the world; its nature is to contemplate the divine things and to see nature in their light. Albertus Magnus cites pagan authorities for his concept of divine filiation, namely, Homer and Hermes Trismegistus, and not the Gospel of John, and he describes divine sonship as the nature of the intellect. There is nothing super-natural in this for him; he calls it the most natural, the *naturalissimum*.[3]

In dealing with particular Christian or revelatory content, the intellect provides and applies its principles. It is not supposed to obey, but to conceptualize itself, the world, and God according to certain rules. This is its philosophical and also its religious life. But how well can this approach be sustained in regard to Christian revelatory material? How consistently did Albertus Magnus apply it? He laid the foundation for a philosophy of Christianity. But how did he proceed in practice? He was inundated with a mass of books and theories, many of which he made accessible to the Western world. But whether he was a coherent philosopher of Christianity is much harder to judge. Suffice it to say here that for Albertus Magnus, the intellect as developed in the Aristotelian-Arabic tradition was part of man's relation to God. That, in fact, it *was* man's relation to God. His treatise *On the Intellect and the Intelligible* paved the way for Eckhart's philosophy of Christianity.

Medieval Philosophers of Christianity?

A philosophy of Christianity—did such a thing exist in the Middle Ages? Perhaps some will concede that it does in the modern era. Leibniz defended God's goodness and wisdom with rational arguments; he talked about the realm of nature and of grace. He really wanted to *prove*, not just to suggest or make plausible. We can assume that he was a philosopher of Christianity, as was Blaise Pascal. We can see a similar trend in Kant's writings on religion, in Fichte's *The Way Towards the Blessed Life*, in Hegel's *Philosophy of Religion*, and in Schelling's *Philosophy of Revelation*. No reasonable person would identify this way of thinking with Eckhart's; to provide an initial idea of it, I shall quote a sentence from Fichte's *Attempt at a Critique of All Revelation* (Königsberg, 1792). Fichte is not interested, as his title might imply, in criticizing all revelation, but in finding a principle by which one could determine the truth of any revelation. In other words: what would a religion have to be like that originated from a God worthy of recognition? Fichte, following Kant, starts from the ethical aspect of revelation: the only revelation that can come from God is one that establishes a moral principle agreeing with the principle of practical reason (§9).

But did such a thing exist during the Middle Ages? Did anyone unambiguously develop criteria by which to recognize the true God? Did any author between 800 and 1500 claim to prove with evidence, for every nonbeliever or dissident alike, that a specific Christian dogma, for example, that of the Trinity, was true? The answer is: without a doubt.

Anselm of Canterbury formulated his program poignantly. He cited faith as his personal motivation, but sharply distinguished it from the question of provability. He claimed that he wanted to argue about God, his qualities, and his Trinity in a way that would derive nothing, *penitus nihil*, from the Bible but would deduce everything through logical and rational reasoning as necessarily true.[4] Even in writing about salvation through Christ's crucifixion, Anselm kept to this program. In fact, he put it in even more radical terms by saying that he wanted to leave Christ out of the equation completely and to argue *remoto Christo*, as though he had never heard of him.[5] Anselm was a devout monk, but he had a strict and clear concept of his methodology, of which his teacher Lanfranc did not approve at all; still, he undertook no changes. *Rationes necessariae, sola ratione:* these were Anselm's key terms. His method was controversial, his results were denied by many, but his concept was clear and can justifiably be called a philosophy of Christianity: Christian content, differentiable from faith by the nature of its purely rational content, and communicable to the laity. Its basis was a simple idea: if God is Truth, and if Christianity is true, then we must be able to recognize that. Within this understanding, Christianity belongs to all people, not just Christians. Whether Meister Eckhart had a similar concept has to be tested in detail and on philological grounds. We cannot presuppose it from the outset. Until now, there was no real danger of anyone making such an assumption; I will test it with the help of Eckhart's texts in the following chapters.

Philosophy of Christianity in the Nineteenth Century

The concept of a philosophy of Christianity seems strange nowadays. It has been abandoned in both Catholic and Protestant theology; even in philosophy, it no longer exists. Leibniz practiced it during the religious wars in order to drive back any theological excess that promoted violence. Ramon Llull (died 1316), an exact contemporary of Eckhart and like him a linguistic genius and gifted writer, similarly strove to convert the Muslims to Christianity through rational arguments and logical, mathematical proofs. He is said to have demonstrated the Holy Trinity and the Incarnation to them with the help of small machines built for combining elemental truths. Whether something like that can work is of no concern here—only whether such a rational approach to

Christianity existed and whether Eckhart can be associated with a comparable type of argumentation, albeit in rather different form. We shall see.

Allow me a preliminary historical note: in *The Way Towards the Blessed Life*, Fichte sought to prove the truth of the prologue to the Gospel of John. Hegel declared that scholastic theology was a philosophy of religion. He cited Anselm and snidely pitted him against Protestant theology, which he said contained only bare dogma and historical trifles. A philosophy of Christianity existed then, and it was even called that. But the fashion had started earlier: in 1777, a certain Erasmus Danielsen had published his *Wahre Philosophie des Christentums für Jedermann* (True philosophy of Christianity for everyone) in Hamburg. I have not seen the text; the title sounds like popular philosophy. Between 1810 and 1860, however, things became more serious and academic. Friedrich Köppen's *Philosophie des Christentums* (Philosophy of Christianity) was published in 1813; Julius Frauenstädt published his *Über das wahre Verhältnis der Vernunft zur Offenbarung: Prolegomena zu jeder künftigen Philosophie des Christentums* (On the true relation of reason and revelation: Prolegomena to every future philosophy of Christianity) in Darmstadt in 1848.

There also existed a Catholic version of the philosophy of Christianity. It emerged in Metternich's Vienna, in two volumes by Anton Günther called *Vorschule zur speculativen Theologie des positiven Christentums* (Prolegomena to a speculative theology of positive Christianity [1826–28], then as volumes 1 and 2 of Günther's collected works [Vienna, 1882]). It found its strongest expression in Johann Heinrich Pabst's *Der Mensch und seine Geschichte: Ein Beitrag zur Philosophie des Christentums* (Man and his history: A paper on the philosophy of Christianity [Vienna, 1830]). Pabst's later polemic pamphlet was called *Gibt es eine Philosophie des positiven Christentums? Die Frage über Leben und Tod des neunzehnten Jahrhunderts* (Is there a philosophy of positive Christianity? The question of life and death of the nineteenth century [Cologne, 1832]). Why was the question of whether a philosophy of Christianity existed one of life and death? It seems like a preacherly exaggeration, but Pabst and Günther's idea was that the rebuilding of Europe after the Napoleonic Wars could not be achieved by torn people. They were torn between knowledge and faith, between Christian inheritance and enlightenment. Philosophers deepened this conflict by ignoring Christianity; the pious consolidated the conflict through their fears of philosophy as corrosive. A philosophy of Christianity reconciled knowledge and revelation and granted humanity peace. It was not enough for science to admit that Christianity was without contradiction. Rather, it had to find Christ's presence within knowledge itself. The idea of the time was that man was self-consciousness. Everything that was present within man's consciousness had to be similar to it, had to correspond to its most basic conditions. It tore him apart and hindered or corrupted his practice in private and in public if important parts of his life and knowledge fell apart. Christian history and Christian ethics were a part of Europe, a part of man. He could neither ignore this history nor graciously acknowledge that it was not absurd. Man himself was said to be this history, and he had to develop this from within himself through science and philosophy, based on the unity of his self-consciousness. Within this process, two conditions were necessary. First, a theory of creation that showed the Creator-God as triune and as one whose Trinity was not only without contradictions, but also a conceptual necessity; second, the theory of the Incarnation. It conceptualized what most Christians consider to be the most important event in history not solely as a mere historical fact, but also as presence. Without being able to show both, Christianity would no longer be assimilable and philosophy would lose its core: the development of content within man's self-consciousness.

The Vienna philosophers of Christianity around 1830 were writing brilliant, fantastical works like Jean Paul, and like Metternich, they were planning a new, monarchical Christian Europe. They strove for a holy alliance of knowledge and faith, which distinguished them thoroughly from similar medieval attempts. But there was one point of comparison: what united them all was a self-consciousness discovered by philosophers from Descartes to Kant, a self-consciousness that recognizes all its content as its own. Around 1300, a theory of the intellect as both condition for and creator of unity was developed. The intellect capable of such unity was not to be understood as a faculty of the soul, but as the ground of unity or substance of the mind-soul. This mind-soul, or intellect, set conditions for everything that could occur within itself. Augustine's doctrine of *mens*, read via Aristotle–Averroës–Albertus Magnus, proved the presence of God within the intellect and interpreted it philosophically as the eternal truth of the Incarnation. Not a single letter of the revelatory texts was changed, but this new way of arguing in an intrinsically philosophical fashion made everything appear in a new light. Humans and angels, God and the devil, had all become subjects of human knowledge.

Reconceptualizing Christianity was nothing new. St. Paul, Origen, John Eriugena, Anselm of Canterbury, and Thomas Aquinas had all attempted new definitions based on a universal understanding of man and the world, of God and revelation. If Meister Eckhart was striving to be a philosopher of Christianity, something I merely touch upon here hypothetically, he would have had to make a similar attempt to discover the truth of Christianity within man's understanding of himself: was the logos that shone within each person not God? Cartesians and Kantians alike considered reason to be that which had to be able to accompany all our ideas. Medieval philosophers of Christianity found in the human mind not the same point of origin, but a comparable one. The few quotations from Albertus Magnus show that there existed an attempt to develop Christian thought and life anew based on this central doctrine of mind.

The Decline of a Model: Evaluations of Eckhart

The search for a philosophy of Christianity in Germany around 1800 was not confined to one denomination. It was a popular topic. Christian Hermann Weiße collected all these attempts in his monumental *Philosophische Dogmatik oder Philosophie des Christentums* (Philosophical dogmatics, or Philosophy of Christianity, 3 vols. [Leipzig, 1855–62]). After 1860, the movement petered out: Neo-Kantians, Neoscholastics, and Positivists all declared that such reconciliations were impossible. The Vienna authors around Clemens Maria Hofbauer, namely, Anton Günther and Johann Heinrich Pabst, were censored by Rome. Catholic authors no longer tolerated a philosophy of the Trinity, nor a philosophical theory of the Incarnation. Around 1840, it was still possible for the famous Catholic theologian Franz Anton Staudenmaier to publish the first volume—containing only 923 pages—of his planned tripartite work *Die Philosophie des Christentums oder Metaphysik der heiligen Schrift als Lehre von den göttlichen Ideen und ihrer Entwicklung in Natur, Geist und Geschichte* (The philosophy of Christianity, or the metaphysics of Holy Scripture as a doctrine of divine ideas and their development in nature, spirit, and history [Gießen, 1840]). Staudenmaier argued: the Bible presupposes metaphysics but also proclaims it. He found it especially in the books of wisdom; the Gospel of John discusses the divine logos that illuminates every human who enters into this world and that thus makes understanding possible not just for Christians. This knowledge, if it contained truth, should be attainable also through philosophy. Staudenmaier employs statements of the Bible that were written late, by writers already under the influence of Hellenistic philosophy, in order to develop his concept of a philosophy of Holy Scripture. I am not sure whether it is satisfactory. I merely point out that Staudenmaier mentions Meister Eckhart, albeit with the greatest distance:

> Among the sects of the Middle Ages, a false mysticism could not remain undetected for long, and one soon raised itself up to such dizzying heights that it made the world aware of its existence all by itself through just one man, who had the mental capacity to stand out among the heroes of speculative thought of all times and who, while abandoning himself to a mystical pantheism and making connections to the Beghards and brothers and sisters of the free spirit, could influence his contemporary environment and posterity only in a very detrimental way that was destructive for true Christian speculation. This man was Meister Eckhart. (640)

Even Staudenmaier, the late idealistic and philosophically open-minded theologian, saw devil's seed. He lets us approach Eckhart not only as a potential philosopher of Christianity, but also with the question whether his mystical pantheism devastates Christian speculation. And beyond that: does Eckhart, as Staudenmaier criticizes, dissipate "the historical side of Christian revelation through his allegory"? (642).

Staudenmaier found even more devilries than the theological experts at Avignon, namely:

The world, for Eckhart, was the Son of God and was God (643)
According to Eckhart, God would not be God without the world (643)
All things were God himself (644)
"Thus, the concept of any revelation is abolished, except for the concept of
    divine self-revelation" (644)

Staudenmaier goes on to criticize Eckhart for distinguishing the Godhead from God. The Godhead becomes God by an eternal process of self-objectification; it returns to itself. "Only now the entire doctrine of the Trinity, and thus the doctrine of Father, Son, and Holy Spirit and their interrelation, has become merely a large symbolic form through which and by which this self-process of divine life is approaching the idea. That is the answer to the big secret: God births out of himself and within himself."

"This is the apex" of Meister Eckhart's pantheistic theosophy (645).

I take these citations as proof of how different philosophies of Christianity can be. We cannot discount Staudenmaier's keen sense of the issue. His critique of Eckhart relied solely on the German texts, but it was thoughtful. I will leave it at that for now. I just want to provide an idea of what a philosophy of Christianity could be. I present this concept here as a merely hypothetical one, as a potential frame. Whether it is accurate must be decided on the basis of Eckhart's works.

3. Self-Portrayals

In interpreting his own works, a poet or philosopher is not always right. But someone who interprets a poem or a philosophical text without considering the self-portrayals of an author is always wrong. They must be taken into consideration and checked against the text. This practice has long been neglected in Eckhart's case. Here I present a few texts in which Eckhart talks about his intentions. He did so repeatedly. It was a convention of academic commentary to state the topic, to name the author's intentions, and to announce what the reader might gain from the book as an introduction to a given work, in the so-called *accessus ad auctores*. Still, the frequency and intensity of Eckhart's self-interpretations were unusual for the time. Eckhart knew that he was deviating from conventional practice and that he was difficult to understand. Nowadays, it makes him more accessible. We hear his own tone; we become acquainted with his ideas, his key terms, and his style from the beginning. But these self-portrayals are not revelations; they need to be compared with Eckhart's writings if we want to define his fundamental concepts more precisely and determine their historical situatedness.

In the following nine excerpts, presented in both my translation and the original language, Eckhart describes what he was trying to do. My collection of his self-portrayals is by no means exhaustive; exhaustiveness would have destroyed the structure of this book. But my approach offers a methodological advantage: my starting point is broader than if I were to posit an initial thesis and then select matching passages. There are many conflicting opinions about Eckhart. Hence, it seems opportune to see how Eckhart himself describes his intentions. Not all interpretative pitfalls are thereby avoided. It could be the case that Eckhart did not accurately describe his intentions, that he did not fulfill them, or that he changed them. We do, however, gain a verifiable point of departure. In the following pages, every reader can compare his own expectations and assumptions—in short, his preconceived image of Eckhart—with Eckhart's representations of himself. Eight of Eckhart's nine self-portrayals are taken from his German sermons; starting in the vernacular may be easier for my audience. That they form the majority here does not mean, however, that Eckhart's German works have a larger methodological benefit than his Latin ones. Their priority is of a purely didactic nature. Let us begin our readings.

German Sermon 3, DW 1:48.8–49.2

I have also often said: knowledge and intellectuality unify the soul in God. Reason falls into pure Being. Knowledge runs in front. It runs ahead and breaks through so that God's only-begotten Son can be born there.[1]

Eckhart says that he has often touched on this subject in sermons: reason is the location of God's birth. It is reason that unites man and God—not a feeling, faith, or a vision. Eckhart is specifying a concept of reason that we will need to consider further. It does not follow from every concept of reason that one is thereby united with God. The Middle High German dictionaries available to me offer no substantive difference between reason (*vernunft*) and intellectuality (*vernüfticheit*). Dietrich of Freiberg differentiated *intellectus* from *intellectualitas;* the latter was the essential, substantially active reasonableness of reason that arose out of its highest degree of "simplicity."[2] In any case, Eckhart speaks about unification, not about the mere knowledge that God is the final ground of the world.

That reason could know God without faith had been a common Christian belief since Paul's writing of Romans 1:20. It was reinforced by the Hellenistic philosophers who were known in the Middle Ages via Cicero and Seneca; Augustine wrote about it; Boethius depicted it as his philosophy. We learn something in this first excerpt about Eckhart's conception of reason: reason is the faculty of the most universal and of what lies behind it. It pushes forward through the jumble of properties and events; it grasps pure

Being. When Eckhart says that it *vellet*, he means that it lunges at the pure essence.

We still need to determine what pure Being is, just as much as *vernüft-icheit*. And yet it is already clear that reason precedes all human action. Its power of penetration, its natural activity, makes the birth of God possible within it—not our desire, not baptism, not ecclesiastical authority. Eckhart describes reason not as collecting, registering, connecting, or obedient listening, nor as the power of tracing the order of the universe within itself. And while reason likely has to go out into the world of experience, Eckhart is instead focused on its power of penetration here. It throws itself into pure Being; it does not look for God in the order of nature. We are far away from proofs of God's existence through nature. Eckhart is speaking as though reason finds God within itself, as though this were its comprehension of pure Being. At least in this text, reason appears to be active. It is that which unites.

German Sermon 73, DW 3:261.11–12

> I say this often and think it even more often: it is a marvel that God poured intellectuality into the soul.[3]

Eckhart admires human reason. It is the best thing in the soul. It is the precondition for the birth of God. It is the content of his constant reflections and often of his speeches as well.

Eckhart calls it a "marvel" that God has given us reason. The word "marvel" has been flattened in modern parlance. Eckhart means far more here than just thinking that it is "marvelous." As our nature and God's marvel, reason shatters the supposed borders between nature and "supernature." It is "supernatural" as a miracle of God. As Albertus Magnus wrote: Oneness with God is most natural to it, *naturalissimum*.

This is reminiscent of the passage from Genesis 1:26: "Let us make man in our own image and after our likeness"—by pouring reason into the soul. But Eckhart is not citing anything here. He knows what reason is. He speaks so that we will know it as well. All people possess it, not only Christians. We have to learn to recognize what value it holds for us. As in the first passage, reason must play its part so that the Son of God can be born in it. Both texts teach the internal relationship between the nature of reason and the birth of God.

German Sermon 6, DW 1:103.1–105.3

Just men take justice so seriously that if God were not just, they would not give a fig for God.

They are so solidly rooted in justice and have so completely gone out of themselves that they have no regard at all for anything, neither the agonies of hell nor the joys of heaven. Indeed, if all the suffering that those endure who are in hell, men or devils, or all the suffering that has ever been or will ever be suffered on earth were to be laid onto justice, they would deem it nothing, so resolutely do they stand by God and by justice.

For the just man, there is nothing more painful and difficult than that which is contrary to justice and that he is not equal in all things. How so? If something can please a man or something else can sadden him, then he is not just. And more: if men are happy at one time, then they are happy at all times; if they are happier during a certain moment in time than during another, then it is an injustice to them.

Whoever loves justice takes such a strong stance in it that the thing he loves constitutes his Being: nothing can draw him away from it; nothing else catches his attention. St. Augustine says: "The soul is more effectively itself when it loves than when it gives life."

Our biblical phrase sounds primitive and ordinary. Hardly anyone comprehends what is contained within it, and yet it is true. Whoever can grasp the difference between justice and the just man will grasp everything that I say.[4]

One of Eckhart's most decisive statements about his purpose. He explicitly speaks about his entire body of work; he does not differentiate between his Latin and his German texts. "Differentiation" here means: the exact relation. Someone who has grasped what differentiates the just man from justice—that is, what kind of relation there is between them—is said to have grasped everything that Eckhart says. Up to this point, "justice" has simply been a term, much like "reason," "pure Being," and the "birth of God." They are concepts that need to be worked out, not simply parroted.

Drawing on our own everyday experiences, we would probably formulate the difference between the just man and justice like this: the just man is a man, and justice is his property. Eckhart could ask in return: when a just man dies, does justice perish as well? Does the definition of a circle perish when a schoolchild throws away his drawing of a circle? When Eckhart thinks of a just man, he considers the latter's justice to be not only his property, the result of his upbringing, or the expression of his noble character. In that case, it would merely be an occurrence in the world of experience, just like thousands of others. For Eckhart, justice is more; it is something close to "reason," "pure Being," or "God."

Eckhart explains how he wants men to conceive of God: God is that which fulfills reason's highest criteria. He must be just. It is only justice that gives the vernacular idea of "God" a specific meaning. It is only through justice that God becomes recognizable and worthy of recognition. Eckhart says this with an inimitable brusqueness: if God were not just, I would not give a fig for him. His audience is supposed to fill in the word "God" through thinking, excise it from its popular sense and its merely figurative use. God does not belong to whatever exists, not even as the pinnacle. Reason must break through to the true content of the term "God." Which is justice.

The ideal life that Eckhart drafts for the just man is remarkable: he is unwavering. Everything that hits him from the outside bounces off him, explicitly even supernatural rewards and punishments, the joys of heaven and the torments of hell. They cannot be the motive of his actions. He is firmly rooted in justice. It gives him support, and what is more, he lives within it. Among Augustine's writings, Eckhart believed that he found the sentence "The soul is more present where that is which it *loves*, than where it *enlivens* a body." The pun sounds much better in Latin: there it says that the soul is more present *ubi amat quam ubi animat*. And while the passage is actually by Bernard of Clairvaux and not by Augustine, it expresses an insight that was nonetheless important for Eckhart: the soul forms itself according to its objects. It becomes what it is after. It does not simply exist. It is not a fixed component of the world; it obtains its essence through attention and rejection. Someone who loves justice, who loves it radically, becomes justice. He reshapes the accidental character of his nature and of his upbringing. As a social and corporeal creature, he remains frail and determined by outside forces. Insofar as he is just, however, he creates his way of life and protects it under every circumstance; therein he remains constant to himself. Someone who falters has not yet made justice his purpose in life. This results in a peculiar form of Stoicism. But the Stoicism here is a consequence, not the core of the idea. What is essential is the ability of the soul to actively give itself a form, to shape itself. It does not stand there fixed, like a tree; it knowingly and willingly throws itself upon others, it *becomes* what it takes up. Many people lose themselves in all sorts of things; but when the soul grounds its life in justice, it *becomes* uniform and becomes justice. Justice is its God—a living God, not a merely imagined one. The soul's entering into justice is metaphorically called the birth of God within it. It is not the metaphor that is essential, but rather the insight into the ability of the soul to form itself—its plasticity, as it were—and into the ability of the just man to become identical to justice. He who has understood this has understood everything that Eckhart has to say.[5]

German Sermon 9, DW 1:154.7–155.3

"As a morning star in the middle of the mist." I am concerned here with the small word "quasi," which means "as." Schoolchildren call this a by-word [an adverb]. That is what I am concerned with in all of my sermons. The most proper terms that one can use for God are "Word" and "Truth." God named himself a "word."

St. John said: "In the beginning was the Word," and he meant that man is a by-word to the Word.[6]

Another comprehensive self-portrayal. Eckhart names the content of all his sermons: God is the Word (*verbum*), man is the by-word (*adverbum*). He is the adverb to the verb, but of the same nature qua word, and as an adverb, he relates his meaning to the verb. Eckhart here is using the grammatical theories of Priscian and his contemporaries, not simply "playing."[7]

Eckhart stresses: As at the beginning of the Gospel of John, God is called "Word," but this is not one of many statements about God; rather, it is the key to knowing God and ourselves: Word and Truth, that is the *aller eigentlicheste* ("most proper" form) of what is to be said. Eckhart goes beyond the superlative when he says what he is trying to do in all his sermons. God is Word, we are word, Word and by-word. Why is "Word" the keyword? It signifies relation. The Word unifies the speaker and the spoken content. It has by-words around it. Word belongs to the intellect. It is making apparent, revelation, showing oneself to another. Someone looking for a metaphor might say that the Word is born anew within him.

We are now familiar with a series of fundamental Eckhartian concepts: reason as the reaching out to pure Being and reason's internal purpose for the birth of the Word, that is, of God, within it; the qualification of the term "God" according to certain criteria, first of Justice, then as Word, as disclosure, as present and intelligible Truth.

Eckhart replaces the word "*got*" (God) with "Word." We are supposed to think "*wort*" (Word) when we encounter the term "*got*." "Word" in its essence refers to the intellect; the one who speaks and that which is spoken occur in the Word. The Word has a relational character; it unifies within itself those that are separate as natural things. The "by-word" is itself Word; it has the same nature. Eckhart conceives of man as Word, not primarily as a thing of nature. As Word, man pronounces natural things. They are present within him, not as natural things, but rather as wordly, mirrored, in a new form of reality.

The prologue to the Gospel of John adopted this insight from the philosophy of the logos of antiquity. Eckhart builds on this age-old wisdom: the Word illuminates every person that comes into this world, not just Christians.

German Sermon 48, DW 2:416.1–10

While I was on the way here today, I was thinking about how I might preach so reasonably that you would understand me correctly. And so I came up with a comparison, and if you understand it correctly, then you will understand my intention and the basis of all the views that I have always preached. This was the comparison of my eye and the piece of wood. When my eye is opened, it is an eye. When it is closed, it is still the same eye. The piece of wood loses and gains nothing from my seeing. Now, pay close attention to my words: if it were to happen that my eye is one and unified in itself, and it is opened and casts a glance at the wood, both eye and wood remain what they are, and yet in active contemplation become one to such an extent that one can truly say: "eye-wood" and "the wood is my eye."[8]

Eckhart knew that his audience had a difficult time understanding him. He recounts what he was thinking while on the way to deliver the sermon that might make his words understood. German sermon 48 is an extraordinarily explicit text. It contains what is likely Eckhart's most articulate self-explanation in his German works. Again, his self-interpretation is related to *everything* that he thinks and says.[9] A comparison explains the basis of his thinking: like the seeing eye that casts a glance at the wood and becomes one with the wood, man, through active performance, through seeing and loving, becomes that which he sees and loves in the mind.

Eckhart is outlining a philosophical problem: I see a tree. The tree exists for itself; the eye has its own being by itself in my organism. We can say that, however, only because we have cast our eye upon the tree. Only then is the tree there, by me. We retroactively separate eye and wood from the eye-wood unity. Is the wood-eye union the truer reality? Or is it merely an image, or simply a thought? Seeing things clearly in this regard, according to Eckhart, is the necessary precondition for understanding everything that he says—not the study of the Bible or dogmatic theology. First and foremost, we need to occupy ourselves with understanding this unity. It is our daily life. It is not a thing of nature, but rather the having of natural things. It is its own form of reality. Conceptualizing it is the only way to make all revelatory texts accessible. Without this initial insight, God is dead and discourses about him are incomprehensible. Here we are at the source of Eckhart's thinking. I will return to it.

German Sermon 53, DW 2:528.5–529.2

> Whenever I preach, I habitually speak of detachment, and that man should become free from himself and all things. Second, that he should be reshaped into the unitary Good, which is God. And third, that he should think of the great nobility that God has placed in the soul so that man might thereby come to God in a marvelous way. Fourth, I speak of the purity of God's nature—the glory that belongs to the divine nature is ineffable. God is a word, an unpronounced word.[10]

Here, Eckhart provides a summary of his sermonic themes. They are diverse but have the following connection: first, man must let everything be, himself and all things. He is able do this because he is active reason that knows that it is positioned above all things. It penetrates the final ground of unity. Detachment forms the entry point for the proper life. The next step is insight into the high status of the soul, which, as reason, is the presence of the Godhead. In the next step, it recognizes the purity of God's nature, its complete correspondence to the criteria—"*got*," that is, the unified Good. It unites truth, concentratedness, and justice within itself. And more: the Godhead is Word, a word with no audible sound, and thus is conceptualized as "unspoken." What "ineffability" means for Eckhart is to be investigated in the context of Eckhart's negative theology.

German Sermon 69, DW 3:176.3–177.5

Fifth: that it [reason] is an image. Ah, now pay close attention and remember this well, for thereby you have the entire sermon summed up: image and image are so fully one with each other that one cannot recognize any sort of difference between them. One may be able to think of fire without heat, and heat without fire. One can also think of the sun without light, and light without the sun, but one cannot think of any kind of difference between image and image. I go even further and say: God in his omnipotence cannot recognize any difference, for they are born with one another and die with one another.[11]

Through reason, man is an image of the Godhead. In this he corresponds completely to the origin that is the Word. Insofar as he is image, there is no distinction between him and his exemplar. The intellect can separate the sun from light, fire from heat. Between exemplar and image, however, there is no difference. Eckhart does not say "exemplar" (*exemplar*) and "copy" (*imago*); rather, he emphasizes the identity of image and image verbally. Even God's omnipotence ends here, for it would be a contradiction if we were image but did not correspond completely to the exemplar. This insight, Eckhart emphasizes, sums up everything with which his sermon is concerned.

"Image"—that is reason as the marvel of being the image of the Godhead. It is possessing worldly things in the manner of the wood-eye synthesis. Image is the Word with its inseparable by-word. On the basis of this active unity, we can speak of wood and eye, of God and his presence, and thus of man's happiness. It is here that justice and truth occur. This occurrence is metaphorically—that is, in a manner requiring explanation—called birth.

The fragment Sermon 16a, DW 1:258.1–11, states something similar: if I lean against a wall, I am indeed close to it, but I am not the wall itself. It is different with intellectual creatures—they are within one another. The soul as the image of God is God. Eckhart adds:

This is subtle. He who understands it has had enough preaching.[12]

Someone who has understood the reciprocity of the image—of the nonbeing wood in seeing—has understood all of Eckhart's sermons. The censors in Cologne objected to this identification.[13]

In Ioh., nn. 2–3, LW 3:4

In explaining this word, the author, as in all his works, has the intention of interpreting that which Christian faith and the scriptures (in both testaments) teach through the natural reasons of the philosophers. "For what is invisible in God is recognized by a creature in the world via the intellect from that which has been created, even his eternal power," that is, the Son, "and his Godhead," that is, the Holy Spirit, as the gloss to Romans 1:20 states. Augustine says in Book 7 of his *Confessions* that he had found the following sentence in Plato, "In the beginning was the Word," as well as a large part of the first chapter of the Gospel of John. And in Book 10 of *The City of God*, he discusses the declaration by a Platonist that the beginning of the Gospel of John up to "and it was a man, sent by God" should be written down with golden letters and displayed in prominent places.

Further, the aim of this work is to show how the verisimilitude of the principles and conclusions and essential properties of the natural things are clearly suggested in the words of Holy Scripture for the one "who has ears to hear" if they are interpreted with regard to the natural things. Several ethical interpretations are provided throughout as well.[14]

Until this point, all of Eckhart's self-portrayals have come from his German sermons and have referred to neither biblical commentary nor the academic disciplines of theology and philosophy, which had been developed and differentiated in the universities since the thirteenth century. They indicated the perspectives under which Eckhart sought to understand the Bible. Here, in the beginning of his Latin text explaining the Gospel of John, Eckhart has to speak more precisely. For the past century, philosophy had had its own

institution in Paris, the Faculty of the Arts. Many books presented arguments exclusively in a philosophical manner. Despite opposition, Albertus
Magnus had helped them gain recognition in the Dominican order. Here,
Eckhart is writing for specialists who inquired after the situatedness of his
reasoning within scientific theories. Eckhart tells them that here, as in all of
his texts (he was evidently concerned with the universality of this intended
goal; here he explains the overarching purpose of his oeuvre), he wants to
explain the Bible, both the Hebrew Bible available to him only in Latin translation and the New Testament, with philosophical arguments. Roughly
speaking, he wanted to extract from the Gospel of John both the creation of
the world and God's Incarnation, both man's redemption and salvation to the
original condition, through philosophical proofs. And he goes even further:
the Bible contains all of natural history. Thus, he wants to show in a second
step that it contains all the principles and conclusions for knowing nature.

Eckhart has charged himself with a double task. He intends to reach
both aspects through philosophical argumentation. He does not revert to a
time before the reception of Aristotle and the commentaries of Averroës.
First, he intends to demonstrate the main truths of scripture philosophically,
namely, God's nature, his Trinity, the creation of the world, and the
Incarnation. Second, he wants to show that the Bible contains all the main
features of knowing nature. He intends to interpret the sayings of scripture
until something emerges that belongs to the realm of natural philosophy, and
sometimes also of ethics.

Eckhart was familiar with the objection that no Christian could philosophically prove the essential contents of the Bible—that indeed he was not
allowed to, for he would be encroaching on a higher realm with philosophical
arguments and would thus violate the dignity of faith, through which one
gains knowledge of God's Trinity, the Incarnation, and the salvation only
through a special form of divine revelation. Eckhart responds to this objection with a series of citations. He quotes Paul's Romans 1:20, underlays the
verse with the Trinitarian interpretation of the gloss, and points to Augustine's
account of his education. With the highest of authorities—St. Paul, Augustine,
the *Ordinary Gloss*—he secured the most difficult point, the philosophical
knowableness of God's Trinity and Incarnation. With the help of the gloss,
Eckhart expands the passage in Romans 1:20, which serves as evidence that all
humans are able to recognize God within the world through natural reason, to
the logos and to the Godhead's Holy Spirit. He strengthens this argument

with recourse to Book 7 of the *Confessions*, in which Augustine confirms that ancient philosophers recognized the logos in the light of natural reason, and thus without revelation.

The second goal of the argument meant: Eckhart wanted to prove that the insights of Greco-Arabic philosophy—specifically those of Aristotle and his Islamic commentators—were expressly pronounced or at least implied in the Bible. One simply had to locate them through philosophical arguments.

With this twin goal, Eckhart threw down the gauntlet to many—not to all, but most—theologians and philosophers of the time, and especially the natural scientists. Since the reception of Aristotle and his commentators in the thirteenth century, a methodological division between philosophy and theology had been the order of the day. Theologians tended to confine philosophy to natural theology, namely, the knowledge of the one God as the ground of the world; to a knowledge of nature, including the doctrine of the soul; and perhaps to ethics and logic. Philosophers were by no means supposed to claim that they could prove the Trinity, let alone explain it better than theologians. There had almost developed a consensus: the Trinity, God's Incarnation, and the redemption were the prerogative of a type of knowledge accessible only through faith. After these concepts were accepted in faithful obedience, reason could prove that they could be formulated without contradictions, but they did not thereby become an object of natural reason to be proved through it.[15] And as far as the investigation of natural things was concerned, it had become an independent philosophical field with its own methods since the reception of Aristotle's *Physics* and his other scientific writings, alongside their commentators writing in Arabic. Two or three years of the Dominican course of study were dedicated to it. Albertus Magnus and Thomas Aquinas, commenting on the enormous textual corpus for this purpose, had established it as a textbook. When we pursue physics, we are not concerned with miracles, Albertus Magnus had exclaimed in order to keep the Bible away from natural philosophy. Eckhart wanted to reunite the recently divided. How he does this in his writings and whether his argument is convincing remains to be seen. The point here is that his program is starting to take shape. His explanation in Latin is more explicit and ideologically clearer than his explanations in German. Still, it corresponds to the German sermons. In both cases, Eckhart is seeking to do more than what preachers usually do, more than paraphrasing the Bible or the creeds and applying them to the present. He wants to grasp the meaning hidden within them. In so doing, he is guided by an emphatic concept of truth: truth as the ground of living, as reason-logos according to the eye-wood model.

Getting there requires distinct, inseparable steps: the internal relation of reason to Justice, Truth, Word, Godhead occurs on the basis of a qualified concept of reason, not as a power of the soul in the soul's substance; the often-used word "God" is in need of interpretation, namely, as Justice, as Being, as Truth, as Word with by-word, and in its relatedness to the intellect; reason conceives of itself as an image identical to its exemplar, which is within it in eidetic fashion, that is, as actual intellectual being, uncreated and uncreatable.

The unity of reflective self-consciousness and ethical orientation follows from this. The way reason—always in the qualified sense—is, it has nothing in common with anything else. Its self-knowledge means: it can let go of everything, even itself. Thus, all secondary motives of self-related actions, even the pious ones, are to be eliminated. The soul is to position its life in Truth, in Justice; then it *is* in Truth. Then it is Truth, and the Truth is within it.

Eckhart is stating the premises for a radical reform of living. Man must first grasp that he is a creature of relations: he becomes that which he decides; he exists as intentional activity. He becomes what he recognizes. He becomes what he intends. He must recognize and develop his dignity. He learns to understand himself as an image of the exemplar, as by-word to the Word, as an essential, not a coincidental, relatedness. In truth, he is the light that penetrates all distinctions. He must cease to think of himself as an existing part of the world. Eckhart insists on the difference between the separate worldly things wood and eye and their oneness in the act of perception. He advances the distinction between the examination of Being and the analysis of intentionality, between ontology and philosophy of mind, between a world of things and the relations that actually exist in the world of thought. Understand what happens when you open the eye that had been shut until now and see the wood. The soul has a greater unity with that which it seeks, knows, and loves than with its physical and psychological organism. It is that to which it consistently places itself in relation.

Ethical consequences are suggested without being fully developed. They do not yet indicate the connection between the conception of reason and detachment. The ethical occurs as a secondary result; it is not the main subject of self-investigation and the new explication of Christian self-consciousness. The bad part is not that humans are bad, but rather that they do not know themselves. Eckhart does not say: "Until now, you have misunderstood Christianity." He says: "You have misunderstood yourselves, and as long as you persist in this error, you cannot provide Christianity with the intellectual and ethical form which is possible today, in 1300." Everything needs to be made anew. Start by thinking about the eye-wood. Its most difficult part is the easiest: we imagine the wood *there* and the eye *here*. We label both as separate, independent things. We have forgotten that we are merely able to keep them separate because they were previously together in the eye-wood unity. The eye-wood unity is not a thing. If someone wants to label it a mode of being at all, then it is a mode of being sui generis. It is the nonmaterial being-within-each-other of eye and wood. The eye, opened and cast on the wood, is, *within itself*, over there with the wood.

German Sermon 52, DW 2:499.10–500.3

Now pay attention, diligently and earnestly: I have already said it several times, and a great master says it as well: man is supposed to be detached in such a way from all things and all works, both internal and external ones, that he becomes God's own site in which God could act. Now I say it differently.[16]

There are stages of understanding. Eckhart despises monotony. Man must leave all things in order to come to rest in oneness. He must negate everything. Eckhart said this often, great authors say it, and it is still the case. Eckhart does not take anything back. Here, in a late sermon in Cologne, he announces the next higher aspect: one must also let go of the letting go of all things. It is not about effort, not about asceticism, but rather about a plain being-at-home that reason does not destroy but perfects. It is and it remains active life, the presence of the self in the desert of the Godhead, and God's presence in the indefinite breadth of the soul, which obtains itself because it has given up everything, even its desire to be a site for the Godhead.[17] In this sermon excerpt, it matters that Eckhart allows himself multiple ways of representation. Different considerations require different propositions. It comes down to an "insofar." I will return to it several more times.

4. Beginnings: Paris and Erfurt, 1292–1298

Two Parisian Sermons

Perhaps we could say that philosophical and poetic texts ask two things of their readers. "Read me," they say, "as though I had just fallen from the sky, devoid of a previous history, devoid of future effects. Receive me as though I were written only for you alone, and as though everything depended on your recognition that I am relevant for your individual life, that I explain this life to you, and that I tell you what belongs to it. Sometimes I may present a strange picture, but you will learn something about yourself." But at the same time, the text seems to say: "Analyze me as a product of past realities: I am interspersed with all sorts of historical, social, intellectual, and psychological conditions. Treat me, albeit in a second phase, as though I were a washed-ashore piece of history. Position yourself against me as an other."

This twinned method is rarely practiced. Against it, we could argue that someone who has drunk in the living *succo* (juice) of the intellectual and linguistic power of an Eckhart or Plato or Kant need not bother with the odds and ends of historical and philosophical detail. But we should remind ourselves that what is considered essential, the poetic-philosophical substrate of Plato's texts, or Eckhart's or Kant's, is controversial and continually being reinterpreted. Not fixed, it is in continual motion, and seemingly small details—dates, manuscript finds, and new biographical data—can all cause significant ripples. Our knowledge or ignorance of certain facts can change our understanding of the basic tenets of earlier philosophers. A failed or successful incorporation of new facts into our commonly held assumptions corrects or conserves certain schools of thought. Without them, subjective appropriations will never experience a corrective; the confident pathos of having captured the essence once and for all remains intact; speech that shuns facts trickles away, vague and imprecise. What previous readings of Eckhart often lack are linguistic discipline, semantic specification, and a philological basis: the way we have labeled and interpreted Eckhart and the categories into which we attempt to squeeze him even today were created at a time when his Latin works were still unknown. And yet they far outnumber his German works, and their tradition is more secure. Within them, a professional author speaks to his educated readers, but they lay dormant in manuscripts at Erfurt and Cusa, until Heinrich Denifle rediscovered them in 1880 and made portions of them available in print in 1886. The preconceptions that were developed when people had access only to the German Eckhart still resonate today. The books on Eckhart written between 1820 and 1890 demonstrate by example what Eckhart scholarship looks like when it lacks the foundation of his Latin texts. The 1857 edition of Eckhart's German works by Franz Pfeiffer made possible more nuanced representations of Eckhart beyond the earlier ones by Franz von Baader, Hans L. Martensen, and Franz Anton Staudenmaier, for example, the studies by Joseph Bach, *Meister Eckhart: Der Vater der deutschen Speculation* (Meister Eckhart: Father of German speculation [Vienna, 1864]), and Georg Lasson, *Meister Eckhart der Mystiker* (Meister Eckhart the mystic [Berlin, 1868]).

These works often categorize Eckhart a priori as a mystic, either in the title or within the opening sentences. Others defined him through specific philosophical currents and called Eckhart's intellectual position "Aristotelian-Thomistic" or "Platonic"; they characterized him as an advocate or enemy of "scholasticism." Many distinguished between scholasticism and mysticism, seeing scholasticism as an abstract art of concepts, and mysticism as intuitive or as immediate religious experience. Still others sought a reformer before the Reformation. All of them lacked access to the Latin manuscripts. To put it bluntly: what these scholars held in their hands was Eckhart's Sunday output; what he did from Monday to Saturday was beyond their knowledge. It had consequences for their interpretations of Eckhart. Everyone ranged between certain alternatives: pantheism or theism, realism or idealism, loyalty or disloyalty to the church. But these decisions were impossible to make without Eckhart's Latin works.

Even small advances within philology and history have consequences. All texts, even the Bible and even Eckhart's, are situated within a specific historical context and have to be read and analyzed carefully within that context. Such a proper historical reading by itself is not enough, but it is the only way to avoid wild speculations, mere subjective appropriations, exploitations of the author in behalf of the church or in antiecclesiastical contexts, all of which abound within scholarly interpretations of Eckhart.

I attempt to follow my proposed twinned method in shifting my focus now to the close examination of Eckhart's works. Eckhart's self-portrayals, which I outlined in the previous chapter, lead us into the depths of mere speculation. They leave many questions unanswered: What concept did Eckhart have of reason? Is man identical to God or not? I want to learn more about the strange being of the eye-wood unity: is it a being or not? How did Eckhart conceptualize the difference between bodily things and intellectual actions? What precise role did faith and revelation play in Eckhart's thought when he wanted to know the Trinity and the Incarnation through natural reason? Did Eckhart perhaps change some of his views throughout his life? Does he not indicate this himself in the First Parisian Question (LW 5, n. 4, 40.5) when he says that he used to think like Thomas Aquinas, but now thinks differently? Do we have to distinguish between Eckhart I and Eckhart II? We can decide these only on the basis of his individual works. Thus, my analysis now proceeds by following the general progression of Eckhart's life and thought, beginning in Paris, *anno* 1294.

Eckhart's main task as lecturer in Paris was to interpret the Bible and Peter Lombard's *Sentences*. His commentary on the *Sentences* has been lost, but two sermons survive from Eckhart's initial years in Paris. As the oldest surviving texts we have of Meister Eckhart, they are of special significance. Both are written in Latin: the older text is a sermon on Peter Lombard's *Sentences*, the *Collatio in libros sententiarum*, which he preached at the beginning of the semester in the fall of 1293; the second is an Easter sermon from 1294. Both sermons are greatly determined by their context and its formal regulations, but they also provide a glimpse of Eckhart's individuality and peculiarity. The *Collatio* on the *Sentences* begins with a verse from Ecclesiastes 38:4: "The Highest has created medicine out of the earth," *altissimus creavit de terra medicinam* (LW 5, n. 1, 17). Eckhart divided up this sentence and, interpreting it word for word, read it as symbolizing the structure of Peter Lombard's theology: beginning with the doctrine of God in the Lombard's first book (*altissimus*), to Creation (*creavit*) in the second, to the Incarnation in Book 3 (*de terra*), and finally to salvation and its healing power (*medicinam*) in Book 4. Such an interpretation was to be expected of a lecturer tasked with explaining the structure of the Lombard's four books. Eckhart's individual streak shows less in his skilled dissection of sentences, which was (while well developed in Eckhart) not uncommon in the Middle Ages, than in his impulse to calculate the height of heaven right at the beginning when encountering the word "*altissimus*," with the help of the Arab astronomer Alfraganus. Eckhart calculates the diameter of the zodiac (*diameter circuli signorum*), if I can trust Josef Koch's conversion of miles to kilometers, as the astonishing distance of 280 million kilometers; he confirms his scale with a quotation from Moses Maimonides. This Jewish scholar taught that the center of the earth was approximately 127 million kilometers away from the bottom part of the zodiac.[1] Would a novice, a young theologian, really speak in such a way about the foundational text of Christianity? Later on, Eckhart focuses on the content of the Lombard's four books in more detail, but it was no more common back then than it is today to start with astronomical calculations of heavenly heights when preaching about the Highest, and to quote a Muslim and a Jewish scholar from a Christian pulpit. This was a theological matter. Eckhart had only to comment on the words "the Highest created," but from the very beginning he combined biblical exegesis with natural science and recognized the superiority of Islamic and Jewish specialists in this regard.

Even stranger was the beginning of the Easter sermon that Eckhart delivered in the next year. The opening verse, from 1 Corinthians 5:7, reads: "Christ the Passover Lamb has been sacrificed. Therefore let us keep the Feast." The feast, Eckhart explains, is the Eucharistic bread of the Mass on this very holiday.

Eckhart's *Introduction* is curious: on the basis of Cicero's two rhetorical books (*De inventione* and *Ad Herennium*), he discusses the criteria for a good speech: it has to affect the hearer directly—*tua res agitur;* it has to contain incredible, that is, marvelous, things; it has to say something new, that is, something unfamiliar; it contains greatness, something that goes beyond nature. Then Eckhart turns toward the Mass: here we encounter something incredible and marvelous, he claims, for God, the "intelligible and incomprehensible sphere," "whose center is everywhere and whose surface nowhere," offers himself to us in the form of bread.[2] Eckhart finds his way to the paschal feast via two strange paths, via Cicero's rhetorical admonitions and via the definition of God by the twenty-four philosophers, which Eckhart frequently—though not always—attributes to Hermes Trismegistus, the thrice-biggest and oldest teacher of humanity. Preachers frequently employ strange digressions to heighten, in Cicero's terms, their audience's suspense, a tendency mocked by Dante and Boccaccio. But Eckhart's path to the Highest in the *Collatio* on Peter Lombard's *Sentences* had led him through Islamic and Jewish astronomy, and now Eckhart deduced God's sublimity from a definition of God that had always been part of human wisdom, a sublimity that makes it seem incredible and marvelous that God offers himself to us in the bread. Eckhart is practicing theology within the educational context of all humanity. He still speaks within the context of Albertus Magnus's boom in cultural expansion. He toys with the most arcane quotations; plenty of non-Christians feature in his sermon: Alfraganus, Rabbi Moses, Hermes Trismegistus. Briefly, Eckhart touches upon the subjects that will concern him for the rest of his life: humility, a virtue of ancient philosophy for which he quotes Ptolemy: "He who is more humble among the wise, is the wiser";[3] the subject "poverty" is implicit at LW 5, n. 7, 140; he stresses the difference between the things of the body and those of the mind (n. 16, 148). In his role as preacher, he provides an example of his type of biblical exegesis, namely, the parabolic and symbolic: after the Crucifixion, Jesus's corpse was wrapped in pure linen, and so the Eucharist is meant only for the pure (n. 11, 143.12). The name "Peter," Eckhart claims, means something akin to "someone who knows," and so the knowledge of one's self and one's own weakness is the right preparation (n. 13, 144.9–11); not a single word about Peter holding the keys to heaven. Boniface VIII succeeded to the papacy on Christmas Eve 1294.

In addition to the pagan masters, Eckhart also quotes a series of Christian authors, particularly Augustine and Dionysius the Areopagite. Remarkable for our purposes is his remark that Albertus Magnus "often" said: "This I know how we are wont to know it, for we all know little" (n. 13, 145.6–7). No one should give himself airs because of his knowledge, and no one should neglect self-scrutiny. Eckhart could have found more confident statements regarding the Eucharist in Albertus Magnus's works, but instead he quotes the humble dictum that exhorts men to become self-aware. This passage is the only indication that Eckhart likely knew Albertus Magnus personally.

Talks of Instruction

In 1294, Eckhart left Paris. There he had read, that is, commented in detail upon, Peter Lombard's theological textbook, the *Sentences*. He then became prior of the convent at Erfurt. His superior, the provincial of the very large Dominican province, was Dietrich of Freiberg, who appointed him vicar of Thuringia. As prior, Eckhart delivered a series of speeches for the Dominican novices, which later received the title *Talks of Instruction* (*Reden der Unterweisung*). They represent the first of Eckhart's larger works, and his earliest work in German. We can date the speeches securely to the time between 1294 and 1298, Eckhart's first and last years as prior.

We are now entering monastery walls that still exist today; young Dominicans and novices were gathered there, likely alongside others who were preparing to take or had already taken vows of poverty, chastity, and obedience. What would be more natural for their prior than to expound to them the higher value of the cloistered life compared with secular activities, and to highlight the duties to which they were committing or had committed themselves, namely, obedience to people of higher rank within the order, poverty as disavowal of private property within a monastic community well provided for, chastity as a life of celibacy? This, we may think, is what needed to be explained to the younger generation. But nothing of this sort occurred, for the speaker was not any prior, but Eckhart—the preacher and brother with a previous career as professor at Paris.

Before turning to the details of Eckhart's speech, we must remind ourselves of the world that surrounded the Erfurt monastery: the time up to 1273 was "a terrible time, devoid of an emperor." It ended with Rudolf of Habsburg (ruled 1273–91), whose territorial power base was splintered. Only amid violent struggles did he manage to prepare the future rule of his royal house of Habsburg. First he defeated Ottokar II of Bohemia, who fell in the Battle of the Marchfeld in 1278. After Rudolf's death, the prince-electors chose Count Adolf of Nassau as king of Germany (1291–98). The authority of the empire was crumbling; imperial power had become dependent on the king's power base, and that of the minor count from the Taunus Mountains was negligible. Through bloody struggles, Adolf managed to bring both Thuringia and Meissen under his control, which caused a clash with the archbishop of Mainz: Erfurt was part of the Electorate of Mainz. Adolf succumbed to the coalition of Mainz, Cologne, and Bohemia, was deposed, and fell in the Battle of Göllheim against Rudolf's son, Albert I of

Habsburg (1298–1308). Yet Albert likewise failed to establish a hereditary monarchy for the Habsburgs; he was murdered by his nephew, John the Parricide, in 1308. The powerful archbishop of Trier, Baldwin, instigated the election of his brother Henry of Luxembourg (1308–13), but the king died during his Italian campaign. The crown was passed to Louis the Bavarian (1314–47). The decades under his rule were fraught with battles against the Habsburgs and the conflict with the pope.

This was the political situation within the empire during Eckhart's lifetime. We shall take a quick look at the history of the papacy as well. Pope Celestine V abdicated on December 13, 1294. He had reigned for only a few months; his resignation occurred under dubious circumstances, probably pressure from his successor, Benedict Caetani, Pope Boniface VIII, who had his predecessor imprisoned. Celestine died in 1296, still in captivity. Boniface VIII (1294–1303) took the idea of the papacy as a worldly power to a new extreme, but found an even more powerful opponent in Philip IV of France, who had Boniface arrested at Anagni in 1303. The French Clement V (1305–14) succeeded Boniface and in 1309 moved the official seat of the Curia to Avignon, where it remained until 1377. Clement led the Council of Vienne (1311–12), which established the dogma of the human soul defined as the form of the body; it also sanctioned the Thomistic theory of the accidental *lumen gloriae*. Clement's successor was John XXII (1316–34), a mastermind of finance and administration who canonized Thomas Aquinas in 1323 and condemned Eckhart in 1329.

After this look at the rather nasty outside world, we shall return to the sanctuary of the monastery walls at Erfurt and to Eckhart's conversations (*Collationes*). The monastery had been in existence since 1228, and because of the importance of both city and monastery, there were enough younger people to provide an audience for Eckhart's subtle deliberations: this alone was an important fact of educational history.

Eckhart transformed the content of the order's vows. He did not consider chastity at all. Obedience he praised as the embodiment of virtue, but it was a new kind of obedience. Toward the end of his speeches, he mentioned poverty, but its meaning, too, was changed. Eckhart reinterpreted the traditional values of his order in accordance with his theory of detachment and letting-be. He developed an outline of his doctrine of life based on his call for self-awareness; he began with an explanation of what he considered "God" to be, and what his God expected of us. His speeches were geared in content, style, and level of sophistication toward younger friars, not toward members of a university.

I cannot recommend the book for lovers of mysticism. It would be confusing if they had to read that they should use their reason resolutely in all circumstances, *bî allen dingen* (DW 5, c. 7, 210.1–2). Their embarrassment would be complete when the text instructs: if they knew in the context of a true mystical vision like Paul the Apostle's (and thus not just during a pious feeling or a subjective vision) that there was still a sick man who needed a bowl of soup, then they would be better advised to abandon the ascent to heaven and fetch some soup for the poor man (DW 5, c. 10, 221.4–8). A single glance at the news today reveals where we can find a *siechen menschen*, a sick man, in need of soup. The times of "rapture" (*Verzückung*), as Josef Quint translated Eckhart's *înzucke*, are over.

We should turn now to Eckhart's main topic, his recasting of obedience. Eckhart begins by stating that obedience *alwege*, that is, *always*—Quint uses the made-up German term "*allwegs*"—causes the best in all things (DW 5, c. 1, 186.4–5). From the sound of it, Eckhart seems to be turning one of the order's virtues into *the* Christian virtue par excellence. There was no precedent for this even before Eckhart. Admittedly, abundant praise of monastic obedience had existed as early as Augustine, the *pater monachorum* who spoke of obedience as "mother and custodian of all virtues"; ideas of *ordo* had long fostered the euphoria for obedience among many theologians who were lamenting Adam's disobedience and strove for an order in which man was subservient in family, church, and state.[4] Even so, obedience had hardly been the superior category in the face of faith, hope, and charity. In any case, Eckhart does not conceptualize obedience as the willing submission postulated in family or politics. And he certainly did not argue from the narrow confines of an individual reason that recognizes itself only in its dependence on a higher reason. The obedience that Eckhart considers central is a *lûter usgân des dînen*, "a complete abandonment of what is yours" (DW 5, c. 1, 188.4). The obedient, in the Eckhartian sense, gives up what belongs to him both willingly and knowingly. Eckhart turned the conventional value of obedience into a voluntary and free disentanglement of the self from all attachment it may have to anything created. He transformed traditional obedience into a theory and practice of self-understanding: obedience, for Eckhart, was a state of being free (DW 5, c. 2, 190.9–12). He touches upon the vow of obedience only marginally (DW 5, c. 1, 187.4); it can be one way for someone to step outside himself, but the most important aspect of it is that any man, not just friars, would no longer want anything for himself (DW 5, c. 1, 187). Obedience, in Eckhart, becomes a letting-be, a radical self-abandonment, and a separation from one's ambitions, ideas, and images, and especially from honors and possessions. What causes the best in all things is not unconditional subordination under men, but a new concept of life, the concept of "letting the self be." And anyone who lets himself be has let everything be (DW 5, c. 3, 195.4–5).

There are certain requirements within this process, and Eckhart names them explicitly: the I is what first gives objects their value. Everything we yearn for is our self-built world. Because it is you who gives value to all things, you hinder yourself when the things hinder you (DW 5, c. 3, 192.3–193.2). Man cannot exist without being turned toward the world; he cannot be without activity. And yet obedience means that he separates himself from himself even during his work; that he realizes the Stoic ideal of imperturbability in himself, not as a concrete effort, but as willing surrender of the will (DW 5, c. 11, 225.10).

Eckhart further presupposes: self-abandonment is not total annihilation; it has nothing to do with self-punishment or being weary of oneself. Rather, it is a kind of exchange of the I for the Godhead. If I let go of myself as the limited I, then the Godhead within me *must* act for me. This is like a compulsion, a *must* inherent in divine nature itself, not a superimposed "having to." Yet God *must*. He *must* determine and perceive my interests; that alone makes the self-abandonment meaningful. God, not some human authority, replaces me in my stead. Eckhart highlights this must of God brusquely: God would lose himself, would lose his nature, that is, his goodness and justice, if he did not fulfill this must (DW 5, c. 1, 187.5–188.2; DW 5, c. 6, 202.3–5, etc.). He always does fulfill it, and the transformed I does not abandon all action; it works God's work, aware of its own freedom. The world is its oyster.

Eckhart's concept of obedience says: start with yourself. Human beings have the curious tendency to search far away rather than nearby. They venture far out and stray from their goal more and more (DW 5, c. 3, 194.1–2). Thus, begin with yourself to let yourself be (DW 5, c. 3, 193.3). It requires self-knowledge. Hence the admonition of the Delphic oracle: "Know thyself!"—*nim dîn selbes wahr* (DW 5, c. 3, 196.3–4).

Yet even this ancient idea, whose long history Pierre Courcelle so aptly described, takes on a particular resonance in Eckhart: it invites the realization that it is each person who inscribes value and who can refuse such estimation. Eckhart urges his reader: recognize yourself as having the power to say no. You can let go of everything, for it is *you* who entangles and constricts yourself in things out there; you have transferred your life, your judgment, and your desire onto them and have tied yourself down. Eckhart would not have been able to say this if some awareness of the significance and power of man's inner life had not been developed by the end of the thirteenth century. Eckhart made his contemporaries aware of it; he encouraged them to recognize themselves in this function of value attribution, to see through and reject every dependence on external things as a self-made shackle. You have to learn the *innere einoede*, the solitude of your interior, Eckhart admonished (DW 5, c. 6, 207.7), meaning not "loneliness" (as Quint translated), but the renunciation of all reliance on external things, a practical understanding and active reassessment within one's social context that does not interrupt one's active function.

Eckhart draws a few conclusions from this: eliminating the world means gaining the world, but we cannot achieve it with a one-time decision. It enters into real life only when it is practiced. Eckhart defines obedience as the highest value and conceptualizes it as "well-practiced detachment" (DW 5, c. 21, 280.8). And this practice, not a momentary idea or supernatural intervention, is what matters.

Eckhart relativizes both disposition and works. The I has to learn and practice thinking and living without "*eigenschaft*" (DW 5, c. 10, 218.8–11). "*Eigenschaft*" (property) is self-reference. It has to be overcome. What matters here is the intention (*meinunge*), not the work (DW 5, c. 5, 200.1–3). Yet we also have to overcome the morally self-aware intention and fulfill the work of providing soup for the sick man. God does not pay heed to the work, but to how you are while you perform it, and what you seek with it (DW 5, c. 16, 247.5–7). You have to let him work your work. He acts for you in you.

Speaking to the young friars, Eckhart relativizes with provocative harshness all monastic exercises, all ecclesiastical practice, including receiving the Eucharist. For those who have turned their lives around and have achieved "well-practiced detachment," stepping on a stone is a more divine work than receiving the Eucharist from someone who lacks this newly defined obedience (DW 5, c. 5, 200.1–3). This reformed self-perception relativizes the difference between church and street, cleric and layman.

Even moral reflections in the form of "what should I do?" grind to a halt. Someone who lives correctly already knows what he has to do. A detached person enters into the flowing earthly life of the Godhead; he does not attach himself to ethical concepts or ideas of what God might want from him. He sets being against active doing (DW 5, c. 4, 197.6–198.9). He has learned to have God "*in wesene*," in essence (DW 5, c. 6, 205.10).

He is united with God. He is one with the One (DW 5, c. 6, 202.7–10). Not just in his will, not just in his intentions and thoughts. He rejects this merely imagined "God" (DW 5, c. 11, 225.3). He is essentially one with him. For God *must* enter into him, and when God does, he can only enter *completely* as the indivisible One (DW 5, c. 21, 281.7–8). He brings along everything good, for he himself is the Good. Eckhart here inserts Thomas Aquinas's idea that grace does not destroy but perfects nature (DW 5, c. 22, 289.2–10). Radically, he demands abandonment and abasement of the self, but not self-diminishment, and not as a heightened asceticism, but as a phase within the life of the just man who has an essential God, not a merely imagined one. Self-awareness remains. He knows: it is *he* who makes the human outside world, and also the psychological one, attractive, even dominant; it is why he can also keep it at bay. It is part of his life to keep his *inwendicheit* (inwardness) present as well (DW 5, c. 21, 276.10–12).

He knows: God's nature is self-disclosure without envy, without reservations (DW 5, c. 1, 187.8–9). That is why he knows what he gains from his self-abandonment. Eckhart speaks of it as a fair trade: he who loses himself receives a *glîch widergelt*, "equal retribution" (DW 5, c. 4, 197.1). He is not looking, of course, for a reward for his "merits." Eckhart eliminated the idea of rewards at the very beginning (DW 5, c. 21, 281.3–5; but see DW 5, c. 4, 197.1–2).

Eckhart addressed the idea of radical poverty early on. He transformed the vow of poverty, just as he did the vow of obedience. He turned it into self-examination, a turn in life toward the ever-communicative God within (DW 5, c. 23, 295–301.2). He relativized everything external, everything schematic, and every prescription; in this sense, he answered the minor questions of his young audience. They asked about penitence and the frequency of communion; they were interested in the relation between prayer and concurrent disposition, the rules regarding clothing and fasting. Again and again, Eckhart urges: there is no one way that would be right for everyone. His agenda fostered individualization (DW 5, c. 23, 302.1–5). Not everything was suitable for everyone. Such an attitude liberates people from any sche-matism. Yet Eckhart was not an individualistic thinker. It would have been incompatible with his awareness: God is the Good par excellence, and he is *everything* Good; reason is the ability to universalize, and nothing is closer to it than God and the universal.

5. The Sermon Cycle on Eternal Birth

New Philological Evidence

When the anarchical socialist Gustav Landauer (1870–1919) insulted Emperor Wilhelm II and was sent to prison in Berlin-Tegel for lèse-majesté, he spent his time translating parts of Eckhart's Middle High German works. He did not get to see them in print; he was a member of the Munich Soviet Republic and was kicked to death in prison after its suppression. In 1920, Martin Buber published them in Berlin as *Meister Eckharts Mystische Schriften: In unsere Sprache übertragen von Gustav Landauer*. In the first sentence of his preface, Landauer declares, "[I will] leave out everything that does not make sense to us. Meister Eckhart is too precious for historical evaluation; he has to be resurrected as a living human being" (7).

Many interpreters of Eckhart have thought similarly, but not many were able to couch their antihistoricism in such grand terms: Eckhart—"too precious" for historical evaluation—to be "resurrected" as a living human being. I take these flashy expressions as a starting point for thinking about the preconditions of historical knowledge. For someone who decides that certain parts of Eckhart's works "do not make sense to us" lays claim to historical knowledge, even if he calls it something else and even if he does not consider his work on Eckhart "historical." What matters here are not disciplinary affiliations but the fact that Eckhart died in 1328 and that mediation between his texts and us is unavoidable.

Everyone who speaks about Eckhart produces such historical knowledge in his present and under present conditions. Eckhart does not simply spill over into the present from "sources" in the past. He is identified, constructed, and evaluated under the conditions of the present. No one simply crosses over into the past. The epistemological capabilities, interests, and constraints of the present shape the image of Eckhart that we create for ourselves. Some authors attempt to draw Eckhart directly into their present. They aim to "resurrect him," but that seems to go beyond human capabilities—at least my own. Eckhart is dead and thus is an object of historical knowledge. Someone who speaks or writes about him is well advised to let us know who is determining the criteria according to which something "makes sense" to "us." Only then will he think about how much his present predetermines the nature of his historical knowledge, and if his interest in Eckhart is genuine, he will want to use all available options for acquiring knowledge. Much of our present, of course, can distract us from Eckhart or obscure him. Yet one of the advantageous conditions of the present is the speed with which new source material that expands our image of the constellation of intellectual life around 1300 is made available. Today, we have a better understanding of the conditions of study within the Dominican order and the intellectual debates at Paris than we did fifty years ago—for example, through the continual editions of works of influential teachers such as Albertus Magnus of Cologne and Henry of Ghent. An account of Eckhart's thinking must not be limited to identificatory paraphrases of individual ideas and motifs. It requires a focus on Eckhart's ideas, but at the same time, every reader of Eckhart who really wants to get to know him has to first go out into the wide, growing field of historical-philological details.

Within the past decades, four initiatives have improved our understanding of Eckhart's thought:

First, the edition and analysis of the sermon cycle German sermons 101–4 by Georg Steer, DW 4:279–610. Steer made the unity and previously contested authenticity of these sermons plausible. They are the focus of the current chapter.

Second, Loris Sturlese's discovery of the Eckhart manuscript at Oxford has improved the quality of important texts among Eckhart's Latin works. He made them accessible in LW 1:2. Sturlese also rewrote the chronology of Eckhart's Latin works on the basis of a painstaking examination of the Eckhart manuscripts at Erfurt.

Third, Loris Sturlese's edition and analysis of Eckhart's trial records in LW 5 shed new light on this last phase of Eckhart's life and thought.

Fourth, the editors of the Corpus Philosophorum Teutonicorum Medii Aevi (CPTMA) made Eckhart's intellectual milieu accessible. It used to be fashionable to cloak Eckhart in the pathos of lofty solitude; nowadays, we can prove that he had connections with others. We find both similarities and stark contrasts between Eckhart and his contemporaries or his Dominican teachers. Studies of his theoretical position within the German order's province have received new impetus in the past decades. New texts are constantly being published. A unified picture of the debates will be possible only after a series of specialized studies. There were German followers and adversaries of both Dietrich of Freiberg and Eckhart.[1]

All these academic initiatives have made our image of Eckhart richer and more animated. I attempt to take advantage of them in the following chapters, starting with the sermon cycle German sermons 101–4.

A Cycle

When Franz Pfeiffer published his edition of Eckhart's German works in 1857 (he knew of the Latin works only from Abbot Johannes Trithemius; they remained undiscovered at Erfurt and Cusa), he placed at the beginning four sermons concerned with the Incarnation of God and suitable for the post-Christmas liturgy. Josef Quint, working on a new edition of Eckhart's German sermons from 1936 onward, doubted their authenticity, especially that of the fourth text. Yet Georg Steer convincingly argued for Eckhart's authorship; subsequent studies have proved him right.[2] We cannot be entirely sure where this group of texts fits into the chronology of Eckhart's life; it is likely that they followed the *Talks of Instruction*. Georg Steer proposes a time somewhere between 1298 and 1305 for their composition, particularly the years shortly after Eckhart's stay in Paris in 1302–3. Steer documents their similarity in style and thought to the *Talks of Instruction* and, to a lesser degree, to the *Parisian Questions* 1–3; an element of uncertainty remains. Steer presents his dating as conjecture; nonetheless, it becomes apparent: the subject of God's birth does not occur only in Eckhart's later sermons.

Like the *Talks of Instruction*, these four sermons are instructional talks with frequently animated addresses to their audiences. Questions of discipline within the order play a certain role, though not a central one. The sermons are not examples of thundering pulpit eloquence, but rather conversations among a few people, focused on a central theme of the Christian faith and Eckhart's thought: the birth of God.

Breaking the Metaphor

Eckhart adopts the birth metaphor but disrupts it with a series of modifications. His first qualification is found in the very first sentence: it has to be a birth that occurs *unceasingly*. The birth of every living creature is over as soon as the newborn has left the womb. A birth *âne underlâ*, "without cease" (101, 335.2),[3] is not a birth, but continuous birthing and constant renewal. It occurs in eternity, but what is being born is not a materially solidified product of divine procreativeness; the birthing is the divine's perpetually new activity. And Eckhart conceptualizes this activity precisely, not through biological metaphors, but as a form of intellectual self-permeation. God is *ein volkomen însehen in sich selber und ein abgründe durchkennen sîn selbes mit im selber,* "a complete looking into the self and a seeing through the depths of his self with himself" (101, 351.88). The second modification of the birth metaphor occurs when Eckhart declares initially (101, 336.4–5): the birth of the Son in the Godhead, which, as dogmatic theology teaches, occurs always, only interests me insofar as it happens within me. *Dâ liget alles ane:* everything depends on it. And when Eckhart says "everything," he means *everything.* In a sermon intended for the Christmas Octave, he does not mention the historical incarnation in Bethlehem anywhere. But the birth in Bethlehem was, as two gospels confirm, a real birth: a human being was born. Eckhart, however, declares that everything depends on "the eternal birth happening within myself." He does not say: in you or in every human being. He relates this statement directly to himself so that everyone will relate it to his or her own self, and he adds: the same eternal birth that is within the eternal Son is also within "us." Eckhart makes this idea even more pointed: God births his Son in us in the same exact fashion as he does in eternity (101, 350.86–87). Eckhart drives home this identity for his audience: *in derselben wîse, und in keiner anderem gebirt got* himself, "in the same way, and in no other way does God birth himself" (101, 352.90). Peter Lombard had successfully disputed this sameness, which Eckhart pronounces elsewhere (for example, German sermon 6, DW 1:109.2–7). For the Lombard, it was not sameness but merely a certain similarity. It became the universal view of the theologians. Pope

THE SERMON CYCLE ON ETERNAL BIRTH 61

John XXII condemned Eckhart's doctrine of sameness in no fewer than four articles of his bull (nn. 10–13).[4]

Eckhart's third qualification reads: the birth of God occurs within the *allerlûtersten, edelsten und subtîlsten* ("most complete, noblest, and subtlest" part) of the soul (101, 339.16–17) if this innermost part lives concentrated in itself. Eckhart was to answer philosophically the question of what was the highest part of the soul. How did he know about it? The answer to this question provides the fourth qualification of the birth metaphor. For Eckhart declares right at the beginning: he wants to speak about it *mit natiurlîchen reden*, "with natural speeches" (101, 342.33), that is, with philosophical arguments. This explanation of his own procedure corresponds to a passage at the beginning of his commentary on John in which Eckhart clarifies his intentions (*In Ioh.*, LW 3, nn. 2–3, 4), but this formulation of method is nonetheless surprising at the beginning of a vernacular sermon cycle about the birth of God. Eckhart even added why he wanted to argue philosophically about God's birth: that way, the audience would be able to recognize that things were as he said. For his own part, he may have trusted Holy Scripture more than himself, but he did not want to argue with the help of the Bible. Why not? The listeners should not simply trust him or the Bible, he declared, but comprehend themselves that it was so. That was his reason for speaking argumentatively, in a substantiating fashion (101, 342.33–35); he knew that his listeners would be more responsive to it. An attitude of curiosity and doubt was increasing during Eckhart's time; he knew it and adjusted to it. He approved of the development. For man, as he had learned from Aristotle, by nature wanted to know *(Metaphysics* A1);[5] by nature, and not because some fashion or received opinion demanded it. Wanting to know—it is what we are. And God, for Eckhart, did not intend to destroy or humiliate the nature that had been created that way—he intended to perfect it. God made man so that he would know (102, 420.127). When Eckhart afterward praised unknowing and said that our salvation rested in ignorance—this had to be an ignorance derived from knowledge. It was a qualified unknowing, not mere nonrecognition or the blocking out of insight, but transformed knowledge (102, 420.130).

Eckhart does not say that his listeners should *imitate* Christ's life and virtues in order to resemble him. There is no mention of convergence, of likeness, of participation, or of emulation of Christ, only of an identical flow of life that everyone can find operating within himself and recognize within himself. Everyone? Eckhart qualifies his statement: natural speeches are, of course, generally accessible, for that is their nature, but Eckhart intended to drive knowledge knowingly into the darkness of unknowing, and not "everyone" could tolerate that. Although Eckhart elsewhere declares the universality of knowledge, he significantly limits the accessibility of his speeches here; he addresses only *gute, vollkommene Menschen,* "good and perfect human beings" (101, 336.8). And he repeats this qualification: he is speaking today only for perfect people. He does not say that he is presupposing Christian faith. Instead, he says in good Aristotelian fashion that he takes it for granted that someone has formed the habit of doing good works and of *living*—in good Franciscan fashion—according to Christ's teachings (101, 354.112–355.15). This is a surprise. One may feel compelled to join Quint in doubting the authenticity of these sermons, for Eckhart usually presents his teachings as if they were for everyone. He did not want a hierarchy of the knowing and the unknowing. Philosophical knowledge was supposed to be accessible to all, even to sinners; but here it sounds as though he wanted to philosophize only for saints.

His expression itself is remarkable: only "perfect human beings." The "perfect" as distinct from common married Christians were well known to the ancient Manicheans and medieval Cathars. There were Christian thinkers who wanted to reserve their knowledge for esoteric groups and who claimed that Jesus and Paul themselves did not speak for everyone; they did not cast their pearls before swine. Even Nicholas of Cusa had a similar tendency; it is the reason why he wanted to have Eckhart's Latin works removed from all public libraries. Yet ecclesiastical administrators during Eckhart's lifetime condemned lay associations of the "perfect," who assigned great knowledge to themselves and claimed freedom from church prescriptions. It was a prevalent issue around 1300, as in Boniface VIII's bull *Saepe sanctam Ecclesiam* of August 1296 and in the constitution *Ad nostrum qui* of the Council of Vienne in 1311.[6] I am not saying that Eckhart's speech belongs among such heresies. I only want to say: he chose a strange way of expressing himself when he claimed of the free morality of the perfect that their virtues flowed freely from their character, without their assistance (101, 354.114). It sounded like quietism, which had been condemned by the church; such diction was dangerous after 1311. It must have sounded suspicious, like an apotheosis of man, when Eckhart denied the very possibility of sinning for every man in whom God's birth occurred (101, 367.216–23). Did not Christians always have to fear that their potential for sin threatened them?

The Nature of God

God is good. He discloses himself without envy according to his nature. He *must* disclose himself if he wants to be God. Otherwise he would be denying his essence. God is mind (101, 345.52–53 and 351.88). Which means: he concentrates within himself the multitude of ideal structures and recognizes himself as their unity. He is word, that is, essential disclosure (103, 484.85–95). Secular philosophers, as Augustine confirms, discovered this on the basis of natural reason, and Eckhart finds it also—like Augustine—in the prologue to the Gospel of John. The philosophical knowledge of God shows: God creates the logos, and he is not a rock of motionless being, no anthropomorphically imagined heavenly emperor of immemorial decrees, but the perfect introspection into the abyss of his self. He is thought that comprehends itself through itself, as we read in Aristotle's *Metaphysics* (Book 12, part 7). He knows himself even in his darkest depths, not through occasional operations or secondary additions, but perpetually and purely through himself. He is fully present (101, 351.88). He is mind, and hence indivisible as perfect wholeness. When he is present, then he is *wholly* present. He does not randomly give something—he gives himself. He produces a nature that is like him. The metaphor of sonship demonstrates this vividly. It marks the result of a philosophical theology that knows: God is mind and his nature is indivisible self-disclosure. These bases of ancient metaphysics and the doctrine of the logos become a Trinitarian philosophy in Eckhart that explains God's disclosure *mit natiurlichen reden*, "with natural speeches" (101, 342:33). This disclosure, for Eckhart, was not a special feature of Christianity, but a feature of man's traditional philosophical awareness of God as formulated by Hermes Trismegistus, Aristotle, Cicero, and the Greek church fathers, but also by Avicenna, Averroës and the *Liber de causis*.[7]

Someone who presents the birth of God as philosophical understanding changes what he is interpreting. If the listeners know that it is true, when they have recognized within themselves the truth of the logos philosophy that Augustine, according to *Confessions*, Book 7, had found in the Platonic books, then what matters is not dogmatic finesse, not the threefold nature or nomenclature of the divine persons, but only the knowledge of God's dynamic self-realization in the simple human experience of the self. Then Eckhart's listener *knows:* the divine begetting of the logos in eternity is identical to the birthing of the Godhead in him. Coarse people have to believe it; Eckhart's students can know it. In this context, the term "birth of God" does not relate to a former event in the past. It is not a purely otherworldly process. It is not complete like a traditional birth. Instead, it continuously occurs anew, unceasingly (101, 335.2). It is a metaphor for God's nature, at once constantly in motion and at rest.

Mind as the Place of Birth

Thereafter, Eckhart examines the question: where does the birth of God occur? His answer: it occurs within us—not insofar as we are natural creatures, but within us as mind (101, 356.125). And so not in the soul insofar as it perceives the external world and desires something within it, but, as Eckhart says, within the ground of the soul. Not as a supernatural, additional gift; God gives himself to the *seele in ir natûre*, "the soul in its nature" (101, 339.18). The soul's nature, which is essential here in its role as the place of birth, is, strictly speaking, the head of the soul: reason.[8] Eckhart distinguishes this reason from reason as a faculty of the soul. In calling the ground of the soul reason, Eckhart implies something other than the "faculty of the soul." Here, "reason" signifies man's most noble part, the *wesen* (essence or being) in opposition to the *kreften* (powers). For Albertus Magnus, Thomas Aquinas, Dietrich of Freiberg, and Eckhart, this was the intellect, and the intellect, for Dietrich and Eckhart, was the intellectual ground of the soul, its substance. Eckhart also calls it "the heart of the soul"; Dietrich of Freiberg used this phrase for the active intellect that produced the soul's substance and that was itself substance and not an accidental faculty of the soul.[9] It was the Greco-Arabic *intellectus* and also the mind (*mens*) that Augustine knew so well in his *De Trinitate*, but that he simultaneously considered the hidden part (*abditum*) of the soul (101, 343.38–40). "Mind" means: the living, essential Word and by-word, and "Word" signifies disclosure and announcement (101, 362.163–67).

The ground of the soul, this substantial *mens*, is logos-like but remains hidden. Human beings themselves obscure the ground of their souls. They scatter themselves in the external world, and so their unity is shattered—instead of looking for the truth within, the only place where it can be found. Instead of conceptualizing the mind as the living unity of all faculties, they know it only as an accidental power, even though Augustine described the mind, the *mens*, as *substantial* thinking and striving. Eckhart finds incisive terms for the hidden nature of the ground of the soul (101, 365.195–98 and

366–67.207–16). It remains hidden entirely within certain ways of acquiring knowledge. Eckhart defines its type of concealment more precisely: it is never, according to Eckhart, made known only through revelation. Eckhart did not doubt that natural reason could recognize the ground of the soul, that is, itself. Human beings recognize natural reason's "thatness" with certainty. We also know what it is: not stone or mere affect, but mind. We know that we must not confuse it with a thing of nature, but we cannot define its essence more closely. The providential point of this boundary is to incite us to hunt after it (101, 361.154–60). And at least we know that it is not simply a dull piece of nature, but the essence of the mind-soul, and thus actuality and energy, even during phases of reception.

Eckhart says that it does not have any *werk*. This means: it does not affect the external world primarily or directly. But the divine light within the ground of the soul emanates into the soul's faculties and changes the outside world (102, 414.60–63). The hidden ground does not remain hidden. Eckhart says that the "masters" did not uncover it. He cannot have been thinking here of Aristotle, Augustine, Averroës, or Dietrich, who knew much about it. By no means did he think that the philosophers might not have known it, but that the theologians had. His statement that the "masters" did not know the ground of the soul refers to the educational practice at the close of the thirteenth century, of both the philosophers and the theologians. They discussed the intellect as a "faculty of the soul" that was turned outward, but not as the heart and head of the soul.[10] And yet within it, in substantial reason, the birth of God occurs. There was no reason to speak of Paris in a vernacular sermon; Eckhart spelled out for himself his own distance from the schools. He had to justify for himself why people there did not speak of God in the same fashion as he did. Why did his doctrine seem strange there, rare, even monstrous?

The birth comes about only under certain conditions: the mind turns outward because of its powers (the faculties of the soul); it tears itself apart in interior struggles. Therefore, it has to reject the dictates of the external world and its commotion (101, 357.133). And it has to do so radically and consistently. There is no room for compromise with the common way of life, which submits itself to external things. Alarmed, a member of the audience asked: Indeed, I grant that the mind has to withdraw itself into itself, yes, but is there no return to the external world? *Ach herre, muoʒ es alles abe, enmag dâ kein widerkêren sîn?* Eckhart's answer is no. You have to let go of everything. There is no return (103, 478.45–46).

Three Key Terms

The first of the four sermons takes its cue from a homiletic theme that consists of two biblical quotations. The first states: when all things were keeping silent, there came into me from above, from the royal throne, a hidden word: *dum medium silentium tenerent omnia . . . de caelis porro ad me dictum est verbum absconditum* (Wisdom 18:14–15). Eckhart extracts three key terms from this and another biblical passage (Job 4:12): medium, silence, hidden word. The keyword "medium" he translates with the noun "means" and gathers from the text, in a daring exegesis, that no means, no middle stands between the divine Word and the ground of the soul: the birth occurs unmediated. The second keyword is "silence," and Eckhart interprets it as follows: when the Father enters into the ground of the soul, human beings act receptively. They listen and are not to speak in the process. They receive and are not to act. The third key term is "hidden word": the Word that is born within us is more easily recognized in unknowing than in knowledge. I provide a short analysis of these three key terms.

There is no *medium*. Becoming one happens in unmediated form; nothing created steps in between the soul and God, the Father. This means first of all: the ground of the soul must not be drawn outward by its powers. It has to break off its relations with the outside. In that sense, it is active; it removes obstacles. It interrupts the three types of intellectual relations with the outside: it intermits the worldly conditions that are produced by the intellect, memory, and will. The rule calls for a hard break, and any weakening of it is forbidden. In addition, the rejection of any intermediary between the Father and the ground of the soul within the context of theology signified a modified version of the doctrine of grace as it had been developed since the reception of Aristotle. The question "What is grace?" had long been answered in two ways. On the one hand, grace was God's benevolence, that is, the goodness and love that he himself was and that he bestowed on humanity. It was an "uncreated grace"; it was an essential benevolence or God's goodness. On the other hand, grace could mean the effect that this benevolence was said to create in men, that is, an impulse to act or a certain disposition in those who received grace. Peter Lombard did not strictly define this efficient grace ontologically; it was no accident of the soul for him, not something created, but the presence of the Holy Spirit within the recipients of grace. During his trial, Eckhart invoked this doctrine of grace by the Lombard. Most theologians of the thirteenth century, however, even Bonaventure, defined grace ontologically and in fixed terms. Grace, they said, on the one hand was God's benevolence, that is, his nature. On the other hand, the effect of this divine benevolence within man was not a substance, for no substance could be within another substance. What remained, then, were two conceptions: divine grace was either a temporary divine impulse or a disposition toward good actions. Grace, insofar as it is within man, certainly belongs within the category of accident; it is a quality of the soul (so, for example, in Thomas Aquinas *Sth* I–II 110, 2 ad 2). It was created as such. Grace (*gratia*) is something created within the soul that is given freely (*gratis*), Aquinas wrote (2 *Sent.* 26, 1, 1). And if grace is created, then it can only be an accident of the soul, for it is added to man's essence and presupposes it. The ontological analysis of this given grace for Aquinas resulted in an interpretation of grace as a reality within a being as that being's property, *actus subjecti in esse accidentali* (ibid., ad 3). And more precisely, grace belonged with the first type of the category "quality": *Gratia est in prima specie qualitatis* (*De veritate* 27, 2 ad 7). Thomas Aquinas said as well that the relation of the soul to its final aim occurred without mediation, without something else stepping in between them. Yet for him, this immediacy consisted of God creating the accident "grace" immediately as an additional property. That meant that God immediately created a mediating quality of the soul. For Eckhart, that was not enough. Grace had a role in strengthening the powers and removing obstacles, but the ground of the soul did not include anything created.[11] The Thomistic solution did not suffice for his pathos of immediacy. Only God himself can bless the soul: immediately, unmediated, without *medium*.

The differences in the concept of grace resulted in different interpretations of Christianity: Thomas Aquinas believed that something immediately created by God entered the soul, whereas Eckhart's God himself entered the soul unmediated. Eckhart's sermon initially calls for a break with the love of the worldly, but also invites a renovation of the Christian self-understanding. If Eckhart had focused simply on cultivating the souls of individual people, preferably in remote nunneries containing women prone to deep feeling, he would hardly have fallen into conflict with the guardians of Christian truth. But he offered a new interpretation of Christianity and preached a new conception of the Christian way of life.

His second key term exemplifies this: silence. His admonition "You shall keep silent. Let God act and speak," "*dû solt swîgen und lâ₃ got würken und sprechen*" (101, 355.116–17), contains a twofold challenge. First, to interrupt every contact with the outside world, to become ignorant of all things, to no longer know anything even about one's own life, to no longer overfeed oneself with images of worldly things or with oneself. The faculties of the soul constantly produce worldly images and pull the ground of the soul outward. Resisting it is a necessity; not passivity, but active withdrawal: "Detach yourself from the turmoil of external works! Flee and hide yourself from the storm of internal thoughts when they create strife!," "*vliuch und verbirc dich vor dem gestürme inwendiger gedanke, wan sie unvride machent*" (101, 357.133–34). We have to consider every word of it: not every work is to be avoided, but active change is necessary. What Eckhart demands is inward action (102, 416.83). Thoughts are a hindrance if they create strife. Even fleeing is an action. The well-counseled soul fabricates imagelessness. It rejects the flow of images that it constantly receives from the intellect, memory, and will. It has to know that it cannot contemplate everything at once. The narrowness of consciousness demands that it be decisive: its powers are closely connected with it; it loses itself through the powers to the outside if it does not object. It cannot at once both look outward and develop an internal, intellectual action (102, 417–18, 101–11).

The soul does not have an image of itself. Images are determined, well defined; but the soul itself is indeterminate, indeterminable, not well defined. In another sense, it is itself an image: it does not have an image of itself, for it is the unfixed image of the eternal God. Thus, not an image. But its unfamiliarity with itself and, relatedly, its imagelessness do not preclude it from knowing very well that it exists (its thatness) and from comprehending its unfamiliarity with itself as an impulse to hunt after its own essence (101, 361.154–60). Eckhart highlights, in coincidental formulations, that unknowing and the manifestness of the self exist simultaneously. It is not true that Eckhart "denies all self-recognition by natural means."[12] We do not *know* the self, but it *shows* itself:

It emerged and was hidden. *Eȝ schein und was verborgen.* (101, 362.168)
It hides itself and nonetheless reveals itself. *Eȝ birget sich und wîset sich doch.* (101, 364.182–83)
Only when one no longer knows it does it *show* itself and reveal itself. *Dâ man niht enweiȝ, dâ wîset eȝ sich und offenbâret eȝ sich.* (102, 419.125)

The self shows itself as darkness. The birth of God presupposes an entering into this self-darkness. That is what silence means.

But it means more. The soul must know—and execute that knowledge in an internal act—that it has to prepare for the birth of God by breaking with any dependence on externals, but that it cannot itself effect its own transformation. *It* is not what induces the act of birth. God effects it; the soul receives it. God *must* effect it wherever it is possible. His nature demands it; it is who he is. He does not withhold anything; he does not disseminate himself in an act of random selection. But he is the Creator, and the Son is the Created. We ourselves become the Son, we step into the role of the Created: we become the Created. Eckhart also calls this being created as the Son a *lîden* (suffering). Like Dionysius the Areopagite, he says that we *lîden*, that is, we suffer, God (102, 421–22.134–45).

It is important that we think along with Eckhart to determine what "*lîden*" can mean here. There are interpreters of Eckhart who are not interested in the minor difference between "suffering" God and receiving a blow to the head. To think along with Eckhart means that we do not suppress questions of this kind and that we look more carefully at the text. For suffering God happens in the mind, in the head of the soul. God, who does not destroy but perfects nature, does not cut off the head of the soul but gives it its divine form. The mind is by nature incapable of suffering, *impassibilis*, as Eckhart says in good Aristotelian fashion.[13] It cannot *lîden* at all. It can receive, but this receiving is, according to its nature, an action. Nothing falls into it from the outside. It has to appropriate what is supposed to be available to it. Its nature demands that it actively receive what is supposed to be available to it into its essence. Latin-speaking Peripatetics often repeated that knowing was a certain kind of suffering, *est quodam pati*, but they explained that what was meant in this case was receptivity, and *passio* here meant receiving something, *recipere*.[14] The active intellect, Eckhart says, can never cease in its activity, because it is its essence. It is always active. It is similar to the divine Father; it effects a new essence in things.[15] The hidden essence of the soul, the *abditum mentis*, is always shining, as Eckhart says in reference to Augustine.[16]

Someone who has followed along with Eckhart's train of thought knows: receiving is also an action; he pays attention to Eckhart's choice of words—the Middle High German word "*lîden*" is not always identical to our "suffering." No theologian will admit that the Son of God is "suffering" from his own creation in all eternity. He is created, and he intellectually accepts his being created. He sees and affirms his receiving of the wholly identical divine nature. And so does the divine man. Our modern word "suffering" invokes improper associations. Eckhart was able to write: God as Father acts, the Son *lîdet*, that is, he *is* born (German sermon 40, DW 2:279.1). Suffering in our modern sense is unfamiliar to God in eternity (*Book of Divine Consolation*, DW 5:48); he had to become man in order to experience it, and only in that way does he *lîden* within the suffering man (5:51, 53, 54). The word "*lîden*" takes on a different nuance depending on whether it is used by God or by the mind, and these nuances are not always synonymous with the modern term "to suffer," not even when Eckhart writes that he is *lîdende* in hearing but active in seeing (102, 421.143–44). The mind (*nous*) was called *apathés* in Aristotle, and Eckhart calls the *intellectus* "*impassibilis*"; modernizing and sentimentalizing tendencies loom large when we claim, in an overly literal translation, that mind-*nous*-*intellectus* is "suffering." Our salvation depends not on our (external) works, but on our suffering of God, *daʒ wir got lîden* (102, 422.145), but this receiving is at the same time our highest activity. Blessedness consists not of doing but of receiving, *beatitudo siquidem consistit in receptione* (Latin sermon 11, 1 [first biblical passage discussed], LW 4, n. 112, 105). This type of "suffering," *passio*, does not take away anything but perfects: *Passio illa nihil abicit, sed perficit.* That is why it is sweet (n. 113, 107). Eckhart's final word regarding the suffering of God is: blessedness is not a kind of being overcome, but of being presented with a gift—it is understanding and becoming one. Bliss is the naked substance of God, *nuda dei substantia*, and it is found, received, touched, and used by the intellect. This receptivity is simultaneously the highest work: *Dîn lîden ist alsus dîn obersteʒ werk* (102, 425.162).[17]

Eckhart knew: he was speaking in a world with a new mercantile bent. Therefore, he accentuated—updating Dionysius the Areopagite—that we do not make, acquire, or earn our own felicity (101, 354.108). The heavenly realm suffers violence, he said, but he was referring to the precondition of felicity, to the irreversible break (102, 418.115–17; 103, 478.45–46; 103, 490.149), not to the intellectual receptivity within the beatifying birth of God.

Allow me a few words about Eckhart's third key term: God enters as a hidden word, *verbum absconditum*. The ground of the soul is unfamiliar, and it is united with the unfamiliar God. The birth does not occur if we imagine before our eyes the philosophical-dogmatic tenets of God's properties (103, 475.15–477.30); it is not a mere act of the intellect, not a result of academic study. The genesis of the deified Man, the *homo divinus*, is not rational in this narrowly rationalistic sense. Eckhart distanced himself from the knowledge of God obtained through reason, as traditionally taught in the schools. But he certainly did not contest the possibility of knowing God and the soul via philosophy. In Aristotelian fashion, he postulated the dependence of thinking on things—that is, thinking as a faculty of the soul—in order to prove the unfamiliarity of God and of the ground of the soul. He insisted that this type of understanding first entered into darkness. He elaborated: God was an abyss, and the soul was also an abyss, and they united in an abysmal, that is, inscrutable, fashion. The traditional sciences of the schools needed to be silent; their knowledge had to recognize itself as unknowing before God's light would reveal itself. It arrives like a powerful flash that inverts everything that existed before it came (103, 488.124–37). New light inundates us incessantly (102, 412.32–36). The last words are not powerlessness and darkness, but perfection and heavenly feast: hospitality and celebration at the divine court (102, 415.78), here on earth. Even though God at times withdraws himself, the birth of God means that God is born; it is the new beginning of the divine man. The heart of the soul remains but is transformed: *you* are reborn. Transformed knowledge develops out of learned unknowing (102, 420.130). The intellectual nature is perfected, not destroyed (104, 576.125–278). Admittedly, it requires the radical break. The necessity of the turnaround is not abolished. The entering into the inner desert (103, 482.34) and darkness (*caligo;* 103, 478.39–44) remains. Love is stronger than death. It survives the complete detachment from things and from traditional knowledge (103, 492.168–72).

The Birth Cycle in Retrospect

Allow me another look at the four speeches. They were conceived as a group and thus form an exception among Eckhart's sermons, which are otherwise all individual works. They formulate Eckhart's position and contain a series of questions about that position. They reject any simplifications. They insist: felicity is not to be had without radical renewal. They show Eckhart as a teacher among inquirers, and they tackle a central theme. They are not an early, youthful work; they are suitable as an introduction to Eckhart's German sermons.

We can imagine the circumstances of their composition. A young professor had soaked up the philosophy and theology of his time during a lengthy course of study; he finally reread, we can assume, Dionysius the Areopagite, especially his *Mystical Theology*. There he read the demand to bid sensory perceptions farewell, to renounce rational thinking, and to unite oneself with the One noncognitively. To do so, he should divest himself of himself and of all things and let himself be carried up "to the remaining ray of divine darkness."[18] But Eckhart does not say: "I am practicing mystical theology." It would have been easy to parrot it. Mystical theology was an established discipline. Eckhart quotes Dionysius, but he adapts him to his own interests. He does not say: "I am showing you how to renounce thinking, for thinking only serves the study of the external world." On the contrary, he announces that he will argue with the help of natural reason. He had a solid foundation through years of training in Peripatetic philosophy. It had taught him not only that our thinking starts with sensory experience, but also that it does not end with it. Like Aristotle, Eckhart knows that man by nature desires the highest knowledge. He derives a detailed image of the human soul from Aristotle and his commentators. He distinguishes reason as the essence of the soul from reason that, together with memory and the will, forms the threefold unity of the *krefte*, the powers of the mind.

In the last of our four sermons, Eckhart speaks of the active and suffering reason. It altogether clarifies his position: we know that suffering God is not the same as suffering from a disease. Eckhart explains that divine filiation was knowable philosophically, for philosophers had shown him that the soul, by nature, was "empty and free." Under these intellectual preconditions, Eckhart could not simply quote Dionysius. He had to resolve the conflict between the Areopagite's nonunderstanding ascent and his insight that God wanted us to be knowing. To achieve this, Eckhart had to sketch a concept of knowing unknowing, for which quotations from Dionysius could serve as secondary confirmations, but not as its "source" per se. Eckhart was neither the first nor the last to do so. John Eriugena, Albertus Magnus, Thomas Aquinas, and Dietrich of Freiberg had similarly pored over the works of Dionysius. Eckhart needed Dionysius's line of interpretation in order to formulate his philosophy of man's deification. Its foundation, however, was the idea that God is mind and creates the logos as the Father, and that this logos enlightens all human beings that have come into this world. He had read it in the first part of the prologue to the Gospel of John, which he knew had absorbed the Hellenistic speculation about the logos; and he knew that Augustine's approval of the philosophy contained in the "Platonic books" had secured its place within Christian thought. But someone around 1300 who wanted to speak philosophically about the divine darkness of Dionysius had to combine it both with the insights that Aristotle and his commentators had gained about the intellect and with an analysis of Augustine's mind as the substantial core of all mental activities. Eckhart knew that Augustine had not conceived of the mind as a faculty of the soul. He also knew that both Thomas Aquinas (*Sth* I 77, 1) and, after him, Bishop Tempier of Paris (in 1277) had forbidden anyone to teach that any creaturely activity was identical with the essence of the human mind.

Eckhart did not need to invent a philosophy of divine filiation. That God created the logos and that the logos was shining within the soul of every human being—this common ground, which he had found in both Plotinus and Augustine, formed his starting point. As mentioned before, Albertus Magnus spoke of a philosophy of divine filiation—not in a theological work, but in his commentary on Aristotle: someone who is connected to the divine intellect himself becomes divine (*divinus*). Such a man appeared to be *the Son of God rather than of a man*. Albertus Magnus was not quoting the Gospel of John here but Homer, a heathen, and the context was an explanation of the Peripatetic theory of the intellect. For it was the intellect, he said, that connected human beings with God.[19]

The four German sermons sketched out this context, but it was impossible for Eckhart to develop it further into an elaborate argument. A natural knowledge of God and the soul was not up for debate here: it was not contested but presupposed. As an introduction to the theory of divine darkness, Eckhart was able to exaggerate to some extent the tendency of human thinking to depend on externals and the *lîden* of the ground of the soul, that is, its receptivity, so that he could culminate by stating: "Your greatest receptivity is your highest activity" (102, 425.162).

Finally, Eckhart discussed questions of medieval ways of life within the four sermons, especially in sermons 103 and 104. He did not devalue monasticism and penance completely; he considered them good as long as they assisted the birth of God. Once that birth occurred, every individual had to decide for himself whether he still felt bound by a particular monastic vow. A dispensation from all things ecclesiastical, the importance of which Dante stressed in his *Paradiso*, was not intended here. We may read in some academic works on Eckhart that he considered it his duty to provide theologically sound instruction for heretical or suspect groups of his time, the friends of God and the Brethren of the Free Spirit, and to integrate them into the church. Apart from the fact that Eckhart nowhere stated his purpose in such terms, and indeed voiced decidedly different intentions, he also explicitly granted the "children of God" the authority to make individual decisions regarding their vows. It must have been alarming for the ecclesiastical authorities.

6. Too Grand a Plan: Prologues to the *Opus tripartitum*

Three Programmatic Texts: A New Chronology

Meister Eckhart thought of himself as a philosopher. People have made him into a counselor of souls, a minister to nuns, a theologian, a combatant against heresy, a preacher, a reformer before the Reformation, and an icon for the depth of the German soul. Perhaps he was all those things; for the moment, it is anyone's guess. Even if he were one or all those things, however, we still know him best through his philosophical writings. He explained that his commentary on the Gospel of John belonged to this group as well. And he began his sermon cycle by announcing that he would argue philosophically (German sermon 101, DW 4:342.33–35). By "philosophical arguments," Eckhart probably understood something different from what we mean by that term today. It remains to be investigated; "philosophy," after all, did not always mean the same thing throughout its long history. That Eckhart would have confused theology with philosophy in the intellectual climate of around 1300, however, is extremely unlikely.[1]

Between 1302 and 1305 or shortly thereafter, Eckhart embraced the opportunity to explain his intention three times. The explanation needed to be written or spoken in Latin, since only that academic language had become flexible enough to possess the precise concepts needed. It was also the official language of a Parisian professor and head of a religious order. As mentioned earlier, Eckhart became a master in Paris in 1302, and in 1303 was elected provincial of the German Dominicans. His short tenure as a master might surprise us, but it was typical; and it did not harm the university. In 1311–12, Eckhart became a Parisian master for the second time, but we shall concentrate on his first years as professor and provincial here.

The three texts to which I refer are the following: first, Eckhart's prefaces to the so-called Tripartite Work, the *Opus tripartitum*—that is, the *Prologi in Opus tripartitum*, especially the general prologue, the *Prologus generalis* to the entire work (*Prol. gen.*, LW 1:148.1–165.15), and the preface to its foundational section, the *Opus propositionum* (LW 1:166.1–182.8); second, the first three *Parisian Questions*, the *Quaestiones Parisienses* 1–3, talks that Eckhart delivered in Paris in 1302–3 (LW 5:37–71); third, the sermons and lectures on one chapter of the Old Testament book Jesus Sirach, or Ecclesiasticus (that is, *Sermones et lectiones super Ecclesiastici 24:23–31*, LW 2:231–300), which are associated with Eckhart's leadership of the provincial order from 1303 to 1311, but which, as Kurt Ruh has shown, begin with a text from 1302.[2]

Detailed research by Loris Sturlese on the Eckhart manuscripts from Erfurt has substantially altered the chronology of the Latin works. This research has moved up the date of the beginnings of the *Opus tripartitum*, namely, the prologues, and the first version of the *Commentary on Genesis* (LW 1 and LW 1, pt. 2), to the time period mentioned above. The *Commentary on the Book of Wisdom* (LW 2:303–634) was also in progress. The *Commentary on the Gospel of John* and his *Second Commentary on Genesis*, the *Liber parabolarum Genesis*, belong to a later period, lasting until sometime after 1313 and, in some cases, after.[3]

The dating of these texts is more difficult than I am presenting it here, for Eckhart continually reworked his texts, and in referring to his own texts also cited what he still *wanted* to write. Nevertheless, Sturlese has shown that the *Opus tripartitum* was not begun late, and its beginnings lie in the period around 1302–3, which allows me to begin with the two prologues from the beginning of the *Opus tripartitum* in order to illustrate Eckhart's concept of philosophy and its relation to revelation.

Eckhart begins with a series of fundamental explanations. They deal with the primary determinations (I am not saying: the first, most universal concepts) such as Being (*esse*), Oneness, Truth, Wisdom, and the like. At the forefront are the four so-called transcendentals—Being, Oneness, Truth, and Goodness—that Thomas Aquinas had developed in his *De veritate* I, I, but Eckhart's list is longer; it also includes Idea, Wisdom, and Love.

Primary Determinations and Accidents

Eckhart's first ontological premise is: the primary determinations must not be confused with accidents (*Prologus generalis*, LW 1, nn. 8–9, 152.8–154.12).[4] Eckhart is not warning against simply conceptualizing these as the most universal generalizations of our thought. For him, they are actual grounds of reality and thus primary determinations, which beings and thinking have in common. We are not to think of them as properties added to an already complete, existing being, like the green color of leaves on a tree during the spring. Eckhart is not fending off a nominalist theory of transcendentals. He was not aware of it; it hardly existed around 1300. It would have completely destroyed Eckhart's approach. From the very beginning, Eckhart assumes a "realistic" epistemology, namely, the correspondence of being and thought.

The most universal determinations do not depend on the existence of individual things; rather, they make these things into beings, into unified and true creatures (nn. 9–10,154.1–156.3). For things to be, to preserve their unified essence, and to have value, the primary determinations need to have made them so. The imagination—in contrast to intellectual insight—stops with individual things and misleads us into thinking that all other superordinate determinations are subsequent, secondary, and accidental. From the very beginning, Eckhart warns against the confusion of imagining and thinking. He interjects several times: never stop at imagining! *Nequaquam est imaginandum* (n. 8, 152.10; *Prologus in Opus propositionum* [*Prol. prop.*] n. 24, 180.6). This second demand is related to the first: someone who thinks of the primary determinations as properties implicitly assumes the primacy of individual things, which is a precondition that many consider Aristotelian but is actually nominalist or empiricist. Eckhart knew Aristotle too well to see him as one of those who think of the most universal determinations only as "somethings" in individual things. Thus, Eckhart takes up one of Aristotle's theses as a next step, which he illustrates with the following sentence: when I call something "white," nothing is predicated other than its "being white."[5] Eckhart describes this concretely: let us suppose that a shield is white. When I call it "white," I am only indicating its white color (*albedo*). It does not receive its entire "being white," insofar as I am thinking of white, because it is a shield, but receives it only from the *albedo*, from the "whiteness."

The Crucial "Insofar"

This precondition sounds inconspicuous, but it was extraordinarily important for Eckhart. His example of *album-albedo* pervades both prologues.[6] One might object by noting: "If I say of a dog that it is black, I am not merely indicating blackness, but rather the blackness of a specific dog." This objection, however, would not pertain to Eckhart's idea. When he formulates it explicitly, he writes that white, insofar as it is white, *in quantum album*, receives everything from whiteness (*Prol. prop.* n. 23, 179.7–9). The first thing to note in his linguistic-logical-ontological premise is contained in "insofar." Insofar as a thing is called white, it has everything from whiteness. This "insofar" plays an important role in Eckhart's thought all the way up to his inquisitorial trial.

The second pivotal step is to extend this analysis of dependence to all the primary determinations: insofar as something exists, it has this from Being; insofar as a man is wise, he has this from Wisdom. In a theoretical linguistic inquiry, Eckhart shows that this does not hold if linguistic forms of "to be" like "is" and "were" are used only as copula, that is, as mere connectors of parts of a sentence (*Prol. prop.* n. 3, 167.2–5). Being, oneness, and goodness, insofar as they occur as attributes of a subject, depend as such on Being, on Oneness, etc. If I say: "Martin is wise," then he as such depends completely on Wisdom. Or Wisdom is within him. Or Wisdom, insofar as it newly occurs within him, has "birthed" him as a wise man. Eckhart does not put it like that here. He manages without the birth metaphor. Birth serves as a metaphor in other texts, no more and no less, for the entering of a thing or a human into the pyramid of light of the primary determination.

A List of the Primary Determinations and Their Functions

A frequently discussed question in the Middle Ages and the Renaissance went as follows: is there a hierarchy among the primary determinations? Even Pico della Mirandola wrote a treatise entitled *De ente et uno*.[7] Which of these determinations is the foundational one and, in this sense, the first? In an overview of the whole work's succession of chapters in the prologue, Eckhart lists fourteen conceptual pairs, the first of which appear in this order:

Being and Nothingness
Oneness and Multiplicity
Truth and Falseness

Goodness and Evil
Love (*amor* and *caritas*) and the sin against it

(*Prol. gen.*, LW I n. 4, 150.1–5)

It is notable that all determinations—except God—have an opposition, but for now we are concerned only with the fact that Being is listed before Oneness. This points to a primacy of Being over Oneness and Goodness. In its favor, it could be argued that nothing can be good if it does not exist. One would have to say that Goodness and Truth have their foundations in Being, but Eckhart proceeds with Boethius: Being is also grounded and firmly established in Oneness and through Oneness (*Prol. prop.* n. 9, 171.3–5). There is reciprocity, a mutual consolidation of Being and Oneness. Then we could attribute primacy either to Being or to Oneness, depending on one's perspective. Something is a being through Being and is one through Oneness, like white through *albedo*. The traditional characterization of Aristotle's *Metaphysics* was that it was the knowledge of beings as such, of *ens qua ens;* Platonic and Neoplatonic thinkers spoke of the primacy of the One, of the *Hen;* Eckhart follows Boethius in linking both principles in reciprocity. This discussion has consequences for the philosophical doctrine of God, which we could call "theologics" if we follow Aristotle, who designated the first philosophy as a *theologike episteme*. Still, before Eckhart gets to that point, he explains the relationship between primary determinations and individual beings more closely:

Primary determinations like Being and Oneness are "prior," not in a temporal sense but rather as that which is presupposed and which effects. Being receives nothing from that to which it gives being; it is not added to anything that existed before it (*Prol. gen.* n. 8, 153.2–4). It precedes—Eckhart's rejection of the idea of preexisting things already said as much. There are no intermediate steps between the primary determination and that which it principiated. There is no intermediary, for it would have to have being already. Eckhart's pathos of immediacy stems from this: wherever they are present, the primary determinations act immediately. What they have realized, that is from them, *ab alio*, but they themselves are not from another, *non ab alio*. We cannot conceive of them as divided. Thus, not only are they not separated de facto, but neither could they be tomorrow; their division is inconceivable because it is impossible by their nature. From this it follows: wherever they emerge, they are there wholly.

Active and Receptive

Eckhart's prologue sketches a metaphysics of the primary determinations in reciprocity. He outlines his metaphysics of Being, Oneness, immediacy, and wholeness. The primary determinations are principles, and they are the foundation of everything else; no piece of empirical evidence could refute them. They do not require any authority for their justification; they themselves justify the truth of all authorities. One cannot imagine them as being "above"; they are present firsts. They are not present like a thing in a container, but completely permeate that which has been set; while present within it, they effect being and oneness.

In this context, Eckhart specifically emphasizes the following points. The primary determination is realized only within itself. Nothing that it has brought into existence has being or oneness without it. Therefore, the established, considered separately, is a mere nothing. The established does not resemble the primary determination, does not partake in it. The primary determination is the only thing that is real and that grants reality. If something is, the primary determination is completely present within it. Then not only is the primary determination's product or its similarity within us; the primary determination itself is present. It rules, but as that which descends and attracts to itself. It shapes the effected thing, it assists it as a whole with its wholeness. It tolerates that there are others that act, but within it and below it. Keeping this in mind, urges Eckhart, is "utterly necessary," *potissime necessarium est sentire* (*Prol. prop.* n. 24, 181.1). Everything that the primary determination itself effects, it effects not toward the outside, but rather into itself. Being has no outside. Again, those imaginative ideas taken from the working methods of craftsmen are problematic. The effecting of the primary determinations is not a producing, which would represent an externalization of something from within them. Their effecting consists of making what has been established resemble them, of making what has been established into a being. Eckhart teaches elementary concepts of reciprocity: the Oneness in Being and vice versa, the being in Being and vice versa, the receptive or "suffering" in the active (*Prol. prop.* n. 10, 171.6–10). Someone who has not learned from the prologues that the active pulls the passive toward itself, that is, that it makes it active, cannot interpret Eckhart's birth cycle in the proper Eckhartian sense. He will think in terms of alternatives, typical for the ontology of things, and say: either the ground of the soul is active (as in Dietrich of Freiberg) or it is passive, as allegedly in Eckhart.

Readers of Eckhart must think of the passive as activated; they must think hierarchy (the primary determinations are givens, they are those which determine), but they must simultaneously keep in mind the primary determination's own active de-hierarchization: that which is above pulls that which is below closer to itself, and vice versa.

Being descends and raises beings up to itself by endowing beings with Being. This Being has to be conceptualized as perfect. That which it has established as being does not add anything to it; it does not give to it anything of Being, Oneness, value (*Prol. prop.* n. 4, 167.9–168.5). It cannot be denied any positive attribute; it must be denied every negative attribute. It is not evil, negative, or formless; rather, the *negatio negationis* is in order for it (n. 12, 172.7; n. 15, 175.13–15). It is abundance that radiates itself, *dives per se*.

Analogy

Along with Eckhart, we shall look more closely at beings which are one and good. Being, Oneness, and Goodness are within them, not above them, not beyond them. Beings as such, not conceivable outside Being, would be nothing. If they *are*, they are in Being and Being is in them, indivisible, wholly present. They depend on it, they are attached to it like properties to a substance, let us say: like green to a tree. Aristotle contemplated what that would mean for the linguistic designation "green." He found: if one asks about that which actually is, then the tree *is*, and the green is *on* it or *in* it. When we say of the green that it *is*, we mean the being of the tree. Aristotle spoke of a *pros-hen* homonymy, a related sharing of the same word, and added that when we call a medicine "healthy," we mean the health of the living being that may potentially benefit from medicine. What alone is "healthy" is the living creature, not the chemical agent, which nonetheless should have something to do with health. Later authors, including Eckhart, called the Aristotelian *pros-hen* homonymy "analogy." This did not correspond to ancient Greek usage, in which *analogia* originated in mathematics and designated a quadrinomial proportion, for example, *a* is to *b* as *c* is to *d*. Scholastic authors, especially Cajetan, designated these as *analogia proportionalitatis* in distinction to the simple *analogia proportionis*. Someone approaching Eckhart's texts with this conceptual apparatus in mind must ask himself which type of predication exists in the relationship of beings to Being, of an individual good man to Goodness. It can only be the *pros-hen* homonymy, but with the emphasis that if I designate something limited as "being," it must refer to Being itself; within something that has being, Being is as little present as health is in medicine. The orientation of this proposition is clear: it destroys the idea of independent individual things across which a universal concept could be folded retroactively: an abstraction. As though he had to defend himself for not having handled the being of things tenderly enough, Eckhart adds: I am not revoking the being of things with this explanation; rather, I am acknowledging and exalting it.[8]

Primary Determinations and Theologics

Being, Oneness, and Goodness are active primary determinations, not abstractions. Thus, one has to say that this is God. Up to this point, Eckhart was philosophizing only about the most universal conditions for worldly structures. But, remaining a philosopher, he goes further and says: this is an outline for a philosophical theology, and hence a theologics independent of revelation in its argumentation.

Its first proposition is: God is Being. What there is to say about Being— that it establishes beings, lives directly active within them and thus does not tolerate a *medium*, cannot be divided and thus always gives itself wholly—all those were statements about God, for God is Being, *Deus est esse* (*Prol. gen.* n. 12, 156.15–158.4). God is Being in the same way that he is Oneness and Truth and Goodness. Thus, if I say of a tree that it *is*, then I mean Being itself, which is God, in a *pros-hen* homonymy comparable to that which Aristotle taught for the being of the green in relation to the tree. As Aristotle saw the being of the green in the being of the tree, so Eckhart sees the being of things in Being itself, from which he constructs his concept of God. What in religious language is termed "creation," he describes as the entering of Being into something that has being, of Oneness into the many, pulling the many to itself and thus making them one. The introduction to theologics consists in the understanding that I must not speak of Being or of *ens* in general in the same way that I can speak of this or that individual being. Thus, Eckhart verbally places the *esse* (*ens*) in opposition to the *ens hoc* not in substance, but only to practice and warn against reification. In substance, they are in each other. That is what pious people mean when they say that the world is created. This needs to be explained. Otherwise, the imagining thinking, that is, thinking that creates mental images, edges forward and makes us believe that the creation of the world consisted of God externalizing things from within himself. But he placed them into Being, and thus into himself. And not in the past, as though creation had long come to an end, but rather he places the being into himself, namely, into Being, wherever something is. Eckhart readily cites a sentence by Augustine on the creating God: God did not make the world and then walk away, *non fecit atque abiit* (*Prol. gen.* nn. 14–19, 159.7–164.4).

God is Being and Oneness. Wherever something is and something is one, he shows himself as present, as whole, as indivisibly, attractingly present. In Eckhart's time, the concept of pantheism or the even more finely spun concept of panentheism did not exist. Eckhart removed the issue that was later designated by those terms by differentiating between *ens* and *ens hoc*, between primary determination and individual thing, but he made it clear that Being was not distinguished in the way that individual things were differentiated. Someone who demands that there be a difference between God and the world is still attached to the idea of independent individual things that God placed into Being at some point. But here God is Being, present, always setting things into himself anew. Someone who is fixated on difference has not conceptualized Being.

This theology is short and clear. And it argues philosophically. Eckhart praises its simplicity. It easily solves all or almost all questions that can be asked about God, and it does so in the light of natural reason (*Prol. gen.* n. 22, 165.9–12). There is nothing here of the abyss, nothing of the blinding darkness of Dionysius. Dionysius does not feature at all here, only Aristotle and Avicenna, Augustine (a specific type of Augustine) and Boethius—and also the *Liber de causis*.[9] With that, a cleansing storm descends on the frizzy multiplicity of propositions attached to different ideas about God. Moses says that God created the world in six days, but he said this for simple people; we know that Being is directly present in continual self-positing. People say that God created the world, but we know that Being continuously posits itself anew in the present. People think that God released the world from within himself, but we know he actually placed it into himself. A new assessment of the "new," as the first half of the fourteenth century managed to achieve world-historically, announces itself when Eckhart writes that every work of God is new: *omne opus dei est novum*.[10] Historians of theology have searched for salvation history in Eckhart's works but have found only rudiments in need of interpretation, for Eckhart's Being is *always* Being. Hegel and Heidegger talk about the history of Being, not Eckhart. For Eckhart, the human intellect, far from being fixated on temporal things, disregards every here and now, as Avicenna taught; it conceptualizes the timeless, Being and Oneness: *abstrahit per consequens a tempore*.[11]

Concept and Structure of the Tripartite Work

The prologues are responsible for clarifying Eckhart's intent, explaining the structure of the book, and signaling his procedure. Enough has been said about his manner of approach: everything occurs in the light of natural reason; it is—in other words—philosophizing (*Prol. gen.* n. 22, 165.11–12). Eckhart's stated intention is that in finally yielding to his brothers' beseeching urgings, he will summarize for them what he says in teaching situations, in sermons, and in conversations. He intends to say things that no one else has said yet, *nova et rara*, since they stimulate the soul more than familiar topics (*Prol. gen.* n. 2, 149.1). This is not how a traditionalist would speak. Eckhart is expressing an awareness of his status as an outsider. He does not want to be asked first what "sources" he has. Being always begins anew; and so, too, does the intellect that disregards time.

Early on, around 1302, Eckhart anticipated objections. Some of the things that he proposes, he says, will appear monstrous and false, but someone who quietly examines them will find that they agree with truth and with the Bible (*Prol. gen.* n. 7, 152.3–7). Again, there is a hierarchy: first proven truth, then Holy Scripture. After all, Holy Scripture speaks differently to one who knows that God is Being. Because he has to show this, Eckhart divides the entire work into three parts:

Part One is called *Opus propositionum*, the work of propositions, and it provides the philosophical foundation outlined in the prologue: fourteen tractates on primary determinations with their respective opposites. Only God has no complement; nothing is his opposite.

Part Two, the *Opus quaestionum*, the work that articulates the problems, puts some of the propositions advanced in Part One in conversation with the common tradition. Its structure follows the order of Thomas Aquinas's *Summa theologiae*. It seems as though Eckhart never wrote this second part.

The third part is partially available. It is the work of expositions, the *Opus expositionum*. Here Eckhart shows: the overall concept he has developed opens up Holy Scripture in a new way. It easily dissolves difficulties and thus makes possible a new formulation of Christian doctrine, one that argues philosophically. Especially important are the commentaries on Genesis, the Book of Wisdom, and the Gospel of John. At the start of the last, Eckhart repeats once more the intention behind all of his writings: to demonstrate *per rationes naturales philosophorum.*

Eckhart outlines the following structure:

Part One demonstrates that God is Being (*Prol. gen.* n. 12, 156.15–16).

Part Two discusses the question "Does God exist?" and thus addresses the problem of proof of the existence of God. We already know that Eckhart's path does not lead him via cosmology, but rather through Being (n. 13, 158.5).

Part Three interprets the first sentence of the Bible: In the beginning, God created the heavens and the earth. We already know that this cannot refer to a temporal beginning, and that creation is to be interpreted as the presence of Being (nn. 15–19, 159.7–164.4).

Regarding the planned structure, Eckhart impresses upon his readers: the last two parts depend argumentatively on the philosophical foundation of Part One. Without the first, the second and third parts hardly have any value, as his example shows: *Deus est esse—Utrum Deus sit—in principio creavit Deus* (nn. 12–14, 156.15–159.7). One has to marvel at the pious audacity of those Eckhart interpreters who believe that they can defy this logical connection, which Eckhart so carefully and explicitly made, and who say that his biblical interpretation is what is decisive in Eckhart's thought. It is indeed important for him, since he occasionally expanded it, but it always depends in its argument on his philosophical grounding. Placing his biblical interpretation in status and argumentative progression *before* the doctrine of the primary determinations—that means contradicting Eckhart. It is a transformation of Eckhartian thought in the interests of a Biblicist Protestant theology.

Philosophy of Form and Essence

Eckhart's prologues are rich in motives. I would like to highlight just two more that demonstrate the genuinely philosophical character of his works and rarely attract attention.

In addition to an outline for a metaphysics of form, which, contrary to some Franciscan teachers, excludes a number of substantial forms (*Prol.*

prop. n. 14, 173.14–175.3), there is a short but very thoughtful ontological analysis of accidents. Eckhart says of them that substance is contained in their definition (*Prol. gen.* n. 8, 152.11–14). He said this on the basis of Aristotle's *Metaphysics* Z 1, 1028a35, but Aristotle's commentators also joined the conversation about this remark. Dietrich of Freiberg presented this thought in his early work *De origine:* it is possible to define properties without mentioning the substance that bears them. For example, I can define a color without including in its definition the pigment or the thing that has been colored. If I wish to describe it, however, from the standpoint of the *being* of the property, *in ratione qua esse habent*, I need to name its substrate as well. Here again we encounter the "insofar" that is so characteristic of Eckhart, this time expressed with the phrase *in ratione qua.*

It has often been said that "medieval" philosophy explained that every creature is a being from another, an *ens ab alio.* Eckhart says this as well: every *album* is from the *albedo*, every being from Being. And yet Eckhart adds a piece of finesse: *What* a thing is, that it does not have from another, *Res id quod est, ut ait Avicenna, a nullo alio habet (Prol. gen.* n. 13, 159.1). For a certain phase of metaphysical observation, Eckhart agrees with Avicenna's concept of essence: a being may have its being from Being, but its essence, *id quod est*, it has in itself and not from another. Conceptualized as essence, the created has a certain autonomy. It has this specific whatness, which it does not have from another. God cannot create a circle to which the definition of a circle would not apply. Augustine, as cited by Eckhart, says: nothing is so eternal, so unimpeachable, so above every arbitrariness as the circle. What belongs to man as man, what an intellect is as intellect, is an eidetically formed whole, an invariable structure that even the Creator cannot change.

Prologues and Sermon Cycle: Two Ways of Thinking

Each of Eckhart's works has to be considered on its own, not interwoven with Eckhartian texts that had different audiences and belonged to different periods. That does not preclude us from looking from the prologues to the sermon cycle. Sturlese has established their temporal proximity.

The prologues have an entirely different intellectual feel from that of the sermon cycle. They breathe a climate of philosophical insistence, of constructive courage, and of lightness. A hint of self-ridicule can be detected when the author declares that he wants to prevent his book from spilling over and turning into a giant ocean of writings, *pelagus quoddam scripturae* (*Prol. gen.* n. 7, 151.13). He stresses his originality and innovation, the dependence of scriptural interpretation on philosophy. In keeping with a point made in German sermon 101 (DW 4:342.33), Eckhart explains that he will argue by using natural reasons (*Prol. gen.* n. 22, 165.11–12). Dionysius is missing from the prologues, and Avicenna from the sermon cycle on the birth of God. There is a common conviction that God gives himself only wholly (*Prol. prop.* n. 4, 168.1–2), and that the first does not tolerate an intermediary between itself and what it has established (*Prol. prop.* n. 13, 172.15–173.1). The prologues make no use of the birth metaphor; it is not necessary either for describing the descent of the wholly remaining intellectual Being and Oneness. The logos is not an issue here. The sermons speak of the intellect only as the location of the Incarnation, not—as the prologues do—as the faculty of metaphysical, supratemporal understanding (*Prol. gen.* n. 9, 154.1–4). I am not drawing any conclusions about the genesis of the prologues and the sermon cycle from these analyses. Eckhart could have cultivated separate ways of thinking at the same time, because he spoke about different topics in front of different audiences.

7. Parisian Debates, 1302–1303

A Famous Text: The First Parisian Question

Eckhart's First Parisian Question, written during the fall of 1302 and surviving only in a single manuscript, is among the most famous texts of medieval thought ever produced. Scholars have interpreted it in different ways. Martin Grabmann, who discovered the text in Avignon at the same time as Ephrem Longpré, saw in it the ominous influence of Averroism, and thus proof of Eckhart's affinity for heterodoxy; Walter Schulz praised it as the birth of the God of modern metaphysics. It induces generalizing interpretations. It is prudent to examine it closely and carefully.[1]

Eckhart's question was: are intellectual knowing and Being identical in God? And are they identical in substance or also in the progression of our reasoning? Eckhart provides his answer in three steps.

First, he sums up the arguments that Thomas Aquinas provided: five from the *Summa contra gentiles* and a sixth from the *Summa theologiae*. They all boil down to this: because God is the first of all beings, he has to be of the utmost simplicity. There is no act—either as a form of doing or as a property—that can be added to his essence, and thus his knowing is his being. Within God, everything is identical to his essence, especially knowing, which is an act that remains within, an *actus immanens*.

Second, Eckhart offers an argument that he brought forth elsewhere, *quam dixi alias*. He does not say that he has written it down somewhere else, only that he has said it before. If he had already written another Latin text that contained this idea, one good candidate would be his first commentary on Genesis. Eckhart had supposedly begun that work at this point, and he voices a similar thought in it (*Expositio Libri Genesis* [*In Gen. I*], LW 1, n. 11). At any rate, he positions himself alongside Thomas Aquinas and quotes what he has argued before: if Being (*esse*) is a perfection, then it must include understanding. Because God is the most perfect being, he is also intellectual knowing (*intelligere*) (LW 5, n. 3, 39.8–10; all citations in this chapter are to LW 5).

Third, Eckhart says: I no longer agree with my former position, *non ita mihi videtur modo*, that God is knowing because he *is* in the most perfect sense, but that God *is because he thinks*. His knowing is itself the basis of his being: *Est ipsum intelligere fundamentum ipsius esse* (n. 4, 40.7.) These are staggering statements, but no one has doubted their authenticity. To justify his idea before he has laid out his actual argument, Eckhart quotes a series of authoritative texts and provides a brief commentary. First, he cites two short sections from the Gospel of John. The Evangelist said: "In the beginning was the Word, and the Word was God." Eckhart points out that he does not say: In the beginning was being (*ens*), and God was that being. The *Word* in its whole essence relates to the intellect (n. 4, 40.7–11). The second preliminary *argumentum ad homines* is that Christ said about himself: "I am the Truth." But truth, Eckhart says, belongs to the intellect; it indicates relation or includes it within itself (n. 4, 40.11–12). Then follows a strange sentence that I have to quote here in its original form (n. 4, 40.12–41.2):

> *Relatio autem totum suum esse habet ab anima et ut sic est praedicamentum reale, sicut quamvis tempus suum esse habet ab anima, nihilominus est species quantitatis realis praedicamenti.*

> A relation, however, has its entire being from the soul and as such is a real category, just as time, although it has all its being from the soul, is nonetheless a subspecies of quantity, that is, of a real category.

The sentence is strange for several reasons. It shifts from the statement "I am the Truth" to a general theory of relation. Truth, Eckhart says, either is a relation or includes a relation, but a relation stems *entirely* from the soul and *as such* is an actual "predicament." In the fourteenth century, relations were increasingly considered products of the intellect; only related things were real, like father and son. Every philosopher admitted that there existed relations purely of thought, as, for example, between the logical parameters of genus and species. But no one who argued for *real* relations claimed that they were *entirely* derived from the soul. Instead, people said that relations were in part derived from the intellect but had their basis in things. Eckhart rejects this view. He says: a relation has its *entire* being from the soul. In the traditional view, he should have proceeded with "and therefore it cannot be a real state of being." The condition for realness was to be a predicament, that is, one of the ten categories of Aristotle's categorical table. Eckhart adheres to this terminology to delineate his diverging opinion clearly: precisely because a relation is entirely from the soul, it is a real predicament. And the same, for Eckhart, is true for time: it receives its being from the soul and is primary reality because of it, namely, as a subcategory of the real category of quantity.

Eckhart's incidental remark about relations and time seems superfluous. He sets out to talk about God's knowing and about God's relation to truth, but instead discusses the soul and its knowledge, which informs being. Its special feature is that it does not merely constitute abstractions. It does not merely form conditions within our thoughts. It constitutes real predicaments, that is, primary states of being, namely, relations and time. This theory is not Thomistic, but anti-Thomistic, as we can see from the exceptionally thorough study by Anton Krempel, *La doctrine de la relation chez S. Thomas d'Aquin* (Paris, 1952). I have commented on this passage from Eckhart elsewhere; it occupied my thoughts for many years, and it put me on the scent of Dietrich of Freiberg when I decided one day that I could not understand it and nobody so far had sufficiently explained it to me. More about it can be found in my book on Dietrich (Flasch 2007a, 56–59).[2]

Eckhart (or merely the text in its present form) again makes a mental leap. In the Gospel of John, it is said of the *verbum* that everything came into being through it: *Omnia per ipsum facta sunt*. One should read the passage, Eckhart counsels, in the following way (*ut sic legatur*): everything it made received being retroactively, *Ipsis factis ipsum esse post conveniat* (n. 4, 41.4–6). It is an ingenious play on the Bible; Eckhart confirms its validity with another quotation, this time from the *Liber de causis*: being is the first of all created things, *prima rerum creatarum est esse*. Eckhart deduces from this: when we come to being, we come to the created. Being is the first thing that is creatable according to its essence, *habet primo rationem creabilis*. What was created de facto is not important—only what is creatable according to its nature. That is being. It is opposed to "wisdom," for wisdom is something whose essence precludes it from being creatable. Someone who attempts to conceptualize wisdom as created, Eckhart shows, comes across the following contradiction: he has to presuppose the existence of wisdom within the creator of wisdom, and so it is effective before its own creation. For Eckhart, wisdom belongs to the intellect and is uncreatable: *sapientia autem, quae pertinet ad intellectum, non habet rationem creabilis* (n. 4, 41.10–11). Now, one of the Old Testament Books of Wisdom states that wisdom was created from the beginning of the world (Ecclesiasticus 24), but Eckhart remains unfazed. He rearranges the word order of the biblical verse somewhat and reads it as saying that wisdom was there before the created world. To him, the biblical text also confirms that God is intellect and intellectual understanding, not a being or being (*ens vel esse*).

This was Eckhart's preview of his authorities. He treated them with great liberty. Then he finally begins his argument. His goal is to show that knowing is positioned higher than being; that it belongs to a different order altogether, *est alterius condicionis* (n. 5, 42.1–2). Eckhart panders to the conviction, common among his contemporaries, that nature is a work of intelligence: intelligences were thought to move the celestial spheres, and thus all earthly processes were influenced by intelligence. They were ordered. Against this common assumption, Eckhart presents his counterargument, but he opens with "some people may say" and first presents the common idea as he finds it in Thomas Aquinas: being per se takes precedence *over* life and knowing; knowing takes precedence only within the individual who is already constituted in being; if, therefore, one imagines various things as already having being, then the thinking ones among them are of a higher rank. To this opinion, Eckhart objects emphatically: "I, however, believe the exact opposite." For Eckhart, word and intellect take precedence over being. But what does it mean that knowing belongs to a different, higher order? Eckhart responds in two steps: first, he reminds us in Aristotelian fashion that mathematical objects cannot be considered according to intent or good, and that something that has being is identical to the good. Good and evil exist in the things themselves, but true and false only in the soul. With mathematical objects, we enter into another world, a world that encourages us to adapt our thinking, for within it people do not inquire after efficient or final causes, as is common in the context of the natural things.

Theory of the Image

As a second step, Eckhart describes the nature of images: if we perceive an image as something that has being, it draws our attention away from what it represents. The image, Eckhart says, "approaches the opposite of being"

(n. 7, 43.13–14). It was a tenuous position to take. Contemporaries could have made the criticism that something either is or is not. But Eckhart successfully describes the special status of the image. It still has, so to speak, a foot in the world of natural things; it consists of wood or stone or canvas; it has an efficient cause and often also an aim. But as an image, it does not have being; rather, it is the relation to the thing it represents. The representation steps outside the natural context from which it comes, and this stepping out is characteristic also of the epistemic image produced in knowledge, the *species* of contemporaneous epistemology (n. 7, 44.2–5). It develops through real processes of the soul and the body, but detaches itself from them and becomes "objective." *Insofar* as it is knowledge, it belongs to a different world. In questions such as this one, philosophical analysis has to be detached from the imagination, *hic imaginatio deficit*. We are dealing with God's knowledge, which is not dependent on things but creates things. The effected as such is not within the true cause. God effects being, and so being is not within God (n. 8, 44.10–14). Eckhart explains that he is not concerned with regulating the use of the term "being"; he wants to highlight instead the foundational otherness of knowing. Were someone to call knowing "being" (*esse*), he would not object. What is important to Eckhart is the sequence and order of the justifications brought forth to defend an opinion like this: if you want to call knowing "being," then it pertains to God *because he knows* (n. 8, 45.1–5). The principle is the nothingness of the principiated. God as the principle of being is not "a being." Creatures have being, and it is within God in the shape of intellectual understanding. We can call this being-as-thought-within-God "being in its pure form," the *puritas essendi*, and in this sense say that God has being (n. 9, 45.6–15). But then, being is within God not as being but as intellect. It is within him as the being of a house is within an image. What matters is the how: being in God is known, but it does not have the *ratio entis*, the characteristic determination of a being; rather, it is within God as epistemic content.

Then Eckhart lays out his theory of analogical propositions. If we call a medicine healthy, then health *is* merely in the living creature, not in the chemical agent. Properties are not beings; only their substance has being. If things have being, then God has no being. Eckhart has a special interest in the relation of property to substance. It is the source of the *pros-hen* homonymy. In it, a property is construed as something merely close to reality, not something real itself. Properties grant a certain "being so," but they do not grant being (n. 11, 46.7–48.11). Martin Grabmann coarsely but aptly called it the theory of the "beinglessness of the accident." In doing so, he correctly identified it as having originated in the Averroistic interpretation of Aristotelian ontology. Nowadays we know that Dietrich of Freiberg developed it carefully and extensively. Eckhart provides an abbreviated version of it and denies that it takes from the accidents anything that should rightfully be theirs.

Eckhart makes a last attempt to describe the higher nature of the intellect: he reminds his audience that according to Aristotle, the eye has to be devoid of color to be able to see all colors (*De anima* II 7, 418b 27). The intellect must not be a specific physical nature if it is to be able to comprehend all physical natures. The knower is the living negation of the known. Thus, when we say that God is the nothingness of being, we only negate what does not pertain to him, and such negations, as John of Damascus taught, were utterly exuberant affirmations (n. 12, 47.14–48.9). And according to Eckhart, that is what God wanted to express when he did not tell Moses his name and instead said: "I am who I am."

Finally, I have to mention a subtle hint that Eckhart provides in his overview of the authorities that are to confirm his subsequent argument: he quotes the sentence from Jesus Sirach (Ecclesiasticus) that I mentioned above, which suggests that wisdom was created before the world. Eckhart adds that we could also interpret "created" as "begot" (n. 4, 41.12). And so we find again the metaphor of begetting and thus of birth. It stays in the background here, but it belongs with Eckhart's other key concepts: the *rationes naturales*, the requirement of philosophical proof, the full significance of "insofar"; the insufficiency of the imagination in the context of thinking; the productive significance of negation; the interpretation of analogy that stresses the nonexistence of the analogate within the first part of the analogy; and the insignificance of the vocable, even of the term "being," when the logical progression of the argument is clear and secure.[3] It goes so far that Eckhart can announce that he will prove that being and knowing are identical in God—*dicendum quod sunt idem re*—even while his argument is moving in the opposite direction. That is possible only when *this* proof is less important than the correction of the imagination in light of the special condition of concept and image, of intellect and perception. The First Parisian Question teaches neither the beinglessness of God nor the beinglessness of the accident. Scholars have long wondered whether Eckhart eventually gave up on the idea of God's beinglessness and later recognized that God was being. Those were neoscholastic proposals. What mattered for Eckhart was that God is being *because he thinks*. Or, in other words, we can say that God is being if we know that it is the higher consideration to say of him that he thinks. Eckhart later, in the *Liber parabolarum*, explained his thesis of the First Parisian Question in this harmonizing way.[4] For all being is derived from the intellect.

The text urges its readers to think about the gap within the system of categories regarding the being in the soul, the *ens in anima*. As long as there is not at least an attempt to close this gap with a theory of a characteristically different, negatively defined *intellectual being*, Christians have no sufficient concept of their God, of themselves, and of the world. Only *insofar* as this was concerned did Eckhart speak in Paris as a master of Christian theology, a theology that knew its God as intellect and Word, but that could not say what it meant without a new theory of the "intellectual being."

The Second Parisian Question

Now, one would think, Eckhart is going to talk about angels, for his Second Parisian Question is entitled: "Is the Understanding of an Angel Its Being?" Eckhart states the question more precisely: he is concerned with the intellectual knowing (*intelligere*) of the angel insofar as it is its activity. Is this activity identical to the angel's being? The question is focused on intellectual knowing, not insofar as comprehending had turned into a piece of stored knowledge, but as an act of understanding (*ut dicit actionem*). In any case, Eckhart intends to talk about angels, and he announces that he will answer his own question in the negative.

Eckhart was a master of theology; therefore, it was one of his duties to speak about angels. His title sounds as if he wanted to go through with it. But Eckhart does not talk about angels anywhere else in the question except in the first and last lines. He does not mention Dionysius the Areopagite, the teacher of theories of angels, or Augustine, or Bernard of Clairvaux. For support, though not as part of his main argument, Eckhart cites Aristotle.

The text has a curious structure. It does not begin with objections to Eckhart's intended argument; it does not end with their resolution. Instead, Eckhart opens with a quotation from Thomas Aquinas, *Sth* I 54, 2. The quotation is introduced, as was common, in a cool and detached fashion, without the mention of the author: "some (*aliqui*) teach." Aquinas opposed the position that the activity of any creature—even of an angel—was identical to its being. All creaturely activity was of an accidental nature; there could not be a creature that would, in its essence, be activity. Eckhart declares that he wants to reach his intended goal in a different way. As in the first question, he is speaking in contention with Aquinas, and not as a Thomist. In quoting Aquinas's thesis, Eckhart is placing his emphases where he likes: intellectual knowing is not being, for knowing is an activity oriented toward the outside, but being remains within. Even if one were to view knowing as an immanent act, it would not be being. Knowing is an infinite activity (*actio infinita*), being is finite; it is limited by genus and species. Intellectual knowledge is directed at truth in all the breadth that comes with absolute being; wanting is aimed at the absolute good. Even sensory perception, for Aquinas, is infinite in a certain sense, for the eye is open for everything visible. Aquinas had already juxtaposed the sheer width of the horizon of knowledge with being restricted by species and genus. And where angels were concerned, Aquinas had already spoken of sensory perception, even though it was something that angels lacked. He had widened the context to the intellectual being and attested that it possessed a certain infinity, for *everything* visible was an object of the sense of sight.

Eckhart does not mention angels again in the rest of the text, speaking only of the intellect and of sensory perception; in the end, he openly states that his main focus was our knowing, *nostrum intelligere* (LW 5, n. 10, 54.4). He wants to show that it is not something that has being. The topic has shifted from the one emphasized by Aquinas, who taught that the knowledge of angels was not identical to their being. Eckhart teaches: the knowing of an angel is not being. In its content, however, Eckhart's argument is focused solely on our intellect and our perception. Our intellect is nothing, and our intellectual knowledge is not being.

As elsewhere, Eckhart stresses that he is speaking in a certain respect. He insists on his "insofar": insofar as the intellect is intellect, *intellectus in quantum intellectus* (n. 2, 50.1; so also n. 7, 52.6); *potentia ut potentia* (n. 3, 50.6).

This means that we are talking about the intellect as the actual having of universal objects, and about perception as the grasping of perceivable things. Not about the eye as a sensory organ, not about the equipment of the soul with the faculty of knowledge. Eckhart has transformed the question of an angel's knowing and being into a general negative theory of sensory and intellectual recognition and claims. The intellect as such and also perception as such are neither here nor now, and insofar as they are neither, they are nothing, but insofar as they are natural faculties of the soul, they are something (n. 7, 53.5–8). Eckhart does not claim to be distinguishing natural things from intentional being; he is sparse in his use of specialized jargon, and he prefers to call knowing a "nothing" rather than to introduce a special category of being. But he is de facto introducing a special category, and he brings forth a series of arguments for this position.

The intellect is not any of the things that it knows. It is the nothingness of its objects. We find this position in Aristotle, who does not say anything about angels but instead quotes Anaxagoras: the *nous* is *amigés*, "unmixed," so that it can rule everything. It does not have a specific nature, a *physis*. To prevent us from confusing it with the divine *nous*, Aristotle adds that the *nous of the soul* before it thinks does not belong to those that have being. It is incapable of suffering, *apathés*, which raises questions, because thinking is a kind of *paschein*, a suffering. It "does not have anything in common with anything" (*De anima* III 4, 429a 18 to 429b 25).

We encounter here for the first time some basic determinations of the intellect and of knowing generally. They are quasi-divine attributes, explicitly belonging to the *nous* of the soul: unmixed, having nothing in common with anything. Extraterritorial, says Aristotle. Eckhart goes a step further and says: nonbeing. And the same is true, according to Eckhart, for simple vision: an eye sees a piece of wood. The eye has to be devoid of color to be able to see everything. Its nonbeing is not a fault, but the precondition for its power, which includes everything visible. Its seeing, Eckhart says, occurs outside being.

In this context, Eckhart presupposes a specific concept of being. He indicates it clearly: being is something internal; the object is outside and informs the object relation. Someone who asks for an ontological bearer, as was traditional, has to say: here the object is the bearer, is the subject, *subiectum*, of the object relation (n. 3, 50.7–8). Knowing is wholly determined by the object, not by the being of the knower.

At the same time, Eckhart conceives of both perceiving and intellectual understanding as actions. Aristotle called this conception the common "actuality," *energeia*, of perceiving and the perceived whose being was not the same (*De anima* III 2, 425b 26–27). Perceiving is our activity, *operatio*, even though the starting point of this act comes from the outside. Included in this is the simple idea that receiving is also our activity; many an Eckhart scholar overlooked it, which had consequences.

In the thirteenth century, people explained that knowledge enters us from the outside via the appearance of an epistemic image, a *species*. In the context of sensory experience, people imagined that an image affected the sensory organs in the form of an optical, acoustic, or haptic impression; in the context of intellectual knowledge, people theorized that there was nothing that directly stimulated the knower from the outside, but that the intellect actively formed a universal epistemic image in the mind, an intelligible *species*, and offered this as knowledge to the intellect, insofar as it was potential intellect. Thus, all human knowledge was seen as requiring a *species* that was also shaped by the outside. This *species* theory of knowing was a contentious, often debated one; Eckhart's contemporaries were the first to realize that it was possible to explain knowing without recourse to *species*. Eckhart's epistemology, however, still presupposed the *species* theory, and his metaphysics and ethics were conceptualized in prenominalist fashion as well.

But it is possible to detach his main argument from the *species* theory, for it reads: The *species* and the intellectual possession of a subject matter in no way have being, for a being in the soul (*ens in anima*) is distinguished from real being determined by the ten categories, which is either substance or accident. But something that is neither substance nor accident does not have being. And thus the being in the soul—like perceiving and thinking—is not a being (n. 4, 51.1–7).

Eckhart invokes Aristotle's *Metaphysics* (especially E 2), according to which everything real can be divided into substance and accident. Perceptions and thoughts are then merely abstractions: everything that is neither substance nor property, like the being in the soul, is nothing.

It is clear right away that an epistemic image is not a substance like a tree or a human. Neither is it a property, like the green of the tree, for a property has to have a bearer, a *subiectum*, but an epistemic image has an object, *habet obiectum*. Eckhart employs another Aristotelian metaphor: the epistemic image is in the soul, it has its proper place in it, but it is not in it as though the soul were its bearer (n. 5, 51.11). It is not its property, and thus it is not a being. It is of a fundamentally different species. It evades the categories of being in previous metaphysics that spoke of an *ens in anima* but could not define what that was. I begin to resolve it, Eckhart says, by saying: it is nothing.

The epistemic image is an image. It leads its beholder that looks upon it not to itself, but to the content of the image. An image is the nothingness of a being; it leads the beholder away from itself and to the thing it represents. If the image itself were a being, it would itself be the corresponding object of knowledge. It represents what it portrays; but it *is* not it. It must not be it at all, for it would then hinder the representation (n. 6, 52.1–11). Magritte painted a pipe and wrote underneath the image: *Ceci n'est pas une pipe.*

Eckhart does not dwell for too long on the epistemic image. Science is something real, a solidified and permanent attitude of the soul. It is within. Knowledge itself is nothingness; it is outside, while the being of the knower is inside.

There were still other traditional criteria for being: something that *is* is determined, it is a something, it is limited to genus and species. The intellect—always as such, insofar as it is intellect—is neither being this nor being that. If "being" means "being something determined," then the intellect is not a being (n. 7, 53.1–4).

Eckhart practices a certain elimination process along the lines of the qualifications of being set out by the Peripatetics. Something that has being is either substance or accident. A being is always something. A being, they say, is always something determined, and thus knowing is not a being, for it is indeterminate (n. 9, 53.16–18).[5] Thomas Aquinas had said the same: sight refers to everything visible, insight to all beings.

But Eckhart asks in return (I am paraphrasing his words), how can you say then that everything that has being is a something, and thus something determined? And that everything real is either accident or substance? You have talked about "being in the soul," but according to your ontological schema, images and concepts are nothingness in the soul. Unlike Thomas Aquinas in *Sth* I 54, 2, I am not trying to prove that even an angel is only a creature, but that our current academic ontology is insufficient. According to this ontology, the understanding that it produces would be nothing. Something does not add up here. I have no problem with you wanting to label images and concepts, imagining and comprehending, as beings. But you have to define what kind of being this could be. We could call it intellectual being and would already know the following things about it: it has nothing in common with anything in the world of things; it is the object-related unity of seeing and seen; it does not fit within your categorical binary of either substance or accident; it is in the soul not as though the soul were its bearer, but metaphorically as in its "proper place"; it possesses a *certain* infinity already as perception and a *fundamental* infinity in thinking; it is indeterminable according to species and genus; it cannot be analyzed according to its efficient or final cause (n. 8, 53.9–10). And here a compromise would seem possible: there are natural things that fit in the Aristotelian categories, and then there is the intellectual being that you have called the *ens in anima* without having examined it, because you have applied your natural categories to it without testing their suitability for the sensory and intellectual experience of human beings. From the vantage point of your doctrine of being, intellectual being would turn the world upside down.

The same impulse is operating here: Eckhart is not concerned with narrowing down the meaning of being to something limited or thing-like, to "being-a-certain-something." Someone who wants to call being in the soul "being" is free to do so, but he will have a hard time with his concepts of "real" and of being as substance or accident, which are tailored to natural things. He will have to come up with a new concept of the intellectual being, which we could call *ens conceptuale* or *ens conceptivum* or *ens intellectivum*. We cannot learn from Aristotle's *Categories* what "being" is in its entirety, as *tota plenitudo;* we can learn it instead from the *Liber de causis* and from Proclus, and once we have grasped it, we can find it also in the central books of Aristotle's *Metaphysics*. In a later work, his *Commentary on John*, Eckhart looks back on this debate of the *Parisian Questions* in a similar summary.[6]

Here, in what appears to be an excessively dry critique of the Aristotelian ontology of the schools of the time, Eckhart lays the foundation of his thinking. He is looking for the special condition of the intellectual being, its nonmateriality, its *energeia*-like unity of knower and knowledge. If it is conceptualized in a new and suitable fashion, then we can grasp the meaning of creation and the truth of the Gospel of John through philosophy alone. This reformed thinking precedes the reformed life.

The Third Parisian Question

Eckhart's Third Parisian Question does not survive directly. We know of it only indirectly, through a mention by the Franciscan master Gonsalvus, an Eckhart rival who cites some of his arguments. Eckhart's Franciscan colleague argued that the love of God in this world was more valuable than the intellectual vision of the blessed in heaven. Eckhart, by contrast, defended the order's doctrine of the precedence of the intellect over the will, which went back to Albertus Magnus and Thomas Aquinas. But he was never a mere defender of certain viewpoints. And he did more: he used the occasion to specify his theory of the intellect.

According to Gonsalvus's report, Eckhart formulated the following remarkable statements:

1. Because the good is grounded in being, the intellect takes precedence, since it is aimed at being, and hence at the foundational, the simpler, the higher (n. 6, 59.12–17). Being is the highest primary determination and the proper object of the intellect.
2. Further, intellectual knowledge precedes volition, for its procedure is cleansing and it arrives at the naked essentiality of a thing, *pertingit usque ad nudam entitatem rei* (n. 8, 60.5–7).
3. Thus, intellectual knowledge is being God's form or becoming God's form, since God also is intellectual knowledge and is not being, *est ipsum intelligere et non est esse* (n. 9, 60.8–9).
4. Intellectual knowing as such is subsistent.
5. Therefore, it is uncreatable, *increabile* (n. 11, 60.11–12).
6. It is what makes us pleasing to God, *grati deo*. Take away knowledge, and what remains is nothingness (n. 12, 61.1–3). "Being pleasing to God" is another way of saying being in God's grace.
7. Knowing is utterly devoid of matter; it exists as reflection. There is no reflection in being but only in knowing, which can say whether something is the same or not (n. 13, 61.4–9). Knowing means saying something about something.
8. A series of arguments that Gonsalvus quotes claims that the intellect takes precedence because it is the root of freedom, *radix libertatis* (n. 14–n. 16, 62.1–7).

We probably should not take every word and every nuance of these sentences literally. Sentence 3, at least, agrees with the First Parisian Question. The intellect is termed subsistent (4) and uncreated (5). That can relate only to the uncreatedness of *sapientia* in the first question; it preludes the debates about the uncreated in the soul. The intellect is called "God-shaped," knowing "becoming God-shaped." Sentences 3 and 6 ascribe being pleasing to God not to grace, but to the peculiarity of the intellect, whose nature makes us pleasing to God, *deo grati*. The echo of *gratia* is unmistakable. The Franciscan placed freedom above the intellect; Eckhart replies that freedom has its root in the intellect, which can imagine the many out of which something can be chosen. These are complicated arguments, and their authenticity and tradition are dubious.

In summary: the first Parisian questions seem to be concerned with God and angels, but they are actually exercises in the search for intellectual being. They lead us to the edges of ontology, which cannot grasp image and knowledge. Its consequence is that we imagine God and the soul as thing-like. But that way the best is forgotten.

8. Programmatic Speeches

Jesus Sirach

Praise of Wisdom

Good manners dictate that I now explain to the reader who Jesus Sirach was. In their chronological studies, Loris Sturlese and Georg Steer grouped together four important works that Eckhart supposedly wrote between 1298 and 1305: the sermon cycle on the birth of God, the prologues to both the Tripartite Work and to the first three Parisian *quaestiones*, and his sermons and lectures concerning the biblical book Jesus Sirach, chapter 24, verses 23–31. The latter are two sermons and two lectures that Eckhart delivered as provincial before provincial congregations, likely between 1302 and ca. 1305. This Jesus is not the one whom Christians worship, but a Jewish writer of the second century BC called Jesus Ben Sira. The Greek version of his name was Jesus Sirach; in the Latin translation of the Bible, the book received the title Liber Ecclesiastici. It is a collection of wisdom sayings and maxims. To give an impression of its ornate diction, I quote what wisdom says about itself in Ecclesiasticus 24, beginning at verse 3:

> I came out of the mouth of the Highest,
> And covered the earth like fog.
> I dwelt in high places,
> and my throne was set on a cloudy pillar.
> I compassed the circuit of heaven alone,
> I walked in the bottom of the abyss.

Across the waves of the sea and across all of the earth,
among all people and nations I reigned.
With all these I sought a place of rest,
a people in whose lands I could live.

God the Lord sent this wisdom to Jerusalem, where it combined itself with the temple service. It continues its praise of itself, and Eckhart takes up the following verses:

Ego quasi vitis fructivicavi suavitatem odoris,
et flores mei fructus honoris et honestatis.
As the vine, I brought forth the fruit of sweet odor,
and my flowers became glorious and bountiful fruit. (24:23)
Spiritus meus super mel dulcis,
et heriditas mea super mel et favum.
My spirit is much sweeter than honey
and my inheritance surpasses honey
and the filled honeycomb of the beehive. (24:27)
Qui edunt me, adhuc essurieunt
They who eat me shall yet be hungry. (24:29)
Qui operantur in me, non peccabunt.
They who work in me shall not sin. (24:30b)
Qui elucidant me, vitam aeternam habebunt.
They who illuminate me will have eternal life. (24:31)

Eckhart understood verse 23 as saying that the flower is already the fruit. This paradox provoked him to make the following explanations: Wisdom is God. God is at once source and aim. He is the first and the last. That is why the verse says that wisdom is flower and fruit.

Verse 29 especially occupied Eckhart's thoughts: he who takes a drink of wisdom will increase his thirst. Eckhart took this to mean that wisdom is infinite. Within it, everything always continues. Where it actually is, it is continually re-created. It is not born once and for all; its eternity is perpetual becoming. Eckhart outlines his program of infinitism and dynamic actualism. It was the provincial's implicit challenge to his German confreres not to remain in the status quo. But Eckhart was not keen on exhortations. He was merely outlining his philosophy and delineating his political ideas.

God Is Being

Eckhart identifies God with being (*esse*) several times.[1] Thus, he provides an explanation of the First Parisian Question and its thesis of God's so-called beinglessness. Here the theory of God's beinglessness is discarded as a criterion for genesic explanations. The First Parisian Question did not intend to establish a thesis for a theory of God, but to offer an exploratory philosophy in search of the peculiarity of the being in the soul. The latter can be grasped only via the power of negation; Eckhart does not change his position in this respect. God, however, is being. Eckhart, we must remember, permitted everyone so inclined to call God being, even in the First Parisian Question; he despised linguistic inflexibility. Now he proposes to say "Being" (*esse*) and "Justice" (*iustitia*) instead of "God" (LW 2, n. 67, 296.7–8). The context, after all, is that he is saying "Wisdom" instead of "God," a wisdom that qua its nature cannot be conceptualized as something created. We encounter a threefold unison: God is Being, but as intellectual activity; he is Justice, but not conceptualized as the property of a person; and he is Wisdom that makes hungry the one who eats of it.

God is Being. This tenet remains. But since Heidegger, the sentence has had a different ring to it from what Eckhart intended it to mean. For Eckhart adds four explanations. First, we must remind ourselves that the higher meaning of "being" is "intellectual productivity." Second, we have to conceive of all beings as images of their idea (n. 38, 266.3–7). They are the content of divine speech. Every thing is preceded by its own *ratio*. The ground of reason shines within all things; it encompasses them without being encompassed by them (n. 38, 265.2–7). Third, it has to be added to the praise of human reason that it is capable of grasping this original, ideal being of things. The human mind is the eagle that ascends to the origins of things. It comprehends their grounds in the treetops of the "original and primordial causes, where they lie hidden as pure and naked concepts before their descent into the things," *In summitate causarum originalium sive primordialium, priusquam in res ipsas prodeant,* "*in solis puris nudis intellectibus*" *latentes* (n. 9, 238.2–7).

What Eckhart calls Being is the productivity of the primordial mind, which produces images of ideas that the human intellect grasps as the immanent origin of the experiential things. Being is defined through the intellect, not through presence, not as a whole of facticity, not as its context, which remains empty. The fourth and final explanation for Eckhart's concept of being is that being is nothing other than realized *forma*. Being, for Eckhart, is not effected; he rejects any examination of being in terms of its efficient and final cause. Metaphysics happens only "in the silence of the efficient cause," *in silentio causae efficientis et finalis* (LW 2, n. 283, 616.1). The formula for Eckhart's metaphysics and his theory of love is "being equals *forma versus causam efficientem*." The philosopher, like the lover, does not look for the origin from which something developed, that is, its efficient cause, nor for what it is good for, that is, its purpose. Analyzing efficient and final causes is indispensable for investigation into natural things, but Eckhart is searching for the pure form as the true Being. He construes the divine life and the life of the deified man, the *homo divinus*, as a disclosure of form outside efficient and final causes, *praeter efficiens et finem* (n. 8, 237.4–8). Eckhart's concept of philosophy was different from that of his contemporary William of Ockham: philosophy was the eagle-like ascent to the realm of the grounds of being, the return to living substances that have their purpose within themselves, the elimination of thing-oriented ways of thinking, and the path to a proper life. Such a life would be one lived in justice and in the all-encompassing flow of divine life, outside which is only nothingness. The proper human life is the aimless settling into the perpetually new Wisdom that is also Justice and Godhead. It is the logos and the ideational being. Eckhart, like Albertus Magnus, calls the man living such a life the divine man, *homo divinus* (n. 23, 250.5; n. 26, 253.4–9; n. 27, 254.7), or simply the "just," *iustus* (n. 8, 236.6–10, etc.).

Eckhart's God sheds the regalia of otherworldly imperial honors and endorses man as his own kind. Within the sermon cycle, the metaphor of God's birth indicated it just as much as the programmatic idea of the *homo divinus* in the context of Jesus Sirach. Eckhart's deliberation begins with the distinction between the above and the below, between the principle and the principiated. The above is abundant and giving, the below poor and receiving. Above shines a light, below is darkness (n. 38, 265.8–13). Within this initial consideration, then, there is a hierarchy. But the above is the good that discloses itself; it succeeds at what its disclosing nature wants: it assimilates the below to itself. The active above attracts the initially passive below. The below becomes the eagle that flies up to the hidden grounds of the world. It is our reifying contemplation that does not recognize the coincidental dynamic in the process between the above and the below. It keeps the eagle small. It rejoices when man appears merely as an earthworm.

Analogia Once More

Eckhart uses this opportunity to explain his concept of analogy. It is always a matter of words and their usage. Eckhart distinguishes between univocal, equivocal, and analogical designations. Univocally employed vocabularies signify things whose differences manifest themselves only within a basic common determination. Dogs are always called "dogs" in the same sense, no matter whether they are big or small, black or white. Equivocal propositions indicate things that do not have anything in common with one another. They are ambiguous, as when I call a boat on Lake Lucerne as well as a hotel on its shore a "ship." The most important investigation, for Eckhart, concerns analogical propositions. In their case, the things labeled are not wholly apart. They possess an objective commonality, but it is further apart than that within the concordant *univoca*, which possess mere individual differences within the same basic determination. Things analogically designated are not entirely disparate. They signify different *modi*, different ways of being within one and the same determinateness. For example, we may say of a meal or of urine that it is healthy. Health is the commonality, a common label. But health is neither within the food nor within urine. We call urine healthy only because it indicates health. It relates to health. But health is present within urine as little as it is within a stone. One could call it "related equivocation"; Aristotle, in thinking about the case that we say of both color and a tree that they "are," called it *pros-hen* homonymy.

Eckhart is concerned with propositions that pertain to both God and worldly things alike. We can say of both God and of a man that they are just. We call God and also a mathematical formula true. We can say both that God is good and that a glass of wine is good.

I would imagine the process of arriving at this type of related equivocation in the following manner: some people drank the wine, they liked it, and Christian and Muslim doctors assured them that wine was healthy. On this basis, they called it good, and the label was later transplanted also onto a mother or a deity. But Eckhart rejected this kind of explanation, which was based in experience, with his theory of the primary determinations. Being (*esse*), *unum, verum, bonum*, but also Light, Wisdom, and Justice belonged to these. Eckhart did not think that they had been abstracted, but that they were the primary grounds of all things. These primary grounds function in the same way as health in Eckhart's example. That means that the One, the Good, and Justice are not to be found in creatures, just as health is not in the urine. Things have oneness and goodness entirely from the outside. Now we just learned shortly before that God as Being does not know any outside: *Extra primam causam nihil est* (LW 2, n. 49, 277.13; citations in this section are to LW 2). Thus, Eckhart arrives at the following summary: within a creature—those overly concerned with terminology call this the analogate—there is nothing of that which is in the first part of the analogy. There we find Being, Oneness, Truth, and Justice. But these determinations are not at home in the things, not rooted in them, not original, not *positive radicatum*, as Eckhart says. And yet we call something created "good" and "a being," even "wise." But it is so through God and within God, not by itself and not outside him. Everything that was created lives off God, eats him and becomes ever more hungry, because it *is* not by itself, but always through him and in him (nn. 52–53, 280–82).

The history of analogy in the Middle Ages is a complicated one. We need only read Cardinal Thomas de Vio's (Thomas Cajetan's) work from 1498 about the analogy of names, *De nominum analogia*, to gain an impression of its difficulty and complexity. Cajetan magnified the issue when he favored an analogy of proportions (a:b as d:e) over Aristotle's *pros-hen* homonymy. Eckhart, however, modeled his theory of analogy on the relation of accident and substance. And he did not waver in it. He relied on a theory that was based on Aristotle-Averroës, which Grabmann called the theory of "the beinglessness of the accident." Eckhart formulated it more clearly: the being of the accident is identical to that of its substantial bearer: *idem esse cum ipso esse subiecti* (n. 10, 239.5–6). This meant that Eckhart's interpretation of the primary determinations also pervaded his theory of analogy: creatures by themselves have no being and no oneness. But they have them both in the first cause, which is Being itself or God.

Eckhart remarks that "some people" misunderstand analogy and are caught up in their error even to this day (n. 53, 282.7–8). "We, however, understand analogy in its truth"—this, spoken in front of the provincial congregation of German Dominicans, signified a dissociation from Thomas Aquinas. Eckhart's theory of analogy agreed with Aquinas's in minor points such as the schematic categorization of equivocal statements, but not in its central tenet, in its negative accentuation: just as urine in itself has no health, creatures by themselves have neither being nor oneness.

Love

Eckhart had hinted at his theory of analogy before; here he presents its basic principles, albeit briefly. He does not grant it much room; with its theoretical intricacies, it would have overcomplicated his lectures before the German Dominicans. His main focus was on the simple consequences of his theory of the primary determinations. He was concerned with the infinity of being that encompasses all creatures and that all creatures crave the more they eat of it. This was a result of a metaphysics of longing and of love that extended all the way down into natural philosophy and the theory of stellar movements: the infinite Oneness invites us in like a seasonal wine room offering the most recent vintage. The world's substance hungers after form; the celestial spheres lust after it, and thus they are in constant motion and do not come to rest in their astronomical-astrological position. Eckhart observes the greed of a thirsty drinker during his first sip, and in his speech links it to the metaphysical thirst that constantly grows bigger.

To make this thirst comprehensible, however, Eckhart had to separate himself from the honored brother Thomas Aquinas. For Aquinas spoke "crudely" of it, as though it was his intention to avoid disgust, as though the infiniteness of this continued desire did not originate in the infiniteness of divine wisdom (LW 2, n. 60, 288.12; cf. n. 29, 256.12–257.1; citations in this section are to LW 2). And Thomas Aquinas must have been included among those whom Eckhart says erred in their doctrine of *analogia*. Eckhart unfolds another school of thought: he pointedly quotes Augustine and Bernard of Clairvaux, Dionysius and the *Liber de causis*, Macrobius, and the Jewish scholar Avicebron, or Ibn Gabirol, and his *Fons vitae*. He broadens the historical context: several times he quotes from the *Book of the Twenty-Four Philosophers*, that strange gathering of twenty-four thinkers who were asked to say in a single sentence what God is. Eckhart selects the following pithy sentences: God is the infinite sphere whose center is everywhere and whose circumference is nowhere (Sentences 2 and 18; n. 20, 248.1–8); God is the love that instead of hiding itself, increasingly blesses (Sentence 8; n. 51, 279.14); and (in recalling Sentence 3) God is wholly in everything (n. 10, 239.2).

The God of Meister Eckhart

A Triptych of Eckhart's Doctrine

In the last three texts, we saw how Eckhart presented his project to the Latin-speaking world. We shall take another cursory glance at the *Prologues*, the First Parisian Question, and the *Sermons and Lectures on Jesus Sirach* (*Sermones et lectiones super Ecclesistici* [*In Eccli.*]). As a whole, they aptly describe Eckhart's intention in his own words. They form a triptych of Eckhart's method. It remains to be seen whether Eckhart remained true to it for the next twenty years of his life. At the least, they are mature works that he composed as an adult.

Eckhart declares in all three texts that he intends to proceed as a philosopher, and he adheres to this stated method. He aims to answer all or almost all questions about God with philosophical arguments, and in clear and simple terms (*Prol. gen.* n. 22, 165.10–12)—that is, not with late-scholastic circuitousness, for which he seems to have had little respect. This aspiration appears so impracticable, so immoderate that some Eckhart scholars have felt the need to understate it in order to present Eckhart in a better light. But Eckhart asserted this claim sharply and clearly. We can choose to reject it, but we should refrain from reinterpreting and changing it. The concept of philosophy with which one approaches an evaluation of Eckhart's stated intent matters. His objective does not appear sensible from the perspective of an Averroistic, a Neo-Kantian, or a neoscholastic concept of philosophy. Evidently, Eckhart considered the Trinity a suitable topic for his philosophical undertaking. And it would admittedly be strange if a Christian theologian who set out to reevaluate "all or almost all questions about God" were to exclude the Trinity from his study. For Eckhart, even man's sonship belongs to the system that he intends to prove, which boils down to a reform of all the main tenets of traditional theology.

As an example, we shall consider the birth of God once again. One of the texts indicates the origin of the motif of begetting: if wisdom is present in the world and if it is uncreatable as such, then it is "begotten, not made" (First Parisian Question n. 4, 41.110–12). We are to append "of one essence with the Father." That is the birth of God. It is the justification for this metaphor, which, like all images, does not need to be constantly repeated verbally, but which must be thought through and made redundant.

For Eckhart, this result was achieved through his transformative analysis of the primary determinations to which Justice and Wisdom belonged;

his concept of philosophy had always included ethics. For the metaphysics of the logos, Eckhart invoked Book 7 of Augustine's *Confessions*, in which Augustine identifies the ancient doctrine of the logos with the first part of the prologue to the Gospel of John. But Eckhart pointed his brothers to another useful text; he advised them to read the *Book of the Twenty-Four Philosophers*.[2] One of these thinkers, asked to say in a single sentence what God was, gave the following answer: God is the eternal sphere whose center is everywhere and whose circumference nowhere; God is immeasurable; there is nothing outside of God. This is a good example of an exercise intended to correct the images that are formed by our imagination. For the image of a sphere whose center is everywhere self-destructs before the thinker's own eyes. The propositions of the twenty-four philosophers, especially the very first, proved that pagan philosophers had recognized the threefold form of the divine being: God is the monad that begets a monad and bends it back onto itself in loving ardor. Eckhart followed this path and, taking it a step further, added: the monad that begets a monad is the being in all beings; it portrays itself in humans as wisdom and is within them.

Instead of measuring Eckhart's project with a primarily supratemporal concept of philosophy, I want to investigate what Eckhart may have meant by "philosophy." Aristotle and Averroës spring to mind first, then Augustine and his *Confessiones* 7, the *De Trinitate* X, 12, XIV, 7, and XIV, 14, and—last but not least—the *Book of the Twenty-Four Philosophers*. Eckhart uses its concept of philosophy.

Someone who wants to follow Eckhart's line of thought here has to rid himself of another notion, the conventional division between "natural" and "supernatural" knowledge. Some Eckhart interpreters learned it in a catechism course and now view it as timeless truth that they can apply to Eckhart. As the classic work by Henri de Lubac, *Le Surnaturel* (Paris, 1967), has shown, however, the distinction was introduced and established only in a certain type of theology by Thomas Aquinas; neoscholastic theologians of the nineteenth century pushed it much further than Aquinas and suggested a two-story Godhead: they imagined that the philosophically recognizable *one* God (*Deus unus*) lived downstairs, while the Triune God (*Deus trinus*), only recognizable supernaturally, lived upstairs. Someone who comes to Eckhart with this belief will not understand a thing. For Eckhart, the dividing line between nature and supernature lay elsewhere. And he explained it. In the first two Parisian *quaestiones*, Eckhart describes the specific nature of the intellect, its characteristic *condicio*, in order to conceptualize God. To the German Dominicans, he said: there is nature within the intellect, but the intellect itself is something higher than nature; it is the site of the ideas. It belongs to a higher world, namely, the intellectual world that Augustine and Plato, his source, had described (*In Eccli.*, LW 2, n. 10, 240.1–7). The intellect is supernature. Plato's intellectual world will become Leibniz's "realm of grace." It is possible to condemn this view, but it is what Eckhart said and thought, and it changed the intellectual coordinate system of the time.

What Is God?

God alone is Being, Oneness, Truth, and Goodness. He alone is Justice and Wisdom (*Prol. gen.*, LW 1, n. 4, 150.1–4). He is infinite; he encompasses everything, as the twenty-four philosophers knowingly said. Every reader of Eckhart has to fight his own imagination, which presents justice to him like an additional property of a person that is dependent on that person. To destroy the idea of independently existing substances, as the twenty-four philosophers did, Eckhart brusquely highlights that there is nothing outside of God: *Extra deum nihil est* (*Prol. gen.*, LW 1, n. 20, 164.8). And again: *extra primam causam nihil est* (*In Eccli.*, LW 2, n. 49, 277.13). We must avoid circumlocution and call this a theory of all-encompassing unity. Eckhart's God is Being and Unity, Justice and Wisdom. He is the all-encompassing attraction or love. Just as Eckhart's philosophy results in detailed analyses, in the theory of the accident (n. 10, 239.5–6), and in the exclusion of efficient and final causality from metaphysics and love (n. 8, 237.4–8), so Eckhart's metaphysics is concerned with affectivity and poesy. This is the reason why Eckhart based his speeches before the German Dominicans on the poetic self-praise of wisdom found in Ecclesiasticus. God as the all-encompassing is at once fruit and flower, scent and fruit (n. 19, 247.10–11). All things divine, including deified humans, possess fruit and flower together (n. 18, 246.10–11). In this context, Eckhart spoke of the coinciding of the maximum and the minimum. Nicholas of Cusa marked up the text of *In Eccli.* n. 20, 248.1, in his own manuscript. Eckhart teaches us to describe coincidental phenomena: God is beginning and end, maximum and minimum, flower and fruit.

It was on this basis that Eckhart imagined the creation of the world. God is the original formal act, the *primus actus formalis* (*In Eccli.* n. 50, 278.9); he discloses the having of form, for form, *forma*, is the first thing that establishes a distinction to nonbeing, *forma sola facit distare a nihilo* (n. 55, 284.7).

And again Eckhart admonishes his audience that they should not let themselves be deceived by the imagination. Whatever an artisan produces is found outside himself. But God's creative act must not be construed in those terms. There is no outside to God; he places everything into himself. His making and creating is neither blind nor arbitrary. He devises the world. That is why every thing is preceded by its ground of thought, its idea or *ratio* (n. 38, 265.2–3). The primary determinations attract to themselves everything that follows (*Prol. gen.* n. 10). They alone provide form and establish the distinction to nothingness.

Immediacy

Eckhart's concept of God contained a tenet that threatened to put an end to every traditional intermediary: the first does not tolerate an intermediate, *primum enim medium non patitur* (*Prol. prop.*, LW 1 n. 13, 173.11). Nothing comes between God and the intellect. Therefore, man becomes deified without any intermediaries; he becomes *homo divinus, deiformis* (*In Eccli.* n. 23, 251.11). It is the nature of the intellect to be God-shaped (Third Parisian Question, 60.8). When Eckhart talks in his sermons about the fact that we are not supposed to know anything or want anything, he presupposes that the intellect reaches the primordial grounds of the things like an eagle in ascent. It reaches the top of the cedar, takes hold of its highest branch, and crops off the twigs (Ezekiel 17:3). It reaches beyond the here and now. It surpasses time (*Prol. gen.* n. 9, 154.3–4). It raises itself up to the ideas, that is, to the grounds of being that precede all things (*In Eccli.* n. 9, 237.11–238.7). It has nothing in common with anything, so it can grasp all worldly forms (Second Parisian Question, 50:1–5). The human mind, Augustine's *mens*, is the hidden part within us that is always active. So justice keeps watch in the heart of the just person while he sleeps, *in dormiente vigilat iustitia* (*In Eccli.* n. 27, 255.3). Speaking to the German Dominicans, Eckhart drew the following ethical conclusions: What matters in the context of moral actions is the intention, not the external act (n. 26, 253.4–9). Justice is incorporated into the receiving activity of the mind; here, the flower is the fruit. This justice is before and outside external actions (n. 27, 255.1–5). And thus we encounter here the first of Eckhart's sentences that will make it onto Pope John XXII's list of Eckhart's errors. Sentences 16 and 17 relativized external action to such a degree that the pope did not consider them squarely heretical, but nonetheless unpleasant and utterly suspect.[3]

PROGRAMMATIC SPEECHES 113

Justice, in Eckhart's writings, becomes the life of the mind. Thus, the just man finds peace in works and does not expect rewards; his ethical actions have value in themselves. A quote taken from Macrobius supports this view: the value of something morally good is situated within itself, *rerum honestarum in ipsis pretium est* (*In Eccli.* n. 24, 251.14).

A Look Back

The three texts of this chapter—the prologues, the first three Parisian questions, and Eckhart's interpretation of Ecclesiasticus—all outline a new metaphysics as theology. They sketch the basic lines of Eckhart's ethical thought. They distinguish Eckhart from authors who interpret the Bible traditionally (*In Eccli.* n. 58, 286.14) or, like Thomas Aquinas, "crudely" (n. 60, 288.12: *grosse exponunt*). Eckhart indicates that he thinks differently from most teachers. He quotes Aquinas, without mentioning his name, and exclaims: I, however, believe the exact opposite (First Parisian Question n. 7, 43.3). During the twentieth century, there were decades in which the *analogia entis* was seen as the central tenet of Thomism. Eckhart attacks it: some people, Eckhart writes, still have not understood analogy (*In Eccli.* n. 53, 282.7–8). Just like other Dominican professors, Eckhart distances himself from the standard teachings of Franciscan authors; he rejects the plurality of substantial forms and the precedence of the will over understanding. Still, his opposition is grounded in something else: others do not grasp the philosophical theology that is contained within the doctrine of the primary determinations. They yield to the imagination. They believe in independent individual things.[4] The contrast between Eckhart's philosophy and that of other scholastics does not stem from the fact that Eckhart called his God beingless. That was either hardly understood or was interpreted correctly as Eckhart's search for the intellect's special status in the world, especially because he counseled generosity in the use of the term "being": if you want to call divine knowing "being," I am all right with that (First Parisian Question n. 8, 45.3–5). Instead, the contrast derived from the following: scholastic Aristotelians did not correct the illusion of the imagination that independent substances exist, even though Aristotle intended something different in his *Metaphysics*. Eckhart pushed them toward a denaturalization of their concepts of God, man, and the world; he intimated that Christian science was far from perfect or complete. In addition, he irritated them with paradoxical emphases and a sometimes crass, realistic style, found, for example, in his description of the horse trade, in which the buyers denigrate the horse (*In Eccli.* n. 32, 260–61). And finally, he disturbed plainer, more upright minds with his use of such strange texts as the *Book of the Twenty-Four Philosophers*, which he quoted in his sermons and recommended in his lectures. We know that there was some opposition in Paris to this philosophical work of art. M. T. d'Alverny describes a manuscript in the Bibliothèque nationale in Paris (Cod. lat. 6286) whose medieval owner attempted to render the text of the *Book of the Twenty-Four Philosophers* illegible.[5] If the text was not heretical, it must have at least seemed exceedingly strange.

9. Golden Apples in Silver Peels: The Origin of the World—An Explanation of Genesis

Platonism in Genesis 1

Anselm of Canterbury was always too afraid to say something new in a book. He certainly did not want to teach something that might not "cohere" with tradition or, above all, with Augustine.[1] That was around 1100. In the meantime, considerable social and cultural shifts allowed for an increase in authorial awareness, to the extent that two hundred years later, Eckhart was able to state in his *Prologue to the Tripartite Work* (*Prologus generalis in Opus tripartitum*) that he would write nothing, or at least almost nothing, that one could find elsewhere (*Prol. gen.*, LW 1, n. 7, 151.15). He would compile what he had said about biblical interpretation on other occasions. To avoid the impression that he was disregarding tradition, he would occasionally, or very rarely (*raro*), refer to texts by saints and teachers, especially Thomas Aquinas. Eckhart names his main sources: Augustine's three expositions of Genesis, along with the commentaries by Ambrose, Basil of Caesarea, Moses Maimonides, and Thomas Aquinas on the creation narrative about the work done in six days (*Prologus in Opus expositionum et in librum Genesis*, LW 1, nn. 1–2, 183.4). Eckhart wrote two commentaries on the first book of the Bible, which narrates the beginning of the world. The first one—*Expositio Libri Genesis*, cited as *In Gen. I*—was written in connection with the *Prologi*, and was likely in the works around 1305. We cannot determine a more precise date, since Eckhart constantly reworked the text; there is evidence of later additions. The second commentary was supposed to become the first part of a new comprehensive commentary on the Hebrew and Greek Bible. It is usually cited as *In Gen. II*, but more aptly as *Liber parabolarum Genesis*, here abbreviated *Liber parab*. It belongs to a decidedly later period in Eckhart's life, likely after 1311–13, and was part of a project that underwent changes. I will discuss it after *In Gen. I*.

Eckhart's first commentary on the Bible makes one thing clear from the beginning: it is not a philological commentary. It does not intend to be. Today we read the first sentence of the Bible as "In the beginning God created the heavens and the earth." Eckhart speculates about the first words of the Latin version. He reads *In principio* as "in principle" (in the sense of "at the source") and then poses his first question: *in what principle* did God create the world?

Allow me a short historical remark before I present his answer. In Christian antiquity, there were two biblical interpreters who were better trained in philology and prepared for the Hebrew Bible than Augustine, namely, Origen and Jerome. Nonetheless, cultural development in late antiquity had led to a decline in linguistic knowledge; Augustine's primacy had established nonphilological biblical exegesis in the Latin West. In his early *Commentary on Genesis against the Manicheans*, Augustine defends the Old Testament against the suspicions of the Manicheans by interpreting everything offensive allegorically. His interpretation of Genesis in the last three books of the *Confessions* remains predominantly speculative and allegorical. Afterward, however, he turned to a more literal interpretation and named it accordingly: *De Genesi ad litteram*. Eckhart either did not notice this turn or ignored it; Augustine adhered to the method much less clearly than the title promised. The influence of the Jewish intellectual Moses Maimonides formed something of an opposing force for Eckhart. It made possible a host of more exact interpretations. Still, Eckhart's own philosophical interest and the importance of the Augustinian tradition outweighed the philological connoisseurship of Maimonides. Eckhart remained indebted to it for many individual questions; he stayed close to it especially in interpreting the Bible as the true doctrine of nature, of nature in its Aristotelian interpretation.[2]

And so what is the principle in which God created the world? It is the concept of things or the divine idea, the *ratio idealis* (LW 1, n. 5, 188.10).[3] Eckhart answers his initial question by introducing his own version of Platonism in the first chapter of the work. We need to address its idiosyncrasies.

To support his way of reading, Eckhart cites the beginning of the Gospel of John, which also begins with *In principio* but then continues with *erat verbum*. Eckhart clarifies what "Word" means. In Greek, it was called "*logos*" and meant "the ground of reason," *ratio*. Eckhart does not mention the almighty Creator or the second person of the Godhead. He neutralizes their role in the foundation of the world and at once turns toward the rational structure of the world; generally speaking, the ground of reason is the principle and root of the thing itself (*ratio ipsius rei,* n. 3, 187.3). It was for this reason that Plato adopted his theory of ideas. He conceptualized them as the grounds of reason of all things, as their principles, in respect both to being and to knowledge.

Eckhart illustrates further what such a ground of reason is. It is the essentiality of sensible things (*quiditas rei sensibilis*), synonymous, as Aristotle said, with their definition and their scientific proof (*demonstratio*). Eckhart understands Platonism as knowledge of the rational blueprint of the sensible world. He cites Averroës's commentary on the passage at the beginning of the seventh book of the *Metaphysics*, according to which philosophers until then had always looked for the essence of sensible things and had failed to find it; if they had found it, then the "first ground of all things" would have been found, *tunc erit scita prima causa omnium entium.*[4] That sounds as though Aristotle and Averroës were concerned with a philosophical theology. Eckhart denies this explicitly: many people erroneously believe (*plerique errantes putant*), he writes, that they were referring to God here. That, however, is not the case; rather, the Aristotelian passage has to do with the immanent ground of reason of the things, with the *ratio rei* that is expressed by the definition (n. 3, 186.13–187.12). Believing that the question of essence was in the clutches of theology, Eckhart distanced himself from the "many" who supported this pious reinterpretation. He insisted on immanence.

As if he had not made himself clear enough already, he continues to elaborate. The inner essential ground of a thing is in *this* sense its principle, in that it has no ground outside itself. It also has no relation to any external ground. The metaphysician looks only at the nature of being, that is, at the essence (*entitas*), and does not prove anything through grounds that lie outside the thing, anything through efficient or final causes. Physicists may investigate God as the efficient and final cause of the world; the metaphysician considers only the present idea. He is concerned only with the *ratio idealis*, which is expressed in the definition and which, as Eckhart continues from Dietrich's *De origine* 5, 61 III 199, enables proofs. He pays no attention to anything external, *nihil extra respiciens* (n. 4, 188.2). Eckhart interprets the Platonism that he detects in the first sentence of the creation narrative in Aristotelian-Averroistic fashion. Accordingly, God created the world by contemplating the ideas. These were, or are, specific ideas, one for lions and a different one for men. It would also be possible to say: he created the world in the Son, for the Son is the exemplar and idea of everything. That is why Augustine said that whoever denied the ideas denied the Son. Someone who understands faith correctly cannot dismiss the theory of the ideas as Eckhart presents it here. That God created the world means that it has a rational layout. And it is not vaguely assumed or believed; it can be grasped through definitions and scientifically proved. Philosophy develops it into *definitio* and *demonstratio*.[5]

From these premises Eckhart deduces a specific method for observing the world. God created everything in wisdom. And Augustine therefore instructs us to proceed in the following manner: you can achieve secure knowledge of what God has done if you determine through true rational thought what is the best in each case. Then you can know what God, the founder of everything good, has done de facto. It is a sentence by Augustine, taken from his early *De libero arbitrio* III 5, 13.[6] This sentence is rarely associated with Augustine, and even more rarely with Eckhart. Eckhart places it at the beginning of his biblical interpretation and thereby sets philosophical conditions for the Creator of the world, in the sense that he is the ground of everything good and he has created the world with reason. There are substantial insights to be gained from this. The principle in which he created everything is intellect. The intellect, according to the *Liber de causis*, is the principle of all of nature. The intellect encompasses all things (n. 6, 189.7–15). Eckhart cites Neoplatonic formulas that describe the world-spirit as the ground of nature. But to the divine logos as the realm of ideas of immanent structures, he assigns the function that his source, the *Liber de causis*, attributes to independent spiritual creatures, to governing intelligences as the grounds of nature. He does not seem especially concerned when he accepts the celestial spirits back into the logos. What counts is the result: everything is arranged rationally and is available to be investigated for definitions and proof.

As ancient philosophers knew, this means that God created everything in the logos. God created within himself. There was no intermediary and no

abyss that he had to overcome. He himself was the intermediary, and he himself—without distance and unmediated—is the world. Eckhart then recounts
a discussion in which he was asked why God did not create the world earlier.
Such discussions existed in antiquity; Augustine, who indignantly rejected
them, talks about this. Eckhart describes his two answers. First, God could
not create the world earlier because he was not God before the world. Second,
there was no "earlier" without the world. God created the world together
and simultaneously with the begetting of his Son (n. 7, 190.11–12), for the
Son is the exemplar and the ground of the ideas of everything. The second
answer was parallel to ancient and Christian speculation on the logos. The
first answer, however, is surprising: God could not, because he was not, *non
potuit, eo quod non esset*. This was difficult for pious ears to hear. Eckhart is
fighting once again against the imagination: *non enim imaginandum est falso*.
It is not the case that God first had a picture book of the ideal world structures and then went about realizing them. One must not *imagine* any interval
of time when the point is to *think* timelessness. In the same timeless Now in
which God begot his Son, he also created the world. One can *imagine* that
God existed without the world. But it cannot be *thought*. Eckhart does everything he can not to construe God's relation to the world as having developed
arbitrarily, although there are people who imagine that this is precisely what
proves the freedom of a personal God.

"Image and Likeness"

Eckhart was very selective in his commentary. He dealt only with those
biblical texts about which he had spoken before. The creation of man was
one of those topics. He was created according to the image and likeness
of God, the Bible says. *Secundum imaginem et similitudinem* in the Vulgate
translation. It suggests two levels of correspondence between man and
God, while Genesis 1:26 expresses the same thought with two different expressions. Since Augustine, and probably as early as Irenaeus, "image" had
been considered the higher correspondence, the more explicit rendition
of the exemplar, compared with mere similarity. What did it mean that
man was called the "image of God"? Eckhart did not want to pass over
this question as he did so many others. He connected it with the question of
why man was created last. What does "last" mean in the timelessness of the
eternal Now?

Eckhart thought a lot about the "image."[7] In the First Parisian Question, he explained that the image as material product belonged to the world of things but that it stepped out of it within it, left its natural character behind, and passed over into being nothingness. It does not direct the eye to itself, as a thing, but rather to the copy that it is *not*. If man is called an "image of God," that means that all other earthly creatures have a similarity to a determined idea in God. They are formed specifically and fixed in one species. Augustine, Aquinas, and Eckhart all thought that the origin of species lay in the mind of God. But while stones, plants, and animals each correspond to only one idea of species, man reflects God as a whole, not something of him, but him himself. Why is that so? Because man has a rational or intellectual nature. And this specifically means that the intellect as such—always the Eckhartian "insofar"—can "become everything." The phrase "to be able to become everything" stems from the characterization of the intellect in Aristotle, *De anima* III 5. And Aristotle's name pops up immediately: he says that man is "all things to a certain extent" (*De anima* III 8, 431b 21) and the complete being, *totum ens*. Eckhart describes this with the words of Avicenna: the perfection of the rational soul consists in becoming the intelligible world, *ut fiat saeculum intelligibile*, and in the shape of the Whole looming within it. In the soul, the universe perfects itself as the world of intellect; the being of the whole world, so to speak, enters into the intellective world with the soul, *transeat in saeculum intellectivum, instar esse totius mundi*.[8] We should pay attention to the phrase "intellective world"; this is what the world is called insofar as it is within thinking. The creation of man is his emerging out of God as the image of God's essence, *in similitudinem divinae substantiae*,[9] not as a similarity to a specific divine model, but rather because he is capable of developing the substantial perfections of God—knowledge, wisdom, foresight, and his dominion over other creatures. Augustine expresses it in this way: man is an image of God because he is capable of God, *capax dei*, because he possesses God's substantial perfections—God's wisdom, insight, and world dominion. And it is not the case that he would have received them only in the future; he has them now. Being intellect means: being intellect now. For "intellect" means similarity with the totality of being, *similitudo totius entis*. The human mind, Eckhart says, contains the universe within itself, not this or that individual thing but rather the entire world, which is why the Greeks called man a microcosm (*In Gen. I* n. 115, 270.2–272.6). Hence, man is said to have been created last. In building a house and in nature, perfection comes at the end. Everything else in nature is a lessening of man. It was for this reason that Avicenna thought that nature, via a long detour, could generate man from just earth, for the flesh of men was made from material sustenance. Aquinas, however, disagreed with Avicenna on this point.[10] Eckhart dismisses the quasi-evolutionary naturalism of the Arab physician less resolutely than Aquinas did.

Philosophical Interpretations of the Bible

We shall return once more to Eckhart's central argument in the first commentary on Genesis. The *Opus propositionum* and the *Opus quaestionum* are not available, but the prologues provide clues about how Eckhart wanted to be understood. His interpretation of the creation narrative proceeds from two explicitly formulated premises. First, we know what God is from the analysis of the primary determinations: God is Being, Oneness, Goodness, Knowledge, Wisdom. The essential determination of God is intellect. He carries the world as the realm of ideas within himself. Second, all biblical interpretation has little or no value for those who have not already thought through its philosophical premises as the *Opus propositionum* was supposed to contain them and as the prologues sketch them out (*Prol. gen.*, LW 1, n. 11, 156.4–7). Only thinking overcomes the false imagination to which many people succumb: they imagine God and the world as separate and relate the two as efficient cause and effect. The raw ideas of efficient and final causality, which are indispensable in physics, do not belong in metaphysics, something that Dietrich of Freiberg had established at length in his *De origine rerum praedicamentalium* of 1286.[11] Only knowledge eradicates the idea that God waited until he created the world. Only a close study of Averroës can correct the most commonly held opinion that in speaking about the long-sought essence, he is speaking about God. The crucial groundwork that Eckhart cites is the Platonic theory of forms. He supplements it with the metaphysics of the books on substance by Aristotle and Averroës; with their help, he demonstrates the immanence and epistemological fruitfulness of the forms; they alone allow for knowledge as *definitio* and *demonstratio*. Eckhart makes himself vulnerable by openly subscribing to the Platonism of the *Liber de causis* and of Augustine, especially in *In Gen. I* nn. 2–7, 186–91, and n. 78, 239.8–240.7. And he subsequently adheres to this position: he solves the nagging question about the origin of multiplicity by stating that God is simultaneously Oneness and Intellect (nn. 10–14, 193.11–198.3; n. 90, 248.14–249.10). It is true that only the One proceeds from the One, namely, the universe from God (n. 12, 195.11–196.2).

God contains the many in the manner of the One, for he is mind. What that means needs to be developed based on Anaxagoras and Aristotle (n. 168, 313.12–314.5). God is Being; creation means the disclosure of Being. Eckhart differentiates being as Being in itself, that is, God, and the being of things. There is uncreated Being and created being, much as there is uncreated Justice and created justice (n. 20, 201.6–9). Thus, there is no "pantheism." The philosophical operation that Eckhart claims as the foundation of his biblical interpretation thus consists of the connection of the theory of the logos and the theory of forms with a metaphysics of essence and substance. It leads to the sharply formulated dictum that makes palpable his distance from contemporaneous authors: *in divinis*, that is, in the nature of God, but also in the *homo divinus*, in grace and in salvation, there is no place for the category of causality, only the category of the ideational ground of reason, of *ratio*, which shows itself as disclosure of form. Aquinas described grace in man as the presence of God as efficient cause: *Deus est vita animae per modum causae efficientis* (*Sth* I–II 110, 1 ad 2). Eckhart's philosophical reform consisted also of silencing the voice of efficient causality. Only grounds of an ideational-formal kind are at once wholly immanent and wholly transcendent, *totus intus, totus foris* (n. 61, 228.4). They make possible the qualified concept of the living that has its telos in itself, just as Aristotle conceptualized it in the twelfth book of his *Metaphysics* (n. 112, 265.9–267.11).

Furthermore, the philosophical plot of *In Gen. I* also rests on the combination of the Neoplatonizing metaphysics of Being and Oneness with the doctrine of the intellect as presented by Anaxagoras, Aristotle, and Averroës and as corresponding with Augustine's theory of *mens*. Eckhart's anthropology, like his philosophical theology, is also a theory of the intellect. This becomes especially clear when Eckhart speaks about man as God's image.[12] The Platonizing metaphysics of Being joins the philosophy of the intellect and produces an ethics. Eckhart's ethics presents the concept of the *homo divinus* (n. 16, 199.7); it traces the disquietude of acting to being (nn. 163–64, 310.4–311.15).

All these are avowedly philosophical concepts. They become even clearer when Eckhart pursues biblical interpretation as knowledge of nature. Along with Moses Maimonides, he reads the book of Genesis as a book of natural history: *docet rerum naturas* (n. 199, 345.7). At length, Eckhart discusses the theory of the elements (n. 30–31, 207–209), to which he re-turned in a *quaestio* during his second term as master in Paris; I have discussed it elsewhere.[13] He provides reasons for why we do not *see* the celestial spheres (n. 83, 242.9–243.2). He philosophizes about the first matter (nn. 36–37, 213.1–214.10). And he strikes up the subject that the *Commentary on John* and the German sermons will unravel: the unity of the knower and the known. Eckhart uses this Aristotelian-Averroistic insight to explain what the Bible means when it says that the two become one in one flesh (n. 199, 345.6–347.5).

A Second Commentary on Genesis

After a number of years—he had already authored the *Commentary on John*—Eckhart announced that he planned to write a new cursory commentary on the entire Bible. The part that he wrote was a new interpretation of the first book of the Bible. He titled it *Liber parabolarum Genesis*. He understood this to mean not what a modern reader might think, namely, a collection of the allegories and parables that occur in *Genesis*, but rather a symbolic interpretation of the events that the book narrates. He wanted to write it for a more advanced audience, for *periti*, and to show that God, who is Truth itself, included all truth in his revelation. The Bible indicated the truth of divine things, the *divina* (or, as Eckhart says, metaphysics), and of the knowledge of nature and ethics. The new commentary was supposed to demonstrate this through selected passages: the Bible as an all-encompassing explanation of the world whose veiled meaning is recoverable through symbolic-philosophical interpretation, which reads the narrative as a parable.

To provide an example: the Lord God famously dipped Adam into a deep sleep before he formed Eve from his rib. Eckhart considered this an actual event at the beginning of human history. But he thought that Moses in his wisdom had written it down so that we could learn the fundamentals of natural history from it. For Eckhart, Adam's sleep means that in nature, every active principle, because it is partly matter, suffers a certain lessening of its force. Its effectiveness is put to sleep. Therefore, Moses writes, "God dipped Adam into a deep sleep" (n. 116, 582.9–12). And when we read, "In the beginning God created the heavens and the earth," then the "heavens" means the active principle, and the "earth" the passive one, of all created things. Moses wanted to tell us that God, the *one* principle, created a binary of world grounds (n. 26, 496.9–13).

Eckhart gives a precise account of his method in the second biblical interpretation; he does not say that Genesis teaches metaphysics, physics, and ethics. This threefold division of the fields of knowledge was a late-antique division of philosophy that continued to apply in the thirteenth century. Eckhart says that the Bible suggests this (*innuitur*). He considered it his duty to uncover those suggestions; that is what he understood biblical interpretation as parable to mean. He said that he wanted to pierce the peel of the wording and gain the pulp of truth (*Prologus in Liber parabolarum Genesis* n. 1, 447.4–6; the rest of the citations in this section are to this text). He knew that he needed to have already proved the interpreted contents. His new biblical interpretation had philosophy too as its foundation. To that end, he pointed to the reasoning in the *Opus propositionum* and the *Opus quaestionum* (n. 6, 455.13–15), but also provided the reasons in the new book, albeit in a shortened version, allowing us to comprehend their intent. They imply that through Genesis, he ascertained a comprehensive philosophical account of the whole world. I will present its main features in a moment; first, I provide a few remarks about Eckhart's unique method of biblical interpretation.

Eckhart identifies, he says, the Bible's insights regarding the principles of the *divina*, the *naturalia*, and the *moralia*. The "divine things" (*divina*) include the Trinity and the Incarnation, which Eckhart demands to know through natural reason. Instead of *divina*, he also says "metaphysics," but not in the sense in which it was used at the time nor as it is used by contemporary academics, but rather in the sense of Eckhart's own conception of the primary determinations. The fundamentals of knowing nature are so important to him that he can occasionally say that he is looking for the grounds of nature and ethics, the *naturalia* and the *moralia*.[14] He wants to prove first through grounds of reason and then through the Bible and finally through the church fathers (n. 58, 526.7). He rarely abandons himself to quasi-poetic association as, for example, when he says of Sarah, the free woman, that she is like wheat among the grains, like the white among the colors, the gold among the metals, the heavens among the corporeal entities (n. 187, 657.11–12). Such comparisons are rare; Eckhart almost always hastens to the deeper philosophical meaning that there is to uncover. What is the text suggesting when Rebecca says that two peoples are in her womb? To Eckhart, it signifies the twofold being of all things: on the one hand the ideational—their being, whether in the ideas in God's mind, in the mover of the heavenly sphere, that is, in a highest intelligence, or in man's intellect—on the other hand their changeable material being (n. 202, 674.3–7). Eckhart is again placing his Platonic ontology into the Old Testament narrative. When Genesis says that man and woman will be one flesh, the parabolic interpretation even in Eckhart's first commentary on Genesis, invoking Maimonides, consists of uncovering the universal-ontological principles: active and passive, form and matter.[15] Eckhart wants to make sure that these contradictory principles interact harmoniously. He uses this analysis to describe the relationship between the soul and God: the passive is not supposed to remain purely passive; the active activates what was previously passive. It is a point of significance for a philosophy of religion: at times, Eckhart presents man and his intellect as empty and passive, but we need to mentally supply his explanation that the lower is perfected and ennobled by the higher. Because the passive initially adheres to the higher, it is in it and works together with it (n. 94, 559.11–13).

Understood symbolically, the narrative of the Fall of man contains the theory of man and the traditional disparagement of woman. For someone well versed in philosophy, the serpent, the woman, and the man point to the three principles in mankind, sensuousness (snake), lesser reason (woman), and essential reason (man) (n. 145, 614.6–9). Eckhart knew the unsolvable questions that the theologians of the twelfth and thirteenth centuries had posed about the Fall. He lists a few of them: What language did the snake speak? How did Eve answer the snake? What type of fruit did she hand to her husband? What language did God speak to Adam? All this, he says, has a deeper meaning. It shows the essential properties of God, of higher and lower reason as well as of the sensory powers of mankind (n. 159, 629.3–15). Eckhart encourages the keen reader to further investigate all of this for himself, and indeed in such a way that he will interpret the narrated events as indicative of a universal, philosophically determined knowledge. That is what it means when Eckhart writes that the reader should take the biblical narrative as parable. He is supposed to let go of the narratives as events and facts. Every truth that he finds is God's truth and is written in the Bible. Understanding the Bible as parable does away with many questions and doubts. Eckhart reports that many of his contemporaries were perturbed by such problems. He responds that they should read these kinds of stories as metaphorical, for that is their historical, as well as their exact and literal, meaning. If someone said "the meadow laughs," then the literal meaning would be that the meadow is blossoming. What is meant is lost on the person who takes the letter literally (n. 136, 603.1–5). Thus, Eckhart claims that his parabolic interpretation is the literal one. And to a literal interpretation belongs everything that is true. Since everything that is true stems from God, who is Truth, every true sense of the Bible is the literal sense of the word (n. 2, 449.4–8). Thus, everyone has the right to interpret the Bible in his own way. God wrote the text so fruitfully that he put everything into it that everyone's understanding can find within it (n. 2, 450.5–10).[16] It is designed as manifold. We are to study the poets in order to understand the Bible. The poets were theosophists as well; they provided instruction about the divine things, nature, and ethics through allegory. Eckhart likes to cite Horace, Virgil, and the poems of Boethius. There is almost an air of early humanism in Eckhart's discovery of the poets' theology; Eckhart, after all, lived in the time of Dante, who died in Ravenna in 1321. In the plain language of the Bible—that is, the *sermo humilis* (n. 1, 448.5), which Erich Auerbach uncovered for Romance philology—lies every truth for every person. Eckhart accorded the freedom that he allowed himself in his textual interpretation to everyone else. In this context, he did not mention the magisterium.

Metaphysics, the Doctrine of the Intellect, and Ethics

The universal metaphysics on which Eckhart based his parabolic interpretation of scripture was mentioned in the context of Rebecca's body. It is a Platonism of two ways of being that Eckhart, along with Augustine, thought of as Platonic: according to it, there is an intelligible and a sensible world. The sensible world is not devoid of truth. It is similar to that which is true, but it is the world of opinions. The intelligible world is the world of knowledge and of the true virtues (*Liber parab.* n. 67, 533.11–534.2; citations in this section are to this text). As is usual among Platonists, the ethical observation is integrated into the ontological. Eckhart puts a special emphasis on the theory that the essentiality of a thing, its *essentia*, is not determined from the outside and is not *ab alio*. It is an idea made sensory, the *ratio* of the thing (n. 68, 534.3–7). This is Avicenna's theory, as Eckhart himself remarks; but he also invokes Augustine's statement that nothing is as eternal as the definition of the circle. That is where the primacy of the universal over the individual lies, in scholastic terms: of the universal *natura* over the *suppositum*. Eckhart thought of the universal as realized. In this sense, only all individual humans taken together are "man."[17] The doctrine of the primary determinations is less prominent, but it is still there: the Good, insofar as it is the Good, is termed "uncreatable." Eckhart is concerned with the creation of the world; and thus he enlarges upon his theory of the causes (*causae*) and causing (*causare*). He could not continue replacing the term *causa* with *ratio*. *Causa* was a high-level term, not least because of the *Liber de causis*. And it was not necessary to eliminate the term for good. He had expelled efficient and final causality from metaphysics, and therefore *causa*—except when referring to the observation of nature—had the meaning of ideational *ratio* and *forma* anyway (n. 121, 586.9–11). Much as in the *Commentary on John*, Eckhart here interprets every acting as speaking (n. 47, 514.3–9). Eckhart's philosophy consists of universal verbalizing; even nature appears as something that speaks. The essential causes (*causae essentiales*) especially are disclosures of themselves; they disclose themselves wholly, undivided.[18] This proves advantageous for the philosophical version of the concept of God: God is the highest, bodiless ground of things, *causa prima* (n. 42, 509.1–5). In his *Liber parabolarum Genesis*, Eckhart carves out two moments above all others: God's creation of the world must not be imagined as an *e-ficere*, as a placing-outside-of-himself. The rejection of this idea is his first point. God is Being; he does not act outwardly, because there is nothing outside of Being.[19] This immanentism is simply the logical conclusion of infinitism and of the identification of God with Being. The second point of clarification renders many a discussion about God's beinglessness superfluous. Eckhart explains: God is Being, and it remains that way. He is, as Eckhart specifies, the "true, the only real, the original" Being. But above all we must remember that he is intellect and that this consideration is the higher one (n. 214, 690.3–6). This was also the teaching of the first two Parisian questions; Eckhart is simply summarizing them once more here, this time in connection with universal verbalization: God is the speaker who, in speaking, wholly discloses himself.

If someone says that God commands, then his commanding is to be interpreted in light of his intellectual nature: his is not an external commanding. He is not ordering about. His ordering consists in providing things with their form, *dando rebus formas et naturas* (n. 93, 559.5–6). But does Genesis not report that God ordered Adam not to eat from the Tree of Knowledge? Indeed, but it has to be understood correctly: the prohibition of eating from the Tree of the Knowledge of Good and Evil means: God called attention to the fact that man should not seek his purpose in a place where good and evil exist together. Man should not let himself be captured by sensuous pleasure; he should not live according to his sensuous side, but rather according to reason and intellect. He should not stop permanently at anything created (nn. 98–99, 563.8–565.99). God's ban on eating thus means: man is supposed to live according to the determination of his essence, his *ratio* and his intellect, and to want the pure good.

The intellect defines man (n. 113, 579.6). It makes him into the likeness of God and, indeed, as stated before, into God's naked substance, whereas all other creatures represent God according to a specific perspective. The intellect is man's connection to God; he does not receive his likeness of God from the outside; it is not granted to him retroactively. He is God-shaped according to his essence and does not seek God only via external nature (n. 194, 666.9–12). The intellect is the highest in the soul, the *supremum in anima* (n. 139, 606.1). Eckhart calls it the "root of life of the mind-soul," *radix vitae animae rationalis* (n. 82, 543.13)—something that has a precise sense for readers of Dietrich of Freiberg: the intellect is more than one of the three mental faculties of the soul. Those grow out of the intellect. It is their substantially active root.[20] A heart that does not beat constantly would no longer be a heart.

The intellect has priority over the will by virtue of the will's indeterminacy (n. 83, 544–45). As the lowest in the order of intellects, it needs sensory experience in man (n. 113, 579.6–10; n. 138, 604–5). Eckhart praises the intellect hymnically: "Its habitus of the principles, which are naturally known to all, is the seed of the sciences. Through them, man is authorized and enabled to judge truth and falsity with his speculative intellect, and with his practical intellect he determines what is good and what is evil. The light of reason within us lets us share in the highest, divine light. It is the seed both of the virtues and of the sciences" (n. 200, 672.9–673.1).[21] God wants us to know. Eckhart praises knowledge, like Dante's Odysseus, seated in hell (n. 113, 579.6–580.6). What Plato described as anamnesis, man recovers from the hidden part of his mind, from the *abditum mentis*, as it is called in Augustine (n. 217, 694.10–11). Relying on Aristotle and Averroës, Eckhart describes the intellect as unity of the knower and the known (n. 56, 524.8–11; n. 147, 616.4–617.5). It is his central subject—in the *Commentary on John*, in German sermon 48, and elsewhere.

The intellect is the root of freedom. In complete contrast to Luther, Eckhart emphasizes the power of man not to be defeated by temptation: *in hominis potestate et libertate est non vinci in temptatione* (n. 176, 647.3–4). The goal of acting freely is to become a deified man, *homo divinus* (n. 27, 497.1–3, and many other places). Within the deified man, the just man and justice are one (n. 91, 555). For him, the Good itself is the goal and in itself is its own reward (n. 171, 641.9–14). He does not look for external reward (n. 131, 596.11–15; n. 171, 641.1–4). Punishments, too, are intrinsic to acting (n. 105, 571). The good life consists of a consequent inner orientation, of inner being, not of doing. Action implements the way to being and life. God does not order any external act (n. 165, 634.11–12). This became one of the charges in the trial. And Eckhart knew anyway that he had critics. He declares that many people will oppose him, *multi luctabuntur* (n. 58, 526.4). These "many people" are other theologians, not simply his denouncers in Cologne, who emerged only later. Eckhart knew it and was outspoken about it: he was a philosopher of Christianity against his time, against the prevailing theology, from whose notice Eckhart's otherness did not escape.

In Genesis, Eckhart found his philosophical theology, his theory of the intellect, and his ethics. He did not want to prove them with the Bible (n. 4, 454.6–10). He also used it to verify his conception of nature, of the first matter, and of the composition of the universe in the four stages that Proclus described: *Deus, mens, anima, caelum* (n. 212, 689:4–5; nn. 209–10, 684–85).

Comparison of the Two Commentaries on Genesis

Eckhart's involvement with texts from the ancient Middle East served him well. They made him more flexible in his use of language. They sharpened his poetic sense, as his lectures on Ecclesiasticus show. He certainly steered the biblical authorities into the direction that he wanted. He did not read the Bible while on his knees, but rather showed what it rationally intended to say. He determined what was reasonable through his philosophical conception, whose primacy in biblical interpretation he often stressed, de facto implemented, and postulated as literal interpretation in a higher sense. He described his biblical work poetically with the sentence that he was looking for golden apples with silver peels. This meant that he had to break through the rind of external words in order to find his philosophical ideas "suggested" there. These were the golden apples. He needed only to bring them out and explain them.

In this sense, the *Liber parabolarum Genesis* went further than the first commentary on Genesis, which had proceeded selectively and speculatively enough but which relied more on the narrative events of the Bible. The second commentary was supposed to become part of a second comprehensive interpretation of the Bible. Eckhart wanted to follow through consistently with the philosophical interpretation of scripture that he had attempted earlier. Still, the first commentary did not become obsolete because of the second. Eckhart did not criticize it, but rather referred several times to his "first edition" in his second commentary.[22] He did not break with this earlier work, but in his second he found his radical, mature form, his philosophy of Christianity for an advanced audience, his consistently conducted philosophical work on the Bible, which he claimed would reveal the "actual" literal sense of Genesis. The *Liber parabolarum Genesis*, as mentioned, emerged in a second attempt and chronologically late. Yet since important German sermons were also composed late, studying Eckhart's second commentary on Genesis is an essential preparatory exercise for understanding his German sermons.

10. Wisdom: *In Sapientiam*

The Commentary Mode

Eckhart had a special interest in the Old Testament Book of Wisdom (*Sapientia*) and commented on it extensively. He may have been working on it at the same time as he was writing his first commentary on Genesis and his interpretation of Exodus. We cannot date Eckhart's commentary more securely within the chronology of his works, but Loris Sturlese has shown that we can assume at least that it may have been written earlier than traditionally thought; Eckhart may have begun this group of three commentaries in Paris as early as 1302; the commentary on the Book of Wisdom (*Expositio Libri Sapientiae*) is especially comprehensive; Eckhart must have worked on it for many years.

Eckhart's principles in interpreting the Bible did not change from the first commentary on Genesis to that on Exodus and the one on the Book of Wisdom: he freely selects the verses for which he wants to provide comments; he does not write a continuous running commentary. We should not expect philological learning in the style of Origen or Jerome. Eckhart names as his methodological example the liberalness of speculative biblical exegesis that he found in the last three books of the *Confessions*. But Eckhart's concept of biblical exegesis is more philosophically rigorous than Augustine's: he wants to determine the philosophical truths contained within the text. No prayer interrupts his treatise. Eckhart has a more elaborate concept of philosophy than Augustine, thanks to Aristotle's *Metaphysics* and its Islamic interpreters as well as the previous studies by Albertus Magnus, Thomas Aquinas, and Dietrich of Freiberg; he integrates selections from Augustine, the *Liber de causis*, and Proclus into it, but also the main ideas of the *Book of the Twenty-Four Philosophers.*

Primary Determinations

In his commentary on the Book of Wisdom, Eckhart continues his philosophical inquiry, especially regarding traditional topics of ontology: being and essence, form and matter, difference and similarity, image and exemplar. He reinforces his conviction that Being (*esse*) is the most basic and fundamental of all determinations: the characteristic quality of the primary determinations pertains first and foremost to Being. He continues his battle against the advancement of reified ideas, as though Being were a retroactive abstraction of many things or as though it were added to things in the form of a property.[1] It is a rejection not so much of the representation of things in the imagination as of their dominance within philosophical thought. It means: every thing, *res*, is preceded by its conceptual structure or the idea of that thing. Eckhart especially applies this critique of simple "realism" to perfections such as Being and Oneness, Wisdom and Justice. All these, to Eckhart, are not properties that are added to a person or a thing. Justice is not within the just man; rather, the just man enters into Justice. Wisdom always was and always is; it has to be detached from the conditions of time and space. Even man's nature is ontologically "earlier" than the individual man, and all men are situated within their universal nature. We could say that Eckhart is merely repeating the principles of his universalistic idealism. Some people, however, have a strange understanding of idealism, and so this academic term has as little value as all others. I understand "universalism" to mean the antinominalist primacy of the universal over the individual. What I for the time being have called idealism, means in Latin that the *ratio dei* is more essential than any individual thing. Eckhart's philosophy has little to do with idealism as the supposed opposite of realism or ontology; rather, it teaches us the primacy of Being. This means that Being is the first and most universal determination, without which all other determinations, the Platonic *koina*—that is, the first concepts, such as Oneness and Goodness—cannot partake in reality; they would merely exist as things of thought or wishful ideas. When Eckhart says that everything is through Being, otherwise everything is nothing, then further explanations are necessary.

This concept of Being is close to that of Oneness; they have a recipro-cal relationship. A tree that has no being is nothing. However, it is also noth-ing if it loses its oneness. A cut-up tree is not a tree, merely wood. That something *is* and that something is *one* is almost the same thing: everything that is has to be one in order for it to be. And with oneness, the concept of wholeness or undividedness ensues; form—not in its colloquial usage here—is the exercised undividedness, so to speak, that has entered an individual; it indicates structure and knowableness, since everything that is disintegrated cannot exist and cannot be grasped in either word or thought. What is divid-ed is destroyed; thus, form implies the recognition that the being and one, the formed and knowable, is something good.

This so-called theory of the transcendentals was derived from the Platonic and Neoplatonic philosophy of antiquity and finally from Plato's doctrine of the *koina*. It adapted motifs found in Aristotle's *Metaphysics*, and we can find many variations of it within the writings of medieval authors; the most popular of them all is the account that Thomas Aquinas offers at *De veritate* I, 1.[2]

Theories about Primary Determinations

During the Middle Ages, roughly three philosophical ways of interpreting the primary determinations like Being or Oneness developed. The first school of thought supported the thesis: what is real is the individual things. And be-cause we can say of all individual things that if they are, they have being, we construe Being as the highest abstraction. And similarly with unity, since things only are as long as they exist undivided, undestroyed. Accordingly, primary determinations are an ultimate conceptual schema. They are sus-pected of being tautological when used in sentences—something has being because it is. But this is an empty and boring option of bringing an individual content like "tree" under a most universal term.

A second school of thought took up a contrary position: Being is the most fundamental basis of all things. It is the objective precondition of indi-vidual things. It is all-encompassingly present and constitutes everything else. If someone were to consider "content" to refer only to individual deter-minations such as house or dog, then he would have to say that this all-encompassing being would be devoid of content. But Being is no such thing; it only posits that something is set and is not nothing.

The definition of Being as the primary determination of all reality fell out of use after Kant's critique; Schelling and Hegel rehabilitated it, and Heidegger, late in his career, brought Being back as the true but forgotten content of philosophy. But even he could not say more regarding the nature of Being than that it is itself. Some Thomists, at a time when ontology and existentialism were in vogue, wanted to detect in Thomas Aquinas's work the philosophy of a universal but real being that was not an abstraction. And Aquinas did indeed say that *esse* was the reality of all forms, the positing, so to speak, of everything, and the reason that anything is at all and not, rather, nothing. Etienne Gilson's *L'être et l'essence* (Paris, 1948) was the manifesto of this school of thought. The authors of this view did not want their real, all-constituting being to be confused with God. Instead, although the cause or the ground of this most universal being could be called God, being as a general, immanent determination was a philosophical principle out of which one could perhaps develop a philosophical theology or theo-logics—but that was not identical to God. Aristotle had made beings as beings the object of metaphysics, but only Being made beings into beings by being added to them as something interior and real. These writers had to distinguish the being of a cat from "being-a-cat" and were fond of the formula that being as absolute positing was something fundamentally different from the essential character or the structure of a cat. Its internal structural principle, its ideal form, they called its essence and distinguished it from its being. They added that essence without being would merely be a thing of thought or a concept. Being was that which factually posited the contents of a thing. In this context, the word "factually" meant something like "contingent," and did not mean that it could be proved with the methods of modern science. Being thus conceived is what makes it so that x is not merely a content of thought. It actuates all structures, all essences. It is real, they say, but as a common, immanent, superconceptual ground. It is not God, but the term " being" can serve to form a suitable name for God when we conceive of a first "being" to be distinguished from the world, one that is independent of all individual things and exists wholly from within itself; a "being" whose essence it would be to exist. It would exist, they said, but not randomly, like all finite things to which actual existing is added; instead without chance, essentially, through itself, so that God's Latin name could be *"esse per se subsistens."* The authors of this school of thought therefore distinguished universal being from the necessary being that exists through itself, or God.

Eckhart shares his special interest in Being as the fundamental primary determination with the second school of thought, a determination that first posits all being of the world in its reciprocal relation with other determinations. Still, something that shows such a fundamental and all-encompassing effect would be—Eckhart would continue his argument in modern terms—its own Godhead besides God. If Being is to be real and not merely an abstraction, then Being is "God." More precisely, we could then interpret the popular concept of "God," derived from writings intended for simple people, in the following manner: instead of the conceptually unresolved vernacular word "*got*," God, we posit "*esse*," Being. And thus we encounter a third way of interpreting the primary determinations. Nothing is so unified—nothing is so allocated to us and is so in accordance with us, nothing is so intimate and closely connected—as Being itself (*In Sap.*, LW 2, n. 194, 529.7–9). Eckhart recommends substituting primary determinations' names for one another as a method. We may as well say Being instead of "God" or Oneness or Justice or Wisdom: *loco dei ponamus "esse" et "iustitia"* (*In Eccli.*, LW 2, n. 67, 296). This was not uncommon among philosophers; Plato said "the idea of the Good" instead of "God" when he was not referring to the gods of popular religion; Aristotle, "the prime unmoved mover," Avicenna, "the necessary being," Aquinas, "being that exists by itself." Eckhart simply says, "God is Being," and adds the admonition that we should not consider primary realities to be additional properties in things.

But new questions arise from this position. If God is "Being," then only nothing or nothingness exists outside of him. Yet we say about a tree that it "is." Eckhart's position within the theory of analogical predications, which I previously mentioned and which Eckhart himself presented also in his vernacular sermon and furthered in the Latin explanations of Ecclesiasticus, can help us explain the situation of the tree. Within a tree, he says, being is as unreal as health within the chemical agent of a pill. We direct the eyes of our minds to the tree, but then see, at the exact moment that we say of it that it is, that it refers to something else to which alone the term "being" pertains. This again raises more questions than it answers. It occupies Eckhart especially in his *Expositio Libri Sapientiae*, to which we will now turn.

God Is Being

Everything strives for Being. A stone that moves, a plant that grows, an animal that begets or births a young—they all want their being. Eckhart attributes this insight to Avicenna, but he also presents it as his own (*In Sap.* nn. 256–57, 588–89). He had apparently faced criticism that his identification of the primary determination *esse* with God robbed the worldly things of their being. Eckhart opposed this criticism and claimed that he was not denying things their being, but that he was establishing it (n. 260, 59192). A cat has its own being; it is shaped by its substantial form (*forma substantialis*) of a cat, and it was begotten in reality. Thus, Eckhart explains that it has its being on the basis of its substantial form and its begetting, *per formam substantialem et generationem* (n. 29, 350.1). Therefore, Eckhart speaks of a form-like being in the nature of things outside (n. 32, 353; cf. n. 194, 529). Is this a return to the second theory of being that I outlined above?

Eckhart plays with the different meanings of the word "being," *esse*. In Paris, he had taught in 1302–3 that being, *esse*, always meant a limitedness, a "being-this-one." Thus, he had established the beinglessness of the intellect, but he conceded that knowing itself could be called being as long as it remained clear that this being was due to knowing. We also encounter the concept of being in its limited sense in the *Expositio Libri Sapientiae* at least at times, for Eckhart states that being possesses the characteristic quality of creatability, *esse habet rationem creabilis* (n. 24, 344). As we have seen, other primary determinations, such as Oneness, Wisdom, and Justice, are supposedly uncreatable. If God is called the *esse*, it is also uncreatable. Different meanings of "*esse*" are operating here. Readers of Eckhart have to learn how to handle the flexibility of the concept. Eckhart's theory of analogy posits clearly that being "outside"—and we already know that there is no outside—as if located in the nature of things, is not being, just as urine is not "healthy"; such "being" is merely called being with regard to living creatures. Once we step over onto the other side, when we contemplate the actual meaning of being, then being becomes the central concept to define the popular word "God" theoretically. Then it follows—to use Aquinas's formulation—that God, conceptualized as Being, is the actualizer of all substantial forms, the *actualitas omnium formarum* (n. 189, 525.1–2). Outside of Being, there is only nothingness.

Someone who discusses the creation of the world must not forget this original meaning of Being. We can define creation as *rerum ex nihilo productio*, as the bringing out, the producing, of things out of nothingness (n. 25, 345.6–7). Not, however, as though God *had* placed something *outside*. "Many," Eckhart says, imagine creation as an effecting, as it were, toward the outside (n. 122, 459.1–2). This idea fabricates the existence of an outside realm, but such a realm cannot exist if God is conceptualized as *esse*. It also posits creation as an event in the past. But we have to imagine things without temporal conditions. The reason for this is that when we say "being," we do not mean becoming, but a completed becoming: a having become. We do not consider "being" as a being only in the future, for being-only-in-the-future implies *not* being in the present. Being is being now, presence. Living is living now. God always creates, continuously. God himself is always new, *Deus semper novus* (n. 161, 497.2). He constantly places the world into himself anew, into Being. This concept of Being, confined to certain key terms, means the following:

Actualism, for being in constant presence perpetually actuates itself anew.

Infinitism, for being in its original meaning encompasses all. It is impossible even to conceive of anything outside of God, *nihil potest esse extra deum* (n. 34, 328.8–9). We call that infinite outside of which nothing exists (n. 146, 484.3).

Critique of the imagining thinking, which imagines an outside of God, that is, of Being, in order to be able to ascribe being to the worldly things.

Intellectualism and idealism, for Being is Being because it thinks, and it thinks the ideational norms of the worldly things. Ideas are *before* the things. They are not merely logical grids of genus and species, but also formal principles before the things, *partes formales priores toto* (n. 118, 454.12). They make possible the knowableness of the world and the definability of things.

Dynamism, for overcoming temporal conditions means conceptualizing being or God and his image as continuously active. He did not create the world; he creates it. He did not become man; he perpetually becomes man. He will not come on Judgment Day; he is always coming and always present. When we say "the Good itself" instead of "God" and imply dynamism, then we recognize: God is love (n. 104, 441). In calling him the One, we understand him as a substantial power of unification. He is the One to such a degree that he is of the highest and indiscriminate simplicity. And in implying dynamism, we comprehend: Being is intellect. Thus, we reach a higher perspective that does not merely stop at the names of God such as Being and the One. God, conceptualized as Being and intellect, continually effects his oneness with man; he is the infinite, the infinitely active Oneness, based on the Aristotelian model of eye-wood (n. 266, 596.5–10). As intellect and dynamic Oneness, he does not have a designated place, but there is no human mind in which it would not be present in a special way, as we can read even in the pagan Seneca: *nulla sine Deo mens* (n. 52, 359.9).

Indistinctism, for Being is not distinct from the beings. In German, the word "distinct" (*verschieden*) can also mean "deceased, dead." I have read about conferences on mysticism in which the main concern of some speakers was to argue that Eckhart should have let his God be "distinct" from the world.

Being, Oneness, Number

In his *Expositio Libri Sapientiae*, Eckhart elaborates on the themes of distinctness and indistinctness: God's name is Being, *esse* (n. 177, 512–13). This does not exclude the existence of individual substantial forms of the worldly things (n. 29, 350) but in fact constitutes them (n. 260, 591). While it is characteristic of the limited concept of being, however, that a being thus construed is different from the others, and that these are thus distinct from one another, the infinite Being is indistinct. It is distinguished from things by its lack of distinction. It is *indistinctione sua distinctissimus*. The nature of God is "not-being-distinct." The more indistinct he is, the more distinct he is (nn. 38–39, 359–60; nn. 154–55, 489–91). That is why God is the One. Something that is distinct is many different things, and thus finite. The infinite by its very nature is uniform, all-encompassing, indistinct. It is not an other to anything else. It is inconceivable to call it the "wholly other."

If we do not strictly conceptualize God as One, we do not correctly define him as Being. Eckhart uses an image to explain reciprocity when he says that Being has its "seat" in the One: *sedes ipsius esse in uno est* (n. 296, 631.2). He is the One, that is, he is one in every way, *unus omnibus modis*. Again, Eckhart positions himself in opposition to "many," not against many among the people, but against "many" of the theologians and philosophers: they do not understand number. They do not know what it means that God is without number, wholly without number, even without the number three, even without any theoretical countability that we could think of (n. 114, 451.1–13;

n. 112, 449.3). All distinction ends with him. It is the reason why the term the "One" is a better name for God than "Truth" or the "Good" (n. 149, 486–87; n. 151, 488; n. 177. 512–13). And yet the One always presupposes and implies Being. Only insofar as this is true does Being retain its priority (n. 177, 512–13), especially over "Good" (n. 149, 486.12–13).

God and Grace

Following these explanations, Eckhart identifies anew what he understands "God" to be. He is Being, he is the One, he is the One to the extent that the question about the origin of the many disappears (nn. 36–37, 356–59). He is unity, the identity with everything. He is nondistinct from everything (n. 38, 360.1). Within him, everything is one, *omnia unum* (n. 96, 430.10—431.1). Within him, the maximum is the minimum, and he is the coincidence of opposites; as the most moveable, he is immoveable (n. 132, 469–70; cf. n. 271, 601.4–7). He is the Good itself. We can find him in the following way, according to Augustine (*De Trinitate* VIII 3): we think of good wine and good bread, then we abandon the determinations of "wine" and "bread" and immediately think "God." For what we are thinking then—the good devoid of determinations—that is God (nn. 98–99, 432.4–435.4). To borrow a phrase from Bernard of Clairvaux: what is God? God is that without which nothing is (n. 90, 423.8). Or as Avicenna said: God is the First, without genus and without substance, without quality or quantity. There is no "where" for him, no opposition, and no definition.

In sum: God is the active, infinite Being that is intellect because of its infinite simplicity. Then he is Wisdom, and as the infinitely active and present wisdom, he is wisdom that continuously reproduces itself, that discloses itself infinitely and indivisibly, that is wholly, in the silence of any efficient causality, *in silentio causae efficientis* (n. 283, 616.1–4); he is unbegotten Wisdom that begets wisdom (n. 65, 396.6; n. 92, 425; n. 105, 441.6–13). He is the wisdom that is continuously being birthed (n. 279, 611.6–8). Eckhart thus combines the doctrine of wisdom of the Hebrew Bible with the theory of the logos, which enters into the world and explains even his theory of grace through the substantial affection of this God.[3] This is Eckhart's traditional method: we should say "Being" and Wisdom rather than "God." We do not find here the idea of an anthropomorphically construed emperor of the world who bestows his grace on a select few, chosen from among the overall damned humanity according to unknown rules. In Eckhart's writings, the word "grace" has to be broken down based on his concept of God. Eckhart's high philosophical conception of God rejects those concepts of grace found in catechisms—be they Tridentine or Lutheran.

Eckhart conceptualizes God philosophically as Being, Oneness, intellect, and dynamic Wisdom, and he therefore conceptualizes him as a seamless Trinity, without external or foreign sources coming in between. God is life, infinite in itself and flowing back into itself (n. 184, 519.3–521.6); he is life in the qualified sense. To understand this, we have to begin to conceive of God as the being that is unity and sameness with everything and as the essential indistinctness within which everything is (n. 38, 360). Ideas of number have to be kept away from this begetting original dynamic: the three that the "many" mention are indeed one. Eckhart often cited the phrase from the New Testament "*Hi tres unum sunt*" in his attempt to correct simple ideas of the Trinity. Eckhart found the Trinity in nature: wherever we find a creator and his creation, they agree in their delight in each other (n. 27, 347.4–6). Everywhere in nature, we encounter begetting, sonship, and the unity of the begetter and the begotten (n. 29, 349.10–350.9). If this begetter is Being, then he does not allow for an intermediary between himself and things; we are familiar with this view from Eckhart's sermon cycle on eternal birth, in which he supports his position with a quotation from the Book of Wisdom: "when deep silence encompassed everything" (nn. 284–85, 616.5–619.4).

Making Problems Disappear

Eckhart's *Expositio Libri Sapientiae* is comprehensive. We cannot provide an adequate account of it in a few pages. A more thorough study would have to investigate how Eckhart praised himself for making disappear many of the problems that his contemporaries faced in philosophy and theology (n. 37, 357; n. 188, 524). These types of remarks are Eckhart's way of marking his opposition to the average Parisian education in theology and philosophy. In Eckhart's opinion, many problems debated there were not worthy of discussion; they could easily be made to disappear. He often points to the opposition that existed between his way of thinking and the ideas of the "many." We should stress also that Eckhart construed God, Being, as everything in everything, a view that served as a model for Nicholas of Cusa. Eckhart's metaphysics of the forms does not project an abstract pattern into things

(n. 135, 473–74; n. 271, 601). We should remind ourselves also of Eckhart's non-Thomistic theory of time. In his First Parisian Question, Eckhart brief-ly summarizes what Dietrich of Freiberg developed in a detailed argument in 1286: time is nothing within the things; it is *wholly* constituted by the soul, but it is not therefore merely a thing of thought, but the reality of nature.[4]

11. Departure: *In Exodum*

Eckhart before an Archaic Book

As mentioned before, Eckhart twice interpreted the first book of the Bible, Genesis, and twice began a commentary on the entire Bible. He must have had serious reasons for such an enormous undertaking. I skipped far ahead in the chronology of his works in order to compare the two commentaries on Genesis, but now I must go back several years to describe the work that directly followed his first commentary on Genesis. Just as Exodus, about the flight out of Egypt, follows Genesis in the Bible, Eckhart is supposed to have written—or at least begun—his commentary on Exodus directly after his first Genesis commentary.[1]

Eckhart discusses important subjects; faced with archaic ideas and narratives in this book, he clarifies his own thoughts in the process of commenting on them. Exodus is filled with dramatic stories: God calls to Moses out of the burning bush. He tells him his name: "I am who I am."[2] If someone asks Moses about his God, he is supposed to answer: "'I am' has sent me." Moses goes before pharaoh and works his miracles. The ten plagues afflict Egypt. The Israelites leave Egypt, taking the Egyptians' gold and silver, and cross the Red Sea with dry feet, the water swallowing up the pursuing Egyptians and their horses and wagons alike. God supplies the Ten Commandments with thunder and lightning, to the sound of trumpets: the fright of God on Mount Sinai.

None of these events are of much interest to Eckhart. His method of reading is rather "scholastic": he is looking for universal theoretical issues. God gives his name, and it raises the question of the relation between names and things. God, it is said, is recognized in darkness (*in caligine*). What does that mean? It presents us with the problem of a positive and negative theology. I now turn to Eckhart's answers to these questions.

"I Am Who I Am"

What does it mean when God says to Moses: "I am who I am"? Eckhart certainly does not think that God is refusing to answer the question. His God does not say: my name remains incomprehensible to you; my name is of no concern to you, for you will not understand it anyway. Instead, Eckhart understands God's self-naming as though God were explicating his essence. Eckhart elaborates on this divine self-naming (*In Exod.*, LW 2, nn. 14–25, 20–30) and first highlights that God calls himself an "I." What does "I" mean? "I" is a pronoun that signifies pure substance, devoid of properties, without any further or external determinations, without any additions. And this pertains only to God because he alone is outside the coordinate system of species and genus and because there is no accident in him; he is devoid of contingency.

Eckhart interprets every single word of God's sentence: I am *who*. "Who" is wholly indistinct. This complete infiniteness pertains only to God. God is WHO.

The repetition of the "I am" is noteworthy: "*sum*" is the predicate. God thus says: "I AM, EGO SUM." Pure Being, naked Being, belongs only to the single subject that is pure Being. God's quiddity (*quiditas*), what he is, is his pure thatness (*anitas*), that he is—that is, the "whether something exists at all"-ness. Eckhart refers to Avicenna: God has no other essence than his thatness, his *anitas*. This pure That simply means Being. The biblical book does not explain God's name. Eckhart takes the first key to it from the Islamic philosopher Avicenna, whose distinction between *essentia* and *esse* was popular in the Middle Ages and beyond. Eckhart explains God's name thus: within God, essence and existence are identical. His essence does not require additional determinations; it is his existence. He is Being.

What does the repetition of "I am" signify in the sentence "I am who I am," "*sum qui sum*"? Eckhart answers that it signifies two things. On one hand, the exclusiveness of the affirmative sentence "God *is*," with the exclusion of all nonbeing, all deficiencies. The sentence negates any negative of God. The *negatio negationis* pertains to God, as Eckhart says elsewhere. God is not a rock of mere presence. He is Being in the qualified sense that excludes anything negative.

On the other hand, the repetition of *"sum"* signifies the reference to itself, the re-flection, return to, and dwelling in itself. God steps outside himself so that he gains traction within himself. He does not lose himself in his movements. Eckhart means that this infinite Being is moved in itself. It whirls around like boiling, bubbling water. It urges, like being in labor and wanting to give birth (*bullitio sive parturitio*). It is not fixed and not infertile. It is boiling, roaring, in violent motion: *fervens*. It fiercely streams back into itself; it melts, so to speak, and flows back into itself: *in se fervens et in se ipso et in se ipsum liquescens et bulliens* (n. 16, 21.11–12). It is light that, by shining into itself, wholly pervades itself and turns back onto itself as a whole. There is nothing within it that would not participate in this self-enlightenment and turning back onto itself. It exists *wholly* as a reflection onto itself as a whole.

Eckhart does not employ the term "Trinity" here, but he effectively says what he considers to be the truth of the Trinity; he knows that there are many misconceptions about it. He disregards those and instead describes it with flowery images: God's being is moving, effervescent, and prolific. It flows back into itself as the totality of a turning back or reflection. When we compare this to Eckhart's language in the first explanation of the *sum qui sum* in nn. 14–15, 20, up to the description of inner motion in n. 16, 21–22, it is noticeable that he has changed his register. His language is not biblical in the sense of historical biblical studies. At first, he speaks in the scholastic diction typical around 1300 for discussions of Avicenna's *esse-essentia* theory, but then he freely describes the inner conditions of the flow of the Godhead and the internal conditions of life. And at n. 16, he indulges in metaphors. His language becomes poetic. In reference to Neoplatonic images, Eckhart shows that he is a master also of the Latin language:

reflexiva conversio—the turning back of Being onto itself
mansio sive fixio in seipso—a home, a settling into itself through thinking
bullitio sive parturitio sui—a surging up, a birthing oneself
in se fervens—effervescent within itself
in se ipsum liquescens et bulliens—flowing into itself and surging up
lux in luce et in lucem se toto se totum penetrans—light in light, shining into
    itself, completely pervading itself
se toto super se totum conversum—which turns back onto itself as a whole with
    all that is within it

Followed by this description of life, which is:

exseritio—an overflowing
res in se ipsa intumescens—something that swells up in itself
se profundit in se toto—that plunges itself into its complete depth
antequam effundat et ebulliat extra—before it pours itself out and wells over
 into the outside.

Even the "spilling out into the outside" is a metaphor: the flowing out of the divine persons, which was supposed to be *ratio*, the factual reason of the creation of the world (all at n. 16, 22).

The Monad That Begets a Monad

For the first step in his interpretation of God's name, Eckhart relies on Avicenna: that meant that existence and essence were one and the same in God. For the second step—the swelling up of the self, the bubbling, and the flowing-back-into-itself of the Godhead—Eckhart relies on the Pseudo-Hermetic *Book of the Twenty-Four Philosophers*. Its first sentence is "The monad begets the monad and bends it back upon itself as love" (or as a blaze of light).

The *Book of the Twenty-Four Philosophers* is a treasure among the philosophical texts of the Middle Ages. It was ascribed to Hermes Trismegistus, the thrice-greatest, the forefather of all wisdom. It contains ancient features, and its editor, Françoise Hudry, wanted to date the text to the third century. More likely, it stems from the end of the twelfth century. Still, in that case, it is even more peculiar, since a Christian author would have had to invent twenty-four non-Christian thinkers who, according to this literary fiction, came together to define what God is. This literary scenario tests what the heathen philosophers could achieve through pure thinking, without revelation, in their knowledge of God. And it is the first sentence of these twenty-four sayings that Eckhart invokes, since it is here that the swelling, flowing-back-into-itself of the Godhead is expressed in this way: "The monad begets a monad and bends it back onto itself in a blaze of love." Oneness is moved in itself and returns to itself. It "begets," and "begetting" and *parturitio* are important keywords for Eckhart. The word "monad" is not surprising here; it does not originate with Leibniz, but is an ancient concept, from Proclus at any rate.

It is important to see how Eckhart proceeds step by step: "I am who I am," "*Sum qui sum*" needs to be explained. Through an ontological analysis, Eckhart shows that it expresses the purity of Being and the exclusion of everything negative. This he proves and explains through Avicenna. In the next step, he shows the return, the bubbling up and flowing back of pure Being into itself. He confirms his position with the passage supposedly by Hermes Trismegistus about the monad that flows back into itself.

Then he continues that because this sentence is true, *propter hoc*, the prologue to John says: "In him was all life." All things in the world exist in this world fountain that flows out and back again. Eckhart thereby puts forward a qualified concept of life. It includes teleological-Aristotelian themes: life is that which contains its telos within itself, that which is an entelechy. Here, however, Eckhart emphasizes the expansion of the living into itself. The living thing stretches itself, shows itself, steps outside itself and into itself. More specifically, it impresses its own unique nature into itself in order to make its own dynamic form flow toward the outside and, brimming over, pour out its vitality (n. 16, 22).

Eckhart explains the phrase "*sum qui sum*" further: this time he draws on a formulation from Augustine's *De Trinitate* VIII 3. There, Augustine guides his readers to a knowledge of God in the following way: think of a good soul and a good angel. Then let "soul" and "angel" go, think only of the good Good, *bonum bonum*, nothing else, and then think of the *summum bonum*, the pure *bonum* mixed with nothing else, which depends on nothing, which is self-sufficient, but which comes back to itself in a complete return, as do all spiritual creatures according to the *Liber de causis*. According to Eckhart, we are supposed to carry out a similar series of thoughts with the determination Being. "*Sum qui sum*" signifies pure, unmingled Being, in the same way that "the good Good" signifies pure Good. Eckhart is not exchanging the primacy of *esse* for that of the Good; he is showing its uninterminangledness and abundance through a similar movement of thought. Eckhart varies this thought further: it is a different question, as determined already by Aristotle, if one asks "what is something?" or if one asks whether *x* is. Avicenna developed this closing remark further: essence in all creatures exists only coincidentally, only de facto: God alone is essence whose own peculiarity is his existing. In everything created, Avicenna said, essence and existence had to be differentiated; Being was something given by another, but essence was independent of everything else. The essence, which the name indicated and the definition expressed, was not dependent on anything. Eckhart clarifies this through the example of the circle. No one is able to change its definition, not even God. Thus, if someone asks who or what God is, then in this one case it is appropriate to answer: God is Being (n.18, 24.7). Thus, God's answer to Moses was true.

Eckhart then analyzes this answer syntactically: the subject of the sentence is essentiality, *essentia*. The predicate is assigned to the subject, here the *essentia*, and in this case the predicate and the subject are identical. The subject of the sentence is of an absolute simplicity; therefore, nothing can be added to it, corresponding to the principle of Boethius: *forma simplex subiectum esse non potest*, "the simple form cannot be a subject." The essentiality already contains every determination within itself; it does not take on any other perfection, and this is expressed in the structure of the sentence. There is no extrinsic perfection that might be added to the essentiality of God; he is enough for himself. Thus, the subject here is sufficient without an extrinsic predicate (n. 19, 25). In speaking about something created, something always has to be added; there is no peculiarity—such as the will, for example—that alone suffices for the work. This self-sufficiency, *sufficientia*, and thus necessity are expressed in the name of God. Eckhart agrees with Avicenna's tendency to say *necesse esse* instead of "God" (n. 21, 27.9–10). God is Being in the fullest sense, and that means: he is intellectual understanding (n. 21, 28). Eckhart closes this series of thoughts with the suggestion that God is Being, which means that he does not exist only in the future and was not in the past; rather, he is present in timelessness (n. 22, 28–29).

From n. 34, 40, to n. 78, 82, Eckhart expands his inquiry to all the names of God. Which of them are valid, which are not? In doing so, he enters into an inquiry that had been a staple of theological discussions since Peter Lombard, in the tract *De nominibus Dei*. Eckhart builds on one of these, namely, that of Thomas Aquinas. Aquinas had grounded everything in God's omnipotence, and to this, Eckhart writes, he would like to provide a few addenda. First, he wants to determine what the philosophers and a few Jews—in fact, only Maimonides, but the combination of the Greek philosophers and the Jews is notable—said about the question of what it means when we call God good or generous. Second, he wants to present what Christian thinkers said about this. And third, he wants to discuss a problem that Augustine and Boethius bequeathed to Christian thinkers when they taught that there could be only two suitable categories in talking about God, and indeed only two, namely, substance and relation: the Godhead as the sole essence, and the divine persons (Father, Son, Holy Spirit) as substantial relations.

I will begin with the context of the third problem, which Eckhart addresses from n. 58, 54 onward. It is of great interest, in part because it shows Eckhart in conflict with the traditional teachings on the Trinity up to that time. I will discuss it only briefly, however, because Eckhart became entangled in the difficult questions concerning the theory of categories; a more detailed account would go beyond the scope of this book. To sum up Eckhart's critique, which was directed even at Augustine and Boethius, in the simplest formula: philosophical thinking searches for the One. It is not satisfied when it is shown two in its attempt to find the One. This is the result of research, but Eckhart approaches it philosophically, at first asking, what is a category? And in doing so, Eckhart insists that a category is not something that has being; rather, it is a logical frame. It is a most universal genus and, as such, is not a reality. Thus, it is necessary to talk differently about categories and about things that have being. The pioneers of the Christian doctrine of the Trinity failed in this regard. They thought in realistic concepts and took Aristotle's ten categories to mean ten beings, and therefore they found ten beings in God. Yet there are not ten beings—there is only *one* Being. For the nine categories that more closely determine the substance do not have being themselves, but rather are only of the being. This again is the theory that Grabmann criticized as the theory of the beinglessness of the accident. Accidents have no being and give no being; rather, they receive their being from their substance (n. 54, 58–59). Like Aristotle and Averroës, Eckhart concludes: in the context of analogical determinations, the actual meaning is really provided in the first analogate only—so, for example, health resides in a living creature, not in going for a walk (n. 54, 60). Thus, the Oneness of Being can be presented. There is only *one* essentiality in God, and in this essentiality there is no multiplicity, no number. Eckhart contemplates what someone would see if he saw God. Answer: he would see a singular perfection that contains everything, and this perfection would not be this or that, but rather a One above everything else (n. 57, 63). Someone who saw two would not be seeing God. For he would see a distinction, whereas in God there is no distinction (n. 58, 65). The opposing theory, which speaks of two predicaments in God, talks about these categories as though they had being.

This theory goes against the Oneness of God, which is neither a primordial number nor constitutes a number. The infinite cannot contain distinctions. These are derived from our comprehending, beginning with the senses, and only in this way do our names for God have a real correspondence. The famous question whether the attributes are different in God or only in our comprehending of them is thereby solved (n. 58, 63).

With this I return to the first of the problems raised by Eckhart: what claim can the positive designations of God have, for example that he is called "good"?

Eckhart opens his inquiry with the advice that one should assume what the *Liber de causis* teaches, namely, that God is *above* every name. That does not mean, Eckhart states, that God is without all names. The *Book of the Twenty-Four Philosophers* posits that words do not designate God, because he towers above and because we do not comprehend him in the intellect, given the dissimilarity between the created and the Creator (n. 35, 41–42). The surprising thing in this preview of his inquiry is that Eckhart teaches the unknowability of God with examples from the twenty-four philosophers, but refuses to designate God as unnamable. God is not unnamable, but rather allnamable, *non est innominabilis, sed omninominabilis* (n. 35, 41). Eckhart agrees with Avicenna that the first and best name of God is Being. Other names, like *substantia*, are effectively negative; thus, the sentence "God is substance" says that God inheres in no other essence. If I call God Being, I negate the nothingness. That is the *negatio negationis*. Thus, only sentences with negative words are really true, as Maimonides says.

Eckhart's reasoning proceeds syntactically. First, one has to be clear; sentences do not directly depict things. They correspond to our concepts and terminology, and our knowledge begins with the senses and thus with the many (n. 63, 67). Eckhart investigates how something is predicated by something. Attributions have a certain chance of being accurate on the basis of similarity. Nothing, however, is similar to God, and we cannot say of anything that it is like God, *Deo autem nihil est nec dici potest simile* (n. 39, 44). Or someone may suggest that those names of God are true that relate to his effects. Eckhart shows how many different effects can originate from the same element via the example of fire. There is no clear similarity between fire and its effects. The result would be even more confusing if we knew nothing about human thinking and had to trace its effects back to a single principle. We would then have several names for our intellectual capacity, but they would apply only to our external view of its effects, not to itself.

Eckhart's main argument combines syntactic and metaphysical thoughts. The main metaphysical argument states that if we are supposed to know God from his effects, then the effect must be distinct from God. Yet if God is Being, then everything that is distinct from him is nothing. Between nothingness and Being there is no intermediary and nothing comparable (n. 40, 45). The result: all names used affirmatively do not apply in an actual sense to God. They place nothing into God, and how should it be possible, after all, to add something else to that which is infinite? The positive names of God may be perfections in us, but we do not know whether they are in God. Using the example of the properties of a dog, Eckhart shows that anger against everything that goes against his master is a good property in a dog; in us, this anger would be a mistake. Many of our assets are only remedies for our weaknesses and shortcomings; they are assets only in this sense. How are we supposed to know what kind of perfection is also one in God? Saying that God is irate or compassionate posits nothing in him. To be compassionate is a perfection in us, not in God (n. 44, 48–50). Affirmations would be addenda to the infinite Being if something real corresponded to affirmations within God. And yet there is no disposition to be added to infinite Being, for multiplicity, number, and difference would thus enter into it (nn. 48–51, 51–54).

Some authors say without thinking that biblical interpretation forms the center of Eckhart's efforts. To begin with, this view contradicts Eckhart's explicit declaration that biblical exegesis would have little or no value without the philosophical foundation of the *Opus propositionum*. Furthermore, it is necessary to pay closer attention to what Eckhart's biblical interpretation consists of. Eckhart's discussion of the name of God "I am who I am" (nn. 14–25, 20–30) and of the affirmative designations occupies a characteristically prominent place at the beginning of his explanation of Exodus—in total, more than fifty pages of the main edition. This allows for more precise assertions.

The dramatic events of Exodus and the experiences of God in the Old Testament do not appear in Eckhart. He inscribes Avicenna's metaphysics of Being, *esse*, after which everything strives and which is all-encompassing Oneness, into the name of God and elaborates on it with the help of the first sentence of the twenty-four philosophers via a philosophy of the Trinity. He works out the animatedness or the reflective character of Being and thus establishes what can be known about the Trinity if one keeps every notion of number away from the divine Oneness. The result of this long discussion of positive sentences about God is absolutely negative: everything positive that is said of God is not said in an actual sense and places nothing into God himself (n. 44, 48).[3] The combination of Avicenna's metaphysics and Maimonides's negative theology prevails. Nevertheless, it is said that God is namable with all names. This, however, presumes an awareness of the fact that sentences do not directly depict reality but rather our conceptions of reality. In n. 36, 43, Eckhart highlights three definitions taken from the twenty-four thinkers in order to prove their negative sense. From among the Christian authors, Eckhart occasionally names John of Damascus, who, according to Eckhart, recognized that Being was God's first name, and he cites Bernard of Clairvaux as well. He criticizes Augustine and Boethius extensively; they spoke of two categories in God because of their confusion of categories and beings, not recognizing that God is One in every way. Their thesis is to be rejected completely because it disrupts the Oneness of God; it is true only insofar as sentences about God reflect our conceptions, which do not place anything into God: *propositiones respondent primo et per se non rebus, sed rerum conceptionibus* (n. 55, 60.6–7).

Eclipse of God

Someone who approaches God will find himself in darkness. Many theosophical writings confirm this view. Eckhart himself mentions it when he explains the sentence from Exodus "Moses approached the darkness in which God was" (nn. 235–38, 194–97).

Initially, Eckhart clarifies Moses's concrete situation: clouds and dark wafts of mist covered Mount Sinai. Thus, in Eckhart's view, the sentence states that God stands by the aggrieved and all people in need. Further, the story signifies that many stand by God when it is advantageous for them but not when he demands something difficult of them. Then people withdraw, just as the apostles abandoned Jesus during his Passion. Only after these considerations does Eckhart turn to God's darkness and interpret it as a surplus of divine light. There is no darkness in God at all—only light. But this light is inaccessible to our intellect. Eckhart again quotes from Moses Maimonides: "The intellect that approaches God butts against a wall." But the obstacle stems from us, not from God. His light blinds our intellect, Eckhart states, just as sunlight repels our eyes. That is why our intellect enters into complete ignorance, the *perfecta ignorantia* of Dionysius the Areopagite, when it approaches God (n. 237, 196.12).

PART TWO

12. Interlude: Writing about Eckhart Today

Someone reading a book about Eckhart wants to know what he said and—since he was not only a preacher, but also a thinker—how he justified what he said. Such a reader is hardly interested in why an author has decided to add another book to the long list of titles on Eckhart. My book describes a phase in the history of European thought; it provides a series of episodes from the history of Christian self-understanding. In short, it is a historical and philosophical book. Still, all historical knowledge begins in the present and leads back to it. And further, it begins with an individual and the historical conditions surrounding his life and works. Therefore, I must briefly interrupt the chronology of Eckhart's works here and turn my attention for a few pages to form more than to content. After all, it is not just useful for the author of a book to ask himself why he is writing a particular book and why he is doing so today. His readers benefit as well, for the author's musings destroy the illusion under which the reader may have found himself so far, that Eckhart himself was speaking to him from within the book about Eckhart. A reader is always faced with a mediating figure, even in cases in which he merely has a collection of quotations before him.

This book endeavors to stay close to Eckhart's texts; it makes use of their most recent editions. It benefits particularly from the latest edited volumes of Eckhart's German sermons (DW 4) and above all from the completed edition of Eckhart's commentary on John (LW 3) and of the trial records (LW 5). It combines philosophical considerations with a philological and historical method. That alone is reason enough why it is a *contemporary* book about Eckhart, written under the conditions of the present.

The past decades have witnessed many discussions of the term "mysticism." I look back on them now; the coefficient of time shows itself again. In the past, I advanced several objections—not against "mysticism," but against the description of Eckhart as a "mystic"; it had become an empty platitude. I advocated earlier that this description was expendable in our studies of Eckhart. It is a relatively late term; it collides with Eckhart's self-portrayal; it hindered rather than furthered research on his life and teachings. The objections to my position were insignificant. Most of the time, a specific university department would claim Eckhart as its own; sometimes, people pointed to Dionysius the Areopagite or Gerson, in whose works we can certainly find a *theologia mystica*. But they motivated me to define the designation "philosopher of Christianity" more precisely—a result of long discussions. Their funniest component was the fact that some people asserted that I had in fact raised substantial objections to the concept of mysticism in relation to Eckhart, but had neglected to work out a new concept of "mysticism." As though I had not just said that the concept was expendable.

Someone writing about Eckhart today can shed some ballast. Some of the preconceived notions that have long cast their shadows on any study of Eckhart have disappeared. Among these were not just the concept of mysticism and—another platitude—its derivation from the depths of the German soul, both of which were associated with the special language used to describe them. There was also the idea of the German tongue taking precedence over Latin. There was Eckhart's supposedly being assigned as a spiritual guide for nuns, tasked with the care of their souls. There were attempts to affiliate some of Eckhart's statements with his "mystical experience of becoming one" or with his audience. But we have no knowledge of either; the texts that survive do not talk about this experience or his public. There was the exaggerated focus on Thomas Aquinas over Albertus Magnus and Dietrich of Freiberg because of the obvious lack of knowledge of the philosophical and theological developments between 1274 and 1328. Attempts to trivialize Eckhart's condemnation by the pope through finesses in legal history led to confusion. To use biblical terms: Winfried Trusen strained at the gnat of various procedural codes and swallowed the camel of the attempted destruction of Eckhart's lifework. Then there were attempts to restore the orthodoxy of Eckhart, a man whom the church had condemned. This tendency has deep origins. It remains to be discussed further.

A contemporary book about Eckhart can devote itself in more detail to his argumentative steps and to the beauty of his metaphors. It can neglect those aspects that have been collecting dust. It could promote itself by pointing out that all earlier works that attempted to present a complete picture of Eckhart had come too early, before the textual base was secure.

Nowadays, there is a better chance that those philosophical concepts that Eckhart himself called the premises of his entire thinking will be highlighted: his theory of the primary determinations, the metaphysics of intellectual being, the elimination of efficient and final causalities from metaphysics, the recasting of the relation between substance and accident, the non-Thomistic conception of analogy, the meaning of the "insofar," his interest in nature, the character of his parabolic interpretation of the Bible.

In these points, Eckhart distinguished himself from the ever more prevalent Thomism of the schools. Eckhart's dissent from Parisian teachings shows clearly, as otherwise found to the same extent only in Denifle, albeit with a different assessment. Eckhart set himself apart from the developments in Paris. That is what those interpreters missed who read Eckhart's works as instructions for souls in search of God. In this context, Eckhart's real historical situation—determined by social necessities and intellectual debates—disappeared. Denifle and Grabmann are right in this regard: for the historical Eckhart, his divergence from the traditional path of common scholasticism and his explicit polemical position against it were defining. He thought differently from the overwhelming majority of philosophers and theologians around 1300. He even said so himself. And it is what makes his condemnation understandable. It was not caused by the base motives of the friars who were denouncing him, not primarily by conflicts with the Franciscans, not by biased legal proceedings, but by judicial application of the standard of orthodoxy taught in the schools.

I wanted to show this in detail. It is the reason why I returned again to the texts after a series of Eckhartian studies. I related the texts back to the scholastic development of the time—not as its conforming product, but as its contrast. And so a new overall picture of Eckhart emerged. It was not supposed to be too extensive. I therefore chose to focus wholly on Eckhart. I am not writing about Augustine or the Areopagite; I hardly mention Suso and Tauler.[1] No "triumvirate of mystical stars" shines forth here;

approaches to the Far East are best left to others who know its languages. Someone writing about Eckhart today, it seems to me, has to focus on his writings, on the basis of a study of the development of medieval thought. Reference to Nicholas of Cusa seems beneficial, too. It might help overcome the popular but inappropriate and modernizing category of Eckhart's "paradox" by replacing it with a description of Eckhart's language as occasionally "coincidental speech."

People today want to know about Eckhart. Many, using the language of advertising, consider him "in." Someone writing or reading about Eckhart will want to know why that is the case. This is how I explain it to myself: the more confusing our daily lives become and the more people experience themselves as objects and victims, the more they develop a need for mysticism. They search for an alternative way of life and present the Eckhart scholar with the question whether to indulge this very real need or not. I think that he must not ignore it. But neither should he cater to it like a servant. He has to create some distance. Someone who wants to escape the hectic pace of his present life in an industrial society, who is looking for meditative relaxation or psychological self-awareness, approaches Eckhart with the wrong premises. He will make crude demands of him; he will ignore his philosophical premises and their historical situatedness or will soon forsake him. It is exactly this situation that a historically conceived book on Eckhart can remedy: it shows those who have tired of city life and seek tranquility and God that Eckhart was a philosopher who lived and thought under wholly different conditions. He possessed the typical education in philosophy and theology of any Dominican of his time; he took up the intellectual certainties and methods of his contemporaries, reshaped them, and, equipped with his philosophical reform, set out to redefine the main concepts of the Christian doctrine of faith and life for his contemporaries and to make them comprehensible to academics and laypeople alike. It is a hermeneutical act of violence to extract Eckhart from this situation and to use him as a remedy for the diseases of the present. Because history has brushed Eckhart's medieval context aside, many things do not make sense. A reader of Eckhart today could perhaps save himself from this self-created embarrassment by getting involved in the historical details. Then again, the hectic modern life that he seeks to escape in fact prevents him from doing so. As a consequence, Eckhart becomes associated with the occult, the esoteric, the arcane, and the seemingly sublime. The industry of mysticism and its supporting writers exploit it.

Someone reading a book about Eckhart today enters into this constellation. Someone writing about Eckhart today has to evade this pressure; he will push for details and Eckhart's original tone. By letting the historical world around 1300 appear foreign, he will clarify the experience of difference that consumers of mysticism would otherwise suffer in silence.

The broad interest in Eckhart has another root as well: the intellectual and linguistic situation of the Christian churches. I am not referring here to their social activities or their skillful self-displays on television, but, for once, to their "truth." This truth predominantly stems from the fourth and fifth centuries, at best from the sixteenth, and is hardly communicable because of the comprehensive developmental shifts in its central points—God and the soul, the Fall and original sin, the Incarnation and salvation, heaven and hell—no matter whether one attempts to explain it in Latin or German. The churches themselves shirk explanations by resorting to imprecise formulations or pleasantries, such as love and family, peace and the preservation of creation. They think they are serving God by spreading optimism. Their mix of old doctrinal baggage and modernizing adjustments seems unsatisfying for contemplative Christians. They look around and read Far Eastern sources and Eckhart. Initially, they are delighted with Eckhart's simplification and expansion of the Christian-Augustinian-Scholastic tradition. They think they are finding in Eckhart what their church "actually" means. They seek in Eckhart a more liberal Catholic or a more profound Protestant. Upon a closer look, however, they are unable to find either. Faced with the extensive breadth of medieval scholastic beliefs, including purgatory and the doctrine of the Eucharist, Eckhart transformed them through a philosophy of Christianity that was contradictory to the developments that theology and philosophy had undergone in the thirteenth century. Church authorities held this transformation against him. Since the 1930s, Catholics like Otto Karrer, Alois Dempf, and Wilhelm Bange have tended to interpret the pope's condemnation of Eckhart as a misunderstanding or a bureaucratic hiccup. Likewise, Lutherans ran into problems: Eckhart's thinking is incompatible with some of Luther's crucial positions—the relation of faith and reason, God's predestination and human freedom, the sacrifice of the cross and ethics.[2] Eckhartism fits the basic religious-philosophical tenets of the two Christian denominations only as long as it is understood imprecisely. The label "mysticism" protects this lack of precision from its own demise. What we can gain from a study of Eckhart for our present times may be this: it removes muddled attempts at reconciliation. Historical difference is opposed to them. Luther does not stand any closer to Eckhart, as has been assumed, because Luther valued the *Theologia deutsch*. Studies of Eckhart can explain this for the benefit of all, but only if they do not proceed in a dogmatically conciliatory way, in an aimlessly wandering and speculative fashion, or in an inexpressively contemplative form, that is, if they develop and foster a consciousness of the present and employ the tools of the trade proper to historical knowledge.

Someone writing about Eckhart today will find himself faced with linguistic difficulties. These are objectively justified. Therefore, it is not enough to avoid the often unspeakably awkward, antiquated, or corny language of translation, to speak no longer of "a little spark of the soul" or "rapture." The problem lies deeper. It is misleading to continue to use one of Eckhart's Middle High German terms whose literal makeup has remained the same but whose meaning has shifted. It is crucial to take notice of Eckhart's allusions to biblical expressions and technical philosophical terms. Philosophical key terms mislead precisely in those cases in which the word still exists today in seemingly unchanged form, like "mind," for example. Both Middle High German and Latin can create problems. What does "reason" mean in distinction to "intellectuality"? How is the Latin *intellectus* to be translated, or *analogia?* Oftentimes, I kept the loan words "intellect" or "analogy" in order not to render the foreign too familiar, but even those terms can lead us astray. I am convinced that we could paraphrase them completely in the modern vernacular, but that would have led to complications and circuities that would have extended the scope of this book beyond all measure. I contented myself with a few examples and put my trust in the reader's intelligence and flexibility.

In writing about Eckhart, the tone matters as well. The historical stages of Eckhart interpretation and the different directions that each took created a distinct style of talking about Eckhart. Scholars of the sixteenth to eighteenth centuries wrote about him in the dry fashion of a librarian. Franz von Baader devoted his full attention to Eckhart and—with surprise and respect—spoke of him as a great thinker. Schopenhauer promoted Eckhart and secured a presence for him among German philosophers, even outside the Hegelian flock. Joseph Görres called Eckhart "a miraculous, almost mythological Christian figure, half-shrouded in mist." From then on, Eckhart became grand, distant, a lonely old hand. Bishop Martensen extended this tone into a sublime, half-idealistic Protestant one. The nationalist spirit of the sixth decade of the nineteenth century further raised the pitch regarding the "father of German speculation." Then followed the erudite but crude Denifle. He spoke disparagingly about Eckhart even while rendering great services to Eckhart studies. He saw Eckhart as a confused scholastic and retroactively showed the passages in Thomas Aquinas that could have saved him from his errors. He polemicized against the Lutheran theologian Wilhelm Preger in order to remove Eckhart from the interpretations of mysticism by German Protestants. Martin Grabmann did not think differently from Denifle, but he explained his manuscript finds in longer passages and in the more inconspicuous style of a specialist. Once in a while, he voiced his indignation: he had sharp and disdainful words for Karrer and other Catholics who wanted to provide room for Eckhart in their own church.

Since the beginning of the twentieth century, Eckhart has become a fashionable subject. The decade of antipositivism cried out for a reformed life; its language became more vigorous, more direct, and more boisterous. Writers polemicized against historical learnedness in the name of life. Admirers of Eckhart appeared more frequently in newspapers and magazines. They spoke solemnly, for they wanted Eckhart to be an iconic figure for Germany. He was supposed to become something akin to Barbarossa or Luther, to the Bamberg Horseman or Uta of Ballenstedt. In 1903, several translations from the Middle High German were published simultaneously— by Gustav Landauer, Hermann Büttner, and Joseph Bernhart. In 1904, Leopold Ziegler published an article in the *Preußische Jahrbücher* (vol. 115, 503–17) titled "Die philosophische und religiöse Bedeutung des Meisters Eckhart" (Meister Eckhart's philosophical and religious significance). Eckhart was considered a "genius" who supposedly founded something like a German Renaissance. Eckhart had allegedly "established once and for all the accent of the German idea of Christ." What Ziegler celebrated in declamatory fashion was "Eckhart's pantheism, his heresy, but also his Protestantism" (508). Eckhart became a role model, a figure of German identity. When Bernhart published a review essay titled "Einige Bücher zur Mystik" (Some books on mysticism) in 1913–14, he expressed his aversion to the increase in mystical books beforehand.[3] In the fall of 1914, Eckhart became tangled up with the rhetoric of German war orators; along with Luther and Kant, Eckhart served as proof of the depth of the German soul.[4] In this context, the tone in which people spoke about Eckhart changed. The diction and style of advertising and political propaganda invaded the discourse; the language became excited and shrill. Eckhart was commended; the suspicion of heresy decreased. Catholics, who were becoming less marginalized in politics and culture at the time, did not want to get on the wrong side of a national idol. Protestants of German descent, theologians and Germanists alike, wrestled for Eckhart in an attempt to adopt him for their own church. Hence the attempts to rehabilitate Eckhart and mitigate his condemnation.

Another circumstance changed the language used after World War I in speaking about Eckhart: expressionist prose—whether Ernst Bloch's or Heidegger's—usurped Eckhart with pathos-ridden words. The youth movement discovered Eckhart for itself with a strong, mostly antiacademic desire for appropriation. Eckhart became the object of literary productions. He rose to the level of a fictional character. A popular writer such as Paul Gurk (a pseudonym of Franz Grau, 1880–1953) described Eckhart's loneliness novelistically and let Satan and Michael fight for his soul. Gurk's *Meister Eckhart* first appeared in 1920 and was reprinted during World War II, in 1943. There was a need for such a thing. Inge Degenhardt described the history and the inflated tone of this type of Eckhartian literature, to which the poem on Eckhart by Ernst Bertram belongs. In 1935, Karrer published another review essay of books about Eckhart, just as Bernhart had done twenty years before him. He criticized the Nazi appropriation of Eckhart but also the merely historical attitude toward him: people were talking about Eckhart without really living by him. This type of Eckhartian historicism, he stated, was a mere attempt to escape the present, and it caused endless chatter: "People are talking. People are writing. It is raining. It is raining Eckhart in all the editorial offices."[5] Karrer appears disgusted by the poor German of the nationalist interpretations. He quotes the Bavarian teacher's magazine of December 20, 1934, which babbles about Eckhart as a Nordic man and describes him as "a herald of German ideology, the torch of whose mind shines forth victoriously through the darkness of the Middle Ages." Degenhardt likewise quotes a series of similarly bombastic appraisals of Eckhart from before 1933 (*Studien zum Wandel des Eckhartbildes*, 237–38). This style is not deserving of comment; I cannot deduce anything from it other than historical disenchantment.

The language of Josef Quint remains instructive. Quint (1898–1976, member of the National Socialist German Workers' Party from 1937) was the most influential Germanist who studied Eckhart, and he dominated the field into the 1970s with his editions and interpretations of Eckhart.

In 1927, Quint gave his inaugural lecture in Bonn on Eckhart's language.[6] He took over the central concepts from the book *West-östliche Mystik* by Rudolf Otto, published a year earlier (Gotha, 1926). Quint begins with the differences among types of mysticism. He follows Otto in his evaluation that Eckhart's mysticism was "heavily imbued with feeling," adding that all mysticism was concerned with the "mystical experience of becoming one," which was "always situated in a supra-rational region of the soul" (672). Quint wanted to illuminate the character of Eckhart's "Gothic thinking" in his speculation and language. He talks about the closeness of scholasticism and mysticism, as well as the distance between them, and concludes: "This mystical thinking, the strong inner motion of which stems from a Gothic-Faustian world feeling, goes against the static positing of concepts of scholasticism" (681). For Quint, it found a more faithful expression in Eckhart's German works than in his Latin writings.

My main interest here lies not in the methodological conclusions drawn by the father of more recent Germanist Eckhart studies, nor in his declared irrationalism, but in the language with which Quint wrote about Eckhart. His reifying forms of expression are noticeable: "supra-rational region of the soul," as though the soul consisted of several layers, "regions" with an above and a below. To explain Eckhart, Quint seeks refuge in collective concepts of cultural history such as "Gothic." He is fond of big words; he knows the "Gothic-Faustian world feeling" and the "mystical experience of becoming one." Eckhart's thinking, he says, seeks to "chase down the salvation of an *unio mystica*" (682). According to Quint, Eckhart's "forceful dynamic, in conflict with the stasis of the scholastic system, drives two characteristic, revealing elements into it: an overly audacious, limits-bursting paradox and the dynamic of a Neoplatonic emanationism." To understand Eckhart, for Quint, is to comprehend his thinking as a struggle "against the limited concept" (694).

In 1939, Quint again rose to speak, this time as professor in Breslau. He expressed his satisfaction that the name Eckhart had become "a very familiar sound in all the German lands" and that "the undeniable credit" for this belonged to Alfred Rosenberg (210).[7] Eckhart is an "ingenious analyst of the soul" for Quint; he celebrates "the thrilling momentum of his captivating speeches" (212). Again, Quint starts from a definition of mysticism: it "does not signify transcendence, but immanence of the divine, and it signifies the becoming aware of God within one's own breast in the experience of the *unio mystica*" (215). He knows that Eckhart "possessed the *intuitus mysticus* as a predisposition deep in his essence" (216). As in 1927, Quint saw the struggle against "the delimiting concept" as the essential part of Eckhart's thinking, but this individual trait of Eckhart in 1939 became "the essentially German, the Gothic-Faustian, the Nordic character within him" (217). In the context of the doctrine of poverty, Eckhart's ethics—in Quint's words—were raised "to the absolutely steepest, most audacious, and insurmountably highest" point (221). And alongside these superlatives a bit of blood and soil: "There lives a happy will to fight within this Eckhart in whose veins flowed knightly blood" (225). What constitutes Eckhart's just man? It is "the inner attitude, the mentality, the inner discipline and order achieved through the most persistent practice that can no longer be scattered or destroyed by any chaos" (226). Above all, "the just man serves the community" (229). This was a Meister Eckhart for the training of SS officials.

Two years later, Quint republished his lecture of 1939. He changed very little. He celebrated "Eckhart's powerful resurrection in our time";[8] he praised Rosenberg, who, he said, had shown that German mysticism was to be understood as "an exquisite outgrowth" of the "efficacy of the Nordic nature." "Rosenberg recognized in the figure of this Eckhart the greatest religious genius of the Germans"; Quint approvingly quotes Rosenberg, who called Eckhart the "greatest apostle of the Nordic Western world" (5). Quint then attributes the highest rating to Eckhart: he was "the deepest and most German thinker of the past" (6). He possessed the "unrestrained Faustian-Nordic drive for depth" (16).

Quint worked relentlessly. When he reprinted his 1939 text in 1941 without significant changes, he was conscious of the fact that his fatherland was now actively involved in a war, and so he added something intended to increase its military strength by pointing out that it was no coincidence that "the Germanic idea of loyal obedience" occurred to "the greatest German mystic, with its demands of self-discipline, of proving oneself, and of making a last stand, sacrificing one's life for one's lord in battle" (25). With his Fascist diction, Quint proved the benefit of studying Eckhart in the context of the war. The "German people" were supposed to "recognize their deepest and truest nature" in this "pure mirror" of a militarized Eckhart (38).

In 1952, Quint was back. In Münster, he gave a talk titled "Mysticism and Language," claiming that both concepts "are shrouded in mystery" (48).[9] Quint's authorities were no longer Rudolf Otto or Rosenberg, but

Leo Weisgerber and Erich Rothacker. There is a lot of talk about silence. Quint's focus is the antagonism between mysticism and language. It is the old struggle against the "limited concept," but now Quint speaks of it in even fuzzier, more elevated terms: he describes Eckhart's "mystical thinking" as "wanting to burst the bonds of the linguistic-conceptual thinking of the German inner speech-form" (60). The central concepts—the mystical experience of becoming one, intuition, silence, and paradox—survived the Nazi era unscathed.

We possess four lectures on Eckhart by Quint from three cultural periods: 1927, 1939, 1941, and 1952. In addition, there is his introduction to *Meister Eckehart: Deutsche Predigten und Traktate* (Meister Eckhart: German sermons and tractates [Munich, 1955]), which ends in the gently de-Nazified sentence that man's becoming "an active and useful servant of the community is Eckhart's constant effort, which he pursued throughout his long life as a fighter with true German diligence, with unswerving and passionate determination despite much opposition." I point to these works not because of their contribution to an understanding of Eckhart or to the methodology of Eckhart studies, but merely because of the way in which Quint talks about Eckhart.[10] His work as an editor is not in question here. His attitude toward Eckhart's thinking is insignificant, partly ignominious, and partly preposterous; his style, however, remains worthy of study: exaggerated pathos, neoromanticisms, nationalistic murmurs, antirational scribbles derived from an unclear concept of mysticism. Strange is his usage of dramatizing adjectives: Eckhart's speech is "captivating," his thinking "overly audacious" and "pushing the boundaries," the Eckhart revival "powerful." Everything descends into depth. The Germanists after Quint had their work cut out for them, clearing away this rubble of rhetoric. Someone writing about Eckhart today should not forget this labor of disenchantment and specification, which culminated in the works of Kurt Ruh.

13. Eckhart's Intention:
Commentary on John, Part 1

The Gospel of John and Philosophy

Eckhart developed a new metaphysics, a new philosophy of nature, and a new ethics as the foundation for providing a new interpretation of the Bible and of medieval Christian self-understanding. He was suspected of heresy, as he wrote, only secondarily because of his success with the people, and with "both genders," but first of all because of his fervor for justice. His work was supposed to make a new, true, and just life possible. He conceived of this new life in less individualistic terms than is commonly assumed. Eckhart clearly said what he was looking for: the truth of life, of justice, and of a Christian self-perception: *veritas vitae, iustitiae et doctrinae* (*In Ioh.*, LW 3, n. 184, 153.12).

To that end, he needed to read the Bible anew, especially Genesis and the Gospel of John. Of the four gospels, John's is the most philosophical. It prompted the greatest number of philosophical commentaries, and among its interpreters we find not only Augustine, John Eriugena, and Thomas Aquinas, but also Johann Gottlieb Fichte in his *The Way towards the Blessed Life* (Berlin, 1806). According to Fichte, the Gospel of John provided a new understanding of the world and a new self-understanding of man and his fortune; it contained the model for a new philosophical paradigm. It asked its readers to abandon their superstitious idea of an orienting world of existing things and to think of the human world as a dynamism of mental processes from which ideas about the world first proceeded. It overcame the idea of the primacy of things to which properties adhere. It comprehended man and human thinking in their performance, "but by no means [as] a *thinking substance*, a dead body in which thought inheres."[1] I am not claiming that Fichte offers the key to Meister Eckhart, but there is no harm in thinking about his conception of man and mind before beginning to speak about Eckhart. Studying Eckhart is not rendered more historically correct simply by ignoring Fichte's critique of man's reified self-consciousness and continuing to fall prey to the idea that the "I" is a thing of a soul to which thinking and wanting adhere. The Gospel of John in particular links this critique with the motif of divine filiation: the logos is God and illuminates every person who comes into this world, not only those who believe in Christ. It provides the power for us to become children of God; it takes up the ancient motif of divine filiation; it speaks of new birth and divine life (John 3:5). The farewell discourses in John provide a new concept of reality and unity: "I and the Father are one," and humans are asked to enter into this oneness. They are supposed to become as one as Jesus is one with the Father (John 17:21). The Gospel of John contains the sentence "I no longer call you slaves, but rather friends" (15:15). All that was needed was for one person to develop a rich concept of friendship from the philosophical literature of antiquity, for example, from Aristotle and Cicero, to bring this dictum back to life: the friend as another "I" who holds back no truth from his friend. Did not Jesus promise the spirit of truth that would lead to *all* truth (16:13)?

A series of topics in Eckhart's earlier writings were conceptualized in the language of John: for example, there were the metaphors of begetting and birth. Eckhart spoke of the enlightenment of all people and of unity in love. The language of the gospel gave Eckhart's own language its intimate tone; it tinged his speculations about the "I am who I am" and about the intellect, which, according to Eckhart, constituted man.

Eckhart's commentary on the Gospel of John is his most extensive and most fully developed piece of biblical exegesis; it was a relatively late work. There is no way of knowing the exact dates of its composition, but it probably belonged to the period between 1310–12 and 1318–20, close to the time of the composition of Eckhart's *Book of Divine Consolation* and some of his German sermons. The commentary cites the *Liber parabolarum* (LW 3, n. 174, 143.5) and was likely written after it, although it is difficult to draw definite conclusions from Eckhart's own cross-references.

Eckhart's commentary on John is a personal work, rich in scope and perspectives. I can highlight only a few of its features here.

As is typical of a late work, Eckhart here reaches back to some of his earlier topics. He continues his analysis of the primary determinations begun in the *Prologi* to the *Opus tripartitum*, that is, of Being, Oneness, Truth, and Goodness (*In Ioh.*, LW 3, n. 114, 99.6; unless otherwise noted, all citations are to this work); he affirms the primacy of Being and specifies the order of the others: Oneness, Truth, Goodness. As in the first two Parisian questions, he places knowing above Being (n. 44, 37.1–3). He discusses again the role and precise meaning of negative theology, which was so central to his commentary on Exodus (which relied on Maimonides). What else can it mean if the metaphysics of the Son is valid? The mind, after all, leads to all truth.[2] As in his earlier works, Eckhart highlights the damage arising from the primacy of the *imaginatio;* in part, he agrees with Augustine, who had argued against pictorial imaginings of the act of creation: God did not make the world like a craftsman who does his work and leaves, *non fecit atque abiit* (n. 579, 508.3). He reiterates his universal postulate of rationality, an often-neglected constant in Eckhart's thinking: we can and must claim that God de facto has done everything that we must recognize with good reasons as the best (n. 55, 46.9–11). Eckhart expands on his motif of the relationship between Justice and the just man. He explains his philosophical position anew: Justice and Wisdom do not inhere in the individual person as properties; rather, the just man as such is begotten by Justice. Eckhart poignantly suggests the long-required change of the metaphysical model: he places the metaphysics of being begotten above the substance-accident paradigm, which he does not abolish completely, but relegates to a secondary position. He indicates this shift with the provocative phrase that the individual inheres in these forms, in Wisdom or Justice, Being or Oneness, *inhaerendo eidem ipsi formae* (n. 46, 38.10–11). He clarifies again the logical order of his argument and stresses the difference between Being per se and being-this-or-that (n.52, 43:11–12).

Eckhart Explains His Method

There are three especially important innovations present in the commentary on John: first, Eckhart clarifies definitively what he wanted to say in all his remarks. He explains his program: he will demonstrate the unity of the Gospel and metaphysics. This point forms the focus of the present chapter.

Second, he developed his metaphysics of the *verbum*, which explicitly integrates the natural things into this new concept. And third, he uses the Aristotelian-Averroistic theory of the unity of the knower and the known to explain how the just man is within Justice. The second and third points will be discussed in the next chapter.

Eckhart explains his method. That he was not practicing exegesis in any theological sense acceptable today is obvious from the arrangement of his materials. His lack of interest in the story of Christ's Passion is notable. The explanation he provided at the beginning of his interpretation shows this as well. It deals with the first verse of the Gospel of John ("In the beginning was the Word") and has the following wording, which I provide in its entirety because of its importance:

> In explaining this saying as well as those that follow, it is the intention of the author—as in all of his texts—to interpret with the help of the natural arguments of the philosophers what the holy Christian faith and the scriptures of both testaments claim.
>
> "For the invisible determinations of God have disclosed themselves to the intellect since the creation of the world through his works, he himself, his infinite power," "that means: the Son, and his Godhead," "that means: the Holy Spirit," as the gloss to Romans 1:20 explains.
>
> Furthermore, in Book 7 of the *Confessions*, Augustine claims to have read the sentence "In the beginning was the Word" in the works of Plato, as well as a great portion of the first chapter of John.
>
> And in Book 10 of the *City of God*, he describes a follower of Plato who said that the beginning of this chapter, up until the passage "a man was sent by God," should be displayed with golden letters in a widely visible place.
>
> 3. Furthermore, the intention of this work is to show how the truth of the principles, conclusions, and essential properties of the natural things are clearly revealed—"whoever has ears to hear shall hear!"—in exactly these words of scripture. Some moral interpretations are inserted throughout as well.[3]

Eckhart's explanation, which I briefly indicated in chapter 3, is extraordinarily valuable. It is the demonstratively placed and comprehensive self-portrayal of the *magister*. It says explicitly that he is explaining his intention here, that is, the intention that he pursues in his interpretation of John and in *all* of his works. The commentary on John is a mature work; Eckhart speaks like an author who is able to look back on a large number of writings and thereby explain the objectives of his life's work. It is a mystery why this clear and explicit text, which has been easily accessible since 1936, has not become the foundation for all interpretations of Eckhart's work. This mystery can be solved with precision; I have done so elsewhere.[4] Here we are concerned with the content of this authoritative self-portrayal.

The assertion has two parts. The first can be found in n. 2: Eckhart wants to prove the truth claimed by the Christian faith in its whole breadth— the creation of the world, the Fall of man, the Incarnation of God, salvation, in all, the truth of the Old and the New Testament—with philosophical arguments. The second part, in n. 3, says that the interpretation is supposed to show that these words of scripture, that is, the first chapter of the Gospel of John, contain the principles of all natural things that have being, the conclusions drawn from these principles, and the essential properties, that is, the noncoincidental qualities of all natural things that have being. Furthermore, there are some moral interpretations.

The first part (n. 2) promises to demonstrate the truth of Christianity philosophically. This truth included not only what could be found in the Bible (which was a confusingly large corpus), since Eckhart considered his symbolic readings the "properly" literal interpretations, but also what was contained in the living consciousness of the faith of living Christians.

The second part of Eckhart's explanation (n. 3) proposes to prove the clearly but tersely articulated bases of natural philosophy of the Gospel of John with philosophical argumentation.

Eckhart provides valuable additions to the first part of his self-explanation. He refers to the *Glossa ordinaria*, to Book 7 of the *Confessions*, and to book 10 of the *City of God*. Eckhart combines these three texts in such a way that they demonstrate his conception of the natural knowability of the Trinity. They authoritatively secure the possibility of a philosophy of the Trinity. Eckhart knew that he needed authorities for support if he wanted to speak philosophically about the Trinity. For his plan contradicted a phalanx of scholastic teachers that included his order's teacher Thomas Aquinas.[5] A series of well-known teachers in the thirteenth century had strictly limited philosophical thinking about the Trinity: philosophy recognized that God existed and founded the world, but it could not recognize the Trinity, which we could know only through faith.

Aquinas cited two arguments for this: first, he said, this restriction of philosophical reason arose from the fact that we knew God only through his function of founding the world, but that the world-creating causality of God was a matter of the entire Trinity and not of its individual persons. Second, Aquinas argued that we could attach certain attributes to the first ground of the world and know that he was reason and will, but that these aspects of the divine mind would not have the distinctness that ecclesiastical teachings attributed to the three persons of the Godhead. Reason and will, understanding and love, were divine attributes, not autonomous persons. The Trinity of the church required a real distinction, *realis distinctio*, of three persons.[6] It is a good idea to keep this controversial term of real distinctness in mind when reading Eckhart; it gives his theory that God distinguished himself the most through indistinction its flavor of a concrete polemic of the time. According to Aquinas, the ancient philosophical theory of the logos approached the doctrine of the Trinity, but it did not achieve it. Augustine, on the contrary, had attributed knowledge of the true God, the recognition of the right concept of creation and the knowledge of the logos, to the Platonists. Eckhart thus positioned Augustine against Aquinas. Otherwise, he would have been unable to claim the first chapter of the Gospel of John as a philosophical text. In addition, his procedure shows what level of methodological awareness had been achieved around 1300. There were sharp boundaries for what the natural foundations of philosophy could attain and what needed to be reserved for ecclesiastical authority. Eckhart shifted these boundary stones. He was able to do this in the safety of the book of Romans, the Gospel of John, the *Ordinary Gloss*, and the two passages from Augustine. He constructed his short text as an elaborate web of quotations.

In the Middle Ages (and far beyond), the passage from the book of Romans was considered the New Testament's guarantee of the right and the import of philosophical theology: God's invisible essence could be recognized in the world by every insightful person, not just by Christians. With the help of the *Glossa ordinaria*, Eckhart interpreted the Pauline passage in such a way that the Trinity seemed included in the extent of man's universal philosophical knowledge of God. Eckhart skillfully integrated the *Glossa*, written around 1100, into the Pauline text three times and interpreted St. Paul's triadic concept in the sense of the Trinitarian theology that had been fixed since the fourth century. This entire operation meant that Eckhart was able, against Aquinas, to claim the Trinity as a subject of philosophical knowledge. In this way, he placed himself against his order's teacher, but not against the entire older tradition. Anselm of Canterbury and Ramon Llull had also been convinced that they were able to provide philosophically compelling arguments for the Trinity. Their key term was: necessary grounds of reason, *rationes necessariae*.

Augustine had attributed knowledge of the divine Word to the Platonists. He reports that he found in the prologue to John what he had read in the "Platonic books" (Plotinus or Porphyry). Eckhart capitalized on Augustine's great authority in order to argue against Aquinas, but altered the original sense of Augustine's assertion. Augustine said that the Platonists had recognized the theory of the logos in the prologue to John; they comprehended the close relation between logos and soul; they taught that the logos enlightened every human being who came into this world; but they had not recognized the Incarnation.[7] Had Eckhart followed Augustine's line of thought, he would have been able to say only that he would prove the first lines of the prologue to John by philosophical arguments. But Eckhart wanted more. He wanted what he said, namely, to demonstrate the truth of both testaments, not only the creation of the world, but also the Incarnation. His reference to Augustine did not cover his entire program; it applied only to the first part of his aspiration. It fulfilled a tactical function not only against the Thomistic exclusion of a philosophy of the Trinity and the Incarnation, but also against the consensus in Paris that had developed since Peter Lombard.

Eckhart presented his undertaking as consisting of two parts: first, he wanted to demonstrate the truth of Christianity philosophically (n. 2), and then he wanted to show that the philosophical truth contained in scripture explained the visible world (n. 3). When interpreted as metaphysics, the Bible, for Eckhart, also contained the basis of natural philosophy. In this context, we need to keep away from modern associations of the phrase "natural philosophy." It is not as though the Middle Ages did not have a developed natural philosophy. Especially in the circles of Albertus Magnus and Dietrich of Freiberg, though not only there, a pointed methodological interest in nature was the norm. Medieval knowledge of nature by no means consisted of the moralistic and religious symbolization of nature, as is still occasionally claimed. It had already been essentially overcome in the twelfth century; it had gone out of fashion with the reception of Aristotle around

1250. The crucial book was Aristotle's *Physics*, but also his book *On the Soul*, his *On Generation and Corruption*, and his biological works.

Thus, to a contemporaneous reader, Eckhart, in his text, said: "I will interpret the Bible philosophically, with strict requirements for proof. Second, I will show that the Bible, interpreted in this way, explains all of nature philosophically for everyone who has ears to hear. I presume the truth of scripture for myself as a believer, but this does not prevent me from proceeding rigorously. For I also want to demonstrate the truth of Christianity and its share of worldly wisdom to the nonbeliever, building on the ancient and Islamic philosophers. I will present this as my metaphysics, since the Gospel is metaphysics; it achieves what Aristotle expected of metaphysics; it observes the beings qua beings.[8] My philosophical theology is metaphysics, philosophy of nature, and ethics. Augustine's drawing on the ancient Neoplatonists is my model, but I want to go further and also prove the truth of the Incarnation and, by virtue of this truth, revive natural philosophy. I want to present a philosophy of Christianity that establishes in detail that the Old Testament, the New Testament, and Aristotle teach the same thing."[9]

It is remarkable what Eckhart could have said about his intentions in his program, but what he in fact did not say. He did not say: "I am a Rhineland mystic and am trying to fit ineffable experiences into concepts." He did not say: "My field is negative theology, into which I am entering with the divine Dionysius's lead." He did not say: "I am a devout Christian who is explaining the contents of the Bible with confidence in divine revelation on the basis of faith." He did not say: "I am first of all a preacher and am gathering from the traditional texts the material that friars need for their sermons." He did not say: "As a Dominican, I am a faithful student of Aquinas, but as a spiritual adviser I relate his theology a bit more to the religious life." He did not say, "I am worried about the orthodoxy of many of the inhabitants of the cities and would like to do everything to reintegrate them into it, with the help of an exaggerated, emphatic diction if necessary."

All these assertions were ascribed to Eckhart during the twentieth century. None of them can be found in Eckhart. He wanted to prove the truth of the main tenets of scripture philosophically, to present the scripture thus tested as the embodiment of the thinking contemplation of nature, and to suggest a few moral consequences.

Specificity is advised if someone says that Eckhart presupposed the truth of faith and scripture. Eckhart differentiated methodologically between faith and philosophical knowledge. He wanted to prove the essential features that he considered most important, not the details of what he believed in. To construct this type of proof, it was impossible for Eckhart to *argumentatively* presume the truth of scripture and faith. Instead, he needed to proceed from philosophical premises and, via strictly rational reasoning, arrive at the conclusion that what the Bible suggested was demonstrably true. According to his own testimony, Eckhart presumed the historical truth of what the Gospel reported.[10] But it is crucial to understand what "presumed" meant in this case. It meant that nothing historical in the gospel narrative was an object of his argument. It was of no great interest for him. Concretely, if the Incarnation does not take place within people, then the historical narrative about it has little worth and is of no interest to Eckhart. Eckhart was neither the first nor the last who—logically, not psychologically!—looked for philosophical proofs of the truth of faith that were independent of said faith.[11]

Eckhart explicitly says that this description of his intention is valid for *all* his writings. He makes no exception for his German texts. He does not exclude any of his earlier writings. His programmatic explanation in the commentary on John corresponds to similar proclamations in other works. There is no doubt that he essentially honored them. To understand them, a few preconditions are required:

- A flexible concept of philosophy developed out of Eckhart's thinking, one that is neither modern nor the common scholastic variety, but that was made possible historically by Aristotle and Augustine, the *Liber de causis* and Proclus, the *Book of the Twenty-Four Philosophers* and Avicenna, Averroës, Albertus Magnus, Thomas Aquinas, and Dietrich of Freiberg.
- Eckhart, like other medieval Christian interpreters, approached the Hebrew Bible via the New Testament. He read the first sentence of the prologue to John into the first sentence of Genesis.
- Eckhart ahistorically combined Moses, Jesus, and Aristotle. He recovered his own metaphysics in the Gospel of John, not that of the schools.
- While we do not have the *Opus propositionum*, which was supposed to contain the philosophical foundation of all his biblical interpretations, Eckhart reminds us again and again of his philosophy, so it does not remain unknown to us.
- Eckhart followed through with his program in the commentary on John, but not with the pedantry of an accountant.
Regarding this last point, he inserted portions of sermons into the commentary, although he declared them as such, just as he had clearly differentiated

academic speech from sermons in his speeches about Ecclesiasticus (*In Ioh.* n. 226, 189.5–7; n. 605, 527.10–12). Toward the end of the commentary on John he points out that he will henceforth proceed in abbreviated fashion (n. 555, 436.5–6). It is another source of a certain irregularity in his working method.

Via philosophical argumentation, Eckhart pursues the origin of all knowledge from the divine source from which everything proceeds: philosophical theology, philosophy of nature, ethics, the practical and the theoretical *ars* all the way up to positive jurisprudence.[12] He is at odds with the distinctions among the disciplines that had developed in the thirteenth century.

• In the context of things and biblical sentences, he stresses the wide spread of meanings. He asks everyone to choose what they like from among the many interpretations.

• He explains that he interprets the Gospel of John with the expectation that every diligent researcher will readily find the correspondence of metaphysical theology, ethics, and the philosophy of nature everywhere (n. 509, 441.10–11). He wants to merge these disciplines with philosophical arguments, show their unified origin, and demonstrate that they are the actual truth, hidden beneath the peel of the biblical wording.

• Why does Eckhart place an astonishingly strong emphasis on knowing nature? He claims that the Gospel of John, correctly interpreted, teaches the essence of the natural things, their characteristic properties in being and acting (n. 13, 12.13–15). He summarized his type of interpretation by saying that he was arguing from the natural things, *ex naturalibus, per naturalia, in naturalibus* (n. 160, 131.10–132.6). Again and again he argued from the things of nature, *ostendere ex naturalibus* (n. 160, 131.16). The gospel, Eckhart says, teaches the essential features of everything that has being, the uncreated as well as the created (n. 83, 70.5–6). Its correct interpretation results in a unified science encompassing both the uncreated and the created. The idea of a higher knowledge of unity arises. The point is to show that the light that illuminates every human being contains all knowledge. More specifically, Eckhart shows the descent of the primary determinations into all areas of nature and human production. Or even closer to Eckhart's metaphysics: the primary determinations talk to us in everything. They speak, as natural reason recognizes, in all works of nature and of human production (n. 361, 306.5–8). He shows how the Word becomes flesh and how it dwells in everything that occurs universally and naturally, *universaliter et naturaliter in omni opere naturae et artis verbum caro fit et habitat in illis* (n. 125, 108.11–13). For everything that proceeds from a principle in nature and revelation is naturally and wholly generally, *naturaliter et generaliter*, in this principle beforehand (n. 4, 5.7–10). And against Augustine, Eckhart argues that if Augustine says that he did not find in the Neoplatonic books that the Word came into his possession, then philosophical reason disproves him, for God, who is Being, came into that which has being, and what belongs more to Being than something that has being (n. 96, 83.5–12)? The historical Incarnation is not contested. Belief in it is even strengthened if we gain an understanding of the universal incarnation of the logos. Once again, Eckhart formulates his program; he presupposes the historical narrative of the gospel, but what he is looking for is the truth of the natural things and their peculiarities, *veritates rerum naturalium et earum proprietates requiramus* (n. 142, 119.14–15).

14. Unity according to Kind: Commentary on John, Part 2

A Theory of the Logos

Universal metaphysics and the physics of the *verbum:* these are the core themes of the content, not merely of the method, in Eckhart's commentary on the Gospel of John.[1] We have come across them already in places where Eckhart considered the *verbum* present and philosophically knowable in all works of nature and human production (especially *In Ioh.*, LW 3, n. 361, 306.5–8). All things reveal ideal preformation, begetting, sonship, and retrospective dependence on the origin. Therefore, it is necessary (*necessarium*) to speak of the Creator, the created, and unifying love in the context of God and all worldly things (n. 160, 132.1). For this renewed philosophical thinking, the first thing is not the presence of things and properties, but the infinite Being that must be intellect and that, as begetter, lives in unity with the begotten. It could be called a universalization of a metaphysics of the logos if universalization were not already part of its nature, and yet this expression could be useful, for Eckhart opposes the naturalization of being and intellect and practices a naturalization of the common philosophy of logos as a partial but important aspect. Eckhart shows its productivity for the natural sciences. He formulates the linguistic character of a being qua being, all the way down to the elements. He positions the *verbum* character of the world against the dominant model of inherence.

Language as prefiguration of the world and as detachment from reified thinking was situated in the nature of the logos philosophy, but in order to prove it as a necessary idea Eckhart makes the following argument. It is impossible for someone to say anything without having formed beforehand and within himself a conceptual schema or image as his product or son, so to speak, that represents the speaker. Likewise, it is as impossible to receive and comprehend something spoken unless the hearer forms within himself a conceptual schema or image that, as his creation, corresponds to that which is within the speaker (n. 486, 418.3–6). This experience is ensured by the philosophical idea of correlativity, which always exists between father and son, between speaker and listener. The One of philosophical reason that is informed about itself is always also the Other. Or in Eckhart's words: from the beginning, where the one was, there the other had to be as well, *Ab initio quo fuit unum, fuerit semper et alterum* (n. 137, 116.9–10). That is what I mean here—no more, no less—when I speak of Eckhart's philosophy of the Trinity. It says: where there is the one, there the other must be also, and they have to be one. It is the mental and active unifying of the one with the other; and so the metaphysics of the logos becomes a philosophy of the Trinity. Eckhart eliminates the notion of efficient or final causes, which had determined metaphysics for so long, and replaces it with formal, language-like communication; he conceives of creation as formal emanation (n. 25, 20.5–6). Being, Oneness, the True, and the Good beget the rightly living man and his community, and express themselves within him. That is how man becomes divine, *homo divinus*. It is how the just man enters into Justice, or rather how Justice, pronouncing itself, begets him into itself.

To prove his position, Eckhart considers a series of reforming steps to be necessary within philosophy. The universal categorization of beings qua beings has to be improved in such a way that natural beings are confronted with and distinguished from the being in the soul as being of the proper kind, that is, as superbeing, namely, as the characteristic *ens cognitivum*. The intellectual being—from the simplest sense perception to the ideas and their recognition in God and human beings—which the greatest philosophers knew was not simply an image of the outer world, has to be grasped in its special status of being—if it is to be "being" at all. We have to stop deriving the primary meaning of being from the natural things. Eckhart notes that this is often overlooked and is the source of much error.[2] Strictly speaking, Eckhart critiques two specific errors committed by contemporaneous theorists. First, they fail to carefully distinguish the first division of being overall. They do not see that they have to speak in an entirely (*omnino*) different manner about the intellectual being than about natural things. The first two Parisian questions had tried to drive home this point. Without this philosophical reform, adequate discussions about the intellect or about ideas are impossible. For without it, people lack the understanding that God is mind. Second, many authors speak about accidents as though they were substances. Thus, they miss the original, Aristotelian sense of analogy. The fact that God is Being is rendered incomprehensible.

Eckhart critiques the dominance of the imagining thinking in questions of metaphysics. The imagination pictures things and suggests that Being, Oneness, and Wisdom are added to them as their properties and receive their being from the individual things. That is why coddled thinking does not grasp the precedence of Being over the individual beings nor the productive, begetting force of the primary determinations. It does not understand what it means that the *ratio rei* precedes the *res* as its ground and that there is only *one* Being, which is Word and discloses itself. It fails to comprehend that the justice within us is no different from Justice itself (n. 119, 104.10–13). The model of ontological inherence is not positioned where it belongs, namely, in a secondary place. It is erroneously attributed to the primary determinations. The relation between the just man and Justice is misunderstood, as is that Being is the Word and that we have to speak of it entirely (*omnino*) differently from the way we speak of things. The universality of the Incarnation is overlooked (nn. 125–26, 108–9; see also n. 155, 128.1–3). It is categorized in theoretical terms as a particular individual thing and thus misconstrued in its present sense. But the Word becomes flesh in every work of nature and of human production (n. 36, 30.12–15). Eckhart adds the already criticized error: many authors consider the concepts of efficient and final causality, indispensable only for explaining the natural world, to be instruments befitting metaphysics (n. 336, 284.9–10, and n. 338, 287.1–8). Thus, they do not see the formal character of the natural processes; they do not see their linguistic formedness and do not gain an understanding of formal flow, the *emanatio formalis*. That creation cannot be understood in technomorphous terms remains uncomprehended (n. 25, 20.5–6). It remains unconsidered what life means in its qualified sense, namely, that it has a goal in itself and is shaped by its essential nature, not through efficient causes. Divine effecting is a shaping, the power of formation (n. 336, 285.2–4, and n. 534, 465.9–11). The substantial *forma* provides being and subsistence for the things; it tastes of the divine or of God who himself is Being itself, the source and root of all being.

How to Conceptualize "God"

I have mentioned several times already how Eckhart conceptualized his God. His commentary on John provides an opportunity to attempt a summary of God's character. Two characteristic operations shape Meister Eckhart's God. First, there is the identification of God as Being. But Eckhart conceives of this Being in correlation with Oneness, Truth, and Goodness, and—since his first Parisian questions—understands this Being as performance, as an intellectual dynamic, as propagating Word in universal disclosure of form. Eckhart identifies the primary determinations with the divine Being and the latter with Truth and Wisdom, and hence with divine thinking that eternally has the world beside it and eternally produces it (n. 216, 181). God wants to beget sons according to his nature (n. 117, 102.4–5). As the Word, he is not a rock of autarchy, but essentially related to his Son and to all who enter into the sonship. After all, he did provide them with the power to become his sons. Therefore, being and knowing are the same within the *homo divinus* (n. 224, 187.11–12). Thence the universality of the Incarnation all the way to natural reproduction (nn. 125–126, 108–9). Its effect is formal self-disclosure as the coincidence of efficient, final, and formal causality, but always under the primacy of the disclosure of form (n. 337, 285.15–16).

The second characteristic of Eckhart's God is his undifferentiatedness. Things are opposed to one another; they differ from one another according to genus and species. God, by contrast, is the indistinct who differs from all things in precisely that regard. His *proprium* is the *indistinctio* (n. 99, 85, and n. 103, 89). He is that which has no opposite. That is, to put it in other words, his incomparable and special position; questions of pantheism or panentheism are deflected. Rather, the following way of thinking has to be followed: the infinitism of divine Being, its reflective nature, its complete return into itself as Oneness, Wisdom, and Justice that wants to beget, transform the Godhead into one who speaks and begets; the metaphysics of the *verbum* and the ontology of the formal flow become a philosophy of friendship as another "I" from whom the speaking friend does not keep any truth.

That is why the role of negative theology is changed. Its specific place within the Gospel of John is not easily determined. First, it states that no one has ever seen God, and only the Son manifested him. If it is part of God's nature, however, to want to beget sons, then disclosure of form and self-revelation are part of his nature. And when he gives himself, his indivisible nature has to disclose itself *wholly*. Within the just man, the otherwise un-knowable Godhead becomes known. The just man qua just man is a speaker; he is *verbum* as well. Nothing foreign to him can pronounce the unknown God; the just man does not say anything other than Justice, and he says it *wholly* at that; he pronounces its innermost character.[3] There is no valid negation of him, only a negation of the negative, and that is the core of the purest affirmation (n. 207, 175.2–3). This is the meaning of the *negatio negationis*.[4]

Is Eckhart's God a hidden God? I hesitate to answer in the affirmative. Certainly, every principle is hidden within itself, but insofar as it is a princi-ple, it steps outside itself and reveals itself. That is the standpoint of the uni-versal philosophy of the logos. God is unknown, but the Son, who came out of the Godhead's bosom, revealed him to us. His light shines forth in the darkness and overcomes it—within the Son and the sons. Negative theology retains its value in its breaking down of the substantiality of positive attrib-utes and in its view of human knowledge as the product of our intellect. It reminds this intellect that elsewhere in its sentences, it does not directly rep-resent things, but only its conception of things. The *homo divinus*, however, lives in blissful consciousness of living in the truth. He does not search; he has found. Or rather: the truth that he was searching for and that permeates everything has found him. Insofar as he is son, he does not *believe*. Within the son, faith is transformed into knowledge. The believer is not yet son; for it befits the son to see and to know the father; believing is the way to become a son.[5] The believer has heard that he has been given the power to become God's son. But hearing always comes from the outside, from something foreign. Someone who lives justice, however, knows it from the inside, from within himself. We should not forget: what is called "father" here is the principle that speaks essentially; it is the intellect, in which lie the grounds of reason of things.[6] The path may be arduous; every birth is associated with pain, but at the end—though in *this* life—the believer recognizes the blessed transparency of the principle that begets him. The preparatory transformation (*alteratio*) passes, the birth is here.[7] The way contains part of the goal, but nobody should confuse the two. True knowledge happens from within one's own self, and is not initiated by outside sources.[8] Already in this life, within the bright consciousness of truth and reason, Eckhart considers fulfilled the following prayer: "Father, show us the Son, and it will be enough for us." The life of the *homo divinus* is present, not just future. It may surprise us that Eckhart does not think highly of hearsay, of faith and expectation. That is his philosophy: being is not a going-to-be. To grasp the truth means to grasp it here and now. Living means living now. The abundance of time does not refer to some ill-defined future; it is in the present, in the here and now of timelessness (n. 293, 245.8–11).

Eckhart's Philosophy of the Trinity

I have already mentioned Eckhart's philosophy of the Trinity. Eckhart believes: where there is the one, there is also the other, and they are one (n. 137, 116.8–10). When Eckhart mentions the triad of persons in orthodox diction, he adds "and the three are one." The employment of the number concept cannot be the last word on the matter, for God is *one in every way*, and numbers belong to the world of corporeal *continua*, not to the world of the intellectual being (n. 369, 314.1). Even according to Eckhart, there has to be a certain distinction within the Godhead: the begetter is one with the begotten, the Son, but he is not the same. He has the same nature, for otherwise the begotten, who himself begets further, would not be Son. What we have here is formal flow within the identity. The highest Oneness has to be conceptualized as life, as intellectually returning into itself.

Two arguments of Eckhart's Trinitarian philosophy are starting to show here. The first idea is based on the Being that is mind and that returns to itself in knowledge. The model for this philosophical idea is the first sentence of the *Book of the Twenty-Four Philosophers*, which Eckhart quotes as a dictum by Hermes Trismegistus at n. 164, 135.7: the monad has to be conceptualized as begetting and as one with what it begets. If the monad were not theorized as begetting, it would remain wholly unknown by itself. It would be empty for us. Self-disclosure and formal flow would never begin. It would mean conceiving of God as separate from the world and man. Eckhart calls it "killing God." God creates forms by placing beings into himself as Being. He speaks and is accessible to us. Eckhart derives this Christian, Neoplatonic, philosophical conviction by conceiving of God as the first and archetypal ground of the world, which discloses itself without envy, as we can read in Plato's *Timaeus* 29b. Eckhart argues further that such a rhythmical unit—the giving ground, what has come out of it, and the unity of both—can be found in all things, in nature as well as in human productions.[9] This metaphorization of the Trinity via natural and cultural philosophy we have encountered before: everything that functions as the origin for something begets its product as father or uncreated origin. It is a creation, product or son, for it is another being of the nature of the begetter. Eckhart obviously got his idea from acts of begetting in nature or preindustrial productions; he posits an organic model for all forms of coming into existence. He is consistent because he conceptualizes becoming as the disclosure of *forma*, as *emanatio formalis*, as I said above. Within the latter, *producens* and *productum* are the same in essence (nn. 342–43, 290–292.2). Eckhart considers nature in light of the Neoplatonizing theory of ideas and of Aristotle's metaphysics of form. Accordingly, everything that produces something begets something that is different from it as *exemplar*, but that agrees with it in essence, in its nature. Thus, a metaphysics of the Trinity is unavoidable. Eckhart illustrates it also with the example of the architect: he must have seen houses in order to be able to build a house. But in its planned state, the house that he is building is not begotten and not made by the external house; the house of the architect's plan is the origin without origin that produces the final house. Origin without origin, image without image—such expressions are not hopelessly paradoxical; they are forms of Eckhart's understanding of the productive nonbeing of intellectual being. The imagined house shows how the being of thought is the ground of the being of nature: being descends from intellectual being to the being of things.[10] And there exists an affection between the begetter and the begotten, a kind of love, either natural or chosen. The begetter loves what he has begotten; he loves it in itself and within himself as the begetter, and so love emanates from both of them.

Eckhart extends this metaphor further, based on images in the Gospel of John: Father and Son, producer and product, stand in reciprocal relation to each other. They are *correlativa*. It is impossible to conceive of one without the other. Where there is the One, there is also the Other. The produced is like the messenger of the *producens;* it speaks of it and points to it. It discloses itself wholly, as completely as it can.[11]

And here I break off. A study of Eckhart's philosophy of the Trinity is rife with presuppositions. It is derived from Neoplatonic Christian speculation and takes a renewed look at its rich inheritance—from the Gospel of John to Origen and Augustine to John Eriugena. It was inconceivable for

Eckhart that the Trinity could merely be believed. In that case, the Son of the Godhead would hardly know anything about the latter's interior. Eckhart considered his argument a necessity and repeatedly stressed this *necessario*, for example, at n. 556, 486. The question is not whether I can comprehend this metaphysical morphology, but rather whether it was thought through with consistency under Eckhart's given historical premises, and whether it fits within his overall concept. He did not think that he could grasp the procreativeness of Justice, the self-disclosure of Wisdom, and the descent of Being to the beings in a different model. Human blessedness would have seemed impossible to him. And he was probably right. When God is not conceptualized in Plato's terms as a substantial, not merely as an accidental or arbitrary, affection, he loses his meaningful function in a rational, metaphysical construction of the world as a whole.

The Oneness of the Knower and the Known

I have to mention another of Eckhart's philosophical emphases in his commentary on the Gospel of John. It is the unity of the knower and the known. It is the topic of eye-wood and wood-eye. The origin of this theorem is easily detectable: it is the theory of perception in Aristotle's *De anima* (*On the Soul*). In this context, the Islamic thinker Averroës became indispensable for Eckhart, above all for his commentary on Aristotle's work, especially *De anima* III, 2, 425 b 26. Avicenna was an important model for the meaning of being in Eckhart's philosophical theology and for many individual questions; in his philosophical interpretation of the Bible, Eckhart was often guided by Moses Maimonides; but in his description of the oneness of the just man and Justice, Eckhart could not make do without Averroës. I have explained this connection between Eckhart and Averroës in another work; therefore, I do not explore Eckhart's historical sources here and instead focus directly on his argument.[12]

A prefatory remark: after the reception of Aristotle in the thirteenth century, philosophical anthropology became more intellectualistic than before. Although Aristotle's work is often considered an example of a successful synthesis of the human mind and body, Aristotle considered the mind the "actual" human being. Since then, the view that the intellect is the essential, defining feature of man has hardly been challenged. What is the Good for man is determined by his reason.[13] It is what Albertus Magnus wrote; it is what Thomas Aquinas wrote. Eckhart frequently pondered the love that lets the lover become the beloved; he saw support for his position in Augustine and Bernard of Clairvaux, but they also presupposed the intellectual nature of man, a nature of mind, and what the word "mind" meant, one also learned from Aristotle and his commentator. Here we shall stick to Eckhart, who wrote some beautiful sentences about love, for example, that he who truly loves does not waste any thought on the question whether he is loved in return; it is enough for him to love what he loves (n. 559, 487.9–11).

Someone who knows something becomes identical with what he knows, *actu idem* (n. 107, 91.10), on all levels of knowledge, from perception to intellectual understanding. It is a characteristic of the intellectual being, the *esse cognitivum*, the distinctive difference of which Eckhart defined further beginning with the First Parisian Question: in every epistemic faculty, an image of what has been recognized develops; the object begets it within the beholder, and his epistemic faculty becomes an object itself. It is a different being, but it is not something other than the object. Another, but nothing other. These formulas are derived from the theology of the Son. The *verbum*, people said, was of the same essence, but another person. Eckhart transfers this formula onto every act of knowledge and derives another argument for his philosophy of the Trinity from the analysis of the intellectual being. He uses a simple example taken from Averroës: the bathroom in the soul would be identical with the bathroom in the house if the bathroom in the house did not also consist of matter. In the context of immaterial content, they are entirely identical (n. 57, 47.16–48.10). In this analysis, Eckhart is concerned also with the parallel that just as God the Father begets the Son, every knower begets an epistemic image, and the eye births within itself the wood that it sees. Eckhart was very careful to balance activity and receptivity in the context of a simple act of seeing: the epistemic image that we produce is a child of the object, but it is also the child of the seer. Eckhart explains this idea through the activity of the painter or writer: both have to produce an image within themselves of the thing that they want to paint or describe. This image is produced by them, and only by them, but it is an image of the thing, and thus the image is also a product of the worldly thing. The painter or architect produces the new house from this oneness of thought-house or house-thought (n. 57, 47.2–48.10). The epistemic faculty of the senses, here the sense of vision, receives its content from the sensible object. It does not receive it from the living creature that exercises this sense, and even less from any other creature. It receives the same being that the object has. According to Eckhart, that is why Aristotle said that the sense of seeing and the seen are *actu* identical, *actu idem* (n. 107, 91.10). Our sense of vision does not grant to the tree that it is a tree. The tree does not provide the eye with the power to see. They are, physically speaking, two creatures. But as intellectual being, they are one. Within the act of knowledge, the sense of vision becomes seeing, and the tree becomes the seen. It is this identity that is Eckhart's focus. It is possible only on two conditions: the sense of vision must be able to produce images within itself; it must become active analogously to God, who produces the *verbum* within himself. It cannot, however, already contain objects within itself or else it could not perceive the tree. The knower must not already be what he is supposed to become in knowing. The eye must not contain the color within itself that it is supposed to receive. Thus, on all levels of knowing there must always exist a balance, albeit differently registered, between activity and receptivity. Likewise, the intellect initially has to be empty. Eckhart quotes Anaxagoras, who called the intellect "naked" and "unmixed" in order to give a name to this prerequisite of the epistemic identity. Eckhart further quotes Anaxagoras, who supposedly said that the intellect initially had to be empty not in order for it to stay empty or for it to be filled by a superior power, but to be able to judge everything (n. 305, 254.1–5). The stage of potentiality has the determination to actuate itself in letting itself be actuated by the object. We comprehend the unity of the just man and Justice via the unity of what can be seen and the sense of sight, of the epistemic faculty and the object, of the intellect and the intelligible. They are one, and as Eckhart quotes Averroës, they are one in a higher sense than matter and form in the sensible things (n. 505, 435.13–436.13). The becoming one in both knowledge and love can be understood with the help of this model, for the lover becomes the beloved. As Eckhart points out, Averroës explained this idea further: the knower and the known do not become a third; they become one and yet remain the creatures that they are (n. 508, 440.3–10).

Eckhart made sure to analyze activity and receptivity within the knower as equal. Both are essential elements, but of course the nakedness of the epistemic faculty has to be highlighted first. This nakedness, however, is not to remain, and the cognitive faculty receives its content only when it enacts it. It produces an image. That is not merely a passive process. Without question, it is obvious that in the context of knowing and loving, the word "passivity" must mean receptivity. Receiving is an activity, not mere suffering. The focus is on activities of life, not of stones that have to suffer the blows of hammers. It would seem to go without saying, but some specialists apparently have forgotten it; Eckhart was certainly conscious of it.

Not every modern interpreter of Eckhart shares his subtlety in analyzing the receptivity of knowing. Several Eckhart expositors impose a pathos of passivity onto Eckhart, thinking that it will bring greater honor to divine grace if it is perceived as paralyzing the intellectual nature that it created. There even arose a crude tale that Eckhart did not know the concept of the active intellect. Or, in even more rash terms, that according to Eckhart, happiness consists of the soul being deprived of its head—for that is the active intellect. According to what Eckhart actually said, however, grace does not destroy the nature of things; it does not change substantial structures (n. 543, 474.10). In this respect, Eckhart abides by Thomas Aquinas: grace does not devastate, it perfects.

The terminology of *pati* and *passio* is noteworthy. Eckhart says of the divine *verbum* that it "suffers" its creation. Insofar as the Son is created, he "suffers" (n. 582, 509.7). Everything he has, he receives (n. 473, 406.4–5). His passion, however, is not a suffering in the current sense of the word; it is an active, understanding receptivity and happy divine life. Eckhart quotes Averroës: certainly, the human mind is the lowest of all intellectual beings. But Averroës was the last person who would have wanted to deny the mind's activity. Eckhart does not intend it, either. As emphasized before, Eckhart highlights that the passive and lower are actuated and raised up by the higher and active. The lower is transformed and adapted to the higher (n. 155, 128.10–129.3). What is important is active exchange, not a cementing of existing hierarchies. What is "above" in metaphysical terms discloses itself to everything below, according to its nature; all beings are part of the Golden Chain.[14] Within this chain, the lower link has an affinity, its natural proximity, to the next higher. That is why they touch. It is part of the passive's nature that it is restless and pushes toward form (n. 574, 502.7–11). There is a natural correspondence between the above and the below, the active and the receptive. The passive has a disposition for the activity of the active; it is connatural to it, *actus activorum sunt in patiente praedisposito* (n. 368, 313.7, and n. 464, 397.6–7). The phase of *passio* passes; the *alteratio*, which can be painful, ends, and the birth occurs (n. 474, 407.1–7).

Some interpreters of Eckhart have the existentialistic-theological tendency to darken the overall picture of Eckhart. Eckhart's commentary on the Gospel of John in particular contradicts this tendency. These interpreters understate Eckhart's qualification of negative theology and neglect the motifs of friendship and full disclosure. They stress the eternal search and read over Eckhart's own statement that a person *will find* God if he looks for him (n. 507, 439.3–4, and n. 509, 441.4–11). We are active in the same manner that God the Father is active. Eckhart can go so far as to say: we are cofathers with him, *compatres sumus* (n. 573, 500.8). Eckhart does not impose a limit on the human intellect in order to distinguish it from the super-natural. He does not have the same concept of a "supernature" as the neoscholastic theologians. He sees the intellect itself as supernature; our intellect is higher than all nature, *altius natura* (n. 45, 37.13–14), *superius omni natura* (n. 500, 431.6–9); grace is "supernatural" as well (n. 593, 517.4–10). God, however, does not destroy the intellect's image. Both belong on the side of intellectual being. Someone who comprehends its special status will speak of activity and passivity in terms entirely (*omnino*) different from those used in the context of the natural things.

Eckhart and Natural Philosophy

Eckhart's universe is formal flow and exchange of forms; both pertain to nature as well as to the intellectual-spiritual life of humanity. His philosophy of love and of the natural things is easily relegated to the background in expositions of Eckhart's philosophical system, but he himself derived the model of his idea of identity from the unity of the sensible thing and the sense of sight (n. 121, 106.1). We should at least remind ourselves once more of just how much Eckhart's commentary on the Gospel of John is a work of natural philosophy, including the explanations of natural phenomena such as wind and fire. Like others before him, Eckhart wanted to precisely define the difference that exists between the illumination of a stone and its warming (nn. 70–71, 58–60). This type of observation of the natural world led him to a metaphysics of the self-disclosure of Being, the effect of which is like the sunshine: it would be extinguished if Being were not present. Something similar happens in Eckhart's philosophy of love in that it creates a balance between the knowing and the intellectual-affective activity of human souls and leads further to a philosophy of the Trinity: God is the active balancing of knowledge and love. For whatever someone thinks or loves is born within him as an image and becomes a shared product of the object and the act of knowledge (n. 573, 500.8–13).

I cannot leave my discussion of Eckhart's commentary on the Gospel of John without raising the question what exactly within it could have appeared to the pope and his theologians as "devil's seed." The men in Avignon did not concern themselves with Eckhart's most extreme speculations. Even so, they condemned the close relation of the Eckhartian God to the world. They condemned Eckhart's belief that God has the world of ideas eternally present, as though Eckhart was teaching the immortality of the visible world in theses 1–3 (*Acta Echardiana*, LW 5:597–598.28). Article 13 (LW 5:598.52–55) expressly condemns Eckhart's concept of the just man and the *homo divinus*. In Sentence 28 (LW 5:599.92–94), they rejected what Eckhart had preached, namely, that one could call God neither good nor better. This precedence of negative theology was more prevalent in the commentary on Exodus than in his commentary on the Gospel of John. Nonetheless, the basic positions of Eckhart's thought were the same in the commentary on the Gospel of John. In addition, the men in Avignon found fault with Eckhart's more practical views, such as his rejection of the prayer of supplication (nn. 605–14, 528.1–537.9), and his refusal to accept the ethical-religious value of external acts (n. 307, 255.1–3). These formed the basis for theses 7 and 9 (against the prayer of supplication) and thesis 16 of the bull of condemnation (LW V 5:598.34–35, 39–42, 63).

15. A New Christianity for the People: German Sermons, Part 1

The German and the Latin Eckhart

It was a foolish idea to claim that Eckhart's German and Latin texts were in competition with one another.[1] There was of course a certain type of imbalance that occurred between them: his Latin writings were discovered when there were influential interpretations of Eckhart based exclusively on the familiar German texts. When the books that Eckhart had written in the learned language of the Middle Ages finally appeared in print, many a reader discovered that the Latin competency required for reading them came neither easily nor quickly. At times, there was a tendency to protect the precious jewel of the depth of the German soul from foreign infiltration by the Latin world.

Eckhart himself clearly differentiated between sermons and academic arguments; this distinction determined the organization of his work on Ecclesiasticus and it recurs as a motif in the commentary on John (LW 3, n. 226, 189.5–7; n. 605, 527.10–12). The German sermons belonged to a different textual genre and were less bound by the requirement to provide sound proofs, but this difference did not rule out Eckhart, as shown, wanting to demonstrate the Christian truth with philosophical arguments in his vernacular sermons as well. Eckhart speaks more directly, more vividly, more energetically, more poignantly, and more personally in German than in Latin. He personally testifies to the reform of his thinking and publicly practices the reformed living that follows from it—hence, the many self-portrayals in the

German sermons. The idea that Eckhart was able to express his "deepest depth" only in German, his mother tongue, however, was based on ignorance of the development of Latin in the Middle Ages and on nationalistic narrow-mindedness. This view is indefensible in theoretical terms. It was grounded in sentimentality and neoromanticism. Factual evidence goes against it as well: some of Eckhart's contemporaries were demonstrably able to translate Eckhart's difficult German sermons into Latin quite well.

The earlier notion that Eckhart's German sermons were primarily delivered and collected in convents has been disproved. Loris Sturlese was able to show that Eckhart had no special assignment for the *cura monialium* (care of nuns). Nowadays, no one would still explain Eckhart's German sermons through the alleged psychology of his female audience.

Someone who accepts the help that Eckhart's Latin texts can offer is proceeding more securely. To give an example: while the commentary on John is primarily focused on a reform of metaphysics and the consequent reform of Christianity, as well as on a new philosophy of nature, it contains reflections on ethics that make it easier for the reader to understand Eckhart's German sermons. I omitted these from my discussion of the commentary on John in order to briefly summarize them here.

The grounds of reason, Eckhart writes, convince us that the good man, the *homo divinus*, is not an isolated individual but rather exists in a community. Eckhart's theory of sociality presupposes his philosophical theory of wholeness. According to this, every member of the community simultaneously serves itself and others. Everything that Christians do or suffer pertains to all of them. Everything belongs to them in common, *omnibus sanctis aut bonis sunt omnia omnium bona communia* (LW 3, n. 386, 329.6–7). This social aspect lies in the idea of the Good itself: someone who loves the Good loves the good in all others. Someone who wants to have wealth, delight, and honor only for himself does not love the other as he loves himself. Envy is contrary to human nature and to the Christian ethics of love (nn. 385–96, 328–37). Eckhart's ethics operates more in communitarian than in liberalistic terms. It emphasizes the reality of shared human nature; its conception of a living whole eliminates the opposition between self-interest and community.

As in questions of metaphysics, Eckhart prominently positions himself against the prevalent opinions of the time in questions of ethical principles. He specifically discards egoistic constructs of moral behavior and the love for God. He shows that earlier Christian thinkers understood love incorrectly.

He rejects Aquinas's explanation that love for God means that we *depend* on God with our entire being, as Aquinas indeed says (*Sth* I 60, 5 ad 4). Aquinas also included this dependence in his schema of efficient and final causality (*Sth* II–II 27, 3). According to this, sons love their father because he is their efficient cause. God is loved for his own sake because he is the final cause of everything. And Aquinas acknowledges that it counts as love for God if God is loved because of present or expected benefits. If that were the case, Eckhart objects, we would love God only for the sake of the benefit that we derive from him: we would love not God, but ourselves (LW 3, nn. 542–44, 473–75). For Eckhart, the correct justification has to be: God is Being, and as Avicenna emphasizes, everything loves Being. The Islamic thinker teaches us how to understand love for God better than Thomas Aquinas. Eckhart's dissociation could not be greater: he thought that the dominant Christian theologians understood neither the Christian God nor love.

For this reason, Eckhart also rejects the idea that man should act well in order to receive earthly and heavenly rewards. The ethical good is an intrinsic value, not a means to an end. Eckhart brusquely distinguishes the morally good (*honestum*) from the useful and the pleasing by calling on Aristotle and Cicero: *honestum est quod sua vi nos trahit* (LW 3, n. 476, 409.3). He is pointing to the reality of collective nature. He cites Aristotle's idea that on the basis of our common nature there exists no difference between humans; he criticizes the individualism of ownership and praises poverty. Individual commodities cannot make man happy; he must *abandon* all of them in order to have the Good itself (LW 3, nn. 385–96, 328–37). This is connected to Eckhart's theory of the ethical neutrality of external acts (nn. 583–86, 510–13), which John XXII condemned as the sixteenth proposition in his bull.

Questions of Dating

Now, on to Eckhart's German sermons. More than one hundred twenty surviving texts could claim Eckhart as their author, even though their textual form in many cases is not secure. There are too many for me to address them all; I content myself with initially saying something about their general characteristics and then focusing in on the central passages of two selected sermons, 48 and 86. This simplification is defensible because we now possess three volumes of the *Lectura Eckhardi* (1998, 2003, 2008), which provide a good reading aid; I translated and explained sermons 6, 39, and 52 for this series. I also translated and commented on Eckhart's sermon *Von dem edeln menschen* along with his *Book of Divine Consolation* (Munich, 2007, 93–114, 148–52). Louise Gnädinger published forty German sermons in translation with Manesse Press in Zurich; her German is better than that of Josef Quint, which Niklaus Largier retained in unchanged form for the two paperback volumes published by the Deutscher Klassiker Verlag (Frankfurt, 1993).

Research of the past decades has furthered our understanding of Eckhart's German sermons. We have shed the earlier idea that these texts were unreliably transmitted solely through transcripts; today we are certain that Eckhart wrote the majority of them himself, even if none of the manuscripts written in his own hand have survived. This view had always been probable given the difficulty of the sermons' subjects and the subtlety of their argumentation; today it is the scholarly consensus.

Loris Sturlese has debunked the idea that the German sermons had a special connection to nunneries. There is no doubt that Eckhart preached to women in Dominican churches as well as in convents, some of which he named. But the sermons show no detectable linguistic or content-based connection with women or women's issues in the fourteenth century. The veneration of Mary plays a certain role, as it does in his Latin works, for example, in the speeches on Ecclesiasticus; but with Eckhart it has the appearance— as does all veneration of saints—of a temporary transition. The following detail is amusing: Heinrich Denifle was the first to point out Eckhart's connection to nuns, but he was trying to suggest that Eckhart was a second-rate theologian; this motif was later rewritten for Eckhart's greater honor. It suggested an empathetic understandability of difficult texts. Both were wrong.

Joachim Theisen and Loris Sturlese emphasized the *liturgical* frame that the sermons have. Quint had ordered the sermons according to how well they were attested in the trial records. Compared to this, a case can be made for a sequence ordered according to the ecclesiastical year and its saints' days; in a few instances, this liturgical frame even allows us to date the sermons, because we know the day on which the feast of a specific saint fell in a specific year. The result, however, is of interest only if we know the year. Regarding the sermons' content there is little to be gained from this; Eckhart's sermons habitually depart quickly from the occasion of the feast.

The dating of individual sermons remains a difficult problem. There would be nothing more desirable than to arrive at reliable dates and to be able to thereby construct a genesic analysis. It is easy to come up with groups to which individual sermons should be assigned, but these assignments cause difficulties. In addition, the chronological differentiation between Eckhart's time in Strasbourg and Cologne is uncertain. Eckhart was certainly in Strasbourg, but we know neither how long he was there nor in what function. As chronological blocks, Koch and Quint distinguished the following four groups:

1. Sermons in the vicinity of the Talks of Instruction, until about 1298.
2. Sermons with a clear echo of the first Parisian questions, ca. 1304–5.
3. Sermons of the Strasbourg period, approximately 1313–23.
4. Sermons of the Cologne years, approximately 1323–26.

Kurt Ruh toppled this model in 1999 by interpreting the place designation "Cologne" in the manuscripts as a later scribal addition.[2]

The regions of Eckhart's activity differed significantly in their dialects; they still do today. But the location of a sermon cannot be determined by the dialect used in a manuscript, since we do not possess Eckhart's authorial copy and do not know to what extent he or a scribe adapted the text to a region's dialect.

The attribution of a sermon to the second group (Koch and Quint's arrangement) occurred on the basis of its proximity to one of Eckhart's theoretical positions. But they can be interpreted in several ways. Eckhart himself relativized the assertion that God could not be called "Being" by saying that he could be called "Being" if only one were to know that God is what he knows. This position does not provide a secure category for chronologically distinguishing individual sermons. And it is true in general that Eckhart gave himself a great deal of freedom both to affirm and to deny a position with his emphasis on the "insofar." The reader has to find out which "insofar" pertains to a given sentence. For these reasons, it is nearly impossible to infer a sermon's date or region from one of Eckhart's propositions.

All this does not mean that there can be no dating at all; it may simply remain approximate. I agreed above with the proposed dating by Georg Steer for the sermon cycle on eternal birth. But if the text of a sermon names a monastery in Cologne as the location of the sermon, it is still not certain—according to Kurt Ruh's objections—that Eckhart delivered this sermon in Cologne. And moreover, when was it delivered? Koch and Quint said between about 1323 and 1326. Quint assembled this group in DW 1:373ff.; Josef Koch attempted further precision.[3] In this context, it was assumed that

Eckhart had spent an entire decade in Strasbourg, 1313 to 1323. Until Kurt Ruh's objection, sermons 10, 11, 12, 13, 14, 15, 22, 51, and 52 counted as having been given in Cologne, though perhaps before 1323. Scholars have increasingly grown more uncertain. Every chronological or geographic attribution has to be discussed on the basis of the individual sermon. My book is not the place for that, and it may always remain possible to doubt these results. Therefore, I now turn to the characteristic *content* of the German sermons.

Intention to Prove Argumentatively: Biblical Interpretation

The German sermons instruct and call on us; they do not popularize an abstract metaphysics; they show ways of living and say why they are neglected. Eckhart's Latin works provide their background, but they do not say exactly the same thing. The German sermons are freer in their expression; Eckhart more frequently speaks in the first person; he brings in rhetorical embellishments that were certainly possible but less obvious in the regulated Latin language. At times, the German sermons go further in their theoretical positions than the Latin works do. Some of the German sermons stem from Eckhart's last years in Cologne, during which he composed in Latin only those works that served his defense during the trial. Many readers of the German sermons were surprised when they ventured into a reading of the Latin texts. Initially, the works appeared too cold, too formal, too strict, and too scholastic in their diction. They indeed require greater practice and familiarity with the terminology, issues, and writing style around 1300. The danger of being disappointed increases if one begins by reading a less accessible Latin text first; one should begin not with the less well-developed Latin sermons (LW 4), but rather with the commentary on John (LW 3).

Eckhart's German sermons are the most beautiful and personal texts that we have by him. They address the reader directly. They get straight to the heart of his intention. They depict him before his audience: how he struggles to speak comprehensibly and how he begins to speak about himself. They are among the most valuable pieces of medieval German literature, which is not lacking in treasures if we think of the *Nibelungenlied*, of *Tristan and Isolde*, and of Wolfram von Eschenbach.

Eckhart does not present himself as a proponent of the faith; rather, he wants to show that one can know what faith says. That was his method in the eternal birth cycle; and it becomes only more intense here. Coarse people need to believe what Eckhart presents; enlightened people know it.[4] The sermons update the biblical message, but Eckhart quickly moves away from the homiletic theme. He does with it what he wants. Whether the Bible speaks of a house, a city, or a widow, Eckhart always interprets it in this way: it is about the soul. When Paul narrates that he has been to the Third Heaven—this passage, in its literal meaning, was an important model for Dante's journey through heaven—Eckhart explains that this signified a third degree of knowledge (German sermon 61, DW 3:37.1–3; the sermons are henceforth cited by sermon number and DW reference). When there is something crude in the Bible, then he simply has to "open it up," *auff thuon* (51, DW 2:466.5). When a biblical parable recounts the story of a man who bought five yokes of oxen, then these signify our five senses (20a, DW 1:337.5–7). Yet Eckhart can equally say that this refers to crude people, people who are simply oxen (51, DW 2:465.6). Things and statements have many meanings: polysemy. Because of this, a medieval interpreter had a lot of freedom, which biblical philology has since taken away from him; Eckhart exploited that freedom to an extreme degree. He interprets the names of places like Naim (18, DW 1:303.1–304.4), of people like Moses or angels like Gabriel, according to his own needs or ideas. Regarding the word "Peter," many people would certainly expect that a "medieval" person would think of Christ's representative on earth and his key, but Eckhart interprets it philosophically: "Peter," that is, knowledge (3, DW 1:48.7). He corrects the wording of the Lord's Prayer: for *fiat voluntas tua*, the German has "*dîn wille der werde!*" but it would be much better as "*werde wille dîn*" (30, DW 2:99.1–3). One can read this as a mere suggestion for a better translation, but Eckhart allows himself still greater liberties: a biblical phrase that the *Symbolum apostolorum* adopted says that Christ is seated at the right hand of the Father. Eckhart explains this by demythologizing it: *Er ensitʒet niergen*—he sits nowhere (35, DW 2:179.5). He wants to conceptualize Christ as logos, not as a fixed bodily creature. Eckhart allows himself the freedom to simply reverse the logical progression of main clauses and subordinate clauses in the Bible: *Nû keren wir das wort umbe* (3, DW 1, 48.6). Scripture, he thought, is a sea of truth; everything one gathers from it is true.

The individual argumentative stunts are not what matters here. No civilization can make a single text into its binding foundation of life if it interprets the text literally, in the exact philological sense of the word. It has to develop "interpretations"; it is the only way to keep the text flexible and usable. In light of this general premise of medieval biblical exegesis, Eckhart was able to unfurl his own art of interpretation. There was no other way for him to develop his new philosophy of Christianity. This philosophy names the conditions of life and thought necessary for understanding the Bible. It is not a specialized science, but is concerned rather with understanding and proper living: someone who has not let go of everything will never be able to understand Jesus (12, DW 1:193.5–7); why one needs to let go of everything and why this letting go does not signify a loss—that is explained by Eckhart's philosophy of Christianity. In the sermons, he introduces his philosophy metaphorically, and metaphors make up the brilliance of his prose. Yet they must not lead to a renewed dominance of the imagination over intellectual knowledge. Eckhart attracts with these metaphors—he calls knowledge a "key" (3, DW 1:52.9–12). He says that whoever conceives of God as "Being" knows him only in his "antechamber" (9, DW 1:150.1)—yet another image, but the reader or listener must overcome all images through theoretical work. At times, Eckhart piles up images to make their relativity visible and palpable, for example, in the case of the soul (for example, 17, DW 1:283.4–284.6), but also of the birth of God and the spark of the soul. These are all images of the imagination. At the beginning they are indispensable, but as beautiful as they may be, they need to be dissolved. When Eckhart says, for example, that the Good has three branches, he is describing the tenets of the first chapters of Aristotle's *Nicomachean Ethics* with an image. Eckhart explicitly asks for parables to be destroyed: to get at their core, their shells need to be cracked. We must try to grasp the bare nature of things (51, DW 2:473.5–6). Eckhart's sermons do not lull us to sleep; they challenge us to think and live correctly. Both presuppose, in the manner of the Aristotelian intellect, a thorough removal of the given and the imaginable: Eckhart once compared his sermon to spicy nutmegs, since one would need to drink something after biting one (26, DW 2:32.6–33.1). The sermons initially disturb the familiar, and it is necessary to make an effort to understand them. They demand a lifestyle in which people break with all self-reference; love God without any thought of benefit, insight, or consolation; and thus turn toward all people so that the suffering of the most distant people beyond the oceans becomes as significant to me as my own or that of a friend. This seems like basic, traditional Christian ethics, but Eckhart preached because he knew that around 1300 it required multiple breaks. It called for a break:

- with the exchange and business mentality developed in the money economy and urban culture of the thirteenth century, in which people gave something in order to receive something in return.
- with the monastic subspecies of this mercantile mentality, which offered fasts and prayers, "works," in short, to God in order to receive rewards in the heavenly kingdom. Eckhart diagnosed their irreligious crudeness above all in the ecclesiastically sanctioned custom of supplicatory prayers.
- with the practical *and* theoretical patterns of thought of this mercantile outlook. Eckhart's philosophy of Christianity included the insight that the mercantile disposition was associated with the misrecognition of truth (1, DW 1:8.5–9.2). Eckhart wanted to show this argumentatively in the new age of more widespread rationality. He rejected self-reference, which he called "*eigenschaft.*" In theoretical terms, he destroyed the traditional imagining thinking, which he said "some" had, namely, the opinion that they were *here* and God was *there* (6, DW 1:134.6–7).

The sermons criticize the theology of the time, not just the wrong kinds of living. They correct the dominance of the imagination of stable, ontologically autonomous things, which hinders man from understanding himself and God and from grasping that his "neighbor" lives beyond the ocean, too. This wreath of theoretical problems intervened in everyday life. That is why Eckhart also dealt with these issues in the German sermons.

But Eckhart does find fault with incorrect ways of life, along with their theoretical presuppositions. He criticizes great scholastic theologians without naming them (as was common) in his vernacular sermons. Famous clerics stumble, he writes, when they have to tell people who they are as humans. They do not understand the nature of the mind-soul: it is a desert and nameless, and it has nothing in common with anything else (28, DW 2:66.5). They misconstrue the temporal preeminence of the mind (5b, DW 1:94.8–95.3). "Some clerics" do not know that there is something in the human soul that stands above man (29, DW 2:88.3–10). Jesus says that he is disclosing *all* truth to us (John 15:15), but theologians, Eckhart criticizes, weaken Jesus's statement by claiming that he only revealed to us what we need on our way to salvation. Cost-benefit calculations occur here as well. No, Eckhart says, Jesus revealed everything to us that he heard from his Father (29, DW 2:83.1–8). The clerics wrongly outline the ground for our love for God by basing it on self-love. These teachers of Christianity do not understand the concept of love for God and one's neighbor. And there are many learned people who do not comprehend it (30, DW 2:102.8). Eckhart paints a pathetic picture of contemporary theology in his German sermons: many great clerics understand neither God nor man. They do not grasp the essential point of Christianity: love for God and for all humans. They do not see the connection between the creation of the world and the birth of God in man. For everything that God does is aimed at his birth within man. That is why the Bible was written. It is why God created the world, the angels, and all of nature—so that God would be born in the soul, and the soul, in turn, in God (38, DW 2:227.6–228.5). Eckhart wanted a complete metaphysical explanation: the birth of God in man as the purpose of the world. Such a position contains philosophical premises. They are mentioned explicitly in the sermons.

Eckhart continues his thoughts on the primary determinations—Being, Oneness, Truth, Goodness. He explains that Being takes precedence in this series (3, DW 1:56.1–8; 8, DW 1:130.5–132.10): wood that exists is better than gold without Being (8, DW 1:134.8–10). Under the condition of the primacy of Being, the primary determinations have an inner connection. Regarding their reciprocity, Eckhart expresses himself in such a way that Oneness almost takes over this primacy (21, DW 1:368.5–370.4). In any case, Oneness is the second-most important determination, before Truth and Goodness. Thus, the most important name of God is "Being," though always linked with Oneness, Truth, and Goodness (1:361.6–362.4).[5] God is Being, and Being is "God's ring" (8, DW 1:130.7). Only God can grant Being, and this fact precludes creatures from being able to provide Being. Therefore, there is no intermediated creation, contrary to what Avicenna thought (1:130.9–131.4). Eckhart, however, certainly surprises his readers when he speaks with apparent regard about a great master who knew how to teach mediated creation while preserving the concept of a God who alone grants Being (18, DW 1:300.3–301.5). Allah is at rest. He lets his attendants do the work, and he is the Lord for precisely this reason. Latin sermon 36 treats the same theme without distancing itself from this great master and even names him: it is Avicenna (*Metaphysics* IX 4).[6] German sermon 18 is a later text; Joachim Theisen dates it to March 6, 1326.[7] There, it seems as though Eckhart shifted his position, but because I am unable to date 18, I will refrain from offering hypotheses about this development. The divergence is certainly in need of explanation.

God is Being. Is God Being? In German sermon 9, Eckhart, following the *Book of the Twenty-Four Philosophers*, teaches that God stands high above being (9, DW 1:142.5–143.4, 145.4–146); only crude masters teach that God is pure being (145.7–8). He ends, however, by remarking that he has not thereby contested God's Being but heightened it (146.1–6). This seeming paradox becomes less troubling for someone who has understood that "Being" flows out of knowing, even when Eckhart pushes negative theology to the point that God is neither Oneness nor Goodness (153.4–5). It depends on the "insofar" with which one regards the question. For Eckhart, the aspect of intellectual knowing and of the primacy of negative theology certainly remains the higher one. Someone who thinks of God primarily as Being sees him only in his antechamber.

I have become entangled with Eckhart in "scholastic" discussions. The German sermons gave him the occasion to say directly what his God was. I offer a few of his turns of phrases: people who make God into a means to an end, who use him like a candle in order to search for something for themselves, will not find him (4, DW 1:69.1–3). The humble man compels God so that God *must* give himself according to his nature, and indeed must give himself *wholly,* for he is indivisible (71.6–8). God *must:* that is the message. His grace is not a random selection of blessed individuals out of a mass of sinners. God *must;* this motif recurs again and again, not in the sense of an external compulsion, but rather from his nature, which he follows freely. Thus, he gives me everything that he gave Jesus, without exception; he gives the soul the power to birth; and thus it births itself and all things (49, DW 2:436.10–438.2). He is love, and thus it is more necessary for him than for me to give everything. God as love makes the human soul crazy about God himself and makes it rage; he makes it so that it loses all sense because of love; it becomes *unsinnig und tobic* (60, DW 3:13.2). God pursues us; he drives us and lets himself be caught—that is his delight (42, DW 2:301.5–8). But he can also die in the soul; humans can kill him.

In addition, Eckhart offers additional extreme expressions: God and the soul can be conceptualized only as reciprocal, correlative. In our thinking, we can separate sunshine and sun, but we cannot understand God without the soul (59, DW 2:631.8–632.2). Our mind breaks through all multiplicity and numbers, and it must also break through God in order to come into the desert of his quiet Oneness (29, DW 2:76.2–77.1). What was above shows itself within (14, DW 1:237:8–9). God is de-heightened, not in himself but in us; man is elevated. The soul does not want to tolerate an instance higher than itself. It simply cannot bear it (32, DW 2:143.1–7). God is in me, I am in God,

I am not lower than he is (27, DW 2:49.2–50.5). The earthly model for the experience of the oneness of the soul and God is the color in the eye (12, DW 1:201.1–8) or the Aristotelian example: wood-eye. It signifies God's complete oneness with the Son. When it is said that no one knows the Father except the Son, then we are included in this unity, for we know the Father (3, DW 1:49.3–4). The soul has two functions: insofar as it moves the body, it is dependent on externals in several ways, but as the ground of the soul, it is one with God, and it is one to such an extent that it separates all additional properties from God (21, DW 1:361.2–5). If God is called a "hidden God," it is because he is hidden in the ground of the soul (15, DW 1:253.5–6). The soul also has to surpass itself; it needs to separate everything from itself: its life, its powers, its nature—all of them must go (44, DW 2:343.8–344.3). Not as though it were destroyed—it destroys itself. The soul dares to be extinguished, and God becomes its ontological support, its sub-stance (1, DW 1:14.2–8). It is neither weakened nor destroyed, but rather born anew in God, and it births the one who has birthed it (22, DW 1:382.9–383.10). Its humility gives God his divinity (14, DW 1:240.9–10).

Someone who speaks of God but does not talk about his oneness with the ground of the soul is not speaking of the true God. The ground of the soul has nothing in common with anything; it is not like anything else and is thus like God (6, DW 1:107.5–6). In this unity, I am positioned above God, *insofar* as we conceive of God as the origin of all creatures. Man must free himself of God if there still exists a difference between God and man (52, DW 2:502.5–9). Because they do not know this, great theologians have difficulties understanding Paul, who wanted to be separate from God for God's sake (59, DW 2:628.8–629.6). Eckhart assesses the apostle's desire as perfection. It was another blow against Aquinas, who had taught that this remark by Paul referred to the period when the latter was an "unbeliever," *in statu infidelitatis* (*Sth* II–II 27, 8 ad 1). Aquinas spoke in this way about pious Jews; to him, they were in a state of infidelity.

All this had consequences for Eckhart's theory of the Trinity. The ground of unity of the intellectual soul searches for the pure One, the only thing with which it is contented (15, DW 1:251.15). Eckhart again attacks unnamed theologians who talk about the three persons and forget that the three are one. Some clerics, he writes, understand the "three" as though they were dealing with three cows. But even if there were hundreds of persons in God, they would all be one (38, DW 2, 234.4–5). The number three is a preliminary, quasi-metaphorical determination. The mind penetrates it and comprehends a "number without number." The mind is a power in the soul—not a proper ability, but rather a creature, a being that has the peculiarity of detaching from being. It is the thought-being of such concentration and unity that no being can penetrate it. Only God lives in it, but even God cannot go in if he partakes of a particular manner, that is, if he is more closely determined. He enters the soul not with anything that has been added to the pure being of unity, but alone, with his bare divine nature (42, DW 2:307.6–308.7).

The philosophical interpretation of the wood-eye unity of God and the ground of the soul diminishes the Trinitarian formulas of the early Christian church councils. Aquinas had demanded a real distinction between the divine persons in the Trinity and had denied natural reason the ability to arrive at this knowledge (*Sth* I 32, 2). Eckhart disagrees with him, even in the German sermons, by reconsidering distinctness and teaches instead: oneness *is* the difference, and the difference is the oneness. The more difference there is, the more unity there is, but regarding the Trinity it is a difference without difference (10, DW 1:173:3–5). Aquinas required that the difference be *as* difference, Eckhart that difference be *without* difference. To conceive of this is a question not of obedience to faith, but of philosophical expertise. As in the context of his justification for the commandment of love, it becomes apparent here what philosophy of Christianity means for Eckhart. It signified the end of a specific type of Trinitarian doctrine and a false rationale behind the commandment of love. Even Pope John XXII agreed, disregarding those of Eckhart's theses (23 and 24) that denied any *distinctio* in God (LW 5:599.75–82). It is not a coincidence that the key word here is also "distinction." But Eckhart's philosophy of *distinctio* was not the end of every type of doctrine of the Trinity. Eckhart explains what "difference without difference" means: the Father comprehends himself. The eternal Word proceeds from him, yet always remains in him, and out of both flows the Holy Spirit, also remaining inside (15, DW 1:252.1–7). The begotten is not the begetter, and insofar as that is true, there exists a distinction. But the begotten returns and knowingly and lovingly abolishes the difference. The highest unity is reflection; it returns into itself. *It has the you in the I*, not separated materially but as intellectual being and belovedness, like the color in the eye. The Godhead is flow of forms. It is Being that has support in itself for everything, and at the same time is a grace that melts out and discloses itself to all creatures. Being is the Father, Oneness is the Son with the Father, Goodness is the Holy Spirit (18, DW 1:301.6–302.9).

Eckhart connects this motif to his determination of the relationship between knowledge and the will. Even in the vernacular sermons, Eckhart's treatment of theoretical terms moves far beyond the quarrels between the Dominicans and the Franciscans. He is concerned with a certain rehabilitation of love and will: these are of equal essentialness in their oneness with knowledge. At one point he also calls love the highest power of the soul.

He sharply accentuates the difference between the ground and the powers of the soul, but he speaks differently about it, depending on the "insofar" of the particular observation (7, DW 1:123.6–124.2; 10, DW 1:162.7–163.5; 11, DW 1:177.6–8; 16b, DW 1:274.9–275.11; and elsewhere). It needs to be comprehended in the same terms as the difference between the Godhead as Being and as being-above, and is not suitable for genesic hypotheses. Knowledge, in good Aristotelian fashion, certainly is the greatest joy (3, DW 1:51.4–7). Knowledge is better than the will, for it detaches; it elevates itself from the individual thing to the universal, and it separates God from the determinations added to him, even from Oneness and Goodness, whereas love searches for God in "the clothing" of Goodness. Truth and Goodness are two of God's gowns, but reason searches for him in his nakedness.[8] "But two are better than one, and knowing carries love within itself" (19, DW 1:314.7–8). The will is free; that is its advantage over knowledge; knowledge is dependent on its content and on sensory experience in man. This explains Eckhart's discarding of the theory of the primacy of the will (36a, DW 2:191.5–12). Knowledge precedes the will and acquaints it with that which the will loves (45, DW 2:363.8–364.4). Reason is the head of the soul (45, DW 2:370.11–371.9). Eckhart, motivated by Augustine's *De Trinitate*, always thinks of the ground of the soul also as the origin of the will or love.

Two philosophical motifs are decisive in the German sermons: first, the theory of God's being, which is posited by his knowing and which Eckhart interprets as the return of the reflection to itself; second, the metaphysics of the ground of the soul, which Eckhart establishes with the Aristotelian theory of the unity of the knower and the known. The debate over whether Eckhart believed that the ground of the soul was created has no special meaning: as the head of the soul, it was created with the soul, but insofar as it is one with God, like the eye with the color, it is God himself in God. This understanding is not restricted to a specific period of Eckhart's work, and so it is not suitable for genesic hypotheses. The debate has governed research on Eckhart for a long time; it does not deserve to be pursued further, just like the discussions about whether Eckhart was a pantheist, panentheist, or theist. These categories are too crude for Eckhart's thought; we have to describe it in its argumentative structure and judge it according to the intellectual conditions around 1300. In doing this, we need to pay attention to terminological presuppositions. Thomas Aquinas and Dietrich of Freiberg explicitly related an expression like "the highest in the soul" to the *intellectus agens;* Dietrich understood it as the substantial and active ground of the soul.[9] It was a lasting Aristotelian inheritance, whereas Eckhart's spark of the soul carries the archetypes of all things, which are the principles of all individual things. To this extent, Eckhart's thinking integrates a Neoplatonic Augustinian philosophy.

Sermons and University Learning

Eckhart was probably aware of the difference between university learning and public speeches, but he wanted to carry over as much as he could of university learning into his German sermons (16b, DW 1:270.6–8). Over and over, he reports which questions are discussed in the "schools." He thereby enmeshes himself and his interpreters in subtleties that may seem strange to the modern reader. Then the question arises of what is *essential* in all these sermons. The question is asked schematically and deserves a schematic answer: first, a concept of reality substantiated by mental reality is essential; second, Eckhart's sermons as a doctrine of life or ethics is essential. These touch upon each other. For Eckhart teaches that we should let go of bodily things and thus not tie our way of life to them; rather, we should take up those things in the ways that they are eternal, as ideas and contents of the logos (16b, DW 1:264.2–3). For Eckhart, this conversion is essential, this break from the dependency on the visible world. Eckhart does not make it go away; he instructs us to grasp and affirm it in its lasting structures. This is a call to reform life as well as knowledge.

We shall remain for another moment with this change in our mode of thinking: in its theoretical terms, it initially means comprehending the peculiar mode of intellectual processes in their distinctness from the world of things. Eckhart prominently sketches out the contours of this distinctness: the bodily things lie apart, whereas intellectual realities inform one another and exist within one another without eliminating one another. They are not in competition (16a, DW 1:258.5–6). They are not rigid, but quietly flow. They are the coincidence of calmness and movement, as expressed in the Aristotelian formulation of the unmoved mover and especially as explained by Boethius. They form phenomena of coincidence; for example, they return to themselves at the same time as they come out of themselves (53, DW 2:530.1–6). Therefore, God's exit is his entrance, and the more all creatures endowed with reason come out of themselves, the more they go back into themselves in their works. It is their nature to abolish the difference between inside and outside in their effecting. These types of Eckhart's considerations at once form a philosophical theory of God, a theory of the intellect, a philosophy of nature, and an ethics; they condense his philosophy of Christianity into a few sentences. Eckhart simultaneously profiled the ethical consequences of his thinking: "you often ask how you should live." In Sermon 16b (DW 1, 271.1–273.6), Eckhart answers: you should live like an image that is wholly determined by its object—indeed, that is identical with it. And so you should not be from within yourself and you should not be by yourself. You should belong to nobody. You should be objective, like an image. Eckhart narrates a personal story. Yesterday when coming to the monastery, he saw sage and fresh herbs growing on a grave. Someone who loves someone loves everything that belongs to that person; he even decorates his grave. A dog loves everything that belongs to his master and hates everything that is abhorrent to him. And so we should be wholly withdrawn from the sensible things. As long as there is still something creeping into the image of the eternal Word that is you and that is not the eternal Word, you are living wrongly. Only that man is a just man who has destroyed all created things for himself and consequently has only the eternal Word in mind: he is more and more formed into, and formed anew in, Justice. Such a man receives what the Son receives; he himself is the Son. According to Eckhart, when Jesus says, "No one knows the Father except the Son" (Matthew 11:27), then you must not only be like the Son. No. *You must be the Son yourself.*

This is the short version of Eckhart's ethical conception. The correct life begins with letting go of one's love of the self. Someone who has let go of it has let go of the whole world; he stands opposite to it. The divestment of all things is the condition for unification and salvation. Eckhart's ethics states how love has to be: as love for God, it breaks with the custom, institutionalized in the ecclesiastical prayer of supplication, of treating God as a means to one's end. For whoever uses God as a means is shoving him under a bench (5a, DW 1:82.10). Detached from the "I," from time, and from number, God's love loves man as man. It treats every man as a member of humanity and thus realizes a philosophical universalism, that is, the real commonality of the shared essence of a species; it loves all men equally because it loves the humanity within them (5a, DW 1:79.4–8; 12, DW 1:195.1–13).

This is Eckhart's simple concept of the proper life. It breaks with the property-based individualism of the urban bourgeoisie as with the monastic justification by works. It radicalizes the message of the propertyless Jesus and the impoverished Francis of Assisi: it is as plain as it is radical. Eckhart surprises us only through the implantation of Stoic ideals into this program. Man, he says stoically, should live unvaryingly (6, DW 1:104.2–7). He should be as though dead; neither joy nor suffering should affect him (8, DW 1:135.4–5).

16. Spicy Nutmegs: German Sermons, Part 2

Theory of the Incarnation

Meister Eckhart's sermons were not acts of lulling contemplation—they were provocations. That is what he must mean when he compares them to nutmegs, into which one cannot bite without washing them down with water. At times, however, our preacher also tells little anecdotes. Granted, he never acted like many of the preachers in Florence who, according to Dante and Boccaccio, reveled in fantastical legends of saints or kept their audiences' interest with interspersed little jokes. Legends of saints also appear in Eckhart's sermons, for example, when he preaches about St. Elizabeth of Hungary, and he also tells little historical stories: he knows of a man who, out of love for his blind wife, cut out one of his eyes (German sermon 22, DW 1:377.4–379.4; citations to the sermons henceforth are by sermon number and DW reference). He chats about his inner life: "As I was on the way here, I was thinking about whether man can compel God" (22, DW 1:385.4–16). He uses humor to characterize people who do not reach the pure form of God's love: they make it across the lake even with half a sail (12, DW 1:195.9). Or he narrates how a farmer had a hedgehog and thereby became rich. For he observed that his hedgehog was sensitive to the weather and could tell when the wind was turning. When this happened, the hedgehog would bristle its quills and turn its back to the direction of the wind. The farmer was thus able to predict the weather; he went to the nearby ocean, sold his knowledge of the wind's directions to the sailors, and became rich.

In the same way, man could become rich in virtues if he paid attention to his errors (32, DW 2:139–40).

Eckhart was rarely this casual. From the outset, he announced that he would argue philosophically in his sermons, and so he did. As a philosopher of Christianity, he presented a new interpretation of Christianity; in this context, he had a host of questions to tackle. After all, he was *not* interested in showing that God's Incarnation had taken place once upon a time, but rather that it was the purpose of all worldly processes as an enduring present (12, DW 1:194.1–2). To do this, Eckhart had to prove the following points by arguing before his audience:

• the human soul can surpass the highest angels (1, DW 1:13.3–7)
• the soul is the world of reason, the *mundus intelligibilis*[1]
• the characteristic otherness of intellectual processes. Intellectual being is being of a higher kind. Grasping it requires a reform of philosophical thought and a constant correcting of images of the imagination and traditional habits of thought.
• the theory of creation and the theory of the Incarnation
• an outline of his philosophy of the Trinity
• the purpose of man's life, including a sketch of the theory of salvation
• the sort of knowledge that he was presenting
• the specific roles of positive and negative theology

Eckhart did all of this in his sermons; I will trace only one of these threads, namely, his philosophy of God's Incarnation. Each of God's births is an Incarnation of God, but Eckhart also needed to explain the significance of God's Incarnation in Jesus.

As I remarked in connection with his ethics, Eckhart argued rigorously for the realism of universals. That meant: he viewed the universals as the real, fundamental determinants of individual things, not as retroactive abstractions. Therefore, we should love *all* people, not just ourselves and our friends. For the real principle of humans is humanity; it is the decisively important concept to be sought after. On the basis of this philosophical position, to which some of his contemporaries objected, Eckhart said that his God was the most universal (9, DW 1:149.5). Under this precondition, he thought about the Incarnation and concluded: God embraced humanity per se, not just a single human being. This premise changes everything that has been said about the events of the New Testament: the Incarnation of God becomes a supratemporal reality; it becomes communication with humanity as a whole; it provides every person with the possibility to be the *homo divinus* permanently; it becomes another expression of man's dignity. It inspires the self-birth of the soul, its going out and its return; this occurs in the natural light of the soul (43, DW 2:328.7). Considering his philosophical realism of universals, Eckhart relates the Incarnation of God to all humanity. He polemicizes against the conventional understanding: people, he says, falsely believe that God became a man only *there*, in Bethlehem. But he becomes man just as much *here* (30, DW 2:94.1–97.3). When Johannes Wenck criticized Nicholas of Cusa's work *De docta ignorantia*, he accused him of universalizing the Incarnation, of taking away its character as a one-time historical event.[2] I would not know what to say against Wenck's objection. I simply maintain that these ideas represent an actual philosophy of the Incarnation on the basis of a realistic option within the quarrel about the universals. This philosophy of Christianity *changes* what it interprets. This was nothing new. Paul, Origen, Augustine, Anselm, and Abelard had also transferred the content of popular belief into their overall concepts and thereby changed them. Even if it was a contested method, it was still possible in their time.

Intellectual Being as Key

I do not want to stray too far from Eckhart's sermons. They are full of speculative ideas, polemical invective, and witty images. As when he proclaims: "The only thing that makes me happy is that God is reason" (9, DW 1:153.11). Or when he polemicizes: A man who understands nothing of inner intellectual processes will never grasp what God is. He is like a man who has wine in his cellar, but has never drunk any of it (10, DW 1:164.5–14). Since it seems more sensible to me to present individual texts and explain them rather than to add to the number of general characteristics, I have selected the central passages from two of the German sermons, 48 and 86.[3]

I have referred to sermon 48 before because Eckhart therein describes his purpose and explains the wood-eye model. I now provide several larger segments of it in my own translation (the Middle High German original can be found in the notes). They are followed by short commentaries.

German Sermon 48 (DW 2:416.1–417.1)

While I was on the way here today, I was thinking about how I might preach so reasonably that you would understand me correctly. And so I came up with a comparison, and if you understand it correctly, then you will understand my intention and the basis of all the views that I have always preached. This was the comparison of my eye and the piece of wood. When my eye is opened, it is an eye. When it is closed, it is still the same eye. The piece of wood loses and gains nothing from my seeing. Now, pay close attention to my words: if it were to happen that my eye is one and unified in itself, and it is opened and casts a glance at the wood, both eye and wood remain what they are, and yet in active contemplation become one to such an extent that one can truly say: "eye-wood" and "the wood is my eye." Now if that wood were without matter and as close to the intellect as the seeing of my eye, then one could truly say that the wood and my eye consist of a single being in the act of seeing. If that is already true for bodily things, how much more does it hold for intellectual things.[4]

Eckhart differentiates the reifying contemplation of the world from his own new way of thinking, which needs to be learned. In the mode of thinking that is guided by concrete things, the wood is something different from the eye. This type of observation, which is calibrated on facts, on isolated individual things, divides the unified experiences of our life; it insists on the ontological autonomy of eye and wood. Its point of view is not wrong, but it is the result of a mental operation performed by us that has severed the cohesion of life and divided it into fixed points. The simplest perception, like my seeing wood, shows the contractedness of this way of thinking: it separates that which is connected in everyday life. It is true: wood remains wood, even when I have seen it. Because of its materiality, it cannot completely enter into my eye. Strictly speaking, nothing of its material goes into the eye at all. As a thing, the wood stays where it is. Hence, the enduring justification for a substantialist philosophy. Eckhart shows, or rather insinuates, that such a philosophy cannot invoke Aristotle; his book *On the Soul (De anima* III 2, 425 b 26–27) describes the oneness of seeing and the seen, of wood and eye as a process of identification: the eye becomes the wood, the soul becomes that in which it places its life's goal. And so it becomes Justice. The soul exists more in Justice than in the human body.

Human life fulfills itself as though it were externalized. It is always already with something else. One could call this the transitory or ek-static nature of human existence. Someone who recognizes this engages in philosophical contemplation regarding the sensory perception of a piece of wood. It cannot be found in the Bible. But why does Eckhart include instructions for becoming aware of one's self in his sermon? Why does it constitute, as he said, the ground of all his ideas? Because he was not only concerned with explaining a series of his basic concepts and saying what the ground of the soul was. Eckhart worked hard on his explanations of concepts, but as will become clear, he wanted more. For him, it was about reforming one's way of life and thinking. When Eckhart refers to "thinking," he argues that we should resist the urge to think analytically, and thereby intellectually enter into the flowing life in which we always already are and about which the reifying composition of life deceives us. Correcting this conception through thinking would make it possible to understand what Christianity is in the first place. For the reifying way of thinking has already grasped everything; it has already determined everything—our self-perception, God, and love—in a pseudorational manner of dividing everything into small crumbs. Eckhart's way of thinking gives us a way out of these established determinations. It changes everything that previously was. Even in places where Eckhart does not omit a single letter or where he speaks in conventional language— because he hardly uses any other—everything is transformed. This type of transformation in one's thinking, lived radically and thought through coherently, is what I am calling Eckhart's philosophy of Christianity. His reform of our ways of thinking has nothing to do with the cobbling together of concepts, which is what the unexperienced and the learned asses have in mind when they hear the word "philosophy," from which they then—with some justification—want to protect their experiences, their feelings, and their religion. Reflecting on the simple act of perception helps push back against this: eye-wood. Now we shall return to Eckhart himself.

German Sermon 48 (DW 2:418.1–11)

On occasion I have spoken about a light that is in the soul. This light
is uncreated and uncreatable. I constantly touch upon this light in
my sermons. This light receives God without anything between him
and itself, without cover, naked, as he is by himself. It is a taking
within the reality of the birthing-into. I can therefore say in truth:

this light has more unity with God than it does with any faculty of the soul, with which it nevertheless is one in Being. For you must know: in the being of my soul, this light is not any nobler than the lowest or crudest faculty of the soul, like hearing or sight or some other power that is susceptible to hunger or thirst, cold or heat. And that is because Being is unified. If one considers the faculties of the soul, insofar as they are in Being, then they are all one and equally noble; if one considers the faculties of the soul in their activity, however, then one of them is much nobler and higher than the others.[5]

I interrupt Eckhart's dense text here with a short explanation. Eckhart says that he is concerned with the light in the soul *in all of his sermons*. This light—let us say, a simple, true knowledge—is de facto uncreated, and more: it is uncreatable in its essence. Let us suppose that a man says something true. Then Truth is in him, and there is no point in thinking that the truth that is in him was created. For who could create truth if he was outside of Truth? Is the untrue supposed to create Truth, perhaps?

Truth here is as little a property of sentences as justice is a merely psychological peculiarity, a property of persons. If Truth is uncreated and uncreatable by nature, then, like Justice, it fulfills the term "God." In that case, Truth is not supposed to be conceptualized as dependent on things, not as a something in the soul, not as a property of sentences or the substance of the soul. It is not something along the lines of "integrity" or "sincerity of one's disposition." Eckhart thinks differently. Reason steps into the light of Truth, into the light of reason, and is at home therein. Reason is in relation to Truth as soon as it is alert. Outside this relation, reason is not reason. Just as the eye, when it is opened, becomes wood and other things, so in every insight is created: Reason-Truth. Someone who grasps this spares himself the endless reifying discussions about the uncreatedness or createdness of the spark of the soul. The reason in Truth is inconceivable in a reified creationism that intends to keep eye and wood separate. In Latin, the saying is *Sapientia, ut sapientia, non habet rationem creabilis*. I will explain this later.

Eckhart insists: it depends on how one thinkingly comprehends reality. One does not learn the correct understanding of the world from the Bible; one must have developed this understanding in order not to read the Bible mindlessly. In this part of the sermon, Eckhart teaches his audience to understand the difference between the philosophy of Being and thinking about active reason: if I think of my eye ontologically, in its "real" unity with my body, then it is here and the wood is there. If, however, I think of it in its living operation, then I see: fixating on the location of my body leads thinking astray. It prevents me from comprehending what I am experiencing in my own body. I have to change my thinking and my life. Then I will grasp that the seeing eye in my body has more in common with the seeing eye of another body than with my hearing, with which it forms a consolidated state of being. It is the nature of things to seem like states of being existing by themselves; in actual experience, they appear as thought, as sought or repelled, as wanted, as gathered into the contexts of experience. Eckhart is not saying that our reason has been bewitched by this reifying tendency. We have simply been trained one-sidedly and taught falsely, and this education fits with a way of life that understands itself as self-assertion. Thus, reason was interpreted for centuries as a "faculty of the soul," something akin to the eye but rooted in the substance of the soul. "Reason" needs to be conceptualized differently from a "power." It is by no means a sort of mental hand that grasps something and thereby comprehends it. As Niklaus Wicki shows in his *Die Philosophie Philipps des Kanzlers* (Fribourg, 2005), the relationship between soul, reason, and "powers" was a contested topic in medieval philosophy because careful readers of Augustine recognized that he had thought of reason and love not primarily as faculties of the soul, but rather as the *one* substance of the soul that reciprocally permeated itself, the likeness of the triune God.

With his dynamism, Eckhart corrects this ontologically fixating way of thinking. He does not want to abolish it. He teaches us to see through it as a habitual belief and a philosophy of the schools that was in need of correction. Without it there would be no point in speaking about the light of reason and the Godhead. Only then must we grasp the following: the light of reason, which turns toward it, lives more in the Godhead, which equals Truth, which equals Justice, than it does in a human body.

Eckhart's thoughts are rushing in this passage. He describes the light of reason as a radical desire for unity. It cannot be stopped by anything in God that looks like plurality, partition, or an externally related property. It accepts God without clothes, naked, without additional determinations, in his absolute simplicity. Here the word "simple" does not have the same meaning that it does in our everyday language. It signifies concentratedness, all-encompassing presence in itself, perfect self-awareness. Now back to German sermon 48.

German Sermon 48 (DW 2:419.1–421.3)

For that reason I say: if man turns away from himself and from all created things—if you do that, then you will be unified and made blissful in the spark of the soul, which neither time nor space ever affect. This spark negates all creatures and wants nothing other than God in his nakedness, as he is by himself. It finds nothing with which it is content—neither the Father nor the Son nor the Holy Spirit nor the three persons together insofar as each exists by itself. I claim in truth: even the unity of the divine nature's procreativeness does not satisfy this light. I want to claim even more, something that sounds even more outlandish, and I claim it in good truth, in the eternal truth, and in the everlasting truth: this light is not content with the simple, unmoving, divine Being that neither gives nor takes. Instead, it desires to know whence this Being comes. It wants to enter into the simple ground, into the quiet desert where a glimmer of difference has never entered, neither Father nor Son nor Holy Spirit. There, in the innermost place where no one is home, only there is this light content, and it is more interior there than it is in itself. For this ground is a simple silence. It is unchangeable in itself and yet changes all things. And it grants life to all those who rationally live in themselves.[6]

The light of reason, which turns toward God, extends beyond the Trinity of the divine persons. It does not let up; it is searching for its ground. It is content only when it has reached the ground of the Godhead's oneness. And it also wants to know whence the Being of the Godhead comes. But did not God enter philosophy so that thinking might stop at God as the final ground? Eckhart wants to know the ground of this ground. Pious people must start to feel dizzy. One can sympathize with the pope's arrival at the verdict that Eckhart wanted to know more than "was proper." What more was he looking for behind or above the Father, Son, and Holy Spirit? Eckhart knows and says explicitly that it sounds strange that he will stop only at the quiet ground of the Godhead, in the desert of endless unity. Reason does not stop anywhere difference still exists. The wholly undifferentiated ground of unity of the Godhead is not far away. It is not difficult to reach. It gives life to all who live rationally within themselves. When reason arrives there, it becomes unified and blessed.

Forms of Life: Mary and Martha, German Sermon 86

I now proceed to the second of the aforementioned sermons—number 86. I must start by saying the following: in the Middle Ages, the two sisters Mary and Martha were considered the archetypes of two forms of life: Mary for an inward turn, Martha for external work. I present here German sermon 86 in a new translation, which I undertook myself, in only slightly abbreviated form (DW 3:472–503).

(DW 3:481.1–482.2)

St. Luke writes in his Gospel: Jesus entered a small city and there was received by a woman named Martha. The woman had a sister named Mary. She sat at the feet of our Lord and listened carefully to his words, while Martha ran around and served Christ, whom they had befriended.

Mary sat at Christ's feet for three reasons. First, God's Goodness embraced her soul. The second reason was an unspeakable desire. She yearned, but she did not know for what. She wanted something, but she did not know what. The third was the pleasant consolation and bliss that she took from the eternal words that flowed from Christ's mouth.

Martha was also driven by three things to run around and to serve the beloved Christ. The first was her prominent age and that her innermost ground was practiced. That is why she knew that no one was as suitable for this activity as she was. The second was the wise prudence that directs external action toward the best thing that love demands. The third was the great worthiness of her friendly guest.[7]

(DW 3:482.14–483.20)

Now Martha says: "Lord, tell her that she should help me." Martha did not say this out of resentment, but rather out of a tender benevolence that urged her to say it. We can call it "tender benevolence" or gentle teasing. Why? Pay attention to the following: Martha saw that Mary indulged herself in pleasure for the complete satisfaction of her soul. Martha knew Mary better than Mary knew Martha. For Martha had already lived long and properly, and living provides the best sort of knowing. Living knows better than pleasure and light what one can receive in this life below God. In some respects, life knows in a purer form than the eternal light. The eternal light provides knowledge of itself and of God, but life lets itself be known without God. When it looks at itself alone, it comprehends the difference between what is similar and what is dissimilar more acutely. This is demonstrated in the writings of St. Paul, but also in those by the pagan masters. In his rapture, Paul saw God and himself in God, in the manner of intellectual knowledge. And yet he did not recognize every individual virtue of God in an image-like idea, at least not exactly. And this was because he had not practiced it in his actions. The pagan masters, on the contrary, achieved such high knowledge through practicing the virtues that they knew every individual virtue more precisely and conceived of it in image-like form better than Paul in his first rapture or any other saint.

This is exactly what happened to Martha. Therefore, she said: "Lord, tell her that she should help me!" It was as though she were saying: "My sister probably thinks that she can do everything she could ever want while she is sitting with you in the midst of consolation. Now let her see whether that is the case. Tell her to get up and go away from you!" She said this out of tender love, even if she did not express it that way. Mary was full of desire; she was longing for something without knowing what it was; she wanted something, but she did not know what. We suspect that she, the dear Mary, sat there—more out of desire than for a reasonable benefit. Therefore, Martha said: "Lord, tell her to get up!" for she feared that Mary might get stuck in her desire and therefore not progress any further. Then Christ answered her: "Martha, Martha, you are concerned. You are looking after many things. Only one thing is necessary! Mary has chosen the best part, which can never be taken from her." Jesus did not say this sentence to Martha in a tone of reprimand. He only responded to her and reassured her that Mary would still become what she wanted to be.[8]

(DW 3:484.1, 484.14–486.9)

Why did Christ say "Martha, Martha" and call her by name twice?
. . . He was implying that Martha possessed everything that there

was of temporal and eternal goods and that a creature should own. When he said "Martha" the first time, he meant that she was complete in temporal deeds. When he said "Martha" a second time, he showed that she was lacking nothing that was necessary for eternal blessedness. Therefore, he said: "You are concerned," and by this he meant: "You stand *by* the things, but the things are not *in* you." Those humans live "*with* concerns" who are unimpeded by them in everything that they do. Those live unimpeded who let all their deeds be guided by the image of the eternal light. These people stand *near* the things, not *in* the things. They stand very close but do not possess any less than if they stood there above at the rim of eternity. "Very close," I say, they are to the things, for all creatures position themselves in between, as intermediaries. And there are two kinds of things that mediate. The first kind encompasses everything without which I cannot enter into God, namely, work and acting in time. "Work" is doing external works of virtue, while "acting" is being active from the inside with rational understanding. The second type of "means" frees itself from all of that. For we are placed into time in order to come closer to God through rational acting and to become similar to him. That is what St. Paul meant when he said: "Redeem the time, for the days are evil." To redeem time means to ascend to God in reason without interruption, to not move about in image-like difference, but rather in reasonable, living truth. "For the days are evil," you need to understand like this: day points to night. If there were no night, there would be no day, and it would not be called day, since then everything would be one light. That is what Paul is concerned with: a life as bright as day has little worth if there can still be a remainder of darkness that covers and overshadows eternal bliss for a great mind. This is what Christ meant when he said: "Go, as long as you still have light!" For whoever acts in the light ascends to God, free and without any medium. His light is his action, and his action is his light.

That is exactly how it was with dear Martha. Therefore, he said to her: "only one thing is necessary," not two. You and I—once surrounded by the eternal light—are one. This Two-One is a glowing mind that stands above all things and under God, at the "perimeter of eternity." It is two, for it does not see God without an intermediary. Its knowing and its Being, or rather its knowing and its epistemic image, never become one. But God is seen only where he is seen intellectually, which means wholly without an epistemic image. In *becoming*, one is as two, and in *Being*, two is one. Light and mind, the two are one, surrounded by the eternal light.[9]

(DW 3:488.7–489.16)

Now we return to our point that dear Martha and all the friends of God with her live *with* concern, but not *in* concern. In regard to them, temporal action is just as great as entering into God, for it brings us as close to God as the greatest thing that is possible of us—excepting only the beholding of God's pure essence. For that reason, Christ says: "You are *with* the things and *with* concern." He means: she was probably distressed and worried with the lower senses; she was not accustomed to the sense of well-being of the mind. She lived *with* the things, not *in* the things; she existed by herself, and the things were by themselves.

Our activity should have these three properties: that one acts rationally and knowingly according to rank. By "according to rank," I mean that our action corresponds to the highest in every regard; by "rationally," I mean that one recognizes nothing better in time; by "knowingly," I mean that one finds living truth in its joyous presence in good deeds. When these three properties come together, they lead just as deep and are as beneficial as all the joy of Mary Magdalene in the wilderness.

Now Christ says: "You are concerning yourself with many things, not with one." That means: a person who orders his life in pure uniformity, without any external action, but for whom an intermediary steps in, cannot take hold up there with pleasure. One thing creates sorrow for man when he sinks into worry and lives therein. Martha, however, stood in confident, steadfast virtue, with a free soul, wholly free of sorrow. Thus, she wished for her sister to achieve this state as well, for Martha saw that Mary was not living essentially. It was a noble reason for wishing that Mary would achieve everything that belongs to eternal bliss. Therefore, Christ said: "One thing is necessary." What is that? It is the One, it is God. It is necessary for all creatures. For if God were to take away what is proper to him, then all creatures would become nothing.

If God were to take away from the soul of Christ what belongs to him, where the mind is one with the eternal person, then Christ would remain a mere creature. For that reason, we certainly need the One.

Martha feared that her sister would get stuck in pleasure and sweetness; she wanted her sister to become like herself. Therefore, Christ spoke as though he wanted to say: "Be happy, Martha. She has chosen the best part. This here will subside. She will receive the highest that a creature can achieve. She will become blessed like you.[10]

(DW 3:491.6–491.17)

Now Christ says: "These many concerns are bothering you." Martha was so essential that no action hindered her. Work and action led her to eternal bliss. This bliss was probably mediated; a noble nature, constant effort, and virtues contributed to it. Mary had to become like Martha before she became the true Mary. For when she sat at the feet of our Lord, she was not yet Mary; she was Mary only according to her name but not in her actual essence, for she sat with well-being and sweetness. She had just been taken into the school and was learning to live. But Martha stood essentially; therefore, she said: "Lord, tell her to get up!" as though she wanted to say: I would like it, Lord, if she did not sit there for the sake of sweet well-being; I would like her to learn to live so that she might possess life essentially. Tell her to get up so that she may become perfect.

As she sat at Christ's feet, she was not yet called Mary. For what I call "Mary" is a well-practiced body that obeys a wise soul. And this is what I call obedience: that the will serves, no matter what the understanding demands.[11]

Eckhart is dealing here with the medieval monastic culture of interiority. He is not rejecting it; he is pushing it further. He understands interiority as the first step, not as the goal. It is essential, but not the highest virtue. This may surprise us, for several reasons. First, Eckhart reverses the hierarchy that the Gospel of Luke (10:38–42) clearly constructs—even according to recent biblical scholarship—between Mary and Martha. Did the early Christians not say that in the story of Mary and Martha, meditation and Christian doctrine took precedence over activities directed outward? Eckhart understood the two women as symbolic figures, as was typical, but he interpreted the gospel in a way that took Martha as the representative of the *higher* level of perfection. Second, Eckhart surprises because he disagreed with a long tradition of ecclesiastical and, especially, monastic literature, which had seen the worldly life prefigured in Martha, and the more highly valued monastic life in Mary. Until this point, Mary had guaranteed the primacy of the contemplative life or of a turning inward. Third, we would have expected something other than the endorsement of the primacy of the active life from an author whom an incorrect classification has persistently called and still calls a "mystic."

What did Eckhart actually say? How did he characterize Mary? The Jesus of the Gospel of Luke assures us that she chose the best part. Eckhart uses the parabolic figure to illustrate his own conceptual hierarchies. With gentle irony, he suspects Mary of sitting at Jesus's feet more for the sake of sweet desire than for "rational benefit." "Rational benefit" is not banal practicability, utility, but rather progress in intellectuality. She listens, ponders, and indulges in mental pleasure. It was not merely a thirst for knowledge or even curiosity that captivated her; she was engaged with her emotions: "She yearned but she did not know for what; she wanted something but she did not know what." Eckhart repeats this sentence twice and thereby gives it a special emphasis. He makes Mary into a *figura* of uncertainty, of good inclination without concrete content; of "infatuation," one could almost say. She has not yet specified her life's direction. This could happen only through restricting, through committing oneself, through abdicating, through the negating of one possibility in favor of another. She lets no "thing" step in between herself and her greatest ecstasy. She is pure remaining-within-herself. She enjoys interiority and nearness to God, and to this end keeps life at bay.

Eckhart goes further in distancing himself from the otherwise much-lauded sister. He lets Martha say of Mary that she thinks she *could* do everything that she wanted while she sits in the midst of consolation. "Now let her see if it is so. Tell her to get up and go away from you!" Mary means well, but is still without the experience of resistance. She does not feel any lack, sees no occasion for acting. She does not sense any conflict, does not need to make any choice. She has consolidated her existence into an invulnerable point and thereby feels well. She is not testing herself and thus overestimates herself. Her good intention has not been practiced and is not realized with body and soul. But this, Eckhart explains via a strange etymology, is the meaning of the name "Mary"—"a well-practiced body that obeys a wise soul." Mary repeatedly avoids practicing. She does not yet correspond to her name. She is not yet the "true" Mary. The praise that Jesus bestows upon her is related, according to Eckhart, to that which she will become. Mary will become like Martha, which means: she will move beyond the stage of pure interiority.

Where will she arrive? What is the end point? It is not as though she willfully chooses to interrupt her contemplation in order to bring soup to a beggar. While this would be correct and would correspond to a decidedly Eckhartian imperative, that is not what is at issue here. She should—according to this text (a thinker does not always say the same thing!)—not *do* anything, but rather *be* something else. She should gain a new consciousness of inside and outside. She will thereby value her lofty inner state differently and position herself in a different relation to the world.

Eckhart explains: she will become like Martha. Martha did not avoid "things." She joined them to her innermost part and associated her innermost part with things to such an extent that they ceased to be only outside. She coordinated the things and her constraints with her highest goals. She left the alternative of *vita contemplativa* and *vita activa* behind. She was the leading figure of a new, third form of life. She exposed herself to life; she looked for it. In this way, she understood something that one can never experience without letting oneself go. Eckhart writes odd sentences about the experience of life: life provides the best knowing. Life itself is knowing; it gives more to think about than pleasure and light, something better, purer than the eternal light could. For Augustine, the eternal light of truth shone only on the inside. It shines there for Eckhart as well. The eternal light, Truth, reveals itself and extrapolates the rational knowledge of God. Life reveals itself—without God. It is composed, so to say, of things, of "godless things." It looks upon itself, shows differences more acutely; without it, everything looks the same. Paul was raptured into the Third Heaven—for that reason, he did not see the perfections of the good man distinctly enough. The pagan teachers of ethics—I am thinking of Aristotle in his *Nicomachean Ethics* and Seneca in his *Epistulae morales*—practiced the virtues, observed them in life, and knew them more exactly than the apostle raptured to heaven. They can tell us more about them.

This is one of Eckhart's difficult ideas. It is hardly possible to find a parallel in the philosophical literature of the Middle Ages. There is probably no sermon that so clearly turns the Gospel of Luke on its head, even if Albertus Magnus's explanation of this passage from Luke laid the groundwork for Eckhart's higher appreciation of Martha.[12] Kurt Ruh and others disputed Eckhart's authorship: the constant praise of Martha at Mary's expense contradicted the text of the gospel too openly. Furthermore, it seemed out of line for Eckhart to choose pagan philosophers over the ecstatic St. Paul as teachers of ethics. But the most astounding feature is this concept of life: the eternal light, the Truth, points to itself and thereby to God, but life points to itself without God and counts here as the higher source of knowledge. Life is a self-referential performance; life is practice. Life is letting oneself go and returning to oneself. Life has its end in itself, is teleologically in itself—in good Aristotelian fashion. Life here is not to be read primarily in biological terms, but more likely as the totality of reality that encompasses God and the world and, in this respect, exists without a specially designated God.

Martha's precedence: she lives in this life. She thereby achieves the "wise prudence that directs external action to the best thing that love demands." The truly wise life consists not in contemplative joy, but rather in the directing of external action to the best thing that we know, that love demands. She goes out to the things, she is with the things, but the things are not in her; they do not suppress her own inner life—they express it. She stands very close to the external things, and the things as intermediaries step in between her and the best that love demands, but she also stands, as it is said, above, at the perimeter of eternity. Does this refer to the highest sphere of the heavens, as in Eckhart's contemporary Dante? No matter—what matters is the change of thinking, which clarifies: temporal acting is just as great as entering into God. Someone who only sinks into his innermost part cannot "live essentially." The "things" create worry for him; he lives in constant opposition, for things are standing about everywhere, and he concentrates himself into his point-by-point existence. Martha steps up to them, orders them into her way of life, and stands worry-free *with* them, not *in* them.

Eckhart's emphasis on time is also striking. He lets Martha be older, concluding that she has already lived long and correctly—which brings knowledge. She knows Mary better than Mary knows Martha. She fears that Mary could withdraw from practicing herself in time. Eckhart gives time a preeminent meaning, as though he were turning against the temporary immersion of oneself in eternity. He says that he understands "reasonable" to mean that one cannot know anything better *at the time*. The position of a man in time who seeks what is reasonable codetermines the result. Time and life as the grounds of knowing—this idea, which was introduced in the twentieth century through the work of Dilthey, finds a distant echo here. And when Jesus speaks about Mary, he relies on the effect of time. He humorously soothes Martha: "Be well, Martha. She chose the best part. This here will subside." For now, she is still in school, but she will learn to live. "To learn to live," to possess life in its essential nature, not merely in its properties, means to become perfect.

Eckhart pursues the thought further, though in another direction: "Only one thing is necessary." Someone who lives in the all-encompassing unity is a glowing mind; he stands *in* things and *above* things. He stands *with* the things, but the things do not live *in* him, overwhelming him. Duality becomes oneness in him. In other people, knowing and being are distinct. Eckhart specifies: since we never have being directly but only in epistemic images, knowing and the epistemic image are different for such other people. But someone who enters into oneness sees God without an epistemic image; knowing and epistemic image, knowing and being, become one. This is Martha: she is no longer a *figura* just of the active life, but of wisdom that has entered into unity, who no longer separates things from the best that love demands. Martha stands there with a practiced virtue, proven in time, with a free soul. She is free because she has found herself in the things that Mary kept away from herself as disruptive, in the best thing, in unity, completely free of worry. The metaphysics of the One in Martha surpasses the difference between *vita activa* and *contemplativa*.

17. A New Consolation of Philosophy

The Book of Divine Consolation: *Chronology and Structure*
The chronology of Eckhart's works has shifted over the past few decades in two ways: important Latin works such as the *Opus tripartitum* have been moved closer to 1300 by about a decade, and the German tractate the *Book of Divine Consolation*, along with its corresponding sermon intended for reading, *Von dem edeln menschen*, is now dated about ten years later than initially thought. Eckhart supposedly wrote it not around 1308, but rather around 1318. Scholars once believed that it was written during Eckhart's years in Strasbourg; now it has been situated closer to Eckhart's commentary on the Gospel of John, with whose content it shares a close textual affinity. We are now approaching the time—and also the concerns—of Eckhart's trial.[1]

The *Book of Divine Consolation* has three parts. The first part contains so much philosophical groundwork that it could offer complete consolation to anyone for any affliction. The second part provides almost thirty individual arguments in the same vein. In the third part, Eckhart offers examples of acts and deeds of wise people who found consolation when they were suffering. At the end of the book, Eckhart addresses some of the controversies surrounding him. He had been attacked for presenting simple people with too lofty topics, and he reacted against the accusation. He objects: if it is forbidden to teach the unlearned, then nobody is ever taught (DW 5:60.25–61.2; Flasch 2006, 91). Eckhart stresses the independent significance of the first part; he expressly states that he is arguing philosophically within it.

The Metaphysics of Sonship

Since I have translated and commented upon the tractate and the sermon *Von dem edeln menschen* elsewhere (Munich, 2007), I limit myself here to a brief explanation of the theoretical groundwork that Eckhart lays out within the first few pages of the *Book of Divine Consolation*, quoted below.

> Above all, we must know: the wise man and Wisdom, the true man and Truth, the just man and Justice, the good man and Goodness, all look at each other. They are related to each other in the following way: Goodness is neither created nor made nor born. Yet it is birthing and births the good man. And the good man, insofar as he is good, is neither made nor created, but is child and son, born out of Goodness. Goodness births itself and everything that it is within the good man. It pours forth being, knowing, loving, and effecting simultaneously into the good man, and the good man takes all his being, knowing, loving, and effecting from within the heart and innermost part of Goodness, and only from it. Good and being good are nothing other than a single "Goodness," wholly one in everything, with the single exception of birthing and being born. The birthing of Goodness and the being born within the good man is wholly a single being, a single life. Everything that belongs to the good man, he takes out of Goodness and within Goodness. There he is and lives and dwells. There he knows himself and everything that he knows. There he loves everything that he loves. There he acts—with Goodness and in Goodness. And Goodness effects all its acts with him and within him, according to what is written and what the Son says: "The Father remains and dwells within me and effects the deeds." "The Father acts until now, and I act." "Everything that belongs to the Father belongs to me, and everything that belongs to me belongs to my Father. It belongs to him insofar as he gives it. It belongs to me insofar as I take it."
>
> Moreover, we have to be aware: when we speak the word "good," it names and includes within itself solely the pure Goodness, without any determinations, no more and no less, but as that which gives itself. When we speak of the "good man," it means: his "being good" is given to him, poured into him, and born into him out of the unborn Goodness. That is why the Gospel says: "As the Father has life within himself, so he has given it to the Son so that he also can

have life within himself." It says "within himself," not "from within himself," for the Father has given it to him.

Everything I have said so far about the good man and Goodness is equally true of the true man and Truth, of the just man and Justice, of the wise man and Wisdom, of God-Son and God-Father. It is true in the same sense for everything that is born out of God and that has no earthly father, into which nothing created births itself, nothing that is not God; in which there is no image, only God, naked and purely alone. That is why John says in his holy gospel: "All those who are born not from blood, nor out of fleshly desire, nor through the will of man, but by God and out of God alone, are granted the power to become 'the sons of God.'"[2]

By "blood," St. John means everything within man that does not obey man's will. By "fleshly desire," he means everything within man that obeys the will only with resistance and struggle, and thus what is inclined toward the desires of the flesh. It belongs to soul and body alike and not only to the soul, which makes the powers of the soul tire and grow weak and old.

By "the will of man," St. John means the highest faculty of the soul. Its essence and activity are not mixed with the flesh; they stand pure in the soul, separate from time, place, and everything that places its hope in time and place or has acquired a taste for them. They have nothing in common with anything else; in regard to them, man is God's likeness; in them, man is of God's genus and species. Yet they are not God himself; they are in the soul and are created with the soul. Therefore, they have to be de-formed of themselves and trans-formed in God. They must be born in God and out of God so that God alone is Father. And so they are God's sons as well, that is, God's in-born, only-begotten Son. For I am the son of everything that forms and births me according to its model and in resemblance to it. Such a man is God's Son, good as the son of Goodness itself and just as the son of Justice, and insofar as he only is their son, Justice is unborn and birthing, and its born son has the same being that Justice has and is. He enters into everything that is proper to Justice and Truth.[3]

In the whole doctrine that the Gospel records and that is understood with certainty in the natural light of the rational soul, man finds true consolation in all suffering. (DW 5:9.4–11:19; Flasch 2006, 9–14)

We have arrived at the core of Eckhart's thinking: he starts out from the primary determinations, a common Eckhartian topic. The determinations—Wisdom, Truth, Justice, Goodness—are interchangeable. Eckhart examines their relation to the individual wise or just man. The term "God" is used late, only after Eckhart has illuminated the relationship between the abstract determinations and the concrete bearer. This relatedness is not effected in the manner of artisanal production; rather, it develops as self-expansion, like the diffusion of light. Biological metaphors illustrate the second type of this cause-and-effect relation: a living creature expands its species by begetting or birthing.

It is possible to criticize Eckhart's initial premises. If someone were to assume that there is no real relation between cause and effect in Eckhart's philosophical system, because "Justice" and "Truth" are only retroactive abstractions, man-made linguistic structures employed to subsume and consolidate true sentences or just deeds into a whole, then Eckhart's entire line of argument breaks down. In pre-nominalist fashion, Eckhart takes it for granted that Justice (Truth, Wisdom, Goodness) is the common and real determinant shared by all just men and then proceeds by eliminating the idea of *making* regarding the activity of Justice (Wisdom, Truth, Goodness). He justifies this exclusion of making by stating that in the context of a type of artisanal, craft-like act, the effecting one always remains *outside*, whereas we only call the just man "just" because Justice is *within* him. The individual just man and Justice directly relate to each other in reality. Eckhart puts it figuratively: they behold each other. *Respicere*, "to look at each another," was a scholastic term for relations. And so Eckhart says: "Justice" is not merely an abstract collective term. Rather, there exists between Justice and the individual just man a real and reciprocal relation within their essential oneness. Justice itself (Truth, Wisdom, etc.) cannot be conceptualized as having come into being. Therefore, both forms of origination that Eckhart highlighted for the individual just man do not apply: Justice is neither made nor born. What underlies this idea is the sentiment of the First Parisian Question, mentioned several times before: insofar as Wisdom (Justice, Truth, etc.) is within the individual, it cannot even be conceived of as something made. It must have entered the wise man in the manner of self-disclosure, which is analogous to begetting. It was not made within him, not placed into him as an additional property, but born into him. Eckhart draws a series of conclusions from this notion:

1. The just man, *insofar* as he is just, is not made and not created, but he is "born" out of Justice. He also has other properties that are made or created, but *insofar* as he is just, he is the *uncreated Justice* itself.

2. It is inconceivable that Justice would have disclosed itself only *partially* to the just man, for Justice (Wisdom, Truth, etc.) is indivisible. And thus it is *wholly* within the just man.

3. If Justice, with all that it is and does, is wholly within the just man, and if the just man receives his justness from and in Justice, then the just man and Justice are *wholly one.*

4. Eckhart grounds his argument through considerations of linguistic logic that we saw first in his First Parisian Question: when we call a body "white," then the adjective merely signifies this quality. We encounter the color "white" in many creatures that are all very different, in a bird's feather or in a rock. When we say "white," we ignore those differences. We are not talking about a feather or a stone, but only about "white." Eckhart employs this Aristotelian rule in the context of the terms "good" and "just": they do not signify anything other than the pure quality, as Goodness and Justice.

5. The relation of uncreated, unborn Justice to the uncreated but born just man is the relation of God-Father to God-Son. Eckhart does not *compare* the relation between Justice (Wisdom, Truth, etc.) and the just man with the Trinitarian relation of God-Father and God-Son; rather, he *identifies* it. The Trinity is not the "model" for his considerations but its real content. Justice, Truth, etc. are the *one* God, and insofar as Justice is within man, he *is* the son of Justice.

6. The just man as such enters into all characteristic qualities, all properties of Justice and Truth. This holds true without any restrictions, for Justice and Truth cannot even be conceptualized as divided.

7. This whole argument, Eckhart says, can be known in the light of natural reason. It applies obviously to his philosophical analysis of the concrete and the abstract. Eckhart's analysis presupposes Aristotle's theory of the predication of adjectives, set out in the fifth chapter of his *Categories;* it is not a report of mystical experiences; it does not form a chapter of the doctrine of grace. Instead, it provides the basis for a rational explanation of the Bible, starting with the Gospel of John.

8. The presence of Justice in man requires that there is something in the human soul that is independent of the body that has nothing to do with time and space. In this regard, the formula of Anaxagoras and Aristotle about the intellect applies, which stated that the intellect does not have anything in common with anything else in order to become everything.

9. The man who becomes conscious of this distances himself from everything created. He "de-forms" himself of himself, insofar as he is created, and of all creatures. He does not wait for events of salvific history; he is positioned beyond time and place, beyond suffering and death. He rejoices in the divine life, which has become *his* life. He possesses inalienable consolation.

These nine theses are contained within the foundational introductory part of the *Book of Divine Consolation*. Many parallel texts, especially Eckhart's interpretation of the Gospel of John, confirm them. We can be certain that they represent the core of Eckhart's teachings. They played a significant role in the accusations of heresy.

The Book of Consolation *and the Commentary on John*

The pages I quoted from the consolatory treatise are a commentary on the prologue to the Gospel of John. As mentioned, it has close textual ties with Eckhart's roughly contemporary commentary on the Gospel of John.[4] I point out a series of agreements between the two texts.

At the beginning of his consolatory treatise, Eckhart talks about the universal determinations—Wisdom, Justice, Goodness, Truth—and about their presence in the individual good and just man. Their relationship is the relation of God-Father to God-Son. In his consolatory treatise, as in his commentary on John, Eckhart initially explains this relationship in analogy to the relation of the universal (being human) to the individual (this man). He briefly describes the presence of the universal in the individual and considers it the real life of the divine Trinity.[5] As in the consolatory treatise, he explains his metaphysics of in-being: everything begotten is *in* the one that has begotten it.[6] The just man exists in Justice. No vision or intuition tells us how this is possible, but only the philosophical analysis of the concrete's containedness within the universal (*abstractum*)—with a realism of universals taken for granted.[7] Eckhart distinguishes between the analogous sharing (participation) of the individual in the universal and univocal reciprocity.[8] For this argument, he invokes the indispensable understanding of Aristotle that the adjective "just" does not signify anything other than the pure quality and that it disregards the bearer of a property.[9]

The consolatory treatise, the tractate of the noble man, and the commentary on John all bring in Eckhart's characteristic examination of the eye, seeing, and color. The eye has to be devoid of color in order to become all colors. It has an essential relation to color by itself, which is the only reason why it can detect individual colors. In seeing, it becomes the seen. *Intellectual* knowing, detached from things, becomes identical to its content, that is, with the mentioned universal determinations of Justice, Wisdom, Goodness, Truth. Sonship is the identity of the intellectual knower with the known, in this case, with the primary determinations. These theories of seeing and intellectual knowing are derived from Aristotelian-Averroistic philosophy. Interpreted as found in Dietrich of Freiberg, they form Eckhart's basis, both in the consolatory treatise and in the commentary on John.[10]

Both his consolatory treatise and the commentary on John initially demand an intellectual and willing conversion of our concept of reality and our relation to reality. The right kind of orientation in life is a turning away from the "this and that" toward true Being.[11] Eckhart does not devalue the earthly individual because of it. He reflects on the presence of true Being, its real presence, and works out the understanding that essence and life are immanent within the individual. I call this Eckhart's immanentism: the stone has its essence, which no one, not even God, can take away from it. It is in itself. It has its own existence and, inseparable from it, its own proper activity, even when it rests.[12] Strictly speaking, it is not from another, *ab alio*. And even more so: something that lives, lives in itself, by itself, for itself. The living being is without ground.[13]

By abandoning the "this and that," we abandon time. Eckhart insists that everything that he brings forward happens in the present. Temporal determinations have no place in the context of God and the intellect; only a present perspective holds.[14] What has been and what will be are of no interest. Salvific history, miracles, and eschatology become metaphors.

In a programmatic move at the beginning of his commentary on John, Eckhart highlights his wanting to present the truth of the Old and New Testaments—that is, Creation, Incarnation, and Salvation—with *philosophical* arguments of natural reason. Right at the beginning of the consolatory treatise, he declares that his tenets are knowable in the light of natural reason.[15] If they are also written in the Bible, Eckhart thinks that's great, for it is good when rational proofs are corroborated by authority.

The commonality of these main motifs is demonstrable; they are hardly genesic hypotheses. What is left for me to explain is why the in-being of Justice in the just man, the Goodness proper in the individual good man, is the life of the Godhead. A simple consideration, one he had already voiced during his first Parisian magisterium between 1302 and 1303, led Eckhart to this idea. Wisdom (Truth, Justice, etc.) as such cannot be conceived of, in the strict sense, as creatable. The exceptional part of this claim is that Eckhart says not only that Truth, Wisdom, etc. were de facto not created, but also that they *cannot be conceptualized as created* according to their essence. In the formal language of Eckhart, the Parisian master, we read: *sapientia . . . non habet rationem creabilis.*[16] This is not a mystical experience, but a necessity that is binding for every reason. The following consideration shows it: if someone were to imagine that God created wisdom (truth, justice, etc.) in an individual person, then he would have to admit that God did this out of wisdom and in wisdom. That would mean, however, that wisdom existed before it entered into a particular individual. There are not two or several wisdoms. Wisdom is Oneness and not conceivable as created according to its essence. This is the simple foundational thought of Eckhart's philosophy. In pronouncing it, Eckhart does not relate an experience and does not refer to the Bible initially. He is simply insightful. Eckhart had expressed this thought in relation to Wisdom in Paris as early as 1302–3, and he expands his idea— in the consolatory treatise and elsewhere—to include Justice, Truth, and Goodness: let us assume that a person does something good. Then Goodness is within his will. We can *imagine* that God has created goodness in his will, but we cannot *think* it. For in thinking, one must say: God was good when he created goodness in man. A critic may still object that what we have here is a mere coincidence of like terms without factual likeness when we speak of the Goodness in God and the goodness of the human will. Someone who chooses this position, however, undermines every rational confidence in saying something about God and the world. Eckhart at least required, in non-nominalist fashion, that there be only *one* Wisdom and only *one* pure Goodness. To say it more precisely: one wise consideration or one good decision within an individual person can always also be analyzed within a sea of contingencies. Eckhart knew this as well. And yet he proceeded to say that someone who thinks Wisdom or Justice itself, purely as such, and who rejects the possibility of a nominalist limitation of reason, thinks Wisdom, taken strictly as wisdom, as the presence of God within man and simultaneously removes the thought "God" from the predominant realm of mere imagination. The causal explanation of the type of production analogous to artisanal manufacture does not apply in the case of Wisdom, Goodness, and

Truth. Eckhart had to come up with something new to describe the presence of the noncontingent among various contingencies. In search of it, Eckhart examines the two determinations "making" and "producing." Truth was not "made," not even the truth of the most humble intellectual knowledge. A simple, true thought was Truth itself, unmade and whole, for Truth is neither makeable nor divisible. If Truth is within me when I pronounce a simple and true sentence, then it can have come to pass only through a kind of self-expansion of Truth itself. Truth is not just in the heavens above, where it bears the name "God," but it is down here; it is with us and in us, and only once we comprehend this will we understand the term "God." Not as though the word "Goodness" *stood in* for the God known from other contexts; rather, we extrapolate the only worthy meaning of God-ness by *thinking* Goodness and Justice, its procreativeness and worldly presence.

We possess a suitable metaphor for self-expansion: humans and animals disseminate themselves by procreating. "Begetting" and "being born" express the same relation that exists between Truth itself and the individual true sentence. Therefore, someone could say: Truth and Goodness are in us, but not because they are "made" and placed into us through some kind of personal favor; rather, they are "born into us" while they remain themselves. This connection to us is essential to them, not coincidental. "Begetting" and "birthing" are organic metaphors, and they are better than the technomorphic images of making, but they can and must be transcended in our thinking: the point is to register the uncreatableness of Wisdom, Truth, Goodness intellectually and at the same time to find them within us humans. These primary determinations—Truth, Goodness, Justice, Wisdom—exist in this world and yet are not conceivable of as created. In this way, they are the presence of God on earth among us. This idea presupposes that we derive our concept of God from the intellect, by thinking Truth, Goodness, Justice. Eckhart said in German sermon 6 that if God were not just, he would not care a fig for him.[17] God as mere energy of the will, as heavenly emperor, or *imagined* as a merely de facto present and coincidentally benevolent person, that, for Eckhart, is not God. What the term "God" can mean becomes comprehensible *intellectually* and acceptable with intact dignity via the criteria of Truth, Goodness, Justice, Wisdom. Nobody can arrive at it through religious ceremonies or belief in miracles. Nobody gains it by bending his knees or reciting biblical passages.[18] To someone who performs the intellectual operation, however, the Bible offers parallels. Eckhart's philosophy of

Christianity can both believe what the Bible says and at the same time want to prove rationally that it is provable through reason in its essential features if interpreted correctly: God created his Son, but he did not make him. This Son is the Word of the eternal Father. And thus Eckhart has arrived at the intellectual substance of the Gospel of John. Now he can explain this gospel and its basic features. Now he can also explain what ancient philosophers meant when they said that no human soul was without God.[19] And he can state that all feelings of hopelessness, of inconsolability, stem from the fact that we do not recognize the truth of this ancient sentence. Insofar as we speak a true sentence or want a good deed, the noncontingent has already spread itself out into us in its characteristic way. Instead, we could also say: God-Son has been born within us, and if he is born within us, then we are God's son, and we are God's son wholly, for the Godhead does not divide itself into parts. Where it is, it is as a whole, wholly. To comprehend this and to understand oneself as son of God in this sense are the essential grounds of consolation that exist in this world. They are derived from the simple understanding that we live in Truth, Goodness, and Wisdom, even when we are looking for them or miss them or declare them to be impossible, and yet they cannot be thought of as creatable by their very essence.

18. Eckhart's Trial: The Charges

Friars Submit Lists of Eckhart's Errors to the Inquisitorial Court in Cologne

A straight path leads from Eckhart's *Book of Divine Consolation* to the inquisitorial trial in Cologne.[1] Someone flipping through the trial records today, which are now available in print in the standard edition by Loris Sturlese (LW 5, cited here according to document and page number), will first find the introductory sentences from the consolatory treatise. With these, two of Eckhart's Dominican confreres opened the list of errors that reported Eckhart as a heretic to the archbishop of Cologne. It happened between August 1325 and September 1326. We do not know for sure how long Eckhart had been in Cologne; the number of years depends on the function he served in Strasbourg. Maybe he had been in Cologne for only two or three years, but ten or twelve seem more likely. In any case, enemies from within his own order denounced Eckhart before the archbishop of Cologne, Heinrich II of Virneburg (1304/6 to 1332); the episcopal inquisition initiated a trial. His denouncers gradually produced three or four lists of Eckhart's doctrinal errors. It emerged later that the Dominicans Hermann of Summo and William of Nidecke were two highly suspicious figures (LW 5, 552–56), but it was too late to change anything about Eckhart's legal proceedings; the trial was under way.

The German Dominican provinces were in turmoil. Discipline had been weakened. The political tensions—whether to favor the pope or Louis the Bavarian—were disruptive; intellectual differences—whether to support or reject Thomism as the doctrine of the order—split the convents. On

August 1, 1325, the pope named Nicholas of Strasbourg the official visitor
(n. 44, 190–92). He knew the lands and the convent in Cologne; he had been
a lector in Basel and Cologne. The two denouncers first handed their list
of Eckhart's errors to him. Nicholas initiated proceedings within the order;
Eckhart wrote an apologia and was absolved. Eckhart's enemies were sent
packing by Nicholas. He had William of Nidecke locked up in a monastic
prison. Subsequently, Eckhart's enemies turned to the archbishop with their
lists of errors; the inquisitorial trial began. Nicholas of Strasbourg attempted
to prevent it: he was charged with obstructing the inquisition.

The first list of Eckhart's errors comprised fifteen passages taken from
the *Book of Divine Consolation* (198–209), six further from an earlier written
defense that has not survived (209–10), another twelve propositions from
Eckhart's second commentary on Genesis (210–15), and finally sixteen quotations from his German sermons, translated into Latin (215–26). In total,
Eckhart's brothers had found no fewer than forty-nine passages that were
suspect of heresy.

Yet it was not enough for them. Soon, his enemies presented the archbishop with a second list of fifty-nine passages excerpted from his sermons
that they deemed heretical (226–45). This second list repeated twenty-one
of the items contained in the first list (524–30), so the number of Eckhart's
errors was not actually one hundred eight. Nonetheless, the dossier created
the impression that Eckhart's works were teeming with heresies—especially
because a third list followed that, though lost to us today, contained passages
from Eckhart's commentary on John that were suspected of heresy (531–34).
There was commotion in the church during these decades; the persecution of
heretics was the order of the day, especially after the Council of Vienne in
1311. The archbishop had to react. And he did.

On February 13, 1327, Eckhart solemnly declared his orthodoxy in the
Dominican church in Cologne; he recanted potential errors and lamented
possible misunderstandings (547–49). He did not acknowledge the authority
of the archbishop's inquisitorial court; as an innocent man and master of
theology, he claimed to be beholden only to the pope and the University
of Paris; Dominicans, he said, were exempt. The Cologne commissioners
rejected his appeal on February 22, 1327 (550–51). The trial was moved
to Avignon in 1327, and thus the legal nature of the trial shifted. The defend-
ant had more rights at a papal court; Eckhart could hope for greater theological expertise there. Almost seventy, Eckhart went to Avignon on foot. A

specially appointed panel began its intense scrutiny of Eckhart's supposed errors and assembled a new list of twenty-eight doctrinal errors from the Cologne documents (557–60). From around the middle of 1327, Eckhart was interrogated in person. The panel of theologians submitted an extensive evaluation of the twenty-eight passages (568–90). Cardinal Jacob Fournier, later Pope Benedict XII, composed an additional report (560–68) that, though lost, can be partially reconstructed. Meanwhile, Eckhart passed away, probably on January 8, 1328, and before April 1328 at the latest, for the pope informed the archbishop of Cologne on April 30, 1328, that the trial would continue despite Eckhart's death. It was a "stark exception" that a heresy trial would continue even after the delinquent was deceased.[2] The pope was relentless in his hunt for heretics. Cologne was pushing for action.

Eckhart's order was split. Eckhart had been a famous professor and a valued preacher among people "of both genders"; he had held high offices within the Dominican order: master of theology, prior of Erfurt, provincial of Saxony, vicar general of Thuringia and Bohemia. The order was worried about its own orthodox reputation, but it could not easily drop Eckhart; and the papal visitor Nicholas of Strasbourg did not want to. Eckhart had followers, both within the order and on the outside. High officials within the order had supported Eckhart's plan—eventually successful—to relocate the trial from Cologne to Avignon, especially since Eckhart's two denouncers were soon exposed as criminals. The list of their transgressions was long. At the same time, however, voices challenging Eckhart had multiplied— surprisingly, even before the pope condemned him, that is, before March 27, 1329. I investigate the way in which Eckhart defended himself against all the allegations in the next chapter.

During Pentecost 1328, only a few months after Eckhart's death, his order adopted a two-part resolution even before the papal condemnation took place: first, Dominican preachers were expected not to speak to the people about topics deemed too difficult (*subtilia*) and that did not contribute anything to the moral advancement of the population; second, those lecturers who discussed dangerous things (*periculosa*) and spoke about topics that sounded evil were to be punished. Thus, the professors within the Dominican order were muzzled by their superiors in the order's administration. They were not to play with fire. They would lose their offices if they tried too hard to be original (n. 63, 594).

Apparently this decree was related to Eckhart's trial and its continuation after his death. The order did not want to relive such an embarrassing episode.

In Cologne, people had other worries. The archbishop was afraid that Eckhart's trial would peter out after the master's death. He appealed to the pope; he had a vested interest in a condemnation of Eckhartism, not simply of Eckhart. The pope assuaged the prince of the church; on April 30, 1328, he wrote to the archbishop that the trial would proceed and would soon be finished (n. 62, 593–94). Eckhart's way of thinking was to be marked as heretical, and it was to be extinguished. This was not just in the interest of two corrupt denouncers. The incident was by no means just a local problem anymore. It had spilled over the confines of the Dominican order into the secular world. Academics and sharp-witted people who had no ties to the Curia and did not look to Cologne declared that Eckhart was a heretic, as mentioned above, even before the pope excommunicated him. More than one theologian thought of Eckhart's teachings as heretical. This was not simply infighting within the Dominican order, or a Franciscan conflict with the Dominicans. Michael of Cesena, the Franciscan superior general, who was quarreling with the pope about the question of poverty, declared in September 1328 that Eckhart was quite obviously a heretic (n. 64, 595, especially l. 7). He used it against the pope that the latter had had one of Eckhart's denouncers arrested on charges of major violations against his order's discipline (n. 56, 552–55).

With regard to content, William of Ockham's critique of Eckhart was more precise. Ockham was interrogated in Avignon on suspicion of heresy at the same time as Eckhart. He knew the individual counts of the accusation, examined each in detail, and concluded that Eckhart was more likely a lunatic than a heretic. William of Ockham, a man famous for his careful manner of argumentation, procured evidence for the German professor's fantastic ideas, fantasies that were hard to believe. According to Ockham, Eckhart taught that the earth existed eternally. He claimed that every just man was transformed into the Godhead and had created the stars with God; God did not know what to do without such a man. And furthermore: within God there were no differences, which meant that the church doctrine of the Trinity was false. Eckhart even claimed that creatures were pure nothingness. Fantastical stuff, all of it (n. 60, 590–91).

A historical fact that tends to attract too little attention is this far-reaching consensus of evaluations and condemnations of Eckhart, even outside the Curia and even among enemies of the pope and fellow suspects of heresy. Eckhart stood against a cultural world. His orthodoxy was in question. Many disputed his new conception of Christianity. Yet their objections came from diametrically opposed sides. This course of events is trivialized in accounts such as that of Winfried Trusen, who finds the trial's main cause among "refractory friars."

The pope's final judgment was issued on March 27, 1329. It said: devil's seed (n. 65, 596–600). The number of errors had remained, but with subtle differentiations: out of the twenty-eight errors, fifteen passages were outright heretical, eleven were evil-sounding and suspect of heresy, and two more were heretical but could not securely be attributed to Eckhart. A little later, the pope demanded that his bull of Eckhart's condemnation, *In agro dominico*, be published in Cologne and that obdurate followers of Eckhart be punished (601–5). As noted above, a lector could lose his position just for teaching something "suspect of heresy." The assumption common among earlier scholars that the pope considered the condemnation to be of mere local relevance does not hold. His bull survives in a manuscript from Mainz.[3]

So much for the external circumstances. The studies of the past decades by Josef Koch, Winfried Trusen, Walter Senner, Jürgen Miethke, and Loris Sturlese have sorted them out. The motives of the individual actors, especially of the archbishop of Cologne, who took a noticeably strong interest in persecution, are difficult to determine with certainty. The political background remains obscure as well. A series of factors played a role: pressure from Avignon; the conflict of the archbishop with the city of Cologne; his clash with Emperor Louis the Bavarian, whose rival claimant to the throne he had crowned and against whom he continued to fight, but who gained sympathies among the urban population while the archbishop supported the anti-imperial papal politics; the role of the Franciscans surrounding Louis the Bavarian; tensions between the archbishop and the Dominicans; factions within the Order of Preachers. In this confusing situation, what matters are the doctrinal contents of the documents, that is, above all Eckhart's defense and the bull of condemnation. Eckhart's twofold self-defense (in the Soest manuscript) has gained authority thanks to the edition and studies by Loris Sturlese. It is not, as previously assumed, a notarial record, but an autonomous text by Meister Eckhart: his last work. It is the self-defense he delivered before the Cologne judges on September 26, 1326; he put it on the record.

A Conflict of Theories: Ten Doctrinal Errors

More important than the personal motives of the actors—which are difficult to investigate—are the following questions: What was criticized and denounced and why? What exactly was condemned? How did Eckhart justify those teachings that were attacked? Did he retract anything? Because of the large number of heretical teachings that were held against him, I have had to simplify the material. It is possible to do so, however, for the extensive lists from Cologne contain repetitions. Here, I first describe the ten main errors with which Eckhart was charged. Then I examine how Eckhart defended himself against these charges (chapter 19). Finally, I discuss the evaluation by the Avignonese theologians and the papal bull of condemnation, *In agro dominico* (chapter 20).

1. Divine Filiation

Eckhart's confreres who ended up accusing him of heresy probably first became suspicious after reading the introductory pages of the *Book of Divine Consolation:* this *Meister* thought of God as not merely the main but the only instance of the primary determinations Being, Oneness, Truth, Goodness, Wisdom, and Justice. They had learned it differently: these transcendental determinations were supposed to pertain to all beings, including the worldly things. Above all, Eckhart taught that the divine first instance of these determinations created the good man as God's son with all the privileges of the only-begotten son. He did not merely consider this father-son relation according to the *model* of the Trinity, as some have claimed in extenuating fashion, but he transferred man as God's son into the Trinity, not in similarity to it, but in correlativity and identity. This expansion of the oneness of Father and Son to include humans seemed irreconcilable with the orthodox concept of God. It was especially offensive that Eckhart taught of the good man that God-Father had *begotten, but not made* him. In this way, Eckhart conferred the traditional attributes of the divine *verbum* onto man and claimed for him, with Trinitarian formulations, that he was not "made" and uncreated. It signified an improper transfer of the divine process onto man. For Eckhart, it was no longer "inner Trinitarian," as some theologians still say today without noticing the spatialization that—from an Eckhartian perspective—lies within their diction. Eckhart carried it to an extreme and denied all differences between the divine Goodness and the good man; according to Eckhart, they were wholly one, the only distinction being between begetting and being begotten. With these propositions, which transferred the life "within God" onto earthly humans, the guardians of the faith began their list of Eckhart's errors (nn. 1–4, 198–199).

Now the Hebrew Bible states that Israel was Yahweh's "firstborn Son" (Exodus 4:22); the prologue to the Gospel of John asserts that God granted all men the power to become sons of God. St. Paul spoke of Christians not as servants, but as free children of God (Romans 9:14). The Vulgate translation of the apostle Peter's second letter teaches that thanks to God's promises, Christians shared in God's nature, *consortes divinae naturae* (2 Peter 1:4). The doctrine of the divine sonship of the blessed was thus well supported by the New Testament. If the baptized are not simply *called*, but *are* sons of God, then "divine filiation" is not simply an image or a metaphor. It had to be more than mere similarity, but instead an actual, substantial origin and reality that could be formulated ontologically. The baptized had to come to share in God's nature; and sons simply have the same nature as their father. Thus, "divine filiation," or "being a child of God," was not just a kind of adoption or a similarity that maintained the difference between Creator and the created, but rather was a being received into the divine nature as *consortes divinae naturae*. Greek ecclesiastical writers had stated several times that God had become man so that man could become God. It has to be explained why Eckhart could offend around 1320 when he taught that man wanted to abandon himself and become God within God.[4]

The answer is that since the times of Peter Lombard, the grace by which men became sons of God had increasingly been interpreted as a created quality, not just in Thomas Aquinas's works, but also within the Franciscan schools. Peter Lombard still interpreted the pouring forth of the Holy Spirit into the hearts of the faithful as its substantial presence; for him, the *caritas* in the souls of the blessed was the uncreated Holy Spirit. Bonaventure, who let grace be an accidental *habitus* only *alongside* the Holy Spirit, wrote that all wise people supported this position.[5] Already in the first volume of his commentary on the Lombard's *Sentences*, however, Bonaventure warily turned against him regarding this question.[6] Thomas Aquinas reduced the presence of the Holy Spirit within the faithful to the mere dwelling of God within the faithful only in his effect—God as the efficient cause. Divine filiation, according to Aquinas, consisted of similarity, *similitudo*, not substantial oneness.[7] For Aquinas, God was the life of the soul, not as an in-dwelling principle, but as efficient cause: *Deus est vita animae per modum causae efficientis* (*Sth* I–II 110, 1 ad 2).

I recommend reading St. Thomas's sentence twice. It sounds straightforward, but he states most precisely that against which Eckhart pushed. We have to remember these expressions when Eckhart demands the silence of the efficient cause, *in silentio causae efficientis*.

Thomas Aquinas asserted himself against Peter Lombard so completely with this theory that some older editions of the Lombard's *Sentences* append to the main text a list of those teachings that were abandoned subsequently by the majority of the scholastic thinkers; this retroactive list begins with the Lombard's thesis that the Holy Spirit is a substantial presence. In light of this development from about 1250, Eckhart's doctrine of divine filiation appeared heretical. Eckhart was out to provoke. In the *Book of Divine Consolation*, he opposes Aquinas's thesis of efficiency with the following sentence: The divine Goodness does not *make* the good man, but it *begets* him: *bonus in quantum bonus non est factus* (n. 3, 198.14–15). An efficient cause remains outside the effected; it produces a separation and distinction between God and the soul. And Eckhart rebuts the *similitudo* theory of divine filiation even more brusquely: the soul, he writes in the *Book of Divine Consolation*, hates likeness, *similitudo*, out of love for the One (nn. 16–17, 205.7–19). And even more harshly he writes against its reduction to mere likeness: the just man as just man is of *one* being with *iustitia*, with all of its properties (n. 9, 202.1–7).

It is never possible to evaluate issues of orthodoxy and heresy within actual history by looking back to the Bible, especially not in a tradition of critical biblical exegesis. Scholastic traditions, regulations taken from canon law, local conventions of speech, methodological advancement, and prejudices of specific decades always play a role. Many factors determine a historical situation. Pope John XXII canonized Thomas Aquinas in 1323. He was striving for doctrinal coherence. He saw that heresies abounded. Chronicles of the fourteenth century teem with inquisitors. Boccaccio's *Decameron* describes how they comported themselves, how they terrorized a city. Peter Lombard's thesis of God's substantial presence within the soul of the faithful was lost to Western Christianity. A scholastic of the sixteenth century, Willem Estius, reports that there was no one left who supported it (1 *Sent.* 17, 1). And although his was not the last word on the subject—learned studies of the

Greek church fathers in the seventeenth century reconstructed the old doctrine—it applies to the course of the fourteenth century.[8] Certain groups, including the theologians, developed distinct doctrines and common convictions within different networks, communities, and schools and during different decades, and Eckhart was moving against the current. He knew and said as much. The friars who denounced him may have had a variety of motives, but they had grown up in an order that had been trying to prevent deviations from Thomism since 1286 under threat of serious punishment, even if it failed to achieve this goal in the fourteenth century. There were dull zealots within the order who, in Albertus Magnus's words, ran up against philosophy like irrational animals; and there were conscientious Dominicans who considered it their duty to obey the order's decrees and submit non-Thomistic teachers for punishment.

In this situation, Eckhart stood against the Thomism that prevailed within the Dominican order regarding a theoretical question, but also against the common, seemingly scholastic consensus. In addition, his liberal use of language was unsettling to many. This was the case, for example, in his German sermon 6 (DW 1:110.8–111.7) when Eckhart explained divine filiation in the following words: we are transformed in God like the bread during the Eucharist. It became one of the charges against him (LW 5, n. 54, 216.7–15). According to the high scholastic doctrine of the Eucharist, what Eckhart's statement meant was: divine filiation effects a transubstantiation within man. Man would cease to be man. But that was not Eckhart's position.

Peter Lombard had already had to overcome significant hurdles in order to establish his thesis of the Holy Spirit's substantial presence.[9] Among academics, the tendency to posit intermediary links was strong; within the social and political life of the day, it was ubiquitous because it paralleled the conditions of life. Awareness of creatures' autonomy and the stability of their essences increased. In this context, grace could mean two things: on the one hand, God's affection for human beings, and on the other hand, a supplementation or perfection of nature. Within man's substance, it could only be a property or an accident. Scholastics grew accustomed to saying that it was an infused and accidental habitus. Beside it, they left the meaning of the word "grace" unchanged as divine favor, or God's benevolent affection. In addition, individual impulses for good actions were called "grace," as, thus, were individual divine promptings to promote man's final purpose. The trend of interpreting grace as a reinforcement of nature went squarely against Eckhart's immediatism. From then on, theologians have defended as a timeless truth the idea that grace was a "permanent form that rests in man, so to speak."[10] Thomas Aquinas put it thus, and the catechism of the Council of Trent repeated three hundred years later, most solemnly, that grace was a divine quality that inhered in the soul, *divina qualitas in anima inhaerens*.[11] Why a property of the human soul should be "divine" was difficult to understand.

I have spoken of Eckhart's immediatism. I take it to mean his rejection of intermediary entities between God and the ground of the soul. Eckhart's divine filiation came about without recourse to intermediary links. Every form of mediation, he stated in the sermon *Von dem edeln menschen*, was foreign to God (DW 5:114.21). This sentence also made it onto the list of Eckhart's errors (LW 5, n. 25, 208.21). In Eckhart's mind, intermediation was a given and indispensable factor in many respects, but not in the context of the mind-soul becoming one with God. For Eckhart, grace makes sons of God; it does not supplement the soul's nature with additional properties. Moreover, Thomas Aquinas had subsumed it technomorphically into the following system: God provides it teleologically as a means for the active achievement of the supernatural goal.[12] Eckhart, however, claimed of his God that any kind of mediation was foreign to him. The ground of the soul is united with God in being, not just in acting, *secundum esse, non secundum operari tantum*.[13] Eckhart's offensive comparison with the Eucharistic transubstantiation said as much.

2. God-World Analogy

The second bone of contention was Eckhart's thesis that God is Being. Something that is unlike Being is nothingness.[14] Nothing exists outside of Being. Thus, the idea that we are here and God is there was abolished. Even Eckhart, however, distinguished between the all-encompassing, noncontracted Being and the formal being of a thing. And this distinction was not merely a concession during his trial. It fought off the danger that Eckhart might be accused of considering every creature to be also the Creator. Still, some anxiety remained. Did he not also say that a creature per se was pure nothingness (n. 73, 225.11–15)? And did this idea not deny the definition of creation as disclosure of Being? Could he in this context invoke the dogmatic doctrine that creation (*creatio*) occurred out of nothingness (*ex nihilo*)? It is obvious that Eckhart departed from Aquinas's doctrine of *analogia* on an important point: he employed the example of urine and health just like Aristotle and Aquinas, but he insisted that there was nothing at all of said health within the urine.[15] Like Aristotle, Averroës, and Dietrich of Freiberg, Eckhart stressed the nonautonomy of accidents more than Thomas Aquinas did.[16] Their being was solely the being of substance. Eckhart derived his model of *analogia* from this understanding of the relation between accident and substance. In this view, there was nothing of Being within creatures, and the problem of whether Eckhart denied creation (*creatio*) returned.

The relation God-world was disconcertingly different for Eckhart from what was expected. In one sense, the world appeared negligible opposite the Godhead, but in another sense, it was as though Being itself absorbed it, the Being that constituted the things and was not merely an abstraction (n. 30, 210.13–17). The doctrine of divine filiation said that God could not be conceptualized without the soul. The theory of ideas and of the divine *verbum* stated that the world was truer in God than in itself; and thus even God could not be conceptualized without the world. Did not the world always exist then? When the line of reasoning based on the thesis of God's timelessness is strictly followed through, then there was no time *before* the creation of the world; and thus it was impossible to claim that God had existed before the world, since *before* is a temporal determination. That is why Eckhart could say that God was not before he created the world (n. 43, 213.9–15). Since the middle of the thirteenth century, however, the Aristotelian-Averroistic thesis concerning the eternity of the world had been a dread for the theologians—often discussed and discarded by the church. Eckhart's idea was derived from Augustine, Averroës, and Dietrich of Freiberg's doctrine of time; however, for almost a century there had been an ingrained cultural attitude that philosophizing heretics were teaching the eternity of the world. It was not the case with Eckhart, but he associated God with the world in his concept of Being and via the theory of ideas. Many worried that he thereby connected God and the world too intimately. Did he not go so far as to equate them? Eckhart raised obstacles to the idea that God was there, and the world here. God created the world, according to Eckhart, by placing it into Being, and thus into himself.

3. Trinity

Eckhart's views on the Trinity were denounced as heretical. Thomas Aquinas had explained at *Sth* I 32, 2 that the special feature of the Christian doctrine of the Trinity—one, in particular, that no philosophical speculation could ever arrive at—was the positing of a real difference, *realis distinctio*, between the three divine persons. If the core of the Christian doctrine was the claim that there were three countable, actually distinct persons within God, then it was a serious charge to say that Eckhart claimed that there was no *distinctio* in God (n. 23, 208.21). And while this sentence had made it onto the Latin list of Eckhart's errors only via a contestable translation, it did represent Eckhart's doctrine correctly. It becomes obvious in the fact that Eckhart, as the evaluation drawn up by the theologians in Avignon shows (n. 97, 587.1–2), defended himself before them with the sentence that there was no distinction (*distinctio*) of persons in God. In practice, Eckhart indeed added "*and these three are one*" whenever he spoke of God as Father, Son, and Holy Spirit. Eckhart recognized a relational distinction, for the begetter was not the begotten, but his interpretation assumed that the divine life in its intellectual execution would always already have removed this distinction. God is one in every way. Someone who sees a distinction does not see the One, but two or three. But God is the One, as Eckhart—invoking Moses Maimonides—taught (n. 46, 214.13–17).

Eckhart deviated from the Thomistic theory of the Trinity on five points:

1. He denied all *distinctio* within the One.
2. Citing the *Book of the Twenty-Four Philosophers*, he interpreted the triune life philosophically as a return of the mind to itself, as a reflection, especially in German sermon 9.
3. He wanted to prove the Trinity with philosophical arguments, something that Thomas Aquinas and the majority of the Scholastics rejected (*In Ioh.*, LW 3, nn. 2–3, 4).
4. He had declared brusquely that *everything* that was written or taught about the Trinity was wrong: *omne quod de trinitate beata scribitur aut dicitur, nequaquam sic se habet aut verum est* (Latin sermon 4, part 2, LW 4, n. 30, 31.1–2). This sentence was not quoted verbatim during Eckhart's trial. Nonetheless, it clearly shows Eckhart's position as an outsider; it was an affront to all theology since Augustine. Other heretics were burned for sentences such as this one, in Geneva as late as three centuries after.
5. Eckhart denied the numerical concept in its uncorrected application to divine Oneness; at most, one could speak of "a number without number"— like Nicholas of Cusa, who did not allow any numerical determinations regarding the Trinity and in his *Apologia doctae ignorantiae* (ed. R. Klibansky,

24.9–10) claimed to have found a quotation by Augustine that read: "When you begin to count, you begin to err." Unfortunately, the sentence is nowhere to be found in Augustine's writings.

It is incomprehensible (or perhaps all too understandable) that in the scholarly literature on Eckhart, we time and again find the claim that Eckhart's doctrine of the Trinity was Thomistic, and that his censors had hunted for heresies within Eckhart's works "with all their might" (W. Trusen). Even a scholar of outstanding merit imposed a harmony where there was none to be found: "*Eckhart partage pleinement la théologie trinitaire dont Thomas d'Aquin offre l'expression technique la plus équilibrée.*"[17]

    It is incorrect. Eckhart's denouncers did not need to make much of an effort to consider Eckhart's understanding of the Trinity heretical. They had a contingent conception of orthodoxy. All they needed to do was to identify orthodoxy squarely with Thomism or even just with the consensus prevailing since Peter Lombard. Perhaps they felt offended by Eckhart's provocative formulation that there were theologians who employed numerical terms for God as indiscriminately as if they were speaking of three cows. "In God, there is neither number nor plurality," Eckhart wrote (*In Sap.*, LW 2, n. 112, 448).

4. God Gives Everything

The Dominicans who denounced Eckhart considered his doctrine of divine birth heretical, especially because Eckhart ascribed all properties of the divine *verbum* to reborn humans.[18] They noted that Eckhart taught that the deified man receives everything from the Father, truly everything that he gives to the divine *verbum*, everything, without exception (n. 47, 233.21–23). They recorded that Eckhart claimed that the deified man is exactly like the Son, without any difference, *sine omni distinctione* (n. 47, 237.14–21). Thomas Aquinas had explained divine filiation as *similitudo* and had thereby retained every kind of distinction. Eckhart tore down these walls with the justification that God was indivisibly one. When God gives, he gives everything. For Eckhart, the son has the same nature as the Father and, removed from time and space, perpetually creates the world with God. He begets the son just like the Father; he wants to be like the Father (n. 55, 217.1–7). This identification of man with God seemed blasphemous. Did Eckhart not thereby disregard Christ's singularity?

5. God without Anger, without Freedom of Choice

Eckhart, as his denouncers alleged, restricted God's freedom. Eckhart did not allow him the free choice to call blessed individuals to eternal life while letting others continue on the road to eternal perdition along with the mass of sinners. Eckhart's God did not know any anger.

Grace as the random selection of the blessed from the *massa damnata* is a doctrine connected with Augustine's name, and Augustine had asserted its authority within the Latin West, even if not necessarily in all its nuances. Thomas Aquinas—despite the frequent invocations of his doctrines within anti-Augustinian liberating tendencies—likewise asserted that grace consisted of God freeing some people from sin while leaving others within it for no reason.[19] Eckhart's God, however, *had* to be good. It was the nature of Goodness to disclose itself without envy. Eckhart's God was free, but his freedom did not consist in rescuing the select. A man who denied everything and detached himself from everything compelled God to grant himself to him. The humble have power over God, Eckhart wrote in German sermon 14 (DW 1:233.10–13). Eckhart's fellow friars who were full of religious zeal had to include this in the list of his errors—twice (n. 57, 314.22; n. 29, 324.19–27). Eckhart made his situation even worse when he added the justification that the humble man and God were one.

6. A Radically Negative Theology

Eckhart's push for a negative theology appeared to his denouncers like another affront against orthodoxy. As in the case of Eckhart's rejection of all kinds of *distinctio* within God, they believed that Eckhart was taking his dependence on Moses Maimonides much too far. They thought that he took his diction to an extreme when he said that God was not good.[20] If there were no difference between the two sentences "God is evil" and "God is good," then there would exist no scientific way of talking about God. It would even be inconceivable how God could have made himself comprehensible to man, that is, how he could have revealed himself. German philologists since Quint have been fond of describing this problematic situation with the term "paradox," but it is not suitable here—not for historical or systematic or linguistic purposes. Eckhart's solution was: God can be called any name as long as we are aware that names merely represent human conceptions of things, not the things themselves.

7. The Ground of the Soul

One serious and weighty charge concerned Eckhart's idea that there was a power within the soul that was uncreated and uncreatable.[21] His denouncers quoted German sermon 15 (DW 1:255.5–7). In this sermon, Eckhart indeed spoke of a "*kraft.*" Around 1300, this term was easily construed to mean faculties of the soul, in the sense of the philosophical psychology of the day. Someone who spoke of the indwelling of the Holy Spirit in the fashion of Peter Lombard, however, could refer to it as "*kraft*" as well—certainly not as a power of the soul, not as something attached to the soul, but as God himself, who propelled men to good thoughts and deeds. This problem pervaded Eckhart's trial until the end, and the scholarly literature on Eckhart for a long time as well. The list of errors contains this problem several times; it quotes German sermon 13.[22] Someone incorporating Eckhart's theory of divine filiation into the established doctrines of the faculties of the soul would have to assume that Eckhart believed in a soul that was a composite of created and uncreated. The repeatedly employed term "*kraft*" was seen around 1320 as either a *lapsus linguae*, a relapse into an older, formerly theologically sound diction, or a philosophical absurdity. What it certainly did not sound like was orthodoxy.

8. Reality of the Universal

What also seemed heretical were the conclusions that Eckhart drew from his realism regarding universals. These conclusions were of a varied nature. For a start, Eckhart insisted that God did not adopt a single human individual in Christ but human nature, for example, in German sermon 5b (DW 1:86.6–87.1). Humanity as a whole was deified (LW 5, n. 55, 329), for human nature was common to all people in the same way. All individuals were included because Eckhart conceptualized humanity as a real universal. This again seemed to threaten Christ's uniqueness, especially when Eckhart put it provocatively: everything that scripture says about Christ also applies to me (German sermon 24, DW 1:421.1–422.3). Something like this must have sounded maddeningly presumptuous to any upright Christian, even without a background in Thomism.

Another conclusion drawn from Eckhart's realism regarding universals was his interpretation of the commandment of love. Eckhart insisted that we must love other people "as ourselves," but "we ourselves" means, according to Eckhart, all people, including those beyond the ocean, because

"I myself" am the same as them, namely, a human being. There was supposed to be no gradation; love should no longer take into account familial relations, everyday structures, or close relationships. In a third document, now
lost, of which we know thanks to the evaluation of the theologians in
Avignon, Eckhart's denouncers quoted a sentence that stated that there were
no steps and no hierarchy in love, *nec gradus est nec ordo*.[23] Eckhart quoted
Bernard of Clairvaux: love does not know any hierarchy (LW 5, nn. 100–1,
342). It was in direct contradiction to Thomas Aquinas (*Sth* II–II 27, 7–8).
In his rigorously universalist ethics, Eckhart seemed to forget that we are
supposed to love our *neighbor*, not the people beyond the sea.

Furthermore, Eckhart distorted Christian ethics by pulling it back
completely into the internal realm and contesting the ethical quality of any
external work.[24] The third list of Eckhart's errors included his tenet that
God does not command any single external act.[25] The second list quoted
from German sermon 6 that man was not supposed to strive for anything,
not honor or benefit or reward, and not even sanctity or inner devotion
(LW 5, n. 89, 339.17–21). And yet everyone had assumed until then that
the Christian life consisted precisely in striving for holiness or inner piety.
And finally, the lists intended for the archbishop recorded the strange
doctrine that Paul wanted to be divorced from God for God's sake.[26]
Accordingly, the just man was not simply supposed to stop striving for
holiness; he was to go to hell for God's sake. Because God in reality was
with the just man, however, hell thus became heaven. Eckhart turned the
Christian life upside down. He muddled everything, especially when he
claimed in the *Book of Divine Consolation* that God was praised also through
sin (n. 12, 203.4–21).

9. Prayer

The list of errors touched upon several other ethical aspects of Eckhart's
teachings; it seemed as though he had misinterpreted not just the Christian
command of love. The submitted quotations proved: he also erred in regard
to prayer. Eckhart stridently distanced himself from religious ceremonies,
the kneeling and bowing. The good man prays to Goodness itself, in his
mind and in truth, through his being, not through moving his feet. Kneeling
and pious nods—those were things for simple people. These unlearned
people needed someone to call out to them: "You are praying to something
you do not know" (n. 28, 209.18–210.2). We have to imagine the religious

practice of Eckhart's day, with all its gestures, to comprehend the shock that Eckhart's call caused: *You know not what you do!*

Similarly scandalous was Eckhart's rejection of prayers of supplication. For Eckhart, asking for something created meant asking for nothing. His fellow friars reported him because he preached that he would have to think long and hard about whether he wanted to ask something of God (n. 64, 221.12–15). It was all the more offensive because Eckhart justified his rejection of prayers of supplication by saying that there was no hierarchy, no disparity between God and the *homo divinus*. God, according to Eckhart, is not the lord, but our friend (n. 101, 342).

God was the Lord; that much was certain for every reader of the Bible. Was Eckhart not depriving him of this exalted traditional title? He even admitted that his soul wanted to enter not just into the role of the Son, but also that of the *Father*. It seemed like presumptuous insubordination, not like the true understanding of Christian love. Petitionary prayers were daily church practice. The church prayed for military victories and abundant harvests. For many Christians, prayers of supplication were the main form of prayer. Christ himself taught people to pray for their daily bread. Eckhart, the professor of theology, dared to contradict him.

10. Figurative Interpretation of the Bible

Eckhart's biblical exegesis ran counter to canonical methods. He invoked the tradition of allegorical interpretation. He emphasized that he did not dispute literal interpretations, but then he let the cat out of the bag and explained that those difficulties in interpretations of Adam, Eve, and the serpent that arise in literal interpretations would disappear if one interpreted them allegorically. Eckhart wanted figurative interpretations to avoid those problems to which the pious willingly submitted, for example, if someone asked in what language Eve and the serpent had carried on their fateful conversation.[27] Augustine had greatly valued allegorical exegesis in the struggle with the Manicheans about the interpretation of Genesis, but had increasingly repressed this type of exegesis thereafter. Allegory was supposed to be permitted secondarily as an additional, edifying contemplation, but it was not to replace the realistic and literal interpretation called "historical." Augustine himself had recognized that allegory, unless decidedly positioned in second place, was a technique for sidestepping miracles. And it was so in Eckhart's thought. He wanted to avoid those difficult questions like the supposed language of the serpent; they were mere distractions from the essential points. And they could not be answered. It was out of the question to fall back on God's omnipotence in the context of the temptation in Paradise. While God could make donkeys and other animals speak, claiming that he miraculously granted human language also to the devil within the serpent— that was taking it too far.

19. Eckhart's Trial: The Defense

A Short Summa of Eckhart's Philosophy

The inquisition did not unquestioningly crush Eckhart. He was given the chance to speak, in Cologne as well as in Avignon—and multiple times at that, both in his long apologia, the *Defense* found in the Soest manuscript, and again, briefly, in the *Votum* of the Avignonese theologians. At an early stage of the trial—in Cologne before January 1326—Eckhart was presented with six theses considered suspect of heresy, which stem from an otherwise unknown apologia of his *Liber benedictus* (the collective title given to the *Book of Divine Consolation* and the sermon *Von dem edeln menschen*).[1]

These six theses form a short summa of Eckhartian philosophy. They come from Eckhart's defense and were reported to the archbishop as suspect of heresy. I briefly summarize them here.

Neither matter nor accident has its own being. They owe their being solely to the substantial form.[2] Because of the successful reception of Aristotle, there was no longer anything heretical about subscribing to the Peripatetic philosophy of substantial form.[3] The context reveals what the denouncers were concerned with: Eckhart was repeating his theory of the primary determinations. According to Eckhart, these are not abstractions; they constitute things and outlast them. While the qualities of things usually receive their being from the substantial form of the thing, the primary determinations do not obtain their being from the bearers of these determinations. They are ontologically "prior," that is, fundamental: they give being. Here the frequently mentioned theory of the accident's deficiency of being comes into operation. Aristotle derived analogical predication from the relation of accident to substance and emphasized that only the being of the substance was the being of the accidental, and that the accident thus had no being in and of itself. In this sense, Eckhart established, as the starting point for further considerations, that the accident gives the individual thing no being; it receives it wholly from Being. The fifth thesis develops this idea further in theoretical terms of analogy: things that happen to have the same name, so-called *aequivoca*, are fundamentally distinct; things that are of the same kind, so-called *univoca*, bear the same name because they are differentiations of the same *one* thing. Here, Eckhart's realism of the universals pipes up again. Analogically designated things are not wholly distinct things and do not represent differentiations of a single thing either, but rather form distinct modes of the same thing. The word "thing" here signifies a real, shared, universal nature. The Aristotelian example is health: it exists solely in a living creature, and only in reference to it do we call urine or a diet "healthy." But then Eckhart emphasizes, in good Aristotelian-Averroistic fashion, that the accident does not bestow being upon the thing; health is not in the urine in any way; the urine is only *called* "healthy" according to it. Health is in the urine as a *sign* of the only existing health, namely, of that in the living creature. In this respect, we can call it its mode without thereby ascribing proper being to it. Thus, sentence 3 (LW 5, n. 27, 209.15–17) holds true: insofar as he is good, the good man receives his entire being from the uncreated Goodness. That is the result of the Aristotelian tenet that the word "white" does not indicate anything other than whiteness, *albedo*. This was the doctrine of the first pages of the *Book of Divine Consolation*.

Two of the theses that follow have already been discussed: with thesis 1 (n. 25, 209.8–12), Eckhart invokes Peter Lombard's lesson that the Holy Spirit, the uncreated, lives substantially in the soul. Eckhart must have known that this idea had fallen out of favor. He was distancing himself from the way that academics spoke about the Trinity around 1320. With thesis 4 (n. 28, 209.18–210.2), he repeated that the good man worships God in his mind and in truth by being good; ceremonies only occupy the imagination of the uneducated.

The denouncers turned the tables. They turned these defenses into new evidence of heresy. They understood that Eckhart was merely repeating his theory of the accident's deficiency of being and his conception of *analogia*. According to this theory, creatures, taken by themselves, were nothing at all.

The Three Premises

"I, Brother Eckhart from the Order of Preachers, answer"—so Eckhart confidently begins his defense. He stresses that, because of the privileges of his order, he is not obligated to appear before the archiepiscopal inquisitors in Cologne. Almost seventy years old, Eckhart looks back on his life: up to this point, no one has denounced him because of his teachings or because of his life; he has the approval of his entire order and of the people. He specifically emphasizes that it is the approval of people of both genders (n. 76, 275.10–16). If he were less famous or less eager for justice, enviers would not persecute him in this way. Eckhart says that he did not only teach justice, but also fought for it. He wanted to reform living and thinking. He speaks of his enemies with disdain: he is amazed that they have not found even more doctrinal errors in his works, for he has written many more works, after all, than those books from which they are citing. But he did compose those books. The German texts of the *Liber benedictus*, the six theses from his first defense, the excerpts from his commentary on Genesis: these texts are his. He intends to demonstrate their truth, but they contain many unusual opinions regarding difficult questions, *rara* and *subtilia* (nn. 78–79, 276.9–23). In the *Prologus generalis* (LW 1, n. 2, 149.1), he announced with the words *nova et rara* that he was teaching something new and unusual; regarding the quotations from his sermons, he reserves the right for himself to prove their authenticity step-by-step. If it is shown to him that he has claimed something that is false, he will gladly yield to a better understanding. Eckhart admits that he can err, but he cannot be a heretic, for that is a matter of the will.

Eckhart's denouncers did not need to be told twice that they had cited too few of his writings. They subsequently delivered a longer and better-elaborated list; a third list with quotations from the commentary on John followed. Before Eckhart addresses the individual theses, he explains the premises of all his propositions. They become self-evident under these three conditions. First, one needs to pay attention to the "insofar." When Eckhart talks about the good man "insofar" as he is good, then this reduplication excludes everything else from the ongoing consideration (LW 5, n. 81, 277.6–8). And so in talking about man "insofar" as he is "divine man," *homo divinus*, his body and everything else is excluded from the discussion without denying its existence. Eckhart then provides examples from the theology of the twelfth and thirteenth centuries to prove the validity and fruitfulness of this abstract way of proceeding.

Eckhart explains here that all his thinking is based on the interpretive power of the "insofar." If it is said of man that he enters into all the properties of the Godhead, then that holds "insofar" as he is son. Eckhart is not recanting, but probably modifying his earlier position. Eckhart specifies the perspective with which he views reality; he concedes that other perspectives are both necessary and possible.

It would be possible to argue against him that his is a merely subjective position; his choice of a given perspective is merely his own individual operation, to which he attributes an enormous degree of reality. Is there not a certain rationalism in the assumption that an abstractly chosen perspective shows the most important aspects of reality? After all, Eckhart deduces fundamental features of human self-conception and rules for conduct from his "insofar." Eckhart wards off this objection by showing that theology has always employed this method. He does not advance a theoretical argument. It is the "rationalism" of scholastic culture, not his private version, that he declares as his first premise. Alongside his realism of the universals, this is the Achilles' heel of his thinking. It allows him to construct a system of thought that encompasses God and the world and man. It sounds simple when Eckhart admonishes that one must pay attention to his "insofar." But therein lay an anticipation of the thinking about reality, a customary way of thinking in scholastic culture, that was of tremendous consequence. It gave him space for excessive propositions, which he only pretends to downplay by explaining that they hold only "insofar."

Second, Eckhart explains, he presupposes Aristotle's tenet from the fifth chapter of the *Categories* (3b 19) in everything that follows: that the term "whiteness" signifies nothing other than "being white." If I call something "good," I mean nothing other than Goodness. It is a conceptual trimming of reality like that of the "insofar." For under this assumption, the individual good man forms a unity with Goodness: *Bonus et bonitas sunt unum* (n. 82, 278.3–6). And thus we have arrived at Eckhart's doctrine of Oneness. It turns a linguistic, logical observation into a metaphysics, as a philosophy of Christianity. Eckhart knows that he is being criticized for conceiving of the connection between man and God as too close, namely, as becoming one. He therefore adds that the unity of the good and Goodness in God himself is a univocal oneness, the unity of man and divine Goodness an analogical oneness.[4]

That sounded more correct than was intended. Eckhart does not add here that he interprets analogy according to the model of the accident-substance relation and construes the accident's deficiency of being in such a way that there is nothing of real health in urine, absolutely nothing. Therefore, there is nothing, absolutely nothing of Goodness in the individual good man unless Goodness has poured itself into him. This poured-out goodness is identical with the Goodness that pours itself; it is begotten, not made. And thus the creature, considered by itself, is nothing; the being that shows itself in the creature is the Being disclosed by God. There is no duality here. And no temporal relation. The key word "*analogia*" must be interpreted here not in its Thomistic sense, but rather in the sense of Eckhart's theory on analogy. The mention of *analogia* thus leads back to Eckhart's concept of essential meaning: the just man as just, and thus thought of in reduplication, is nothing other than Justice. The same applies to a being and Being, to the individual one and Oneness, to the individual wise man and Wisdom. These primary determinations constitute the individual things; they have everything from these intellectual principles.

The third premise that Eckhart names as the foundation for his thinking is a double proposition about everything that is acting or begetting. It is a metaphysical claim about everything that acts, *omne agens*, insofar as it is an *agens*. It has two aspects: first, it says that no efficient cause by its nature finds solace before it has introduced its own form into that which has been effected or begotten by it. If its effecting has been successful, then it has passed on everything that its substantial form contains—again we encounter the strictest universality—to the begotten (n. 83, 278.7–13).

Eckhart claims this of every efficient cause. We would be well advised to think about the begetting of a living thing. Eckhart is positing the disclosure not of all individual properties, but rather of all elements of the substantial form. All worldly efficiency is a disclosure of form, and "form" has the full meaning of the Aristotelian *morphe*.

The second aspect is another example of the Eckhartian art of abstraction. He says: everything that acts, insofar as it is an effecting thing, or everything that begets as a begetting thing is unbegotten; as such, it is neither made nor created. It is not from another; it is *non ab alio*.

From a Thomistic standpoint, every creature stems from another, is *ab alio*. Eckhart says that this is not the case with efficient causes and begetters, and it is only this premise that makes his thinking evident.[5] Thus, we need to look at it more closely.

Eckhart again describes his way of proceeding, upon which his entire thinking depends, as an abstract operation. He conceives of effecting and begetting as a unit that encompasses contradictory elements. Again he claims a metaphysical universality and again everything holds only "insofar" as we think of the effecting as an effecting and of the effected as an effected. The one that effects or begets as such is uneffected and unbegotten. It is not from another; it is the source, principle, or unbegotten father. But insofar as it discloses its shape or substantial form, it is opposed to and yet one with the begotten. Everything that effects begets a unity with an immanent, relative opposition. In every actually occurring change (*motus*), changing and "being changed" are one.

Eckhart is presenting a theory of becoming conceptualized through natural philosophy, interpreting "becoming" as the being united of oppositions within the unity of the process. And hence he gains a metaphysical rule of the highest universality, which already contains a philosophy of the Trinity in its expressions: Father, Son, begotten, not made, one with the Father in relative opposition, full reciprocity of the related, which are one because oneness always leads itself back to Oneness. Someone who can conceive of this comprehends the Trinity and sonship philosophically. Someone who has not conceived of it does not understand a single word of Eckhart, even if he were to recite all his works. Eckhart explains this explicitly when he sums up in his conclusion that from the three said premises, he deduces the truth of *all* the statements that are taken from his books and propositions and held against him. With their objections, his opponents demonstrate only that they are uneducated and that they lack a pious disposition (n. 86, 279.11–14).

We shall look back once more at Eckhart's three premises: in the dramatic situation of the beginning of the trial, they summarize everything that Eckhart claims formed the basis of all his statements, written or oral. They are all of a philosophical character of the highest abstraction. There is no talk of the Bible or of mystical experiences. They are concerned with the philosophical foundations of a new and deepened understanding of the Bible and of Christian truth. Someone who has understood them, Eckhart says, can demonstrate the truth of all the theorems that are being held against him as doctrinal errors.

Thesis for Thesis

Now on to Eckhart's responses to the individual theses. He denied having taught only a single one. Malicious and ignorant—that is what Eckhart said the person had to be who ascribed the thesis to him that a part of the soul was uncreated, as though the soul were made up of created and uncreated parts (n. 92, 281.14–16). There certainly were uncreated and uncreatable things in the soul, namely, the Godhead itself, but it was not a part of the soul, Eckhart declared. If it was called a "power" in the soul, then it was naturally not one of the "faculties of the soul," but rather the Godhead itself, acting within us. Eckhart considered it incorrect to claim that a faculty of the soul was uncreated. It was right, however, that man as intellect was created according to the image of God, who was intellect, pure intellect (n. 137, 298.12–299.4).

What was held against him regarding the fortress of the soul was obscure and dubious. He said that he never claimed it (n. 147, 303.1–5). Admittedly, he had spoken of the nameless ground of the soul, which stood higher than intellect and will insofar as these were faculties of the soul. He said that Jesus entered into this castle, that he gave it his divine Being through his grace, which concerned being more than effecting.[6]

This was not a retraction, just a clarification. By contrast, he declared that what he had said about the prayer of supplication has been misunderstood. Eckhart claimed that he did not say that one should not pray to God, but rather that God knows our needs in advance; he stands in front of the door and knocks, (n. 144, 301.8–12). But Eckhart had argued differently before, namely, by citing the nothingness of created things. His retraction shifts the point in question. He probably saw that he had gone too far.

Both of the mentioned doctrinal points—the uncreatedness of a power of the soul and the prayer of supplication—referred to sermon texts. Whoever thinks of Eckhart today primarily as a preacher must keep in mind that Eckhart thought of his academic texts as more reliably transmitted and more thoroughly formulated than his sermons. In any case, he differentiated academic prose from the style of sermons. He frequently comes back to this point: he need not put up with answering the quotations taken from his sermons. It is only out of generosity that he nevertheless responds to them.[7] When he said that God belongs to the *homo divinus* to the same extent as he does to himself, that was an emphatic way of speaking, *emphatica locutio*, which had the sense of saying that if God effects his works in us, then he must be in us.[8] And when he said that God was so invested in coming to the good man that it was as though he would lose his essence if he did not reveal to us the entire abyss of the Godhead, that was said emphatically; and even the saints spoke in the same way, after all, when they said, for example, that sins cause God great pain.[9] It was also said emphatically that God *must* give himself to us. But the meaning of this manner of speaking is clear: it is God's nature to be good, to disclose himself, and to give us everything.[10] Eckhart sticks to the idea that God gives himself *wholly* and that he gives us everything that he is. This, says Eckhart, is completely true (n. 21, 323.7). He explicitly explains that he stands by the incriminating sentence that God gives him *everything* that he gives to the divine *verbum* (n. 55, 329.11–16). He affirms his sentence that there exists no difference between the divine *verbum* and the soul, *non est aliqua distinctio* (n. 142, 351.12–13). He also defends the sentence that we become transformed into God like the bread of the Eucharist. Only the thinking of his opponents, bound by the imagination, would find the sentence false and absurd that states that the same Son is in us and gives everything that belongs to him (n. 99, 341.24–26).

These are the only passages in which Eckhart ascribes one of his sentences to the emphatic style of preaching. They are all contained in the trial documents. Eckhart had never before said that he spoke emphatically. That is an important fact. For there have been interpretations of Eckhart that made Eckhart look like a good Thomist who, in sermon-like exuberance, let himself get carried away by sweeping formulations, which, as a theologian, he had to revoke and which were misunderstood as heretical. If that had been the case, the accusation of heresy would have been caused by the emphatic style of his preaching and by misunderstandings on the part of the people. But that is out of the question. Among the numerous theses considered suspect of heresy, these are the only ones that Eckhart himself connected to his emphatic style as a popular speaker—once to weaken a prior statement in passing and once more to revoke another one in substance.

With "to weaken . . . in passing," I refer to phrases in the *Defense* that Eckhart was able to advance on the basis of his "insofar" technique without taking back another, more important "insofar." That is the case when he proclaims that divine filiation in man is analogical and not univocal (n. 145, 352.23). Or when he affirms the formula by Peter Lombard that the logos is an image (*imago*) of the Godhead and that we are "to the image," *ad imaginem*.[11]

Eckhart adorns his defense with citations from the Bible and Augustine; it is instructive to see how he emphasizes his agreement with Aquinas several times in order to defend himself. For example, he asserts that Aquinas did not ascribe any proper moral quality to external actions, either (n. 124, 292.8–14). Eckhart is referring to *Sth* I–II 20:4. But it is only a partial agreement, and part of it refers to matters that are not being contested.[12] Eckhart rightly invokes Aquinas's differentiation of equivocation, univocation, and analogy (n. 153, 353.14). But apart from the fact that Aquinas's theory of analogy drove his interpreters to desperation because of its complexity, Eckhart differs markedly from it because he found nothing of the determination in the analogate that shares its name. Eckhart's invocations of Aquinas have a decorative character. We can see this as well in n. 131, 296.9. They were of no benefit to Eckhart during his trial.

Occasionally, Eckhart admitted that one of his sentences sounded bad, *male sonat*, for example, the one in which he claimed that the united soul also wanted to be the father and beget the son that begot it. But he defended even this sentence; it was a conclusion from a previous sentence that no distinction existed there.[13] He took back the sentence that we become transformed into God. That was an error,[14] though only in the eyes of his censors—in *his* sense it was true.[15] For in Eckhart's view, the "insofar" here holds: the just man is not transformed in such a way that he would cease to be a man.

The *Defense* rather strengthened other teachings previously considered suspect of heresy. It did not take back the idea that God is Being. Like earlier texts, it differentiated between formal, inhering being and absolute divine Being (n. 117, 289.6–7). That was not a self-serving declaration at the trial. Eckhart decidedly stuck to his own interpretation of analogy. And so the idea of the nonbeing of creatures as such remained. Eckhart hinted at the idea of intellectual being, the *esse cogitativum*, which was decisive for his theory of "becoming one" (n. 61, 331), but did not elaborate on it any further while under interrogation. Furthermore, he contrasted complete agreement with mere similarity, anti-Thomistically; he pitted "being one" against the Thomistically correct "being similar" (n. 3, 319.5): *Homo non debet esse similis deo, sed unum cum deo.*

That was his old, anti-Thomistic interpretation of divine filiation. It was the Rubicon that separated him from traditional scholasticism, which understood itself as orthodox.

Eckhart formulated his theory of the Trinity unrelentingly and strict-ly: if we are talking about three persons, it cannot possibly signify multiplic-ity or countability. The three are one (n. 53, 329.5–7). He repeated his thesis that the Godhead is *one* in every respect, *omnibus modis et secundum omnem rationem* (n. 122, 291.10–11). This threeness was not supposed to be a num-ber; Eckhart's Godhead does not exhibit any distinctness in itself. It is *one* in all ways and in every respect. It is obvious that Eckhart had abandoned the common scholastic doctrine of the Trinity.

Even more impressively, Eckhart insisted on his universalization of the Incarnation. He repeated several times that the Godhead adopted the universal human nature, not the concrete individual Jesus. It united itself with individual humans only with regard to the universality of divine filiation. Eckhart used his realist conception of the universals, with an em-phasis on Incarnation and *caritas*, as though no other theory were possible: "[You share] being human or human nature with every other person. God himself is shared by all" (n. 72, 336.6–7). This philosophical position produces a specific theory of the Incarnation: God adopted the real, univer-sal nature of man; he wanted to show us what true love is. It pertains to all people, not only to friends. Hence, God wanted to say: "Love them be-cause they are human beings, for you too are a human being!" (n. 69, 335.17). Love for oneself, Eckhart says, consists in loving the universal human nature in all individuals, just as the Incarnation consists in the fact that the real universal human nature is joined with God. We should love human beings for that which is human, not as this or that human, but rather human as human: "Take away what is immanent in you!" (n. 68, 335.99). Especially in the following passages of his *Defense*, Eckhart expresses this philosophy of the Incarnation, which is simultaneously a theory of Christian love, as curtly as possible: n. 139, 299.9–14; n. 65, 333.8–15; nn. 67–70, 334.13–335.25.

This is not the place to procure baskets full of citations plucked from Greek ecclesiastical authors who speak about the deification of all human nature. Eckhart lived in the West. And there, around 1320, this belief was monstrous and "rare." Eckhart attempted to designate his de-nouncers not only as evil and uneducated, but also as heretics themselves.[16] The attempt was futile. His enemies had the same biblical texts in front of them as he did. But they had a different philosophy. It did not operate on the basis of oneness and the disclosure of *forma*, but rather on difference and distance. It relied on mere similarity instead of being one with God. Eckhart formulated the opposition like this: they deem it false and heretical that man can be united with God. And yet Jesus says in the Gospel of John: "You, Father, are in me and I in you, so that they might be one in us as well."[17]

20. The End in Avignon: "Devil's Seed"

The Final Interrogation

Eckhart was given one last chance to speak in the report of the theologians in Avignon. The report dates from the second half of 1327 and logs his last defense as abbreviated notes. As mentioned earlier, the committee had condensed the extensive lists from Cologne into twenty-eight points. There were several causes for the deletion of many of the original items. It hardly could have seemed feasible to the theologians of the Curia to combine their assessment with a debate about the great theologian Peter Lombard's ideas in I 17 of his *Sentences* and the Holy Spirit's presence within the faithful. They cut the repetitions and longer explanations of the Cologne list down to a single sentence; that is why the introductory passages from the *Book of Divine Consolation* no longer appeared among the charges. It is not as if the theologians had become more lenient in their criteria. But their work would become much easier if just one of Eckhart's propositions could summarize the general tenor of his long speeches. The censors left out his strictly philosophical theorems, like the theories of intellectual being, efficient causality, accident, and analogy; they worked only from the Cologne lists and devoted themselves to the theological themes relevant to ecclesiastical politics. We are justified in picturing them as well-educated men; they cite Themistius and discuss the interpretation of Augustine, John Chrysostom, and Aquinas. Their judgment of Eckhart's sentences is uniformly scathing. They label all of them as heretical, two as blasphemous,[1] but consistently add that they are referring to the wording of a given section, *prout sonat*. That was their task; they had to judge each of the twenty-eight articles, not Eckhart as a person. But that qualification did not make any difference in this case.

The gentlemen began with long discussions of Eckhart's claim that it had been impossible for God to create the world earlier than he did.[2] Eckhart's statement shows: he did not think of the creation as a random act of God or the result of a choice. For Eckhart, God's action was God's eternal essence. In addition, he understood the first sentence of Genesis as referring not to the temporal beginning of the world, but rather to the divine logos as its principle idea. The world, as God's idea of the world, was eternal. Moreover, Eckhart reminded the judges: without time there was no before, and once time existed, the world was always there.[3] It was important to the judges that a finite number of units of time had passed from the beginning of the world to their present. Their unusual zeal in this matter kept them focused on the first three articles. This can easily be explained: the eternity of the world was considered a standard erroneous doctrine of the time. Positing the eternity of the world was the error of Aristotle and Averroës. This heresy was expected in Avignon. Nevertheless, the censors made the mistake of characterizing eternity as a long duration and of saying of God that he had been *before* the world, *ante tempus fuit*,[4] without realizing that this "before," as Augustine had emphasized, was a temporal determination with relation to the world, to which God's actions were not subject.

It bothered the censors that Eckhart mentioned the creation of the world in the same breath as the begetting of the divine *verbum*. The second of his incriminating articles stated that God begot the divine Son in the same now of eternity in which he created the world. They confronted Eckhart with the following: the begetting of the Son was an eternal process, the creation a temporal one, a *creatio temporalis*, as they said.[5]

The theologians did not reach a consensus regarding the eternity of the world in this case, but the examination resulted in the condemnation of the first three articles. Eckhart's objection that God's activity was his eternal essence and that the world as the content of ideas was identical to the eternal logos did not interest the judges. They had strict criteria for heresy. Claiming that the world was eternal was one of them.

Considering the breadth with which the theologians discussed the eternity of the world, they treated the question whether the intellect was uncreated rather tersely.[6] Eckhart repeated his thesis that it was absurd to think of the soul as pieced together out of created and uncreated parts; the report remains concise to an extreme and says nothing about the fact that Eckhart had conceived of the unity of the intellect and its intellectual content, including the uncreated, according to the model of the wood and the eye. The analysis of intellectual being was left out. The censors indignantly concluded that for as much as Eckhart denied the article, he had written it down and preached it too many times. And above all, it was heretical.

In the fifth article, Eckhart claimed that it is wrong to call God "good." He explained that was as untrue as calling something white "black." Eckhart now considered this sentence an error, but then explicated it via the theory that God is beyond all names. The theologians rejected this justification by arguing that not all sentences are equally inappropriate. If they were all equally remote from divine truth, then one could not say anything about God at all. Saying that God is good is true to a higher degree than claiming that a white object is black. Because Eckhart ignored this difference, they said, he was no longer able to accept any sentence about God; his intensification of negative theology destroyed instruction in the faith and academic theology; it was heretical.[7] Eckhart's theory of theology merely evinced its impossibility.

"All creatures are pure nothingness," says the sixth article. The censors considered it heretical, for it disputed that the Creator bestowed being on the things. If this article were true, they argued, creatures could neither be nor act; creatures endowed with reason could effect neither benefit nor guilt, deserve neither eternal bliss nor damnation.

The report relates that Eckhart defended his article by saying that creatures depend on God at every moment and thus are mere nothingness by themselves. The censors did not accept this reply: in their opinion, creatures do indeed depend wholly on God, but the real dependence is based in their real actuality, *in reali entitate*. They have real being; they are not nothing, but rather are something. God's act of creation was not aimed at nothing. Admittedly, God and the creatures together are not more Being than God alone, yet God and the creatures together are several things, *plures res*.[8] The judges are correct: something that *is* not, cannot be dependent. With their objection, they show *ex negativo* what it meant when Eckhart taught that God is Being. They do not say a single thing about this Eckhartian premise. For them, Eckhart distinguished between *esse absolutum* and *esse formaliter inhaerens* to no avail.[9] His philosophical investigations about white and whiteness, about good and Goodness, were not included.

Articles 7 and 9 form a thematic unit. They state that even evil is not situated outside divine Being; the glory of God shines brightly even in sin. Eckhart, the report says, justified this idea by arguing that evil facilitates patience. In support of this, article 8 offers the proposition that God is praised even in blasphemy. Against this, the theologians objected that it is foolish to refer to insults directed at God as praise. They rejected the interpretation of Augustine put forward by Eckhart for his justification of article 8; in their view, it contradicted Augustine. Eckhart's position was heretical and, moreover, absurd.[10]

One can see where the censors' interests lay: they wanted an unambiguous theology. They wanted clear differentiations between good and bad actions. They wanted the honor of God to be visibly and audibly maintained. They needed rules for external behavior. And they saw all this threatened by the sequence of articles 10–13. To refute these theses, the theologians rejected the heresy that God demanded only interior actions and no external behavior. That God loves the soul, not the external work. The Ten Commandments, they objected, refer to external work. Eckhart is supposed to have responded that God indeed demands external action as well, but that the visible act does not have its moral quality by itself, but rather through the intention of the soul. The censors thought that this sounded dangerous. Good action must indeed be borne by love, and the external act was not primarily intended by God's command, but God rewards and punishes external actions as well. Inner affect is not enough when an external work is required.

Eckhart did not get another chance to speak here. He could have said that he knew as well that love had to become active, but that his proposition had been another one, namely, that an external process does not impart any moral or religious quality. The work is only good if the human being is good.

On to the group of articles 14–16: here the theologians of the Curia dealt with Eckhart's rejection of the prayer of supplication and the expectations of reward. Eckhart did not want to ask for anything created, for everything created was nothingness, the negation of the Good. God alone is our reward. In addition, asking for something represented subordination under the giver; it understood God as the superior lord, not as an equal friend. The censors rejected all this as heretical but mentioned that Eckhart must have asked God for something on occasion. They accused him of condemning the entire church, the home of the prayer of supplication; of contradicting Christ, who called on us to perform the prayer of supplication. They said that Eckhart denounced the struggle for inner devotion or holiness; but someone who renounces piety and holiness could not seriously expect God as the true reward. Renouncing holiness was a grave sin; Eckhart was seducing people into sin and false doctrines. If Eckhart did not want to receive any gifts from God, because God was not his lord but rather his friend, then that was faithlessness. It was true that we should not be content with earthly things, but without being God's servants (*servi*), we cannot attain blessedness, for even in blessedness God is the Lord and we are servants. Then the theologians explained as a matter of principle that denying lordship and servitude was heretical.[11] For God is the Father and Lord in glory. It was blasphemous to say that we are equal to him as sons and should not make him into our Lord through supplication.[12]

Eckhart's excessive formulation expressed that which was new and "monstrous" in his philosophy of Christianity. The censors could not but reject it. Then they examined a whole series of theses, articles 17–23, about the divine filiation, which Eckhart had presupposed in articles 15 and 16. In his divine nature, the theologians explained, Christ had no brothers; he only had them as a man. It was heretical to teach that God was perpetualy begetting the good man. They pointed out that Eckhart himself had explained that his banal identification of the "noble man" with the only begotten Son of God was an error (article 17, n. 68, 580.25), but then justified it nevertheless. The committee of theologians brusquely rejected Eckhart's theory of divine filiation, and their keyword was that Eckhart denied the *difference*. It was a matter of *distinctio*, in multiple senses; Eckhart claimed that God's work always forms a unity, but in that case all created things would be one without any difference, *absque distinctione*.[13] Above all, he underestimated the difference between God's adoptive children and his own only begotten son. Eckhart—heretically—let them be identical with the divine Word, *absque omni distinctione*.[14] Eckhart's comparison with the transformation in the Eucharist proceeded from the same false premise that man becomes the divine Being without any distinction, *sine omni distinctione* (article 20, n. 75, 582). The gentlemen did not shy away from repeating themselves when it came to accusing Eckhart of denying every sort of distinctiveness; in their rejection of article 20, the key phrase occurs five times: *sine distinctione*. They thereby provided a negative characterization of Eckhart's thinking about unity and becoming one. There was another phrase that they used for this: Eckhart claimed unity where similarity was present. Similarity and difference, *similitudo* and *distinctio*, were the keywords when Aquinas spoke about divine filiation. The censors repeated them as criteria for determining orthodoxy and heresy.

The theologians pointed out that Eckhart claimed that the Father gave him *everything* that he gave Christ—but this was false. The Father indeed gave Christ to us as our savior, along with everything belonging to that task, but not also with his special privileges as the only Son of God. No man is perfect like Christ.[15] The deified man, the *homo divinus*, is not the Word made flesh; he was not born of the Virgin Mary and did not die on the cross; he can never have the properties of Christ in the same quality. Eckhart disregarded Christ as an empirical and unique figure. He was not mindful of what belongs to Christ alone, uniquely to him, *singulariter*, and to no other.[16] The theologians recognized that Eckhart explained his position via the commonality of nature. It was another instance of his realism concerning universals. But, they answered, we share only the human, not the divine, nature with Christ. When Eckhart took his identification to the point that God did not really know what to do without men and that man himself was the begetter of the Divine Word, such nonsense did not merit any discussion (article 23, n. 88), and his "insofar" were of no use to him here.[17] This passage was the harshest dismissal of Eckhart by his censors. They resented that he misconstrued the uniqueness of the connection between God and man in Christ. It was also the only passage in which they referred to Eckhart's *inquantum* method, without accepting it as a justification. It led, they objected, to absurd consequences.[18] The theologians found unbearable what Eckhart had to say about the identity of the noble man with Christ. Just as false was his philosophy of the Trinity, which they condemned in articles 24 and 25. Their main accusation: Eckhart did not recognize any difference among the three persons. He said that whoever sees three or two instead of the sought-after One will not become blessed. Then, the censors critically inferred, the blessed ones in heaven do not see the Trinity (article 24, n. 94, 586). The gentlemen went into detail and emphasized that there is indeed no countable quantum in the Trinity, nor in essentiality, but there is in the persons. Eckhart denied the countability and difference of the divine persons. That Eckhart denied countability in God was as heretical as not recognizing any difference between God and creatures, between Christ and the deified man. The report claims that in his defense, Eckhart brought forth the argument that there is no difference of the persons in God. For these three are *one* God. Again and again the keyword occurs: *distinctio*. The censors confronted Eckhart with the orthodox belief that the multiplicity, difference, and countability of the three divine persons are compatible with the unity of the divine being.[19] Eckhart, in contrast, taught that every type of distinctness is alien to God.[20] Where there is no *distinctio*, there is no multiplicity either.

We cannot ascertain whether Eckhart said in Avignon that there is no difference among the persons in God. If he said it, it was a life-threatening denial of a main dogma of Christianity. The censors recognized that according to Eckhart's tenet, there is absolutely no distinctness in God; he is *one* in every way, *Ubi enim nulla distinctio, ibi non sunt plura distincta* (article 25, n. 100, 587.23–24). The committee did not care that Eckhart reinterpreted the Trinity as the return of the mind to itself. They saw him as being in opposition to all Christian theologians of the time, and in this they were right. Eckhart affirms this himself in Latin sermon 4, part 1. The theologians concluded from this that he was deviating from the faith. What was true was that he was deviating from all recent interpretations of the Trinity.

There was yet another theorem of unity that was poorly received in Avignon: Eckhart's theory of *caritas*. He understood love as union, and in this union there was neither gradation nor hierarchy, *nec gradus nec ordo*.[21] That was as un-Catholic and un-"medieval" a position as saying that God did not want any intermediaries. Against this the censors invoked Augustine, John Chrysostom, and Aquinas; above all, however, they argued that one must love God more than one's neighbor. There was thus a hierarchy in love. Love was not a union, they said, but rather two are loved, *duo ibi diliguntur*, and there was a teleological order whereby the neighbor was loved for God's sake.[22] Eckhart's theory of love destroyed this gradualism. In 1327, it was heretical. The Avignonese specialists mentioned neither Eckhart's realism of the universals nor his thesis that God was the most universal. They proceeded on the basis of theses, not philosophical arguments. It could not be any other way for administrators of truth. They needed unambiguous results. And so it is not surprising that they did not philosophically discuss Eckhart's rejection of remorse on the basis of the supratemporal essence of the mind.[23] They saw only heretical dissent against scripture, against the doctrinal decisions of the church, and against the sacrament of penance.[24] They did not want any mixing of good and evil. They needed a good God for the Christian people, a God who admittedly permitted the existence of evil but who did not authorize man to do evil things or even to tolerate his earlier misdeeds.

At this point, it is possible to look back at the main accusations leveled in Avignon against Eckhart's orthodoxy. To conclude, I summarize them once more (LW 5, 568–90):

He teaches that the world is eternal, articles 1–3.

He claims that part of the soul is uncreated, article 4.

He says that God is not good, article 5.

He explains that creatures are pure nothingness, article 6.

He preaches that reviling God is just as good as praising him, articles 7–9.

He deprives external actions of their moral quality, articles 10–13.

He rejects the prayer of supplication and the striving for holiness, articles 14–16.

He conceptualizes divine filiation as complete identity, articles 17–23.

He denies the distinction and countability of the persons of the Trinity, articles 24 and 25.

He misunderstands Christian love as the denial of every form of subordination and superordination, article 26.

He rejects remorse, articles 27–28.

The Judgment of the Pope: Devil's Seed

"Devil's seed"—that was the pope's last word in Eckhart's trial. The solemn document of condemnation is dated March 27, 1329. After mentioning that Eckhart died, it begins with the words *In agro dominico*, in the field of the Lord. The pope alludes to the New Testament parable of a hostile man who strewed weeds over the seed of truth in the field of the Lord. The pope, as the warden of the field, was fending off the evil seed before weeds and thistles overgrew the field—Eckhart's teachings.[25]

The pope could hardly have expressed himself more brusquely. "With deepest sorrow," he begins his report. To paraphrase his text, in his voice: Recently a man from the German lands by the name of Eckhart, supposedly a teacher of theology and a preacher, wanted to know more than was proper. Instead of soberly adhering to the rules of the faith, he turned away from truth and toward fables. Seduced by Satan, the Father of Lies, he sowed thorns and thistles over the brilliant truth of the faith. He invented many things that fogged the true faith in the hearts of many, above all when he preached to simple people, but also when he put his teachings down in writing. According to the investigation of our honorable brother, Archbishop Henry of Cologne, which was continued in the Roman Curia on the basis of our authority, it is clear from the confessions of this Eckhart that he disseminated the following twenty-six articles in both speech and writing.

Twenty-six quotations from Eckhart follow. They are the articles with which the committee had occupied itself, but in a new arrangement. The pope first names fifteen articles that are heretical without any qualification. These articles teach the following errors (LW 5, 596–600):

The world is eternal (1–3).
God is also praised through revilement (4–6).
One should reject the prayer of supplication and not strive for holiness (7–9).
The deified man is identical with the only-begotten Son of God (10–13).
God somehow wants people to sin (14–15; cf. 4–6).

These are followed by eleven articles suspect of heresy, *prout sonant*, but ones that could perhaps result in an orthodox position with the help of many interpretations. They concern:

the ethical insignificance of external actions (16–19)
the identity of the noble man with the only-begotten Son of God (21–23;
cf. 10–13)
the denial of every difference (*distinctio*) in God (24)
caritas as unity of God and man, without hierarchy (25)
the creatures as pure nothingness (26)

In addition to these twenty-six doctrinal errors, there are two articles that Eckhart denied ever having taught:

The uncreated intellect is part of the soul (27).
We cannot call God "good" (28).

The division into three groups is new; Eckhart had not pleaded in vain before the committee. Two articles were only provisionally condemned as being his. The division into two groups, one group of fifteen and another of eleven items, can probably be traced back to the committee's statement, repeated multiple times, that it was judging Eckhart's propositions *ut verba sonant* according to their wording, not according to the context. But it is wrong when people claim that the pope prohibited only sentences that were "ambiguous." That does not even apply in the case of the last eleven items; they were suspect of heresy and prohibited. In short, they too are devil's seed, but it is only to them that the *prout sonant* applies. It is wrong to claim that the pope examined and rejected the teachings only as individual theses. He says explicitly that he examined their wording *and* their context, *tam ex suorum sono verborum quam ex suarum connexione sententiarum*.[26] Of course, he was not trying to say that he requested all of Eckhart's works and read them all; but he did attempt to get an overall idea according to the twenty-eight propositions.

In the last part of his bull, the pope emphasizes that he let many theologians investigate these theses and that he himself carefully examined them with his cardinals. His own examination, like that of the theologians, found the fifteen theses and the two named last to be heretical, both in their wording and in their context; the remaining eleven sounded far too dangerous; they were very bold and suspect of heresy. He condemns these articles with the approval of the cardinals and prohibits the books containing them. He orders that all who defend these articles will be treated as heretical or as suspect of heresy.

At the end of his bull, the pope discloses that at the end of his life Eckhart confessed to having taught the twenty-six articles, but revoked everything that might generate a heretical sense in the heart of believers. He subjected all his words and works to the judgment of the apostolic seat. The report about his retraction sounds believable; it was formulated with enough reservations. To condemn Eckhart as a heretic was not possible: he had not insisted on his errors, and only someone who stubbornly held to his errors counted as a heretic. And condemning him made no sense anymore: his teachings were heretical, devil's seed, but the man was dead. His books were to be burned.

The pope, the cardinals, and the censors saw Eckhart as being in complete opposition to Christian doctrine. In their eyes, Eckhart conceived of God as too closely associated with the world, which was eternal like God and which he had begotten together with the divine *verbum* (articles 1–3). Eckhart misunderstood the Christian doctrine of the creation of the world when he called creatures pure nothingness (26); he did not correctly separate God from evil and from sin (4–6, 14–15); he destroyed the doctrine of the Trinity by not acknowledging any distinction in God (24). He misinterpreted the Incarnation through his complete identification of the noble man with Christ

(10–13, 21–23). He thought heretically about Christian love (25) and the religious and ethical obligation of external actions (16–19). By rejecting the prayer of supplication and the seeking of external things, as well as piety and holiness, he positioned himself outside the bounds of the Christian faith.

One need not love Pope John XXII. He died in 1334, but Dante had already reserved a spot in the *Inferno* for him decades earlier. Whatever one might think of the holy father, if Eckhart indeed confessed the twenty-six doctrinal errors, any other pope—no matter how high-minded—would have had to condemn him dutifully. Eckhart's dissent was blatant. And it is not true that the pope spared Eckhart's person, as one occasionally reads. I have explained why he could not condemn him as a living person. But the pope saw Eckhart and his ideas as entangled in the clutches of Satan. Incidentally, he never said that Eckhart had gone overboard with mysticism; he said that Eckhart wanted to know more than was proper. This was a biblical phrase that was also applicable to heretics. But the historical fact at hand is that the pope used it against Eckhart, not that it appeared in other places as well. The pope did not concern himself with the philosophical background to Eckhart's teachings, which was at least discussed in rudimentary fashion during the committee's proceedings. Someone who says today that Eckhart was a preacher more than anything is following the pope, not Eckhart himself. The pope feared a dissemination of Eckhart's teachings among the people. He condemned Eckhart without compromise. He was only fulfilling his duty. Eckhart's teachings in unmitigated form had no place in the Christian self-understanding of the Roman Church from John XXII to Benedict XVI.

21. Epilogue

Someone who wants to perceive something new has to *gain* perceptions. He has to want them; they will not descend upon him automatically. He will begin searching for them whenever he encounters something in surprise that he has not yet understood.

Even a nonprofessional reader of Eckhart's German texts will notice that Eckhart is not content with simply stating that he wants to guide the reader to oneness with God, but that he incorporates—it will seem to the reader—preparatory intricacies. For example, Eckhart recommends exchanging the name "God" with "Justice" and assures his reader in German sermon 6 that he will have understood everything that he, Eckhart, says once he has grasped the relation of the just man to Justice. The reader simply has to remember—a new intricacy—that the word "just" was not to be construed as anything other than "Justice"; for this ontological thesis from the logic of language, Eckhart points to Aristotle. In this fashion, Eckhart shows even in his vernacular work that his doctrine of the birth of God, which at first sounds simple and devout, implicates the reader in philosophical premises. German sermon 48 takes this tendency even further. Here, Eckhart demands of his hearers or readers that they recognize that we can speak about trees in the external world only because we have cast our eyes onto a tree and have admitted this tree into our eyes, not as a natural thing, but as an image. We are supposed to recognize the act of seeing the tree's image as a reality of its own kind, one that so far had no place within metaphysics, and to no longer confuse this reality with the type of being of the natural things.

There are many indications of theoretical premises such as these in Eckhart's works. They are not just learned decor, but evidence that he considered his argumentative way of speaking a prerequisite. Without it, he explicitly says, all pious doctrines, all interpretations of the Bible, and all ethical demands are worth very little, or even nothing at all.[1] This attitude corresponds to Eckhart's repeated explanations that he was speaking not in the light of natural reason, that is, he did not presume the Christian faith within his argumentation, but wanted to prove its main tenets philosophically. We can read it thus in the German sermons and the consolatory treatise.

The Latin works indicate this even more markedly. The trial records contain a fragment of an Eckhartian self-defense, now lost.[2] It forms a small compendium of Eckhart's philosophical premises. He first recalls that Peter Lombard, the master of sentences, lived and died in the belief that the Holy Spirit worked within man, and that it was thus something uncreated within the soul. Then Eckhart lists a series of philosophical premises according to which his incriminating sentences are true:

The right theory of accident. An accident—insofar as it has being—is only defined through substance. Substance receives its character solely from the substantial form.
As white (*album*) from whiteness (*albedo*), so the good man, insofar as he is good, receives his being from the divine Goodness.
The theory of analogy states that there is nothing within the urine of the health or sickness that it indicates.
An individual creature receives everything from the universal without giving something to it.

The written defense of the Soest manuscript names three philosophical theorems from which Eckhart derived his philosophy of Christianity:

The strict observance of the "insofar."
The unity of the good and Goodness that followed from Aristotle's principle that "white" (*album*) does not signify anything other than "whiteness" (*albedo*).
The unity of every producer or begetter and the begotten in nature and technology.[3]

I ask the reader to pay attention to the epigraphs at the very beginning of this book. The first of these texts states two philosophical premises that distinguish Eckhart's thinking from that of many others: he distances himself from the metaphysics of other thinkers who are guided primarily by nature. They talk about ideas and the being of knowledge as though they were natural things. And they speak of accidents as though they were substances. Eckhart's philosophical-theological conception is based on the knowledge that intellectual being was special and on the rejection of the hypostatization of properties. Anyone thinking along with Eckhart who fails to keep these in mind as presuppositions of his thought will never have understood Eckhart.

The second epigraph is set against the half-existentialistic theologizing interpreters of Eckhart who forget, fideistically distort, or obfuscate Eckhart's programmatic concept of reason.

The third epigraph invites those who claim that Eckhart's doctrine of the Trinity corresponds to that of Saint Thomas Aquinas to make a greater effort.

The fourth and fifth epigraphs signal Eckhart's dissent regarding the philosophy and theology of his day. Eckhart finds the concept of the intellect lacking in the writings of most famous scholars—the intellect, which Aristotle, following Anaxagoras, said did not have anything in common with anything else. They think in categories pertaining to things; they do not know what mind is and what its separateness means. They do not distinguish ideas and intellectual being clearly from the kind of being of the natural things. Thus, they miss the point of the metaphysics of number and the meaning of the doctrine of the Trinity; add to that the hardly recognized third epigraph. They speak of the three persons of the Godhead as though they were three cows.

In opposition to almost all his contemporaries, Eckhart claims the following central points of difference as his premises:

the impossibility of conceptualizing the primary determinations, under which Eckhart counts Wisdom, Justice, and Love, in the same manner as dependent properties

the theory of the accident, which privileges substance, and the theory of analogy derived from it

the advanced Aristotelian-Averroistic concept of the mind, along with the understanding of the special metaphysical position of the intellect and intellectual being

the recognition of the "insofar"

Similar bases of these metaphysics and the theory of the intellect were developed by Dietrich of Freiberg. His was a theory of the intellect, intellectual being, the accident, and analogy that diverged polemically from the familiar ideas of scholasticism. Thus the question returns whether Dietrich could justifiably be called Eckhart's instigator. The answer is that he was, beyond all doubt. The details of their relationship require further study. Those details, however, do not belong here; a discussion of them would go beyond the structure and style of this book. I am simply sketching the current state of the field and calling attention to a few aspects through which we can evaluate it.

The discussion was reignited when Loris Sturlese published his study of Eckhart's potential familiarity with Dietrich of Freiberg's works.[4] The Bochum School, which published Dietrich of Freiberg's works between 1977 and 1985, had addressed the differences between Dietrich and Eckhart as early as 1977 and had considered the possibility that Eckhart may have retroactively influenced Dietrich.[5] Sturlese showed parallels between Eckhart's first commentary on Genesis (*In Gen. I*, LW 1, n. 115, 270–72) and Dietrich's *De visione beatifica* (1.2.1.1.4 [1]–[3], 3:39.82–40.24). Sturlese considers them secure proof that Dietrich must have read Eckhart. And so new questions arise. Among other things, the chronology of Dietrich's works has to be adjusted: his *De tribus difficilibus quaestionibus*, to which the *De visione beatifica* belongs and which Loris Sturlese and I have always dated to a time around 1296, would have been written about ten years later than we previously assumed. Such adjustments are not uncommon among Dietrich scholars. Even with these adjustments, however, Dietrich's chronological preeminence and that of his intellectual impulses remain. His very earliest work, *De origine rerum praedicamentalium* (*Opera omnia* 3:136–201), secures him a strong position in the genesis of Eckhartian thought. Thanks to a lucky find by Maria Rita Pagnoni-Sturlese, it can be dated to 1286 or shortly thereafter.[6] At this early date, Dietrich could not have read any works by Eckhart. They did not exist yet. *De origine*, however, argues in great detail and with strict criteria in favor of Eckhart's characteristic philosophical premises, mentioned above. Thus, Dietrich must have been the stimulus for them. In short, Dietrich's *De origine* develops crucial, nonsecondary, basic tenets of Eckhart's thinking. No one claims that Eckhart taught the same things as Dietrich. Both thinkers, however, shared vital points of departure; both positioned themselves outside the scholastic mainstream and went separate ways within their common ground. Without claiming completeness, I list here a few theorems taken exclusively from Dietrich's earliest work that undeniably reappear in the changed context of Eckhart's writings:

1. The elimination of efficient and final causality in the context of metaphysics. According to Eckhart, the production of the image occurs when efficient and final causes are silent, *in silentio causae efficientis et finalis*.[7] His metaphysics speak of the essence as being, of shape and formal flow, not of making. In love as in metaphysics, efficient and final cause have no place.[8] Eckhart's lovely expression of the "silence" of these external causess and its application to love advance in original fashion the initial thesis that Dietrich, following Averroës, developed in 1286. See or. 1, 5, 3:138.54–59; or. 1, 8, 3:139.81–89; or. 1, 27, 3:144.246–47; or. 1, 30, 3:145.264–66; or. 3, 8, 3:159.37–44; or. 5, 14, 3:189.90–94. This doctrine, as one can see, is very well attested early in Dietrich's writings.[9] It plays a fundamental ontological role for Dietrich: it determines the meaning of something that has being as a being, of *ens qua ens:* a being in its essential sense is thus that which has its essence due to *immanent* principles, apart from efficient and final causality.[10] It led to Dietrich's unmitigated concept of essence.[11] According to Dietrich, metaphysics contemplates a being qua being and neglects its causes. What follows from this is the characteristic understanding, supported by Avicenna, of the absoluteness of the *essentia*, or. 1, 10, 3:140. Thus, the definition of substance was: it is of absolute subsistence and is called "a being per se," because of its immanent substantial form.[12] Something that really is has its goal within itself, *finis intra*, or. 3, 24, 3:164.186. From this idea follows Eckhart's "immanentism" and his "qualified concept of life."[13]

2. The characteristic analysis of the accident, which was laid out by Aristotle and Averroës but which experienced a particular intensification in Dietrich and Eckhart's thinking, and which Martin Grabmann calls the Averroistic theory of the "beinglessness of the accident" and which is identified in the first Parisian questions. It can be found in Dietrich's writings.[14]

3. What follows from the previous theorem is the non-Thomistic interpretation of *analogia*, in the form in which Eckhart often presented it from his first stay in Paris (First Parisian Question, LW 5, n. 11, 46), especially in *In Eccli.*, LW 2, nn. 52–53, 280–81. It can be found earlier in Dietrich's writings, or. 1, 25, 3:144.231–41; 2, 7, 3:145.19–146.30.

4. In 1286, Dietrich demonstrated the theory of time and relation in detail and in the same fashion as Eckhart later summarizes it in the First Parisian Question, LW 5 n. 4, 41. It occurs in or. Proemium 9, *opera omnia*, 3:137.30–138.2, in the context of Dietrich's thesis of the constitutive function of the human intellect.[15]

5. According to *De origine*, Dietrich's hypothesis of the production of primary reality via the intellect was based on the understanding that nature cannot

distinguish between individual thing and idea, between the *res* and the *ratio rei*.[16] This argument recurs in Eckhart's commentary on John (*In Ioh.*, LW 3, n. 31, 24.10), but Eckhart does not develop Dietrich's theory of constitution from it. He was interested in other things.

6. In *De origine*, Dietrich surprises his reader by discussing the existence of intelligences as hypothetical: *si essent*.[17] Eckhart continued this phrasing, but unlike Dietrich, he was not interested in the theory of intelligences.[18]

7. Dietrich distinguished between imagining and thinking, *imaginatio* and *intellectus*, more clearly and with a more thorough explanation than his predecessors.[19] In Eckhart's writings, it is a constant motif, from the *Prologi* to his self-defense.

In *De origine*, Dietrich not only propounded early his fundamental differentiation between the *ens simpliciter*, also *ens per se*, and the *ens nunc* or the *ens hoc*,[20] but also declared that the *intellectus*, which he was investigating as the *principium constitutivum*, was the *ens simpliciter*, which kept this mode of an "absolute being," even in individuation. The intellect is the essence of the universal and is in itself universal. These ontological premises of a theory of the intellect that Dietrich developed played, as we have seen, a foundational role for Eckhart. I will not pursue them further here; I merely want to show with a few select yet undeniable examples that Dietrich inspired Eckhart. The two of them knew each other well for many years and most likely conversed with each other. Nothing is more natural than students influencing their teachers. This fact does not, however, override the chronological and argumentative priority: it was Dietrich who undertook a metaphysical reorientation *before* 1300. He distinguished a being qua being, the *ens ut ens*, from the this-and-that (*hoc et hoc*) and determined the characteristics of the human intellect based on this difference. Later, in *De tribus difficilibus quaestionibus*, he drew from this theory the necessary religiophilosophical conclusions and uncovered concretely the flaws within the Christian self-understanding. Ruedi Imbach has shown with impressive care how Dietrich diagnosed the grave damages that philosophical shortcomings have inflicted on Christian thinking.[21] By showing what consequences these shortcomings have and how they could be remedied, Dietrich in 1286 created the preconditions for Eckhart's new philosophy of Christianity.

Notes

CHAPTER I. LIFE AND WORKS AROUND 1300

1. S. Kierkegaard, *Der Augenblick: Aufsätze und Schriften des letzten Streits*, trans. Hayo Gerdes (Düsseldorf, 1959), 6.

2. H. L. Martensen, *Meister Eckhart: Eine theologische Studie* (Hamburg, 1842), 1, 5.

3. Josef Koch, "Kritische Studien zum Leben Meister Eckharts," in *Kleine Schriften*, vol. 1, ed. Josef Koch (Rome, 1973), 247–347; Loris Sturlese, *Meister Eckhart: Ein Portrait* (Regensburg, 1993); Kurt Flasch and Ruedi Imbach, *Meister Eckhart—in seiner Zeit* (Düsseldorf, 2003). See also the volumes by Klaus Jacobi, ed., *Meister Eckhart: Lebensstationen, Redesituationen* (Berlin, 1997), and the *Miscellanea Medievalia*, vol. 32 (Berlin, 2005), especially the pointers by Loris Sturlese in LW 5 and in *Homo divinus* (see bibliography).

4. [In German, Thomas Aquinas's most common name is "Thomas von Aquin," i.e., Thomas of Aquin. Flasch prefers the name "Thomas von Aquino," for the reasons discussed here.]

A gentleman about whose level of education I choose not to speculate publicly complained that I always write "Thomas von Aquino." He was missing the "Aquin" with which he was familiar. But if one were to look up "Aquin" in the Brockhaus [the standard German encyclopedia], he would find nothing. For the town "Aquin" does not exist in Italy. There are certainly some Italian place names that have existed in Germanized form for centuries, such as "Mailand" for Milano or "Rom" for Roma; and avoiding these would, it seems to me, go against the standards of our language. The small town in the province Frosinone near which Thomas Aquinas was born, however, does not belong with them. There existed in nineteenth-century Germany an ideologically oriented group of authors who attempted to normalize "Aquin." We could compare their procedure with that of an art society whose members were enamored by Raphael and who claimed, in order to popularize their idol in Germany, that he was from "Urbin." But "Urbin" does not exist anywhere; there is only "Urbino," and likewise only "Aquino."

5. I assembled the literature on the secular and ecclesiastical history of the later Middle Ages in the introduction to my translation of the *Chronicon Moguntinum*, a world chronicle written from the perspective of a Mainz cleric. The chronicle begins eighteen years after Eckhart's death, but it is instructive for the urban and ecclesiastical conditions of the fourteenth century; see Kurt Flasch, ed., *Mainzer Chronik: 1346–1406* (Mainz, 2009), 24.

6. Albert Hauck, *Kirchengeschichte Deutschlands im Mittelalter*, vol. 5, pt. 1 (Berlin, 1954), 480.

7. Thanks especially to Inge Degenhardt, *Studien zum Wandel des Eckhartsbildes* (Leiden, 1967).

8. Meister Eckhart, LW 5:597–600.

CHAPTER 2. A FORGOTTEN CONCEPT

1. It is interesting also because the important book by Rodolfo Mondolfo, *La comprensione del soggetto umano nel antiquità classica* (Florence, 1967), is not easily obtainable in most German libraries.

2. On the role of the cited authors, see Flasch (2006) and the works by the scholars at Lecce: Loris Sturlese, ed., *Studi sulle fonti di Meister Eckhart* (Fribourg, 2008). On Seneca, see Nadia Bray in ibid., 167–92.

3. On Albertus Magnus, see Flasch (2000), 370–76, and Flasch (2006), 67–85. The latter contains an extensive bibliography of the latest scholarship (169–70).

4. Anselm of Canterbury, Prologue to the Monologion, *Opera omnia* I, 7:7–11: *quatenus auctoritate scripturae penitus nihil in ea persuaderetur, sed quidquid per singulas investigationes finis assereret, id ita esse plano stilo et vulgaribus argumentis simpliciique disputatione et rationis necessitas breviter cogeret et veritatis claritas patenter ostenderet.*

5. Anselm of Canterbury, *Cur deus homo*, ed. F. S. Schmitt (Darmstadt, 1970), 2: *Ac tandem remoto Christo, quasi numquam aliquid fuerit de illo, probat* [sc. the book] *rationibus necessariis.*

CHAPTER 3. SELF-PORTRAYALS

1. *Ich hân ez ouch mê gesprochen: bekantnisse und vernünfticheit einigent die sêle in got. Vernünfticheit diu vellet in daz lûter wesen, bekantnisse diu loufet vor, si vürloufet und durchbrichet, daz dâ geborn wirt gotes einborner sun.*

2. The term *intellectualitas*, in contrast to *intellectus*, is common in Dietrich of Freiberg; see I.I.2.I (3) I 23; I.I.3 (2) I 26; I.I.3.I (I) I 27; 3.2.9 (I) I 85; and elsewhere. Eckhart seldom used the term, but, like Dietrich, speaks of simplicity as the *radix intellectualitatis: In Sap.*, ch. 1, "Auctoritates," LW 2:303, and *In Sap.* I, LW 2, n. 5, 326.

3. *Ich spriche daz dicke und gedenke ez noch dicker: ez ist ein wunder, daz got in die sêle gegozzen hât vernüfticheit.*

4. *Den gerehten menschen den ist alsô ernst ze der gerehticheit, wære, daz got niht gereht wære, sie enahteten eine bône niht ûf got und stânt alsô vaste in der gerehticheit und sint ir selbes alsô gar ûzgegangen, daz sie niht enahtent pîne der helle noch vröude des himelriches noch keines dinges. Jâ, wære alliu diu pîne, die die hânt, die in der helle sint, menschen oder vîende, oder alliu diu pîne, diu in ertrîche ie geliten wart oder iemer sol werden geliten, wære diu gesast bî der gerehticheit, sie enahteten sîn niht einen bast; sô vaste stânt sie an gote und an der gerehticheit. Dem gerehten menschen enist niht pînlicher Q6:104 noch swærer, dan daz der gerehticheit wider ist, daz er in allen dinge niht glîch ist. Als wie? Mac sie ein dinc vröuwen und ein anderz betrüeben, sô ensint sie niht gereht, mêr: sint sie ze einer zît vrô, sô sint sie ze allen zîten vrô; sint sie ze einer zît mêr vrô und ze der andern minner, sô ist in unreht. Swer die gerehticheit minnet, der stât sô vaste dar ûf, swaz er minnet, daz ist sîn wesen; den enmac kein dinc abeziehen, noch keines dinges enahtet er anders. Sant Augustînus sprichet: "dâ diu sêle minnet, dâ ist si eigenlîcher, dan dâ si leben gibet." Daz wort lûtet grop und gemeine, und verstât doch wênic ieman, wie im sî, und ist doch wâr. Swer underscheit verstât von gerehticheit und von gerehtem, der verstât allez, daz ich sage.*

5. On German sermon 6, see Kurt Flasch, "Predigt 6: Iusti vivent in aeternum," in LE 2:29–52.

6. *Als ein morgensterne miten in dem nebel. Ich meine daz wörtelîn quasi, daz heizet als, daz heizent diu kint in der schuole ein bîwort. Diz ist, daz ich in allen mînen predigen meine. Daz aller eigenlîcheste, daz man von gote gesprechen mac, daz ist wort und wârheit. Got nante sich selber ein wort.*

    Sant Johannes sprach: in dem anvange was daz wort, und meinet, daz man bî dem worte si ein bîwort.

7. See Susanne Köbele, " 'Absolute' Grammatik bei Meister Eckhart," *Zeitschrift für deutsche Philologie* 113 (1994): 199–202; see especially 202, note 28, for Priscian's definition of the adverb: *adverbium est pars orationis indeclinabilis, cuius significatio verbis adicitur.*

8. *Dô ich hiute her gienc, dô gedâhte ich, wie ich iu alsô vernüfticlîche gepredigete, daz ir mich wol verstüendet. Dô gedâhte ich ein glîchnisse, und kündet ir daz wol*

verstân so verstüendet ir mînen sin und den grunt aller mîner meinunge, den ich ie gepredigete, und was daʒ glîchnisse von mînem ougen und von dem holʒe: wirt mîn ouge ûfgetân, sô ist eʒ ein ouge; ist eʒ ʒuo, sô ist eʒ daʒ selbe ouge, und durch der gesiht willen sô engât dem holʒe weder abe noch ʒuo. Nû merket mich vil rehte! Geschihet aber daʒ, daʒ mîn ouge ein und einvaltic ist in im selben und ûfgetân wirt und ûf daʒ holʒ geworfen wirt mit einer angesiht, sô blîbet ein ieglîcheʒ, daʒ eʒ ist, und werdent doch in der würklicheit der angesiht als ein, daʒ man mac gesprechen in der wârheit: ougeholʒ, und daʒ holʒ ist mîn ouge.

9. On German sermon 48, see Burkhard Mojsisch, LE 1:151–62.

10. *Swenne ich predige, sô pflige ich ʒe sprechenne von abegescheidenheit und daʒ der mensche ledic werde sîn selbes und aller dinge. Ze dem andern mâle, daʒ man wider îngebildet werde in daʒ einvaltige guot, daʒ got ist. Ze dem dritten mâle, daʒ man gedenke der grôʒen edelkeit, die got an die sêle hât geleget, daʒ der mensche dâ mite kome in ein wunder ʒe gote. Ze dem vierden mâle von götlicher nature lûterkeit—waʒ klârheit an götlicher nature si, daʒ ist unsprechelich. Got ist ein wort, ein ungesprochen wort.*

11. *Daʒ vünfte: daʒ eʒ ein bilde ist. Eyâ, nû merket mit vlîʒe und gehaltet diʒ wol; in dem hât ir die predige alʒemâle: bilde und bilde ist sô gar ein mit einander, daʒ man keinen underscheit dâ verstân enmac. Man verstât wol daʒ viur âne die hitze und die hitze âne daʒ viur. Man verstât wol die sunnen âne daʒ lieht und daʒ lieht âne die sunnen. Aber man enmac keinen underscheit verstân ʒwischen bilde und bilde. Ich spriche mê: got mit sîner almehticheit enmac keinen underscheit dâ verstân, wan eʒ wirt mit einander geborn und stirbet mit einander.*

12. *Dit ist subtijl. Die dit verstaet, he es gnoech ghepredecht.*

13. *Acta Echardiana, Proc. Col. I,* nn. 1–74, LW 5, n. 62, 220.6–31; see also S. Köbele, LE 1:43–74, esp. 60.

14. *2 In cuius verbi expositione et aliorum quae sequuntur, intentio est auctoris, sicut et in omnibus suis editionibus, ea quae sacra asserit fides christiana et utriusque testamenti scriptura, exponere per rationes naturales philosophorum. "Invisibilia enim dei a creatura mundi per ea, quae facta sunt, intellecta conspiciuntur: sempiterna quoque virtus eius," >>id est filius<< "et divinitas," >>id est spiritus sanctus<<, ut ait Glossa, Rom. I. Et Augustinus l.VII Confessionum dicit se in libris Platonis legisse in principio erat verbum et magnam partem huius primi capituli Iohannis. Et De civitate dei l. X narrat de quodam Platonico, qui dicebat principium huius capituli usque ibi: "fuit homo missus a deo" >>aureis litteris conscribendum et<< >>in locis eminentissimis proponendum<<.*

   3 Rursus intentio operis est ostendere, quomodo veritates principiorum et conclusionum et proprietatum naturalium innuuntur luculenter—"qui habet aures audiendi!"—in ipsis verbis sacrae scripturae, quae per illa naturalia exponuntur. Interdum etiam ponuntur expositiones aliquae morales.

15. The editors of Bonaventure's works have documented the consensus in scholasticism that there was no *philosophy* of the Trinity; see Bonaventure, *Opera omnia* I (Quarracchi, 1882), 77b on I Dist. 3, pars I, art. unicus, Quaestio III; see also Thomas Aquinas, *Sth* I 32, I c.a.: *impossibile est per rationem naturalem ad cognitionem Trinitatis divinarum personarum pervenire.*

16. *Nû merket hie mit vlîʒe und mit ernste! Ich hân eʒ ofte gesprochen, und sprechent eʒ ouch grôʒe meister, daʒ der mensche alsô ledic sol sîn aller dinge und aller werke, beidiu innerlîche und ûʒerlîche, alsô daʒ er möhte sîn ein eigen stat gotes, dâ got inne möhte würken. Nû sagen wir anders.*

17. On German sermon 52, see the new critical edition by Georg Steer with commentary by Kurt Flasch (LE 1:163–200).

CHAPTER 4. BEGINNINGS

1. Meister Eckhart, *Collatio in Libros Sententiarum*, LW 5, n. 2, 18. Included there are Koch's conversions of the distances from miles to kilometers.
2. Meister Eckhart, *Sermo Paschalis a. 1294 Parisius habitus*, LW 5, n. 2, 136–37.
3. Ibid., LW 5, n. 14, 146.
4. Augustine, *De civitate Dei* 14:12, ed. Dombart-Kalb, *CC* 48:434.12–14: *sed oboedientia commendata est in praecepto, quae virtus in creatura rationali mater quodam modo est omnium custosque virtutum;* compare Thomas Aquinas, *Sth* II–II 104.

CHAPTER 5. THE SERMON CYCLE ON ETERNAL BIRTH

1. The starting point for the following analyses—in addition to the works of Albertus Magnus and Thomas Aquinas—is drawn from Ulrich of Strasbourg's great *Summa*, the four volumes of Dietrich of Freiberg's works, and the monumental commentary on Proclus's *Elementario Theologica* by Berthold of Moosburg. Surveys of the scholarly debates surrounding these figures are included in Imbach, esp. 109–52; Alessandra Beccarisi, "Johannes Picardi von Lichtenberg, Dietrich von Freiberg und Meister Eckhart," *MM* 35:516–40; Loris Sturlese, *Homo divinus: Philosophische Projekte in Deutschland ʒwischen Meister Eckhart und Heinrich Seuse* (Stuttgart, 2007). For the most recent scholarship, see the following newly available texts. For Nikolaus von Strasbourg see CPTMA, vol. 5, 2, 1,

and vol. 5, 2, 2 (Hamburg, 2009); vol. 5, 2 (3) (Hamburg, 1990). On Nikolaus, see E. Hillenbrand, *Nikolaus von Straßburg: Religiöse Bewegung und dominikanische Theologie im 14. Jahrhundert* (Freiburg im Breisgau, 1968); Loris Sturlese, "Eckhart, Teodorico e Picardi nella Summa philosophiae di Nicola di Strasburgo: Documenti per una storia della filosofia medievale tedesca," *Giornale critico della filosofia italiana* 61 (1982): 183–206; R. Imbach and U. Lindblad, "Compilatio rudis ac puerilis: Hinweise und Materialien zu Nikolaus von Straßburg, OP und seiner Summa," *Freiburger Zeitschrift für Philosophie und Theologie* 32 (1985): 155–233; Dagmar Gottschall, "Nikolaus von Straßburg, Meister Eckhart und die cura monialium," in *Meister Eckharts Straßburger Jahrzehnt* (Stuttgart, 2008), 95–118. For Heinrich von Lübeck, see his Corpus, vol. 4, I (Hamburg, 2009). Loris Sturlese provides insights into the open questions raised by the new texts (vii–xxi); see also Loris Sturlese, "Gottebenbildlichkeit und Beseelung des Himmels in den Quodlibeta Heinrichs von Lübeck, O.P.," *Freiburger Zeitschrift für Philosophie und Theologie* 24 (1977): 191–233. For Johannes Picardi von Lichtenberg, see Burkhard Mojsisch, *Meister Eckhart* (Hamburg, 1983), 147–62, and the article by A. Beccarisi mentioned above.

2. Georg Steer, "Predigt 101," in LE 1:247–88; Steer, "Mutmaßungen über die Zeit ihrer Entstehung," in *Deutsche Mystik im abendländischen Zusammenhang*, ed. Walter Haug and Wolfram Schneider-Lastin (Tübingen, 2000), 253–81; Mauritius Wilde, *Das neue Bild vom Gottesbild: Bild und Theologie bei Meister Eckhart* (Fribourg, 2000); Rodrigo Guerizoli, *Die Verinnerlichung des Göttlichen: Eine Studie über den Gottesgeburtszyklus und die Armutspredigt Meister Eckharts* (Leiden, 2006).

3. Sermons 101–4 are found in DW 4. In this chapter, they are cited by sermon number, page, and line of the original in DW 4.

4. Peter Lombard, *In 2 Sent.* 16, 4, vol. 1 (Grottaferrata, 1971), 409; Thomas Aquinas, *Sth* I 93, I ad 2; John XXII, *In agro dominico*, articles 10–13, *Acta Echardiana, Processus contra mag. Echardum*, LW 5, n. 65, 598.43–55.

5. Meister Eckhart, *In Ioh.*, LW 3, n. 300, 251.4–5.

6. *Saepe sanctam Ecclesiam*, in Heinrich Denzinger and Peter Hünermann, eds., *Enchiridion*, n. 866, 383; the constitution against the Beghards and Beguines, ibid., nn. 891–99, 388–89.

7. On the church fathers, see Hugo Rahner, "Die Gottesgeburt in der Seele: Die Lehre der Kirchenväter von der Geburt Christi aus dem Herzen der Kirche und der Gläubigen," *Zeitschrift für katholische Theologie* 19 (1935):

333–418; see also Rahner, *Symbole der Kirche: Die Ekklesiologie der Väter* (Salzburg, 1966), 13–87.

8. Meister Eckhart, German sermon 10, DW 1:173.10–12, and German sermon 38, DW 2:229–230.1. Further evidence is in the source apparatus, DW 4:340.

9. Dietrich of Freiberg, *De intellectu et intelligibili* 2:9–11, in *Opera omnia* 1:152–64.

10. On the *abditum mentis* and for Aquinas's idea that the intellect is the *supremum in anima*, see Flasch (2007a), 216–19. On Aquinas generally, see Flasch (2000), 377–93.

11. Eckhart, German sermon 72, DW 3:252.1–4. More texts are cited in DW 4:346, note 31.

12. Thus Georg Steer, in LE 1:273.

13. Eckhart, LW 4:229.5–7.

14. Ibid., 109.14–110.3.

15. Eckhart, German sermon 37, DW 2:220.1–221.1.

16. Eckhart, *In Sap.*, LW 2, n. 677, 426–29.4.

17. See also Eckhart, *In Ioh.*, LW 3, n. 677, 591.9–11: *Patet ergo quod nudam dei substantiam, plenitudinem esse, quae est nostra beatitudo, deus scilicet, consistit, invenitur, accipitur, attingitur et hauritur per intellectum.*

18. Dionysius Areopagita, *Über die mystische Theologie (I)*, trans. Adolf Martin Ritter (Stuttgart, 1994), 74. Indispensable for the study of Dionysius is the first critical edition of Pseudo-Dionysius's writings: *Corpus Dionysiacum: Pseudo-Dionysius Areopagita*, ed. Beate Regina Suchla (Berlin, 1990–); see also Beate Regina Suchla, *Dionysius Areopagita: Leben, Werk, Wirkung* (Freiberg, 2008). On the more limited influence of Dionysius on Eckhart, see Elisa Rubino, "Davon sprichet der liechte Dionysius," in *Studi sulle fonti di Meiter Eckhart*, ed. Loris Sturlese (Fribourg, 2008), 113–34.

19. Albertus Magnus, *De intellectu et intelligibili*, Lib. II, tract. un. c.9, in *Opera omnia*, ed. Borgnet (Paris, 1890), 9:517b.

CHAPTER 6. TOO GRAND A PLAN

1. On the *Opus tripartitum*, see Wouter Goris, *Einheit als Prinzip und Ziel: Versuch über die Einheitsmetaphysik des Opus tripartitum Meister Eckharts* (Leiden, 1997); see also the references cited therein.

2. Kurt Ruh, *Meister Eckhart*, 102–5.

3. Loris Sturlese, *Homo divinus*, 28–30.

4. Citations are all taken from the edition in LW 1, 148–65. Unless explicitly noted otherwise, they refer to the *Prologus generalis* (*Prol. gen.*).

5. Here Eckhart is citing Aristotle's *Categories* c.5, 3b19: *Prol. gen.* n. 16, 160.9; *Prol. prop.* n. 2, 41.36–42.1; *Prol. prop.* n. 23, 46.26–29.

6. For example, *Prol. gen.* n. 12, 157.9; n. 13, 158.7; n. 16, 160.9; *Prol. prop.* n. 2, 166.6–7; n. 9, 171.7; n. 23, 179.7–9.

7. Good Latin-German editions can be found in the *Philosophische Bibliothek* 573, edited, translated, and commented on by Paul Richard Blum, Gregor Damschen, Dominic Kaegi, Martin Mulsow, Enno Rudolph, and Alejandro G. Vigo (Hamburg, 2006).

8. See Josef Koch, "Zur Analogielehre Meister Eckharts," in Koch 1:367–97; Fernand Brunner, "L'analogie chez Maître Eckhart," *Freiburger Zeitschrift für Philosophie und Theologie* 16 (1969): 333–49. On the problem and history of analogy more generally, see also Jean-François Courtine, *Inventio analogiae: Métaphysique et ontothéologie* (Paris, 2005); Earline Jennifer Ashworth, *Les theories de l'analogie du XIIe au XVI siècle* (Paris, 2008).

9. On the role of the *Liber de causis* and Proclus in Eckhart's work, see Fiorella Retucci, in *Studi sulle fonti di Meister Eckhart*, ed. Loris Sturlese (Fribourg, 2008), 135–66.

10. Eckhart, *Prol. gen.*, n. 18, 162.12.

11. Ibid., n. 9, 154.6. For the role of Avicenna in Eckhart's work, see Flasch (2006), 122–38, and Alessandro Palazzo in Loris Sturlese, ed., *Studi sulle fonti di Meister Eckhart*, 71–112.

CHAPTER 7. PARISIAN DEBATES, 1302–1303

1. There is a considerable amount of scholarship on the Parisian questions. See especially Martin Grabmann, "Neuaufgefundene Pariser Quaestionen Meister Eckharts und ihre Stellung in seinem geistigen Entwicklungsgange," in Grabmann, *Gesammelte Akademieabhandlungen* (Paderborn, 1979), 1:261– 382; Ruedi Imbach, *Deus est intelligere: Das Verhältnis von Sein und Denken in seiner Bedeutung für das Gottesverständnis bei Thomas von Aquin und in den Pariser Quaestionen Meister Eckharts* (Fribourg, 1976); Kurt Ruh, "Meister Eckharts Pariser Quaestionen 1–3 und eine deutsche Predigtsammlung," *Neues Jahrbuch* 10 (1984): 307–24; Emilie zum Brunn et al., eds., *Maître Eckhart à Paris: Une critique médiévale de l'ontothéologie* (Paris, 1984); Kurt Flasch, ed., *Von Meister Dietrich zu Meister Eckhart* (Hamburg, 1984).

2. The decisive parts, written around 1286 are: Dietrich of Freiberg, or. Proemium 9, *Opera omnia* 3:137.30–138, 2; or. I. 19–20.

3. On the doctrine of analogy, see Koch 1:367–97; for the reference to Albertus Magnus, see 393n42a.

4. Meister Eckhart, *Liber parabolarum*, LW 1, n. 214, 690: *notandum primo quod in deo, principio omnium, est considerare duo, ut sic dicamus, puta quod ipse esse verum, reale, primordiale. Adhuc autem est ipsum considerare sub ratione qua intellectus est. Et huius rationis proprietas altior apparet ex hoc, quod omne ens reale in natura "procedit ad certos fines" et "per media determinata" tamquam remomoratum per causa altiorem, ut ait Themistius.*

5. Either the argument in n. 10, 54.1–5, contains an error or the text is corrupt. It goes: Being is in its origin (its ground) not a being. A being is first found in that which proceeds from the ground. Knowledge is caused by objects, and thus the *ratio entis* is not part of it. But it would be logical to conclude: thus the *ratio entis* is not in the object, but rather in knowledge.

6. *In Ioh.*, LW 3, n. 540, 471, and LW 3, n. 514, 445.

CHAPTER 8. PROGRAMMATIC SPEECHES

1. Someone who eats Wisdom (God) continues to hunger. Meister Eckhart, *Sermones et lectiones super Ecclesiastici* [*In Eccli.*], Ecclesiasticus 24:29, LW 2, n. 41, 276.4–5: *sumus autem per esse, in quantum sumus et in quantum ens, esse nutrimur et pascimur. Et sic omne ens edit deum, utpote esse.* See also ibid., n. 49, 277.13–14: *extra primam causam nihil est; quod enim extra causam primam, deum scilicet est, extra esse est, quia deus est esse.* The German translation invents the word "*abseits*" (apart from) for *extra*. The translators write as though there might be something that is "*abseits*" (apart from) Being and therefore apart from God. Eckhart says that there cannot be anything outside of Being or God, for *extra* means "outside of."

2. Ibid., n. 20, 248.1–4; n. 51, 279.14–280.1; see also n. 10, 239.1–2.

3. *Acta Echardiana*, LW 5, n. 65.60–64 and 65.97–103, 598 and 600; in this citation, "n." refers to the trial document number, and 598 and 600 are page numbers.

4. Eckhart, *Prol. gen.* n. 8, 152.8–153.11.; n. 17, 160.13–162.8.; *Prol. prop.* n. 24, 180.6–181.2.; Second Parisian Question, n. 2, 50.1–5.

5. M. Th. d'Alverny, "Un témoin muet des luttes doctrinales du XIIIe siècle," *AHDMA* 17 (1949): 223–48, esp. 230ff.

CHAPTER 9. GOLDEN APPLES IN SILVER PEELS

1. Anselm of Canterbury, *Prologus to the Monologion*, in *Opera omnia*, ed. F. S. Schmitt (Seckau, 1938), 1:8.8–9.

2. On medieval biblical interpretation, see Beryl Smalley, *The Study of the Bible in the Middle Ages* (Oxford, 1952); Henri de Lubac, *Exégèse médiévale: Les quatres sens de l'Écriture*, 4 vols. (Paris, 1959–61); Henning Reventlow, *Epochen der Bibelauslegung*, vol. 2 (Munich, 1994). On Eckhart's explanation of the Bible, see Konrad Weiß in LW 1:9–19; Koch 1:399–428; Eberhard Winkler, *Exegetische Methoden bei Meister Eckhart* (Tübingen, 1965); Susanne Köbele, "Primo aspectu monstruosa: Schriftauslegung bei Meister Eckhart," *Zeitschrift für deutsches Altertum und deutsche Literatur* 122 (1993): 62–81; Yossef Schwartz, "Meister Eckharts Schriftauslegung als maimonidisches Projekt," in *Moses Maimonides (1138–1204)*, ed. G. H. Hasselhoff and Otfried Fraisse (Würzburg, 2004), 173–208.

3. Citations from *In Gen. I* according to LW 1, 185–444.

4. Averroës, *Metaphysicorum liber* VII, t.5 Aristotelis opera cum Averrois commentariis, vol. 8 (Venice, 1562; reprint, Frankfurt am Main, 1962), 156rA.

5. Dietrich of Freiberg had expressed in his *De origine* a connection to Averroës and the idea of the autonomy of *essentia*, right up to the point of capturing it in terms of definition and demonstration. For the role of *forma*, see or. 1, 8, in *Opera omnia* 3:139; or. 1, 12, in 3:140; or. 5, 61, in 3:199; for *essentia* without *causa*, see or. 1, 27, in 3:144.

6. Augustine, *De libero arbitrio* III 5, 13, CC 29, 282.21–22: *quidquid tibi vera ratione melius occurrerit, scias fecisse deum tamquam bonorum omnium conditorem.*

7. See Loris Sturlese, *Homo divinus*, 47–60.

8. Avicenna, *Metaphysica* IX 7, van Riet 510:72–73.

9. The discussion about whether Dietrich had adopted the expression and the theory of *imago* from Eckhart or vice versa is pertinent here. On this, see Loris Sturlese, in *Recherches sur Dietrich* (Turnhout, 2009), esp. 198 and the epilogue.

10. Eckhart, *In Gen. I*, LW 1, nn. 131–32, 284.9–286.5; Aquinas, *Sth* I 91, I ad 2.

11. In Eckhart: *In Gen. I*, LW 1, n. 4, 187–88; n. 68, 232; *Liber parab.*, LW 1, n. 121, 586.9–11; *Expositio libri Exodi* [*In Exod.*], LW 2, n. 32, 56; *In Eccli.*, LW 2, n. 8, 237; *In Sap.*, LW 2, n. 20, 340–41 and note 2; *In Sap.*, LW 2, n. 170, 505; *In Ioh.*, LW 3, n. 443. In Dietrich, early (1286) and keenly

developed: or. 1, 27, in *Opera omnia* 3:144.246–47; or. 1, 30, in 3:145.264–66; or. 3, 8, in 3:159.37–44; or. 5, 14, in 3:184. 90–94. See also Flasch (2007a), index, s.v. "Form and Innensein."

12. Eckhart, *In Gen. I*, LW 1, nn. 115–16, 270.1–274.3; nn. 131–33, 284.9–287.9; n. 144, 298.1–7; nn. 148–49, 300.3–16; nn. 163–64, 310.4–311.15.

13. Flasch (2007a), 617–18.

14. Eckhart, *Liber parab.*, LW 1, n. 134, 600.8–9; see also n. 135, 601.3–5 and 602.4–6.

15. Eckhart, *In Gen. I*, LW 1, nn. 197–200, 343–347; *Liber parab.*, LW 1, nn. 21–26, 491–96; see also nn. 28–40, 497–507, and nn. 41–48, 507–18.

16. See Eckhart, *Prologus in Opus expositionum*, LW 1:183–84. Here we find the explanation that even if the interpretation abandons the first literal sense, it is still true and hits the actual meaning of the letter, *proprietatem litterae* (n. 3, 184.6–11). In n. 5 is the theory of the multiple (not just the fourfold) senses of scripture in which everyone can choose what appears useful to him.

17. Eckhart, *Liber parab.*, LW 1, n. 20, 490.10–12; nn. 53–56, 521–25 and nn. 68–69, 534–35.

18. Ibid., n. 47, 515.5; n. 49, 517.5–15; n. 51, 519.11–13.

19. Ibid., n. 9, 480.8–10; n. 11, 483.1–8; n. 88, 549.11–551.14.

20. Dietrich of Freiberg, *De intellectu et intelligibili* II 2–8, in *Opera omnia* 3:147–52.

21. *Semen autem scientiarum habitus est principiorum, quae naturaliter nota sunt omnibus, per quae habet et potest iudicare homo de veritate et falsitate, quantum ad intellectum speculativum, et inter bonum et malum, quantum ad intellectum practicum. Lumen ergo rationis in nobis, quod est participatio divini et supremi luminis, semen est tam virtutum quam scientarum.*

22. References back to *In Gen. I* occur at n. 8, 479.3; n. 40, 507.6; n. 41, 508.4; n. 74, 539.8.

CHAPTER 10. WISDOM

1. Meister Eckhart, *In Sap.*, LW 2, nn. 41–55, 362–69. Citations to *In Sap.* are to the text in LW 2.

2. Jan A. Aertsen, *Medieval Philosophy and the Transcendentals: The Case of Thomas Aquinas* (Leiden, 1996).

3. Eckhart, *In Sap.*, n. 81, 412.11–413.4; n. 214, 550; nn. 272–74, 602–4; n. 281, 613.7.

4. Ibid., n. 33, 354.4–10; n. 107, 443; nn. 293–96, 626–31.1. In Dietrich already in 1286: or. Proemium 9, in *Opera omnia* 3:137.30–138.2; or. 1, 19–20, in *Opera omnia* 3:143.

CHAPTER 11. DEPARTURE

1. Meister Eckhart, *Expositio libri Exodi* [*In Exod.*], LW 2:1–227. Citations to *In. Exod.* are according to the text in LW 2.
2. On the interpretation of *"Ego sum qui sum,"* see Werner Beierwaltes, *Platonismus und Idealismus* (Frankfurt am Main, 1972).
3. Eckhart, *In Exod.*, n. 44, 48, and n. 53, 57: *Patet quod radix et ratio praemissorum, et quomodo dicuntur affirmationes omnes sive nomina positiva nullo modo deo competere.*

CHAPTER 12. INTERLUDE

1. For this I refer the reader to the reprint of the edition of Suso's work, which I was responsible for, edited by Karl Bihlmeyer first in Stuttgart (1907) and then in Frankfurt am Main (1961), as well as to Loris Sturlese, *Homo divinus*, 169–230.
2. For the relationship between Eckhart and Luther, see I. Degenhardt, *Studien zum Wandel des Eckhartbildes* (Leiden, 1967), 290–93.
3. Joseph Bernhart, "Einige Bücher zur Mystik," *Hochland* 11 (1913/1914): 226.
4. Evidence for this is discussed by Rudolf Eucken and Paul Natorp in Kurt Flasch, *Die geistige Mobilmachung: Die deutschen Intellektuellen und der Erste Weltkrieg* (Berlin, 2000), 27, 216, 322, 325, 328.
5. Otto Karrer, "Eckhart-Schrifttum und Historismus," *Hochland* 32 (1935): 374.
6. Josef Quint, "Die Sprache Meister Eckharts als Ausdruck seiner mystischen Geisteswelt," *Deutsche Vierteljahrsschrift* 6 (1927): 671–701.
7. Josef Quint, "Meister Eckehart: Ein Vortrag," *Zeitschrift für deutsche Kulturphilosophie: Neue Folge des Logos* 5 (1939): 209–231.
8. Josef Quint, "Meister Eckhart," in *Von deutscher Art in Sprache und Dichtung*, ed. G. Fricke, F. Koch, and K. Lugowski (Berlin, 1941), 3:3–44.
9. Josef Quint, "Mystik und Sprache: Ihr Verhältnis zueinander in der spekulativen Mystik Meister Eckeharts," *Deutsche Vierteljahrsschrift für Literaturwissenschaft* 27 (1953): 48–76.
10. I offer a supplement to the consistently favorable representation of Josef Quint in Inge Degenhardt, *Wandel des Eckhartbildes* (Leiden, 1967), 308–9.

CHAPTER 13. ECKHART'S INTENTION

1. Johann Gottlieb Fichte, *Anweisung zum seeligen [sic] Leben* (Berlin, 1806), 91; translated into English by William Smith as *The Way towards the Blessed Life* (London, 1849), quotation on 56.

2. Meister Eckhart, *In Ioh.*, LW 3, n. 75, 63.1–8; n. 86, 74.6–75.1; nn. 195–96, 163–65; n. 206, 173.11–16.

3. Ibid., nn. 2–3, 4; n. 2: *In cuius verbi expositione et aliorum quae sequuntur, intentio est auctoris, sicut in omnibus suius editionibus, ea quae sacra asserit fides christiana et utriusque testamenti scriptura, exponere per rationes naturales philosophorum.*

   "Invisibilia enim dei a creatura mundi per ea, quae facta sunt, intellecta conspiciuntur: sempiterna quoque virtus eius," "id est filius," "et divinitas," "id est spiritus sanctus," ut ait Glossa, Rom. 1:20.

   Et Augustinus l.VII Confessionum dicit se in libris Platonis legisse "in principio erat" verbum et magnam partem huius primi capituli Iohannis.

   Et De civitate Dei l.X narrat de quodam Platonico, qui dicebat principium huius capituli usque ibi "fuit homo missus a Deo" "aureis litteris conscribendum et" "in locis eminentissimis proponendum."

   n. 3: *Rursus intentio operis est ostendere, quomodo veritates principiorum et conclusionum et proprietatum naturalium innuuntur luculenter—"qui habet aures audiendi!"—in ipsis verbis sacrae scripturae, quae per illa naturalia exponuntur.*

   Interdum etiam ponuntur expositiones aliquae morales.

4. Kurt Flasch, "Meister Eckhart und die Deutsche Mystik: Zur Kritik eines historiographischen Schemas," in *Bochumer Studien zur Philosophie*, vol. 10, *Die Philosophie im 14. und 15. Jahrhundert: In memoriam Konstanty Michalski (1879–1947)*, ed. Olaf Pluta (Amsterdam, 1988), 439–63; Flasch, "Meister Eckhart: Versuch, ihn aus dem mystischen Strom zu retten," in *Gnosis und Mystik in der Geschichte der Philosophie*, ed. P. Koslowski (Zurich/Munich, 1988), 94–110.

5. Thomas Aquinas, *Sth* I 32:1. The great scholastics who rejected a philosophy of the Trinity are listed in Bonaventure, *Opera omnia* (Quarracchi, 1882), 77, scholion II.

6. Thomas Aquinas, *In Boetii de Trinitate*, Prooemium qu. I art.4, c.a. and ad 6, as well as ad 8, *Opuscula theologica*, ed. R. M. Spiazzi (Turin/Rome, 1954), 2:326–27.

7. Augustine, *Confessiones* VII, 9, 14:22–23, CC 27, 101 Verheijen: *Sed quia "verbum caro factum est habitauit in nobis," non ibi legi.*

8. Eckhart, *In Ioh.*, LW 3, n. 444, 380.13–14: *Evangelium contemplatur ens in quantum ens.*

9. Ibid., n. 155, 186.5–7.

10. Ibid., n. 124, 108.3–11.

11. Meister Eckhart is a frequently misused author. Because of this, it is critically important to start with Eckhart's own explanation of his self-portrayal or at least to acknowledge this, even if a modern interpreter were then to come to the conclusion that Eckhart did not follow through with his program. I first made reference to Eckhart's self-portrayal in an essay from 1969: Kurt Flasch, "Die Intention Meister Eckharts." This study was published in a place that was not particularly easy to access; other contingencies made it difficult to use it in interpreting Eckhart. Since then, there has been a reversal. The best subject-specific historical works on Eckhart have verified my analyses. Kurt Ruh in particular has explicitly approved of my interpretation: Ruh, *Meister Eckhart: Theologie, Prediger, Mystiker*, 76, and for Eckhart's German works, 122. Other affirmations are found in Mojsisch, *Meister Eckhart: Analogie, Univoẑität und Einheit*, 2–11; Libera, *Introduction à la mystique rhénane*; A. de Libera, E. Wéber, E. zum Brunn, eds., *L'œuvre latine de Maître Eckhart: Le commentaire de l'Evangile selon Jean; Le Prologue* (Paris, 1989), especially the notes to 26–30; see also L. Sturlese, "Meister Eckhart," in *Klassiker der Religionsphilosophie: Von Platon bis Kierkegaard*, ed. F. Niewöhner (Munich, 1995), 298.

12. Meister Eckhart, *In Ioh.*, LW 3, n. 444, 381.4–6: *Patet ergo, sicut frequenter in nostris expositionibus dicitur, quod ex ea eadem vena descendit veritas et doctrina theologiae, philosophiae naturalis, moralis, artis factibilium et speculabilium et etiam iuris positivi.*

CHAPTER 14. UNITY ACCORDING TO KIND

1. See Julie Gasteigt, *Conaissance et verité cheẑ Maître Eckhart*, esp. 81–201.

2. Meister Eckhart, *In Ioh.*, LW 3, n. 514, 445.4–14: *Sciendum ergo quod ens secundum totum suum ambitum prima sui divisione dividitur in ens reale extra animam, divisum in decem praedicamenta, et in ens in anima sive in ens cognitivum, sicut manifeste colligitur ex diversis locis libri De causis et Proclo, item etiam ex V et VI Metaphysicae. Adhuc autem sciendum quod, sicut in VI dicitur, bonum et malum sunt in rebus extra animam in natura reali, verum autem et falsum sunt in anima. Ex quo patet quod pertinent ad ens cognitivum et ad cognitionem, bonum autem pertinet ad ens reale sive ad ens naturale.*

*Aliter autem loquendum est omnino de rerum rationibus et cognitione ipsa-
rum, aliter de rebus extra in natura, sicut etiam aliter loquendum est de substantia
et aliter de accidente. Quod non considerantes frequenter incidunt in errorem.*

3. Ibid., nn. 195–96, 163–65.

4. Ibid., n. 207, 175.5; n. 556, 485.5–10; n. 562, 480.8–13.

5. Ibid., n. 158, 130.13–131.4: *credens nondum est propie filius, cuius est videre et
noscere patrem, Math. 11, nec tamen est expers omnino filiationis, sed se habet ad
illam ut dispositio et imperfectum . . . Est ergo credere vel fides quasi motus et fieri
ad esse filium.*

6. Ibid., n. 192, 161.6–8: *in patre, utpote principio quod est intellectus, sunt rerum
rationes, quae cognitionem respiciunt ex sui proprietate.*

7. Ibid., n. 474, 407.1–7; in addition, see n. 574, 502.7–503.2.

8. Ibid., nn. 405–6, 344.1–345.4: *Postquam vero est virtuosus, habens esse virtutis,
iam cognoscit per esse suum, esse, inquam, virtutis et per esse virtuosi quod idem
est . . . Haec est cognitio vera et perfecta per priora et per propria: quando actus
cognoscuntur per esse, effectus per causam, iam non indiget homo foris testimonio
alieno, sed intus in se ipso habet testimonium ipsius sui esse et virtutis . . . Credere
enim per auditum est foris ab alieno et absentis; videre autem praesentis est, certi-
or scientia est. Propter quod intelligere videre dicitur.*

9. Ibid., n. 164, 135.11–14: *In aliis autem omnibus, quae a deo sunt, secundum quod
plus et plus sapiunt divinum, perfectius et imperfectius, universaliter usque ad
ultima et infima in rebus invenitur in omni actione et productione pater, filius
et amor sive spiritus procedens.* The entire passage is important: nn. 160–64,
131–35.

10. Ibid., n. 518, 447.13–14, but see also the passages at nn. 512–18, 443–48;
nn. 23–24, 19 and note 1; nn. 36–37, 31–32; n. 41, 34.11–15.

11. ibid., nn. 362–67, 307–12.

12. See Flasch (2006).

13. Meister Eckhart, *In Ioh.*, LW 3, n. 51, 42.8: *bonum hominis est secundum rationem esse.*

14. Ibid., n. 264, 218.13–219.12; n. 266, 22.12–221.2 and; n. 318, 265.10.

CHAPTER 15. A NEW CHRISTIANITY FOR THE PEOPLE

1. The state of scholarship on Eckhart's German sermons is discussed in the
three volumes of the *Lectura Eckardi* (Stuttgart, 1990–). They also contain a
comprehensive bibliography of the topic. From the considerable amount
of scholarship, I mention only the following: Burkhard Hasebrink, *Formen*

inzitativer Rede bei Meister Eckhart: Untersuchungen zur literarischen Konzeption der deutschen Predigt (Tübingen, 1982); Friedrich Ion, *Die Predigt Meister Eckharts: Seelsorge und Häresie* (Heidelberg, 1993); Susanne Köbele, "Primo aspectu monstruosa: Schriftauslegung bei Meister Eckhart," *Zeitschrift für deutsches Altertum und deutsche Literatur* 122 (1993): 62–81; Köbele, "Bîwort sîn: 'Absolute' Grammatik bei Meister Eckhart," *Zeitschrift für Deutsche Philologie* 113 (1994): 190–207; Klaus Jacobi, ed., *Meister Eckhart: Lebensstationen, Redesituationen* (Berlin, 1997); Claudia Altmeyer, *Grund und Erkennen in deutschen Predigten von Meister Eckhart* (Würzburg, 2005); Sigrun Jäger, *Meister Eckhart: Ein Wort im Wort; Versuch einer theologischen Deutung von vier deutschen Predigten* (Berlin, 2008).

2. Kurt Ruh, "Zu Meister Eckharts Kölner Predigten," *Zeitschrift für deutsches Altertum und deutsche Literatur* 128 (1999): 42–46.

3. Josef Koch, in LW 4, xxiv, note 1, and Koch, "Meister Eckhart in Köln," in *Studium generale in Köln*, ed. C. H. Hering (Cologne, 1948), 13–14.

4. Meister Eckhart, German sermon 39, DW 2:253.3; see also German sermon 39, DW 2:262.5–6; the German sermons are henceforth cited by sermon number and DW reference.

5. See also 18, DW 1:301:6–302:9, and 19, DW 1:314.1–9.

6. LW 4, n. 365, 314.1–13. Eckhart does not take back the earlier critique but considers the theory reasonable and acceptable.

7. Joachim Theisen, *Predigt und Gottesdienst: Liturgische Strukturen in den Predigten Meister Eckharts* (Frankfurt am Main / Bern, 1990), 280–81.

8. Reason comes to God naked in the place where he clothes himself, but not in the clothing store (*Kleiderkammer*), as Quint insensitively translates *kleithûs*.

9. For evidence concerning Aquinas and Dietrich of Freiberg, see Flasch (2007a), 217 and note 11.

CHAPTER 16. SPICY NUTMEGS

1. See German sermon 17, with commentary by Loris Sturlese, in LE 1:75–96, and DW I, German sermon 22, 381.1–2.

2. Johannes Wenck, *De ignota litteratura*, ed. E. Vansteenberghe (Münster, 1910), contribution VIII 6, especially pp. 39–40. Some passages with a corrected text can be found in LW 5, appendix 3, 610–12.

3. On sermon 48, see Burkhard Mojsisch in LE 1:151–62, and also (with information on more recent scholarship) Gasteigt, *Connaissance et verité chez Maître Eckhart*, 151–83. On sermon 86, see the several publications by

Dietmar Mieth, especially *Die Einheit von vita activa und contemplativa in den deutschen Predigten und Traktaten Meister Eckharts und bei Johannes Tauler* (Regensburg, 1969).

4. *Dô ich hiute her gienc, dô gedâhte ich, wie ich iu alsô vernünfticlîche gepredigete, daʒ ir mich wol verstüendet. Dô gedahte ich ein glîchnisse, und kündet ir daʒ wol verstân so verstüendet ir mînen sin und den grunt aller mîner meinunge, den ich ie gepredigete, und was daʒ glîchnisse von mînem ougen und von dem holʒe: wirt mîn ouge ûfgetân, so ist eʒ ein ouge; ist eʒ ʒuo, sô ist eʒ daʒ selbe ouge, und durch der gesiht willen sô engat dem holʒe weder abe noch ʒuo. Nû merket mich vil rehte! Geschihet aber daʒ, daʒ mîn ouge ein und einvaltic ist in im selben und ûfgetân wirt und ûf daʒ holʒ geworfen wirt mit einer angesiht, sô blîbet ein ieglîcheʒ, daʒ eʒ ist, und werdent doch in der würklicheit der angesiht als ein, daʒ man mac gesprechen in der wârheit: ougeholʒ, und daʒ holʒ ist mîn ouge. Wære aber daʒ holʒ âne materie und eʒ ʒemâle geistlic wære als diu gesiht mînes ougen, sô möhte man sprechen in der wârheit, daʒ in der würklicheit der gesiht daʒ holʒ und mîn ouge bestüenden in einem wesene. Ist diʒ wâr von lîplîchen dingen, vil mê ist eʒ wâr von geistlîchen dingen.*

5. *Ich hân etwenne gesprochen von einem liehte, daʒ ist in der sêle, daʒ ist unge-schaffen und ungeschepfelich. Diʒ lieht pflige ich alwege ʒe rüerenne in mînen pre-digen, und diʒ selbe lieht nimet got sunder mittel und sunder decke und blôʒ, als er in im selben ist; daʒ ist ʒe nemenne in der würklicheit der îngeberunge. Dâ mac ich wærlîche sprechen, daʒ diʒ lieht habe mê einicheit mit gote, dan eʒ habe einicheit mit deheiner kraft, mit der eʒ doch ein ist in dem wesene. Wan ir sult wiʒʒen, daʒ diʒ lieht niht edeler enist in dem wesene mîner sêle dan diu niderste kraft oder diu allergröbeste, als gehœrde oder gesiht oder ein ander kraft, an die hunger oder durst, vrost oder hitʒe gevallen mac; und daʒ ist des schult, daʒ daʒ wesen einvaltic ist. Dâ von, als man die krefte nimet in dem wesene, sô sint sie alle ein und glîche edel; aber dâ man die krefte nimet in irn werken, sô ist einiu vil edeler und vil hœher dan diu ander.*

6. DW 2:419.1–3: *Dar umbe sô spriche ich: swenne sich der mensche bekêret von im selben und von allen geschaffenen dingen, als vil als dû daʒ tuost, als vil wirst dû geeiniget und gesæliget in dem vunken in der sêle, der ʒît noch stat nie enberuorte. Dirre vunke*

DW 2:420.1–10: *widersaget allen crêatûren und enwil niht dan got blôʒ, als er in im selben ist. Im engenüeget noch an vater noch an sune noch an heiligen geiste noch an den drin persônen, als verre als ein ieglîchiu bestât in ir eigenschaft. Ich spriche wærliche, daʒ disem liehte niht engenüeget an der einbærkeit der vruhtbær-lîchen art götlîcher natûre. Ich wil noch mê sprechen, daʒ noch wunderlîcher hillet:*

ich spriche eʒ bî guoter wârheit und bî der êwigen wârheit und bî iemerwernder wârheit, daʒ disem selben liehte niht engenüeget an dem einvaltigen stillestânden götlîchen wesene, daʒ weder gibet noch nimet, mêr: eʒ wil wiʒʒen, von wannen diʒ wesen her kome; eʒ wil in den einvaltigen grunt, in die stillen wüeste, dâ nie underscheit îngeluogete weder vater noch sun noch heiliger geist; in dem innigesten, dâ nieman heime enist, dâ genüeget eʒ jenem liehte,

DW 2:421.1–5: *und dâ ist eʒ inniger, dan eʒ in im selben sî; wan dirre grunt ist ein einvaltic stille, diu in ir selben unbewegelich ist, und von dirre unbewegelicheit werdent beweget alliu dinc und werdent enpfangen alliu leben, diu vernünfticliche lebende in in selben sint.*

7. DW 3:482.14–483.20: *Sant Lukas schrîbet in dem êwangeliô, daʒ unser herre Jêsus Kristus gienc in ein kleineʒ stetlîn; dâ enpfienc in ein vrouwe, hieʒ Marthâ; die hâte eine swester, hieʒ Marîâ; die saʒ ʒe den vüeʒen unsers herren und hôrte sîniu wort; aber Marthâ gienc umbe und dienete dem lieben Kristô.*

Dri dinc tâten Marîen sitzen bî den vüeʒen Kristî. Daʒ eine was, daʒ die güete gotes umbegriffen hâte ir sêle. Daʒ ander was unsprechelîchiu begirde: si begerte, si enwiste wes, und wolte, si enwiste waʒ. Daʒ dritte was süeʒer trôst und lust, den si schepfete ûʒ den êwigen worten, die dâ runnen durch den munt Kristî.

Marthen ʒugen ouch driu dinc, diu sie tâten umbegân und dienen dem lieben Kristô. Daʒ eine was ein hêrlich alter und ein wol geübeter grunt ûf daʒ allernaehste; dâ von dûhte sie, daʒ niemanne daʒ werk als wol ʒe tuonne waere als ir. Daʒ ander was ein wîsiu verstantnisse, diu daʒ ûʒer werk wol gerihten kunde in daʒ allernaehste, daʒ mine gebiutet. Daʒ dritte was grôʒiu wirdicheit des lieben gastes.

8. DW 3:482.14–483.20: *Nû sprichet Marthâ: 'herre, heiʒ, daʒ si mir helfe.' Diʒ ensprach Marthâ niht von haʒe, mêr: si sprach eʒ von einem minnegunste, von dem wart si betwungen. Wir suln im sprechen einen minnegunst oder einen minneschimpf. Als wie? Daʒ merket! Si sach, daʒ Marîâ umbegriffen was mit luste nâch aller ir sêle genüegede. Marthâ bekante baʒ Marîen dan Marîâ Marthen, wan si lange und wol gelebet hâte; wan leben gibet daʒ edelste bekennen. Leben bekennet baʒ dan lust oder lieht allez, daʒ man in disem lîbe under gote enpfâhen mac, und etlîche wîs bekennet leben lûterer, dan êwic lieht gegeben müge. Êwic lieht gibet ʒe erkennenne sich selber und got, aber niht sich selber âne got; aber leben gibet ʒe erkennenne sich selber âne got. Dâ eʒ sich selber aleine sihet, dâ merket eʒ baʒ daʒ, waʒ glîch oder unglîch ist. Daʒ bewîset sant Paulus und ouch die heidenischen meister. Sant Paulus sach in sînem ʒucke got und sich selber nâch geistes wise in gote, und enwas doch niht bildelîche wîs in im eine iegîche tugent erkennende an daʒ naehste; und daʒ was dâ von, daʒe r sie an werken niht*

*geüebet enhâte. Die meister kâmen mit üebunge der tugende in sô hôch bekant-
nisse, daʒ sie eine ieglîche tugent bildelîche nâher bekanten dan Paulus oder
dehein heilige in sînem êrsten ʒucke.*

*Alsô stuont ouch Marthâ. Dâ von sprach si: 'herre, heiʒ, daʒ si mir helfe,' als
ob sie spraeche: 'mîne swester dunket, sie vermüge, swaʒ si welle, die wîle si bî dir
in dem trôste sitʒet. Nû lâʒ sie schouwen, ob eʒ alsô sî, und heiʒ sie ûfstân und von
dir gân.' Daʒ ander was ein lieplich minnen, wan daʒ si eʒ spraeche ûʒ dem sinne.
Marîâ was sô vol girde: si gerte, si enwiste wes, und wolte, si enwiste waʒ. Wir
hân sie arcwaenic, die lieben Marîen, sie saeʒe etwenne mê durch lust dan durch
redelîchen nutʒ. Dâ von sprach Marthâ: 'herre, heiʒ sie ûfstân,' wan sie vorhte,
daʒ si blibe in dem luste und niht vürbaʒ enkaeme. Dô antwurte ir Kristus und
sprach: 'Marthâ, Marthâ, dû bist sorcsam, dû wirst betrüebet umbe vil. Des einen
ist nôt. Marîâ hât den besten teil erwelt, der ir niemer enmac benomen warden.'
Diʒ wort ensprach Kristus niht ʒe Marthen in einer strâfenden wîse, mêr: er antwurte ir und gap ir trôst, daʒ Marîâ werden sölte als si begerte.*

9. DW 3:484.1, 484.14–486.9: *Warumbe sprach Kristus: 'Marthâ, Marthâ' und
nante sie ʒwirunt? . . . Er meinte, alleʒ, daʒ ʒîtliches und êwiges guotes waere und
daʒ creature besitʒen sölte, daʒ daʒ Marthâ ʒemâle hâte. An dem êrsten, dô er
sprach Marthâ, dô bewîsete er ir volkomenheit ʒîtlîcher werke. Ze dem andern
male, dô er sprach Marthâ, dô bewîsete er, alleʒ, daʒ dâ hoeret ʒe êwiger saelde,
daʒ ir des niht enbraeste. Dâ von sprach er: 'dû bist sorcsam,' und meinte: dû stâst
bî den dingen, und diu dinc enstânt niht in dir; und die stânt mit sorgen, die âne
hindernisse stânt in allem irm gewerbe. Die stânt âne hindernisse, die alliu iriu
werk rihtent ordenlîche nâch dem bilde des êwigen liehtes; und die liute stânt bî
den dingen und niht in den dingen. Sie stânt vil nâhe und enhânt es niht minner,
da nob sie stüenden dort oben an dem umberinge der êwicheit. 'Vil nâhe,' spriche
ich, wan alle creature die mittelnt. Mittel ist ʒwîvalt. Eineʒ ist, âne daʒ ich in got
niht komen enmac: daʒ ist werk und gewerbe in der ʒît, und daʒ enminnert niht
êwige saelde. Werk ist, sô man sich üebet von ûʒen an werken der tugende; aber
gewerbe ist, sô man sich mit redelîcher bescheidenheit üebet von innen. Da ʒander
mittel daʒ ist: blôʒ sîn des selben. Wan dar umbe sîn wir gesetʒet in die ʒît, daʒ wir
von ʒîtlîchem vernünftigen gewerbe gote naeher und glîcher werden. Daʒ meinte
ouch sant Paulus, dô er sprach: 'loeset die ʒît, die tage sint übel.' 'Die ʒît loesen'
ist, daʒ man âne underlâʒ mit vernünfticheit ûfgâ in got, niht nâch bildelîcher un-
derscheidenheit, mêr: mit vernünftiger lebelîcher wârheit. Und dâ 'sint die tage
übel,' daʒ verstât alsô: tac bewîset naht. Enwaere kein naht, sô enwaere und hieʒe
eʒ ouch niht tac, wan eʒ waere alleʒ ein lieht; und daʒ meinte Paulus, wan ein
liehteʒ leben ist alʒe kleine, bî dem noch iht vinsternisse gesîn mac, daʒ einen*

hêrlîchen geist bewîlet und beschatewet êwiger saelde. Daʒ meinte ouch Kristus, dô er sprach: 'gât, die wîle ir daʒ lieht hât;' wan, swer dâ würket in dem liehte, der gât ûf in got, vrî und blôʒ alles mittels: sîn lieht ist sîn gewerbe, und sîn gewerbe ist sîn lieht.

Alsô stuont die liebe Marthâ. Dâ von sprach er ʒe ir: 'des einen ist nôt,' niht ʒwei. Ich und dû, einstunt umbevangen mit êwigem liehte, ist eineʒ, und ʒwei-eineʒ ist ein brinnender geist, der dâ stat ob allen dingen und under gote an dem umberinge der êwichheit. Der ist ʒwei, wan er âne mittel got niht ensihet. Sîn bekennen und sîn wesen oder sîn bekennen und ouch des bekantnisses bilde die enwerdent niemer ein. Sie ensehent got, wan, dâ wirt got geistic gesehen, vrî von allen bilden. Eineʒ wirt ʒwei, ʒwei ist ein; lieht und geist, die ʒwei ist ein in dem umbevange êwiges liehtes.

10. DW 3:488.7–489.16: *Nû kêren wider ʒe unser rede, wie diu liebe Marthâ und mit ir alle gotes vriunde stânt mit der sorge, niht in der sorge, und dâ ist daʒ ʒîtlich werk als edel als dehein vüegen in got; wan eʒ vüeget als nâhe als daʒ oberste, daʒ uns werden mac, âne aleine got sehen in blôʒer nature. Dâ von sprichet er: 'dû stâst bî den dingen und bî der sorge' und meinet, daʒ si was wol mit den nidern sinnen betrüebet und bekümbert, wan si niht alsô verwenet stuont in geistes süeʒe. Si stuont bî den dingen, niht in den dingen; si stuont sunder und eʒ sunder.*

Driu dinc suln wir haben in unsern werken. Daʒ ist, daʒ man würke ordenlîche und redelîche und wiʒʒentlîche. Dem spriche ich ordenlîche, daʒ in allen orten antwürtet dem naehsten. Sô spriche ich dem redelîche, daʒ man in der ʒît niht beʒʒers enbekenne. Sô spriche ich dem wiʒʒentlîche, daʒ man bevinde lebelîcher wârheit mit lustiger gegenwürtichheit in guoten werken. Swâ disiu driu dinc sint, die vüegent als nâhe und sint als nütʒe als aller der lust Marîen Magdalênen in der wüeste.

Nû sprichet Kristus: 'dû bist betrüebet umbe vil,' niht umbe eineʒ. Daʒ ist: sô si lûter einvaltic stât âne allen gewerp, hin ûf gerihtet an den umberinc der êwicheit, sô wirt si betrüebet, sô si von sache gemittelt wirt, daʒ si niht enmac stân mit lusted ort oben. Der mensche wirt betrüebet in der sache, der dâ versinket und stât bî der sorge. Aber Marthâ stuont in hêrlîcher, wol gevestenter tugent und in einem vrîen gemüete, ungehindert von allen dingen. Dâ von begerte si, daʒ ir swester in daʒ selbe gesetʒet würde, wan sis ach, daʒ si niht weselîche stuont. Eʒ was ein hêrlîcher grunt, ûʒ dem si begerte, daʒ si stüende in allem dem, daʒ dâ gehoeret ʒe êwiger saelde. Dâ von sprichet Kristus: 'eines ist nôt.' Waʒ ist daʒ? Daʒ ist daʒ eine, daʒ ist got. Daʒ ist nôt allen crêatûren; wan, ʒüge got daʒ sîne an sich, alle crêatûren würden ʒe nihte. Züge got daʒ sîne abe der sêle Kristî, dâ ir geist geeiniget ist an die êwige persône, Kristuss blibe blôʒe crêatûre. Dâ von bedarf man des einen wol.

Marthâ vorhte, daȝ ir swester behaftete in dem luste und in der süeȝe, und begerte, daȝ si würde als si. Dâ von sprach Kristus, als ob er spraeche: gehap dich wol, Marthâ, 'si hât den besten teil erwelt;' diȝ sol ir abegân. Daȝ naehste, daȝ crêatûre werde mac, daȝ sol ir werden: si sol saelic werden als dû.

11. DW 3:491.6–491.17: *Nû sprichet Kristus: 'umbe vil sorge wirst dû betrüebet.' Marthâ was sô weselich, daȝ sie ir gewerp niht enhinderte; werk und gewerp leitte sie ȝe êwiger saelde. Si wart wol etwaȝ gemittelt: eȝ stiuret wol edeliu natûre und staeter vlîȝ und vor genante tugende. Marîâ was ê Marthâ, ê si Marîâ würde; wan, dô si saȝ bî den vüeȝen unsers herren, dô enwas si niht Marîâ: si was eȝ wol an dem namen, si enwas eȝ aber niht an dem wesene; wan si saȝ bî luste und bî süeȝe und was allerêrst ȝe schuole gesetȝet und lernete leben. Aber Marthâ stuont sô weselîche, dâ von sprach si: 'herre, heiȝ sie ûfstân!,' als ob si spraeche: 'herre, ich wölte gerne, daȝ si dâ niht ensaeȝe durch lust; ich wölte, daȝ sie lernete leben, daȝ si eȝ weselîche besaeȝe.' 'Heiȝ sie ûfstân,' daȝ sie durnehte werde. Si enhieȝ niht Marîâ, dô sib î Kristî vüeȝen saȝ. Ich heiȝe daȝ Marîâ: ein wol geübeter lîp, gehôrsam einer wîsen sêle. Daȝ heiȝe ich gehôrsam: swaȝ bescheidenheit gebiutet, daȝ des der wille genuoc sî.*

12. Albertus Magnus, *Super Lucam*, in *Opera omnia*, ed. Borgnet (Paris, 1894), 23:87–89.

CHAPTER 17. A NEW CONSOLATION OF PHILOSOPHY

1. For the whole chapter, see Flasch (2007b).
2. These sentences became articles 1–4 in the list of errors presented by the prosecutors in Cologne, LW 5, nn. 1–7, 198–200. Not word for word, but according to its sense, it becomes article 11 of the papal bull, LW 5:603.65–67.
3. Also in the list of the prosecution, article 4, LW 5, nn. 8–9, 201–2.
4. See Kurt Flasch, "Meister Eckhart: Expositio sancti Evangelii secundum Ioannem," in *Interpretationen—Hauptwerke der Philosophie: Mittelater*, ed. Kurt Flasch (Stuttgart, 1998), 381–401.
5. The *Book of Divine Consolation* and the commentary on John play off each other; see *In Ioh.*, LW 3, nn. 14–32, 13–25. As in the consolatory treatise, Eckhart starts by explaining his philosophical theory of principles concerning the relationship between *concretum* and *abstractum*. He says this (n. 14, 13) and then explains that based on this, one can explain almost everything that is found in the gospel about the divinity of the Son (n. 23, 19; n. 27, 21). It is dependent on the way he arranges his argument: in the beginning there is neither a theologumenon nor a mystical doctrine of life, but rather a thinking

about *iustus* and *iustitia*, about *ratio rei* and *res*, about abstract and concrete, about idea and ideate. And this is then the true, not the merely imagined, theologumenon. Eckhart emphasizes the *universal* character of this *philosophical* conception (n. 6, 7).

6. Eckhart, *In Ioh.*, LW 3, n. 4, 5.

7. Ibid, n. 14, 13; n. 26, 21.

8. Ibid., n. 5, 7; thanks to Burkhard Mojsisch for clarifying this (*Meister Eckhart: Analogie, Univozität und Einheit* [Hamburg, 1983]).

9. Eckhart, *In Ioh.*, LW 3, n. 16, 14.

10. Texts in Flasch (2006), 120.

11. Eckhart, *In Ioh.*, LW 3, n. 208, 176; n. 391, 333; n. 449, 384; n. 611, 533.

12. Eckhart, *Buch der göttlichen Tröstung*, part 2, DW 5:39:1–7.

13. Eckhart, *In Ioh.*, LW 3, n. 19, 16.13: *Hoc enim proprie vivit quod est sine principio.*

14. Ibid., n. 8, 9; n. 18, 15.

15. Ibid., nn. 2–3, 4; Eckhart, *Buch der göttlichen Tröstung*, DW 5:11.20–22, and Flasch (2007a), 13ff.

16. Eckhart, First Parisian Question, LW 5, n. 4, 41.10–11: *Sapientia autem, qua pertinet ad intellectum, non habet rationem creabilis.*

17. German sermon 6, *Iusti vivent in aeternum*, LE 2:32.8–9.

18. A light jab by Eckhart at the overvaluing of liturgical head and body movements can be found in LW 5, n. 28, 310.4–8.

19. Eckhart, *Von dem edeln menschen*, DW 5:111:11; Eckhart, *Processus Coloniensis II*, LW 5, n. 150, 353.15–17.

CHAPTER 18. ECKHART'S TRIAL

1. See Koch, 309–44; Bernard McGinn, "Eckhart's Condemnation Reconsidered," *Thomist* 44 (1980): 390–414; Winfried Trusen, *Der Prozess gegen Meister Eckhart: Vorgeschichte, Verlauf und Folgen* (Paderborn, 1988); Walter Senner, "Meister Eckhart in Köln," in *Meister Eckhart: Lebenssituationen, Redesituationen*, ed. Klaus Jacobi (Berlin, 1997), 207–38; Susanne Köbele, "Meister Eckhart und die 'Hunde des Herrn,' " *Beiträge zur Geschichte der deutschen Sprache und Literatur* 124 (2002): 48–73; Jürgen Miethke, "Der Eckhartprozeß in Köln und Avignon," in *L'età dei processi: Inchieste e condanne tra politica e ideologia nel '300*, ed. A. Rigon and F. Veronese (Rome, 2009), 119–43. Indispensable: Loris Sturlese, LW 5:247–73.

2. Jürgen Miethke, "Der Prozess gegen Meister Eckhart," in *Meister Eckhart: Lebenssituationen, Redesituationen,* ed. Klaus Jacobi (Berlin, 1997), 372.

3. R. Lerner, "New Evidence for the Condemnation of Meister Eckhart," *Speculum* 72 (1997): 363–66.

4. LW 5, n. 10, 202.9–18. Unless otherwise specified, citations in this and the following two chapters refer to the fifth volume of the Latin works, LW 5 (Stuttgart, 2006).

5. Bonaventure, *In 2 Sent.* 26, art. unic. qu. 2, *Opera omnia* 2:635a: *omnes recte intelligentes concedunt, in iustis esse gratiae donum, et credunt etiam, in eis esse donum increatum, quod est Spiritus sanctus.*

6. Bonaventura, *1 Sent.* 17, 1 art. unicus qu. 1, *Opera omnia* 1:294b.

7. Thomas Aquinas, *In 1 Sent.* 17, 1, 1, 157b. I cite Aquinas's commentary on the *Sentences* according to the Parma edition of 1856.

8. Artur Michael Landgraf, *Dogmengeschichte der Frühscholastik,* vol. 1, bk. 1 (Regensburg, 1953), 220–37.

9. Chapter 6, *1 Sent.* 17, 148–52, attests to this.

10. Thomas Aquinas, *ScG* III, 150, 442a; *qualitas inhaerens: Sth* I–II 110:2.

11. The Roman catechism of the Council of Trent, Pars II c.2 qu. 38 (Regensburg, 1905), 1:149.

12. Thomas Aquinas, *ScG* III, c.147, Leonina III, 345–46.

13. LW 5, n. 70, 224.14; n. 112, 345.4–5.

14. Ibid., n. 55, 211.19–20.

15. Ibid., n. 29, 210.3–11, esp. 7: *in urina nihil prorsus est sanitatis.*

16. In Dietrich in his work *De Accidentibus, Opera omnia* 3:53–90. But also already in his early work *De origine rerum praedicamentalium* 1, 5, 3:138.60–139.70, and 1, 24–28, 3:144.225–58. See Flasch (2007a), index, s.v. "Akzidens."

17. E. H. Wéber, "L'argumentation philosophique personnelle du théologien Eckhart à Paris en 1302/1303," in *Meister Eckhart: Lebenssituationen, Redesituationen,* ed. Klaus Jacobi (Berlin, 1997), 108, note 42. He cites the following passages: *In Ioh.,* LW 3, n. 43, 36; *In Exod.,* LW 2, n. 28, 34, and n. 56, 61; *In Sap.,* LW 2, n. 65, 393. But in none of these is the Trinity or the real distinctness that Aquinas demands to be found.

18. LW 5, n. 52, 215.16–18; n. 50, 215.7–9.

19. Thomas Aquinas, *ScG* III, 150, Editio Leonina III, 470.

20. LW 5, n. 54, 243.26–244.3.

21. Ibid., n. 60, 218.16–21.

22. Meister Eckhart, German sermon 13, DW 1, n. 59, 220:4–9; n. 60, 218.

23. LW 5, n. 59, 578.17–19, and n. 101, 588.4.

24. Meister Eckhart, *Liber parab.*, LW 1, n. 165, 634.11–12.

25. Article 13, LW 5, n. 57, 558.30.

26. LW 5, n. 68, 222.17–223.9; n.36, 326.7–16.

27. Ibid., n. 32, 210.21–211.11.

CHAPTER 19. ECKHART'S TRIAL

1. LW 5, n. 24–30, 209–10.

2. Ibid., sentence 2, n. 26, 209.13–14, and sentence 6, 210.12–17.

3. On the significance of Aristotle's *On the Soul* for Eckhart, see Flasch (2006) and Alessandra Beccarisi, "Aristoteles . . . der hoechste unter den meistern," in *Studi sulle fonti di Meister Eckhart*, ed. Loris Sturlese (Fribourg, 2008), 11–38.

4. See Angela Schiffhauer, "Nos filii Dei sumus analogice," in *MM* 32:356–92.

5. LW 5, nn. 84–85, 278.14–279.10.

6. Ibid., n. 122, 347.3–348.5.

7. Ibid., n. 127, 293.18–294.10.

8. Ibid., n. 24, 323.20–324.4.

9. Ibid., nn. 33–34, 325.21–326.4.

10. Ibid., nn. 97–99, 341.3–27.

11. Ibid., n. 132, 296.13; n. 136, 350.9.

12. Thus in the citations to Thomas in LW 5, n. 134, 297.13–14, and n. 109, 344.19–21.

13. Ibid., n. 131, 296.1–9.

14. Ibid., n. 132, 296.11.

15. Ibid., n. 99, 341.24–26.

16. At the beginning of his answer to the second list (LW 5, n. 2, 318–319), Eckhart provides a list of five doctrinal errors made by his opponents. First, they deny the possibility of the union of man with God; second, they deny that creatures by themselves are nothingness. They attribute temporality to the divine act of creation. They claim that the external act adds something of moral perfection to the internal act. And they believe that the Holy Spirit can be given to a person who is not the Son of God.

17. John 17:21, LW 5, n. 152, 354.3–5.

CHAPTER 20. THE END IN AVIGNON

1. Article 1, LW 5, n. 2, 569.12; article 16, n. 64, 580.8; all citations to the articles drawn up against Eckhart are to the texts in LW 5.

2. Article 1, nn. 1–12, 568–71.
3. Article 2, n. 15, 571.12–13.
4. LW 5, n. 17, 571.23.
5. LW 5, n. 21, 572.12–13.
6. Article 4, nn. 22–24, 572.15–21.
7. Article 5, nn. 26–29, 573.3–574.4.
8. Article 6, nn. 30–33, 574.
9. LW 5, n. 117, 289.6–7
10. Articles 7–9, nn. 34–41, 575–76.
11. Article 16, n. 64, 579.28–29.
12. Ibid., n. 64, 580.1–8.
13. Article 19, n. 71, 581.15.
14. Ibid., n. 73, 581.25–26.
15. Article 21, n. 82, 583.26.
16. Article 22, n. 86, 584.18–20.
17. Article 23, n. 89, 585.9–10.
18. Ibid., n. 92, 586.3–8.
19. Article 24, nn. 97–98, 587.1–11.
20. Article 25, nn. 99–100, 587.13–32.
21. Article 26, n. 101, 588.4.
22. Ibid., n. 105, 588.21.
23. Articles 27–28, 589–90.
24. Article 27, n. 109, 589.23–24.
25. *Acta Echardiana*, LW 5, n. 65, 596–600.
26. LW 5:599.99.

CHAPTER 21. EPILOGUE

1. Meister Eckhart, *Prol. gen.*, LW 1, n. 11, 156.4–10.
2. Eckhart, LW 5, nn. 24–30, 209–10.
3. Ibid., nn. 81–86, 277–79.
4. Sturlese, "Hat Meister Eckhart Dietrich de Freiberg gelesen? Die Lehre vom Bild und von den göttlichen Vollkommenheiten in Eckhart's *Expositio libri Genesis* und Dietrichs *De visione beatifica*," in *Recherches sur Dietrich von Freiberg*, ed. Joel Biard, Dragos Calma, and Ruedi Imbach (Turnhout, 2009), 193–219.
5. See Kurt Flasch, "Einleitung," in Dietrich von Freiberg, *Opera omnia* 1:xxvi.
6. See references and discussion in Flasch (2007a), 162–65.

7. Eckhart, *In Sap.*, LW 3, n. 283, 616.1.

8. Eckhart, *In Eccli.*, LW 2, n. 8, 237.1–8.

9. Dietrich definitively formulated this thesis early: *Metaphysicus considerat ens inquantum ens, quae consideratio est entis per essentiam secundum rationem suae quiditatis circumscriptis a re suis causis tam efficientibus quam finalibus*, or. 5, 61, 3:199, 632–34. For more on this, see Flasch (2007a), 119–21 and index, s.vv. "Innensein" and "Immanentismus."

10. Dietrich of Freiberg, or. 1:8–1:9, 3:139–40, and 1, 12, 3:140.126–28.

11. Dietrich of Freiberg, or. 1, 27, 3:144.246–47: *unumquodque enim dicitur ens per suam essentiam, non concernendo aliquam causam.* On this, see Imbach, 153–250, and Flasch (2007a), index, s.vv. "Sein," "Sein und Wesen," "Wesen."

12. Dietrich of Freiberg, or. 1, 30, 3:145.264–66: *Substantia dicitur ens secundum rationem absolutae subsistentiae et ens per se secundum rationem intrinseci actus formalis.*

13. On this, see Eckhart, *Book of Divine Consolation*, part 2, DW 5:39.1–7, and *In Ioh.*, n. 19, 16.13: *hoc enim proprie vivit quod est sine principio;* see also Flasch (2007a), index, s.v. "Leben."

14. Dietrich, or. 1, 25, 3:144.233–34: *Tota enim entitas eorum non est aliud, quod sunt aliquid entis, quod est substantia.* See also or. 1, 5, 3:138.60–139.70, and or. 1, 24–28, 3:144.225–58; or. 2, 21, 3:149.146–51; Imbach, 297–332; Flasch (2007a), 253–76.

15. Dietrich, or. 1:19–1:20, vol. 3: *quaedam sunt entia primae intentionis, quae constituuntur operatione intellectus.* For a discussion of this, see Flasch (2007a), 57–59 and the index, s.vv. "Relation," "Zeit."

16. Dietrich, or. 2, 14, 3:148.93–96; 22, 51, 3:156.370–75; or. 5, 31, 3:189.270–80. See Flasch (2007a), index, s.v. "Natur."

17. Dietrich, or. 1, 14, 3:141, esp. ll. 145–46, 150; 1, 37, 3:168; 3, 37, 3:168.336.

18. Eckhart, *In Ioh.*, LW 3, n. 83, 71.

19. Dietrich, or. 5, 8, 3:182.35–39; 5, 26, 3:187.220–188.233; 5, 58, 3:198.600–8.

20. Ibid., 5, 17, 3:184–85 and 18, 3:185; also 533, 3:190.

21. Ruedi Imbach, "Gravis iactura verae doctrinae," in Imbach, *Quodlibeta*, 153–207.

Bibliography

ECKHART'S WORKS

Citations to Eckhart's works are from the following edition:

Meister Eckhart. *Die deutschen und lateinischen Werke*. Stuttgart, 1936–. The German works are abbreviated DW, the Latin works LW.

Useful also, for both text and notes:

Meister Eckhart. *Traités et Sermons*. Translated by Alain de Libera. Paris, 1993.

Largier, Niklaus, ed. *Meister Eckhart: Texte und Übersetzungen von Josef Quint*. 2 vols. Frankfurt am Main, 2008.

Steer, Georg, and Loris Sturlese, eds. *Lectura Eckhardi: Predigten Meister Eckharts von Fachgelehrten gelesen und gedeutet*. 3 vols. Stuttgart, 1998, 2003, 2008; abbreviated LE.

BIBLIOGRAPHY

Older scholarly works are listed in Niklaus Largier, *Bibliographie zu Meister Eckhart* (Fribourg, 1989). Newer works are added continually to the bibliography of the Meister Eckhart Society. A solid overview of more recent publications is included in Julie Gasteigt, *Connaissance et vérité chez Maître Eckhart* (Paris, 2006), 443–58.

WORKS ON MEISTER ECKHART

Aertsen, Jan A. "Meister Eckhart: Eine außerordentliche Metaphysik." *Recherches de théologie et philosophie médiévales* 66 (1999): 1–20.

Albert, Karl. *Meister Eckhart und die Philosophie des Mittelalters*. Dettelbach, 1999.

Altmeyer, Claudia. *Grund und Erkennen in deutschen Predigten von Meister Eckhart*. Würzburg 2005.

Bach, Joseph. *Meister Eckhart der Vater der deutschen Speculation: Als Beitrag zu einer Geschichte der deutschen Theologie und Philosophie der mittleren Zeit.* Vienna, 1864.

Beccarisi, Alessandra. "Philosophische Neologismen zwischen Latein und Volkssprache: 'Istic' und 'isticheit' bei Meister Eckhart." *Recherches de théologie et philosophie médiévales* 70 (2003): 97–126.

Degenhardt, Inge. *Studien zum Wandel des Eckhartbildes*. Leiden, 1967.

Denifle, Heinrich. "Meister Eckharts lateinische Schriften und die Grundanschauung seiner Lehre." *Archiv für Litteratur- und Kirchengeschichte des Mittelalters* 2 (1886): 417–640, 673–87.

Flasch, Kurt. "Converti ut imago—Rückkehr als Bild: Eine Studie zur Theorie des Intellekts bei Dietrich von Freiberg und Meister Eckhart." In *Albert le Grand et sa réception au Moyen Age: Hommage à Zenon Kaluza*, edited by F. Cheneval, R. Imbach, and Th. Ricklin, 130–50. Fribourg, 1998.

———. "Die Intention Meister Eckharts." In *Sprache und Begriff: Festschrift für B. Liebrucks*, edited by H. Röttges, 292–318. Meisenheim, 1974.

———. *Meister Eckhart: Die Geburt der "Deutschen Mystik" aus dem Geist der arabischen Philosophie*. Munich, 2006.

———. "Meister Eckhart: Expositio sancti Evangelii secundum Ioannem." In *Interpretationen—Hauptwerke der Philosophie: Mittelalter*, 381–401. Stuttgart, 1998.

———. "Meister Eckhart, Predigt 52: Beati pauperes spiritu." In *Lectura Eckhardi I: Predigten Meister Eckharts von Fachgelehrten gelesen und gedeutet*, edited by Georg Steer and Loris Sturlese, 163–99. Stuttgart, 1998.

———. "Predigt 6: Iusti vivent in aeternum." In *Lectura Eckhardi* II, edited by Georg Steer and Loris Sturlese, 29–52. Stuttgart, 2003.

———. "Procedere ut imago: Das Hervorgehen des Intellekts aus seinem göttlichen Grund bei Meister Dietrich, Meister Eckhart und Berthold von Moosburg." In *Abendländische Mystik im Mittelalter: Symposion Kloster Engelberg 1984*, edited by Kurt Ruh, 125–34. Stuttgart, 1986.

———, ed. *Von Meister Dietrich zu Meister Eckhart*. Hamburg, 1984.

Flasch, Kurt, and Ruedi Imbach. *Meister Eckhart—in seiner Zeit*. Düsseldorf, 2003.

Frost, Stefanie. *Nikolaus von Kues und Meister Eckhart: Rezeption im Spiegel der Marginalien zum Opus tripartitum Meister Eckharts*. Münster, 2006.

Goris, Wouter. *Einheit als Prinzip und Ziel: Versuch über die Einheitsmetaphysik des Opus tripartitum Meister Eckharts*. Leiden, 1997.

Grotz, Stephan. *Negationen des Absoluten: Meister Eckhart, Cusanus, Hegel.* Hamburg, 2009.

Guerizoli, Rodrigo. *Die Verinnerlichung des Göttlichen: Eine Studie über den Gottesgeburtszyklus und die Armutspredigt Meister Eckharts.* Leiden, 2006.

Halfwassen, Jens. "Gibt es eine Philosophie der Subjektivität im Mittelalter? Zur Theorie des Intellekts bei Meister Eckhart und Dietrich von Freiberg." *Zeitschrift für Philosophie und Theologie* 72 (1997): 338–60.

Hauke, Rainer. *Trinität und Denken: Die Unterscheidung der Einheit von Gott und Mensch bei Meister Eckhart.* Frankfurt am Main, 1985.

Jacobi, Klaus, ed. *Meister Eckhart: Lebensstationen, Redesituationen.* Berlin, 1997.

Jäger, Sigrun. *Meister Eckhart—Ein Wort im Wort: Versuch einer theologischen Deutung von vier deutschen Predigten.* Berlin, 2008.

Kampmann, Irmgard. *Ihr sollt der Sohn selber sein!* Frankfurt am Main, 1996.

Kern, Udo. *Die Anthropologie Meister Eckharts.* Hamburg, 1994.

Koch, Josef. "Kritische Studien zum Leben Meister Eckharts." In *Kleine Schriften* 1, edited by Josef Koch, 247–347. Rome, 1973.

Largier, Niklaus. "Das Glück des Menschen: Diskussionen über beatitudo und Vernunft in volkssprachlichen Texten des 14. Jahrhunderts." In *Nach der Verurteilung von 1277*, MM 28, edited by J. A. Aertsen et al., 827–55. Berlin, 2001.

———. "'Intellectus in Deum ascensus': Intellekttheoretische Auseinandersetzungen in Texten der deutschen Mystik." *Vierteljahrsschrift für Literaturwissenschaft und Geistesgeschichte* 64 (1995): 423–72.

———. *Zeit, Zeitlichkeit, Ewigkeit: Ein Aufriß des Zeitproblems bei Dietrich von Freiberg und Meister Eckhart.* Bern, 1989.

Lasson, Adolf. *Meister Eckhart, der Mystiker: Zur Geschichte der religiösen Speculation in Deutschland.* Berlin, 1868.

Leppin, Volker, ed. *Meister Eckhart aus theologischer Sicht. Meister-Eckhart-Jahrbuch* 1. Stuttgart, 2007.

Libera, Alain da. *Introduction à la mystique rhénane d'Albert le Grand à Maître Eckhart.* Paris, 1984.

Liebeschütz, Hans. "Meister Eckhart und Moses Maimonides." *Archiv für Kulturgeschichte* 54 (1972): 64–96.

Malte-Fues, Wolfram. *Mystik als Erkenntnis? Kritische Studien zur Meister Eckhart-Forschung.* Bonn, 1981.

McGinn, Bernard. *The Mystical Thought of Meister Eckhart: The Man from Whom God Hid Nothing.* New York, 2001.

Mieth, Diethmar. *Meister Eckhart: Mystik und Lebenskunst.* Düsseldorf, 2004.

Miethke, Jürgen. "Der Eckhartprozeß in Köln und Avignon." In *L'età dei processi: Inchieste e condanne tra politica e ideologia nel '300*, edited by A. Rigon and F. Veronese, 119–43. Rome, 2009.

Mojsisch, Burkhard. *Meister Eckhart, Analogie, Univozität und Einheit*. Hamburg, 1983.

Quero-Sanchez, Andrés. *Sein als Freiheit: Die idealistische Metaphysik Meister Eckharts*. Freiburg, 2004.

Reisch, Donata Schoeller. *Enthöhter Gott—Vertiefter Mensch: Zur Bedeutung der Demut ausgehend von Meister Eckhart und Jakob Böhme*. Freiburg, 1999.

Ruh, Kurt. *Geschichte der abendländischen Mystik III: Die Mystik des deutschen Predigerordens und ihre Grundlegung durch die Hochscholastik*. Munich, 1996.

———. *Meister Eckhart: Theologe, Prediger, Mystiker*. Munich, 1989.

Saccon, Alessandra. *Nascità e logos: Conoscenza e teoria trinitaria in Meister Eckhart*. Naples, 1998.

Schirpenbach, Meik Peter. *Wirklichkeit als Beziehung: Das strukturontologische Schema der termini generales im Opus Tripartitum Meister Eckharts*. Münster, 2004.

Speer, Andreas, ed. *Meister Eckhart in Erfurt*. Miscellanea mediaevalia 32. Berlin, 2005.

Stirnimann, Heinrich, and Ruedi Imbach, eds. *Eckardus Theutonicus, homo doctus et sanctus: Nachweise und Berichte zum Prozess gegen Meister Eckhart*. Fribourg, 1992.

Sturlese, Loris. *Homo divinus: Philosophische Projekte in Deutschland zwischen Meister Eckhart und Heinrich Seuse*. Stuttgart, 2007.

———. *Meister Eckhart: Ein Portrait*. Regensburg, 1993.

Tobin, Frank J. *Meister Eckhart: Thought and Language*. Philadelphia, 1996.

Trusen, Winfried. *Der Prozeß gegen Meister Eckhart*. Paderborn, 1988.

Wackernagel, Wolfgang, trans. *La Divine Consolation: Traduit du moyen-haut allemand, présenté et annoté*. Paris, 2004.

———. *Ymagine denudari: Éthique de l'image et métaphysique de l'abstraction chez Maître Eckhart*. Paris, 1991.

Waldschütz, Erwin. *Meister Eckhart: Eine philosophische Interpretation der Traktate*. Bonn, 1978.

Welte, Bernhard. *Meister Eckhart: Gedanken zu seinen Gedanken*. Freiburg, 1979.

Wilde, Mauritius. *Das neue Bild vom Gottesbild: Bild und Theologie bei Meister Eckhart*. Fribourg, 2000.

Winkler, Eberhard. *Exegetische Methoden bei Meister Eckhart*. Tübingen, 1965.

Winkler, Norbert. *Meister Eckhart zur Einführung*. Hamburg, 1997.

Timeline

ECKHART	POLITICS—CHURCH—SCIENCE—CULTURE
Before 1260 born in Tambach near Gotha	Around 1240/1245, Dietrich born in Freiberg, Saxony
	1250 Friedrich II†
	1254–73 Great Interregnum
	1271–75 Marco Polo in Asia
	1273–91 Rudolf of Habsburg*
	1274 Council of Lyon; Bonaventure†; Thomas Aquinas†
	1276–92 Henry of Ghent teaches at Paris
	1277 bishop of Paris condemns 219 theses
	1280 Albertus Magnus†
	1285–1314 Philip the Fair, king of France
	1285 Godfrey of Fontaines, master at Paris
	1286 Boetius of Dacia†; Siger of Brabant†; Dietrich of Freiberg, *De origine rerum praedicamentalium*
	1292–98 Adolf of Nassau†
	1294–1303 Boniface VIII
	1298–1308 Albert I of Habsburg*
	1300 Boniface VIII, *Unam sanctam*

ECKHART	POLITICS—CHURCH— SCIENCE—CULTURE
1302/3 master in Paris; first three Parisian questions (LW 5); *Opus tripartitum* (LW 1)	1296–1303 conflict between Philip the Fair and Boniface VIII
1303–11 Erfurt, prior of Saxony, a new province recently separated from Teutonia	1304–8 Giotto, Scrovegni chapel, Padua
Sermons and Lectures on Jesus Sirach (LW 2)	1308 Duns Scotus in Cologne* 1308–13 Henry VII of Luxembourg* 1309–77 popes in Avignon
1311–13 master in Paris; fourth and fifth Parisian questions	1311: Marguerite Porete executed in Paris; Council of Vienne, *Anima forma corporis, lumen gloriae;* council condemns eight errors of the Beghards; Knights Templar abolished 1313 Soest, Wiesenkirche (St. Mary of the Meadow) begun
1314–23(?) Strasbourg and/or Cologne; Strasbourg, German sermons (DW 1–3) 1318 *Book of Divine Consolation* (DW 5)	1314–46 Louis the Bavarian* 1316 Ramon Llull† 1317–19 widespread famine in Europe 1318/20(?) Dietrich of Freiberg† 1321 Dante† 1322: Cologne, cathedral choir complete
1323(?)–26 Cologne, German sermons (DW 1–4)	1323 Thomas Aquinas canonized 1324 Marsilius of Padua, *Defensor Pacis*
August 1325–January 1326 first list of errors submitted in Cologne	
1326 second list of errors submitted to the archbishop of Cologne; first summons	
1327 simultaneous trial against Eckhart and Ockham in Avignon (LW 5)	
1328 January 8 (or April at the latest), death in Avignon	
1329 March 29, condemnation by John XXII, *In agro dominico* (LW 5)	

POLITICS—CHURCH—

SCIENCE—CULTURE

1337–1453   Hundred Years' War

1346–78   Charles IV*

1347   William of Ockham[†]; republic in
Rome, Cola di Rienzo

1348   University of Prague; Archdiocese
of Prague

1348–49   Black Death

1349   Thomas Bradwardine[†]

1361   Johannes Tauler[†]

1366   Henry Suso[†]

1378–1418   Great Western Schism

Abbreviations

AHDMA	*Archives d'histoire doctrinale et littéraire du Moyen Age* (Paris, 1926–)
CC	*Corpus Christianorum, Series Latina* (Turnhout, 1951–)
CPTMA	Corpus philosophorum teutonicorum medii aevi (Hamburg, 1985–)
DW	Meister Eckhart, *Deutsche Werke* (Stuttgart, 1936–)
Flasch (2000)	Kurt Flasch, *Das philosophische Denken im Mittelalter* (Stuttgart, 2000)
Flasch (2006)	Kurt Flasch, *Meister Eckhart: Die Geburt der "Deutschen Mystik" aus dem Geist der arabischen Philosophie* (Munich, 2006)
Flasch (2007a)	Kurt Flasch, *Dietrich von Freiberg: Philosophie, Theologie, Naturforschung um 1300* (Frankfurt am Main, 2007)
Flasch (2007b)	Meister Eckhart, *Das Buch der göttlichen Tröstung*, trans. Kurt Flasch (Munich, 2007)
Imbach	Ruedi Imbach, *Quodlibeta* (Fribourg, 1996)
In Eccli.	Meister Eckhart, *Sermones et lectiones super Ecclesiastici* (LW 2, 231–300)
In Exod.	Meister Eckhart, *Expositio libri Exodi* (LW 2, 1–227)
In Gen. I	Meister Eckhart, *Expositio Libri Genesis* (LW 1:185–444).
In Ioh.	Meister Eckhart, *Expositio sancti Evangelii secundum Iohannem* (LW 3)

In. Sap.	Meister Eckhart, *Expositio Libri Sapientiae* (LW 2:301–643)
Koch	Josef Koch, *Kleine Schriften*, vol. 1 (Rome, 1973)
LE	Georg Steer and Loris Sturlese (eds.), *Lectura Eckhardi 2* (Stuttgart: Kohlhammer, 2009), 29–52
Liber parab.	Meister Eckhart, *Liber parabolarum Genesis* (LW 1:447–702)
LW	Meister Eckhart, *Lateinische Werke* (Stuttgart, 1936–)
MM	*Miscellanea mediaevalia* (Berlin)
Prol. gen.	Meister Eckhart, *Prologus generalis in Opus tripartitum* (LW 1:148–65)
Prol. prop.	Meister Eckhart, *Prologus in Opus propositionum* (LW 1:166–82)
or.	Dietrich von Freiberg, "De origine rerum praediamentalium," in *Opera omnia* (Hamburg, 1983), 3:136–201
qu.	*quaestio*
ScG	Thomas Aquinas, *Summa contra Gentiles*
Sent.	*Commentary on the Sentences*
Sth	Thomas Aquinas, *Summa theologiae*

Index